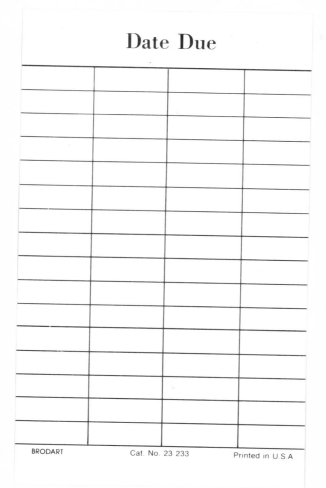

Date Due

BRODART   Cat. No. 23 233   Printed in U.S.A.

On the Man Question
*Gender and Civic Virtue
in America*

Gender
and
Civic
Virtue
in
America

ON THE
MAN
Question

MARK E. KANN

Temple University Press | Philadelphia

Temple University Press,
Philadelphia 19122
Copyright © 1991
by Temple University.
All rights reserved
Published 1991
Printed in the
United States of America

Library of Congress Cataloging-in-Publication Data
Kann, Mark E.
    On the man question : gender and civic virtue in America /
    Mark E. Kann.
        p.   cm.
    Includes bibliographical references and index.
    ISBN 0-87722-807-8 (alk. paper)
        1. Patriotism—United States.   2. Individualism—United
    States.   3. Militarism—United States.   4. Family—United
    States.   5. Social role—United States.   6. Sex role—United
    States.   I. Title.
    JK1759.K26 1991
    306.2'0973—dc20   90-45668

To three generations of
fathers and mothers,
sons and daughters

Sam & Ann, Sam & Anne

Skip & Stephanie, Rob & Caroline,
Joel & Greta, Jerry & Kareen

Jennifer, Erica, Sarah, Stephanie,
Shayle & Julia Rose

And to a magnificent mother
and special son

Kathy & Simon

Contents

Preface

My thesis is that individualism is more problem than promise in America. The problem is that males are usually considered too passionate and selfish to be trusted with individual rights. The liberal solution is to condition men's individualism with civic virtue. Historically, Americans look to fatherhood to prompt male sobriety, consent, and patriotism. They rely on constructions of womanhood to urge lovers, wives, and mothers to sacrifice their own individuality to tame men's appetites and ensure that men heed the nation's call to arms. They also sustain a martial spirit and military ethic to discipline otherwise self-indulgent young males. What I call the other liberal tradition in America incorporates the classical republican demand that men, women, and youth sacrifice for public good.

The origins of the other liberal tradition are located in Restoration England, where pioneering theorists attacked the traditional patriarchalism of church and state only to encounter a series of questions. How could passionate men be trusted with liberty and rights? How could female treachery be subdued and women recruited on the side of civic order? How could youth be habituated to the noble calling of freeholder, citizen, and soldier? John Locke's answers to these questions anticipated American efforts to restrain individualism with an "engendered" civic virtue. Locke forged a theory of "liberal patriarchy" that called on statesmen to engineer men's compliance, on wives to make husbands into sober breadwinners, and on manly fortitude and military adventure to launch youth toward patriotic manhood. The American adaptation was primarily manifested in evolving, middle-class images of fatherhood, fraternity, womanhood, and war.

Here is a preview of my conclusions. First, liberalism and republican-ism were not discrete paradigms. Indeed, liberal individualism demanded republican civic virtue. Second, the triumph of Lockean liberalism in America was not an unalloyed victory for possessive individualism. The nation's Lockean consensus required males to earn their rights and females to practice civic virtue in return for limited autonomy. Third, liberalism depended on martial virtue and militarism to discipline youth and en-sure order across generations. Finally, individualism in America was and is mostly myth, something we talk about and desire but rarely achieve and almost never trust. That makes liberalism a usable past for conserva-tives who look to families, schools, government, and the military to tame individual passions and interests; but it is also a usable past for radicals, feminists, and peace advocates who see civic virtue as the basis for a more egalitarian society.

This study is synthetic. It focuses on seventeenth-century English politi-cal philosophy and nineteenth-century American culture. It draws on the work of intellectual historians who debate the origins of American liberal-ism, family historians who tease images of fatherhood and fraternity from the past, social historians who recover women's victimization and agency, and military theorists and historians concerned with the relationship be-tween society and war. I would not have dared such an undertaking had it not been for the support, insights, and suggestions of colleagues and friends.

Robert Booth Fowler introduced me to Louis Hartz's work and then debated it with me for two decades. I have been fortunate enough to work with John Diggins, Joyce Appleby, and Steven Ross and also bene-fit from the creative counsel of Earl Klee, Peter Breiner, and Matthew Cahn. I have been guided through English political thought by the exper-tise of Stephen Baxter, debates with Richard Ashcraft, a brief encounter with John Pocock, and discussions with Carole Pateman. And I have been helped to reread Locke by the insights of Laura Greyson and Timothy Kaufman-Osborn. Elinor Accampo, Lois Banner, Helen Lefkowitz Horo-witz, and Barrie Thorne escorted me down the avenues of women's history, Harry Brod and Michael Messner accompanied me down the slippery slope of men's studies, and Roger Dingman and Don Higginbotham eased my way into military history. Thank you all.

A second uninterrupted summer at the William Andrews Clark Memorial Library afforded me leisure for further investigations of early-modern English thought, while a remarkable week at the U.S. Army War College provided a unique chance to test my concepts on postmodern officers. A University of Southern California sabbatical leave, a Haynes Foundation Fellowship, and National Endowment for the Humanities Summer Stipend (FT-33223) created the time needed to put ideas on paper. I offer my gratitude for this support.

I must make three special acknowledgments. First, my longtime friend Judith Hicks Stiehm has left an indelible imprint on this book. For a quarter of a century (gulp!), she has urged me to put political theory into an historical, gendered context and also to put questions of life and death, peace and war, at the center of political analysis. Judy, I finally got the message! Second, I have been blessed with the opportunity to work on four books with the special group of people who are Temple University Press. I am especially indebted to Janet Francendese, a brilliant and beautiful woman who has been my editor, friend, and tour guide in Philadelphia. Finally, again, and always: Kathy and Simon, I love you.

Introduction
Individualism, Civic Virtue, and Gender

> *There's no trust,*
>
> *No faith, no honesty in men; all perjured,*
>
> *All forsworn, all naught, all dissemblers.*
>
> —*William Shakespeare,*
>
> Romeo and Juliet

Liberalism was a philosophy of sobriety, born in fear, nourished by disenchantment, and prone to believe that the human condition was and was likely to remain one of pain and anxiety.
—*Sheldon S. Wolin*[1]

Individualism is a powerful symbol of American life. We treasure individual rights to speak our minds, choose our values, seek our goals, and achieve self-fulfillment. We believe individual self-interest is the foundation for economic growth and prosperity. We treat individual suffrage as the definitive characteristic of democratic government. In a sense, individualism is the lifeblood of an American Dream that flows to our children, circulates among immigrants, and courses through the rhetoric of public policy. American historians record its genealogy and sociologists diagnose its effects while business leaders prescribe more of it and politicians praise it. Even critics are obsessed with it. They tell us that individualism has infected the habits of our hearts and forced the closing of our minds.

A closer reading of our history suggests that individualism actually symbolizes a remarkably small segment of American life. It may be the official transcript of public discourse; but it is a legacy claimed primarily by middle-aged males who have settled into family life, achieved some economic success, and feel they have earned the right to resent others' authority. Individualism *does not* describe the historical norms or cultural practices of women and young men. Since colonial times, women have been called on to forgo individual aspirations, economic opportunities, and political influence for the good of family, community, and nation. Young men have been required to prove their mettle by renouncing individualism to anticipate and perform military service. A more convincing symbol for this majority is the self-sacrifice classically known as civic virtue.

Liberalism in America evolved as an "engendered" combination of individualism for older men and civic virtue for women and warriors. It was born in fear that men would abuse individual rights and sow social disorder unless they were taught some bourgeois sobriety. Women's function was to tame the male shrew. A compulsory military education was to test and discipline young men's passions. The liberal ideal was that the influence of self-sacrificing women and exposure to military virtues would transform unruly young males into predictable, productive middle-aged adults who could be trusted to exercise individual rights without fostering anarchy or tyranny in society. In short, liberalism required republicanism.

This suggests a fundamental flaw in the ongoing debate over the origins of liberalism in America. Early American thought may have been rooted in a pervasive Lockean individualism, but it also included demands for civic virtue from women and young men. The republican rhetoric of virtue and corruption may have been a significant influence during the American Revolution but it did not dissipate afterward; it was channeled into continuing cultural expectations that women and young men practice civic virtue. Finally, a recent "third wave" focus on early America's diversity of traditions, including liberalism and republicanism, neglects the systematic connection between liberalism and republicanism. My thesis is that the individual rights of men were conditioned on the sacrifices of women and young males.

The Origins Debate

Louis Hartz's 1955 *Liberal Tradition in America* ordains John Locke as the spiritual father of American political thought, rhetoric, and culture. Hartz's "storybook truth" is that Locke's individualism and social contract theory anticipated the American experiment. In turn, early Americans adopted and adapted Lockean individualism with a vengeance. The historic union of Lockean theory and American practice was consummated in the 1840s when American Whigs put away their fear of the masses and accepted the proposition that men of all classes could be entrusted with individual rights with little chance that they would foment anarchic disorder or class conflict. "The result," says Hartz, "was to electrify the democratic individual with a passion for great achievement and to produce a personality type that was . . . the hero of Horatio Alger."[2]

This gospel of an exceptional Lockean consensus provided a powerful explanation for domestic tranquility and Cold War fever in the early 1950s. The nation's "virtual unanimity" on Lockean individualism undermined class conflict at home and fostered "a colossal liberal absolutism" abroad. But Hartz's origin story lost much of its academic appeal when the Lockean consensus crumbled in the 1960s. That was when liberal individualism, materialism, and representative government were attacked by radicals identifying with Third World socialism, reactionaries demanding order without law, and reborn moralists seeking social redemption. America was hardly unique in 1968, when violence in Prague and Paris was matched by violence in Chicago.

Gordon Wood's 1969 *Creation of the American Republic* explains the dynamics and containment of social conflict in America.[3] Following Bernard Bailyn's work, Wood focuses on classical republicanism in early American thought. On his reading, the Revolution was the colonists' attempt to free themselves from corrupt British rule and forge new decentralized republics. The ideal was that virtuous Americans would rise above self-interest, participate together to found state commonwealths, and balance liberty and authority for the public good. However, the Founders' hopes quickly gave way to disenchantment. They feared that vice, factionalism, and mob rule pervaded the new republics; and their fears drove them to experiment with a Lockean "science of politics" and a U.S. Constitution that freed men's acquisitive appetites but harnessed their political ambitions. The Constitution signaled the "end of classical politics" and the rise of liberal individualism in America.

Wood's creation story suggests that social conflict was neutralized, not eradicated, by the Framers' institutional engineering. That explains the periodic resurfacing of opposition ideologies, popular movements against inequality, and elite efforts to reconfigure consent and coercion as well as the turbulence of the late 1960s. Since then, studies of American republicanism have proliferated. The most notable is J. G. A. Pocock's *Machiavellian Moment*, which traces republicanism from Aristotle through Machiavelli and Restoration England to revolutionary America. Pocock argues that the Founders' ideology was republican; the Framers' emergent Lockean liberalism rent the republican fabric; but a thin republican rhetoric persisted. Steven Ross's social history of Cincinnati suggests that republican ideology proved flexible enough to adapt to industrialization and shape public debate beyond the Civil War. And Dorothy Ross argues that the republican "dialectic between virtue and commerce" reappeared among late nineteenth-century populists.[4] Scholars may debate the exact life span of republicanism, but they agree that Americans had exchanged it for Lockean individualism by the twentieth century.

Republicanism is now being revived as a "usable past" that can serve as a corrective to triumphant Lockean individualism.[5] Robert Bellah supports civic virtue as a remedy for Americans' individualistic flight from social commitment. Richard Battistoni argues for shifting American public schooling in citizenship from liberal norms of individual satisfaction and self-interest to republican ideals of participation and public good. Sara Evans and Harry Boyte want to counter Lockean individualism by restoring republican traditions of community and commonwealth.[6] The view from the academic left is that republicanism is an indigenous language that can be appropriated to foster radical democracy.

Caroline Robbins and H. T. Dickinson point out, however, that traditional republican ideology legitimated the rights of propertied elites, not the power of popular majorities. Following a similar line of reasoning, Joyce Appleby associates eighteenth-century republicanism with the Federalists' aristocratic belief that civic virtue depended "upon the capacity of *some* men to rise above private interests and devote themselves to the public good." Rogers Smith adds that nineteenth-century republicanism in America functioned as a justification for nativism, social homogeneity, and states' rights in the service of racial, sexual, religious, and ethnic discrimination.[7] This hierarchical facet of republicanism is not lost on modern conservatives. The view from the academic right is that republicanism is also a "usable past," one that legitimates restrained individualism and reinforces popular quiescence to traditional authority.[8]

Despite the academic and activist interest it has generated, republican revivalism has failed to reduce Hartz to a historiographic footnote. Critics agree that Hartz helps to explain the ultimate triumph of Lockean individualism even if he exaggerates its effect on early America. More important, Hartz's main themes seemed to be reconfirmed in the 1970s. Students for a Democratic Society's Tom Hayden appeared to assimilate into the Lockean mainstream when he cut his hair, put on a tie, and ran for public office; and militant factions like the Weather Underground suffered isolation and elimination—as if to announce that the Lockean consensus was restored. The "Me Decade" and "the culture of narcissism" demonstrated the resilience of individualism; the quest of women, gays, seniors, environmentalists, religious sects, minorities, and others for inclusion bolstered conventional liberal politics; and Ronald Reagan's revolution symbolized renewed materialism and Cold War hysteria. In this context, it was no surprise that Hartz's defenders regained the intellectual offensive in the 1980s.

They still argue that Lockean individualism dominated early American thought, pervaded public consciousness, and constituted a national consensus, but then modify Hartz's story in three ways. First, as Isaac Kramnick notes, republican ideology did prevail in English and American discourse for much of the eighteenth century, but "Lockean ideas made a dramatic and decisive comeback in the 1760s and 1770s"—just in time for the American Revolution. Second, even if republican rhetoric outlasted the Revolution, it was emptied of classical content. John Diggins memorializes republicanism as a dying language in early America, fatally compromised by the Lockean meanings that infected its concepts and the Lockean individualism that inspired Americans. He writes, "The classical idea of virtue as resistance to political corruption and a patriotic subordination of private interests to the public good had come and gone by 1787." Joyce Appleby adds that republican rhetoric survived nationhood in competition with a Lockean individualism that was ascendant by the 1790s: "In the context of classical republican thought virtue meant civic virtue, the quality that enabled men to rise above private interests in order to act for the good of the whole. By the 1780s this meaning is less clear. . . . By the end of the century virtue more often referred to a private quality, a man's capacity to look out for himself and his dependents—almost the opposite of classical virtue." Finally, the Lockean consensus is considered more flexible than Hartz suggests. It can invite Hamiltonian statism and democratic socialism into the liberal dialogue, though these opposition ideologies must still adapt to Lockean language and meanings.[9]

Gordon Wood now entertains a compromise. "For early Americans," he states, "there never was a stark dictionary of traditions, liberal and republican." The idea that early Americans mixed their intellectual traditions in the process of sorting out individualism and civic virtue has produced a "third wave" of interpretation, what James Kloppenberg considers "an emerging consensus among historians concerning the persistence of diversity in American patterns of thought and behavior during the colonial and early national periods." His analysis is that liberalism, republicanism, and Christianity merged briefly during the Revolution and diverged shortly thereafter. Rogers Smith concentrates on a blend of liberalism, republicanism, and "ethnocultural Americanism," each dominating at particular moments. Richard Vetterli and Gary Bryner argue that Christian benevolence, Scottish common sense philosophy, republican civic virtue, and liberal institutions joined together in early America. Anne Norton contends that liberalism had an immense influence in the puritanical North while ideals of republican civic virtue pervaded the antebellum South. And Jean Elshtain adds a culinary note: "Liberal and republican elements commingle in this American civic stew." [10]

It is important to resolve this debate. Origin stories have consequences. Biblical creationism not only explains human origins but also legitimates notions of good and evil. Evolutionists trace the ascent of beast to man and thereby generate standards of the natural and perverse. Political theorists posit states of nature and historians reconstruct national origins only to shape our perceptions of what is politically desirable and historically possible. The scholars who debate liberalism's origins do more than write history. They give it meaning, name effective causes, and fix the odds on the future. Gordon Wood neatly capsulizes the significance of the liberal-origins debate when he asks whether "we Americans are . . . as inevitably individualistic and capitalistic as Hartz and others thought." [11]

Inevitable Individualism?

Early Americans produced little systematic political philosophy. They formulated their ideas in pamphlets, newspaper articles, sermons, speeches, letters, reports, essays, and short treatises on narrow topics. Few writers cultivated philosophical detachment. Most were politically engaged. They generally assumed rather than stated fundamental values; and they often cultivated ambiguity to enhance their appeal to diverse interests, classes, and regions. That is why the writings of Franklin, Madison, and Jefferson, for example, show up as evidence on all sides of the origins debate. We need to examine American thinkers' philosophical assumptions and cultural meanings to comprehend the contextual significance of individualism and to question its inevitability in American history.

Remarkably, intellectual historians dwell on Lockean liberalism as the philosophical source of American individualism but they do little to analyze the relationship between Lockean liberalism and individualism. The reason is fairly straightforward. Hartz and Diggins, like Wood and Pocock, are uncritical in equating Lockean liberalism with what C. B. Macpherson calls "possessive individualism." [12] Their paradigmatic view is that Locke's social contract theory legitimated individual rights, economic rationality, and instrumental politics. By extension, Locke's triumph in America logically entailed the defeat of contrary republican norms such as civic virtue, commonwealth, and the active political life. The main debate, then, concerns "when" Lockean individualism took precedence over republicanism.

However, a wealth of recent scholarship suggests that Lockean liberalism justified an individualism that incorporated republican civic virtue. Locke's notion of natural individual rights was conditioned on civic restraints embedded in family life, education, the economy, and politics. Locke feared that untamed, possessive individualism would destroy any hope for establishing a peaceful liberal order. Men's selfish passions needed to be reconciled with civic virtue to safeguard public good. Consequently, the triumph of Locke's liberalism in America actually required the perpetuation of civic virtue.[13] We can appreciate the enduring effect of Locke's "conditional" individualism by locating the point where Hartz's narrative of Lockean individualism meets Wood's tale of republican disenchantment.

Hartz identifies Liberal Man as the hero of Horatio Alger. He is the individual with enough self-control to avoid temptation, enough willpower to rise above adverse circumstances, and enough drive to take full advantage of rights and opportunities. He has the economic wisdom to be industrious, save his wealth, make appropriate investments, and work the market to his advantage. He knows that self-denial today is the basis for prosperity tomorrow. He understands that individual rights, opportunities, and property depend on the law-abiding behavior that fosters good reputation, economic predictability, and political stability. In short, Alger's heroic ideal is the sober bourgeois male.

Locke's American heirs rarely assumed that historical men came close to approximating this heroic ideal. They took a dim view of men's self-control, rationality, and civility. Men had a capacity for such heroics but rarely fulfilled it. Any optimism regarding men's sobriety was deferred to the distant future. Meanwhile, flesh-and-blood men were feared as sinful, passionate creatures prone to habitual laziness, ignorance, and alcoholism as well as impulsiveness, greed, deceit, aggression, and violence. Most men were considered candidates for individual license and mob anarchy, some men for aristocratic profligacy, corruption, and tyranny. Hartz captures this skepticism about men's passions when he characterizes the American consensus as the "alliance of Christian pessimism with liberal thought" that produced "a liberal bleakness." Similarly, John Diggins argues that "Calvinism became the conscience of liberalism" by infusing it with the suspicion that men's sins and passions could not be eradicated. And Wood's creation story centers on the Founders' belief that men's vices doomed early republican experiments to failure. He quotes George Washington to that effect: "We have, probably, had too good an opinion of human nature in forming our confederation." [14] The enduring question confronting liberalism was whether men were redeemable.

Many intellectuals believed that the Revolution would bring about men's redemption. But the desire to build cities on a hill was shattered by repeated instances of men's intemperance. Early America had few Voltaires who attacked Christianity's core belief in Original Sin, fewer Rousseaus who imagined bringing heaven down to earth, and virtually no Condorcets willing to embed men's perfectability in history. What Carl Becker calls "the Heavenly City of the Eighteenth Century Philosophers" was mostly a French phenomenon that was occasionally echoed by Jeffersonians. However, the American Enlightenment preferred to mix religious doubt with secular pessimism.[15] It dreamed the rights of men and even fantasized about human progress but almost always woke to obsessions with men's untamed passions and interests.

How could flawed men be endowed with extensive individual rights that invited them to vent their passions and indulge their interests at the expense of social order? The specter of Shays' Rebellion and its violent repression haunted the founding generation. Leading political thinkers believed that men's destructive passions had to be harnessed by forces stronger than self-control, sober rationality, or presumed civility if social stability was to be thinkable. The colonial experience with British rule suggested that traditional state authority was not the solution. Government intervention threatened to deny individual rights, promote political tyranny, and prompt rebellion. Ultimately, American liberalism demanded that men's individualism be subdued in ways consistent with popular consent.

This is where Macpherson's "possessive individualism" becomes essential to American origin stories. A Lockean liberalism that emphasizes individual self-interest, property rights, accumulation, and economic rationality *seems* to explain how flawed men could be trusted to exercise individual rights without fomenting social disorder or inviting government repression. The explanation is that men sublimate their passions into their economic interests. Albert Hirschman explains, "One set of passions, hitherto known variously as greed, avarice, or love of lucre, could be usefully employed to oppose and bridle such other passions as ambition, lust for power, or sexual lust."[16] If men's appetites for ease, alcohol, promiscuity, aggression, and violence were absorbed into an omnivorous materialism, then it would be possible to release their acquisitive desires, provide them opportunities for economic satisfaction, and expect them to recognize their individual stake in stable property relations safeguarded by a limited government. Implicitly, men's possessive individualism transformed them into predictable, productive, and peaceful citizens of the liberal state.

Hartz and Wood assume this transformation. Hartz calls it "the magical alchemy of American life . . . [which] in addition to transforming passive peasants into dynamic liberal farmers was going to transform bitter proletarians into incipient entrepreneurs."[17] Hartz's Lockean consensus, then, refers to a tacit contract among American men to act as if the individual search for wealth was the meaning of life, liberty, and happiness. For Wood, the Framers' major feat was disassociating greed from corruption and allowing men to air their appetites in a "kinetic" environment that involved "such a crumbling of political and social interests, such an atomization of authority, such a parceling of power, not only in the governmental institutions but in the extended sphere of society itself, creating such a multiplicity and a scattering of designs and passions, so many checks, that no combination of parts could hold, no group of evil interests could long adhere."[18] The Constitution created a polity in which men could be greedy because their excessive passions were neutralized by pluralistic competition and political fragmentation. Hartz and Wood may debate whether Americans' Lockean consensus or the Framers' Lockean "science of politics" was the liberal catalyst, but they agree that it was possessive individualism that calmed the beast in American men.

This assumed identity among men's passions, possessive individualism, and compliant citizenship is problematic. Aileen Kraditor suggests that historians tend to "underestimate the importance to individuals of those social forms that mediate between the public sphere and the private sphere, those institutions such as the family, neighborhood, and club."[19] Men's embedded social relations affect how they pursue wealth and whether they pursue it in ways consistent with social peace. Moreover, Albert Hirschman observes that the idea of men's passions being tamed by their economic interests had run its course by the mid-nineteenth century when the unrestrained desire for property was commonly seen as an uncontrollable and terrifying force.[20] That there was nothing natural or automatic about the relationship among men's passions, materialism, and civility was the centerpiece of David Hume's classical critique of social contract theory.

Hume did not believe that men's passions could be wholly subsumed by their economic interests. He argued that men had a passion for property and even a recognized interest in stable property relations. But men were also creatures of habit. And when their habits were upset, they often engaged in aggression and violence despite damage to their economic interests. Men might be restrained from self-destructive behavior by fear and necessity, but these sources of stability were anemic. Fear dissipated in the absence of proximate coercion and opinions regarding necessity were "uncertain, ambiguous, and arbitrary." For Hume, the only solid foundation for economic sobriety and political order was the cultural continuity manifested in sons who "follow the path which their fathers, treading in the footsteps of theirs, had marked out to them."[21]

Even if men were possessive individualists, the problem of social peace was unsolved. Hume argued that economic rationality, by itself, did not prevent men from disobeying laws whenever dishonesty or deceit seemed profitable. For example, men disavowed their marriage contracts to escape financial and emotional obligations; abrogated business contracts to enhance personal wealth; or broke the social contract when an economic calculus determined that crime and coercion paid. The integrity of contracts required men to regard honesty and fidelity as habitual civic virtues. When Hume stated that "the commerce and intercourse of mankind . . . can have no security where men pay no regard to their engagements," he was suggesting that the liberal social contract demanded men's prior loyalty to a notion of public good.[22]

Horatio Alger certainly understood the importance of cultural continuity and civic virtue. Indeed, the frailty of intergenerational bonds and fear of possessive individualism directed his novels.[23] Alger's fictional heroes were often fatherless boys who had no established path to follow. They grew up in moral gutters populated by sinful criminals and fallen aristocrats whose street code was survival, self-indulgence, and a quick buck rather than sobriety. No magical alchemy teleported them from the gutter. They needed pluck and luck, to be sure, but they especially needed the assistance of father figures who subsidized them, guided them, instilled good habits in them, and provided exemplary role models for them. In addition, Alger's heroes were exceptional boys. Even in gutter society, they showed a special sense of Christian piety that kept them from the path of sin, prepared them for their encounter with fortune, and steadied them on the road to middle-class success. They then developed a sense of Golden Rule paternalism and assumed a personal obligation to help other youth as they themselves had been helped. In sum, Alger's archetypal liberalism incorporated both benign patriarchy and habitual civic virtue as necessary reins on male individualism.

Hartz is not insensitive to the difficulties of making possessive individualism the bedrock of American society. He betrays doubts in his mixed admiration for antebellum Southern sociologists who emphasized organic patriarchal bonds among men, then criticized Northern capitalism for its economic individualism, and finally defended slave society. Hartz comments, "No one who reads the beginning of their argument can fail to find it refreshing and no one who reads its conclusion can fail to find it fantastic." Wood is also concerned. He constantly points out the Founders' fear of unfettered materialism, for instance, in this 1786 *Boston Independent Chronicle* article: "We daily see the busy multitude engaged in accumulating what they fondly call riches, by forestalling, extortioning, and imposing upon each other." Wood argues that the Framers' fear of such "licentious" men prompted them to conceive a Constitution that reserved government for the "worthy" few.[24] Unfortunately, Hartz and Wood do not give serious consideration to patriarchy and civic virtue because they assume that Lockean liberalism precluded these values.

Michael Walzer succinctly poses the dilemma of men's individualism and social order: "Without some shared sense of the duty . . . there would be no political community at all and no security or welfare—and the life of mankind 'solitary, poor, nasty, brutish, and short.'"[25] In fact, the liberal tradition in America involved a desperate search for father figures and civic virtue to provide that shared sense of duty. Candidates for patriarchy included actual fathers empowered and restrained by paternal obligations; Whigs and patricians claiming exemplary self-discipline born of good breeding and elevated tastes; successful businessmen emblematic of industry and pragmatism; and natural aristocrats, professionals, and experts counseling patience and promising to govern wisely for the people. Potential sources of civic virtue included religion, education, communal institutions, fraternal groups, and even a cult of masculinity that identified manly "character" with self-discipline and patriotism as personified by Andrew Jackson and Theodore Roosevelt.[26] The search was necessarily desperate because *traditional* patriarchy and civic virtue were steadily undermined by the individuating force of the nineteenth-century marketplace.

Robert Nisbet now suspects the search has failed. He believes that Lockean individualism has produced a "twilight of authority" that relentlessly drives us toward chaos and oppression.[27] Let me suggest that Nisbet is quite mistaken. Locke's American heirs developed a cultural dependence on women and militarism to tame men's individualism by fostering and managing "the making of the American middle class."

The Making of Bourgeois Men

Hartz and Wood forget Abigail Adams's plea to "remember the ladies" and Benjamin Franklin's "plain truth" that men secure peace by preparing for war. This is a major oversight. Their academic debate solely concerns the rise of individualism in the male civilian sector. It disregards the women who reproduced the social order and the young men who risked their lives to defend it. Further, it neglects the historical truth that the primary cultural ethic of women as life-givers and men as life-takers was self-sacrifice for family, community, and country. And it overlooks American liberalism's reliance on women's civic virtue and young men's exposure to martial discipline to promote economic sobriety and restrained citizenship in the male-dominated public sphere.

When gender is introduced to the origins debate, it is "fitted" into earlier stories. Diggins's defense of Hartz interprets Victorian women's reputed "submission, purity, and domesticity" as privatized virtues that fortified men for the possessive individualism of the marketplace. Pocock recovers the importance of citizen soldiering in early American rhetoric, but his goal is to show the residual influence of republicanism on America's increasingly individualistic society. Anne Norton cleverly uses gender as a device to contrast the privatization of family life in the masculine North and the legitimation of republican soldiering in the feminine South only to conclude that privatization, individualism, and masculinity triumphed with the North at the end of the Civil War.[28] In each case, women and warriors are inserted as actors whose episodic presence enriches the drama but hardly affects the possessive individualism at the climax.

However, recent studies of the social history of American women in the eighteenth and nineteenth centuries point to a different climax. They uncover consistent cultural expectations that women engage in self-sacrifice to tame men's passions and thereby contribute to social peace, cure industrial society's ills, and ultimately ready men for the sacrifices entailed in a patriotic defense of the nation in wartime. These cultural expectations were mostly popular idealizations of middle-class morality, but they partly reflected and reinforced the sexual division of labor in middle-class life and influenced the aspirations of socially mobile Americans seeking middle-class status. Idealized above all else was the notion that women were especially capable of cultivating civic virtue and that women's civic virtue was instrumental in producing an orderly liberal society protected by somewhat patriotic men.

From the Revolution forward, American writers attributed to women special domestic virtues that were understood as civic virtues; these virtues had significant public ramifications and involved much more than building private havens in a heartless world that prepared men to return to the marketplace. Linda Kerber's investigation into post-Revolutionary "republican motherhood" draws our attention to the connection between women's domesticity and nationhood:

> To the mother's traditional responsibility for maintenance of the household economy, and to the expectation that she should be a person of religious faith, was added the obligation that she also be an informed and virtuous citizen. She was to observe the political world with a rational eye, and she was to guide her husband and children in making their way through it. She was to be a teacher as well as a mother.[29]

American women were encouraged to become educated in order to teach their husbands and sons some piety, responsibility, and civic-mindedness. By the mid-nineteenth century, women's domesticity was elevated as a solution to men's fall from grace in the marketplace. Mrs. Graves wrote, "The domestic institution, which may be rendered so potential through the properly-directed influence of women, contains within it a counterbalancing power to regulate and control the [male] passions which give too great an impetus of the social machine."[30] Women were to sacrifice their own civil, economic, and political rights to devote themselves wholeheartedly to subduing men's passions. Their sacrifice made their functional contribution to society seem all the more virtuous. Ideal wives and mothers were honored as selfless patriots.

Women's selfless patriotism was not confined to their homes. It was manifested in an impressive array of women's reform movements that were tolerated and even encouraged by male ministers, business leaders, and politicians. Women sought to restore civility to community life by fighting moral corruption among men as well as by standing guard over public decency and order. Their struggles for temperance, abolition, and social housekeeping aimed at taming men's passions, restraining their material greed, fostering social harmony, and enhancing public good. Their strongest argument for suffrage was that they would use the vote to control men's excesses, humanize the economy, and infuse civic virtue into politics.[31] The cultural rule of thumb was that women's civic virtue might serve as a corrective to men's tendency toward anarchy and tyranny. Women's domesticity signified their duty to domesticate private and public man.

High among women's civic virtues was their willingness to urge their sons to do their civic duty during wartime. Here women were aided by the pervasive cultural belief that young men had an obligation to serve as citizen–soldiers. This belief was more than a residue from the republican past. It had a continuous influence on American public life. What Marcus Cunliffe calls "the martial spirit in America" equated masculinity with the desire, skill, and duty to bear arms for the state. Boys' and men's literature encouraged it, the frontier tested it, and paramilitary organizations provided civilian outlets for it.[32] The martial spirit was reinforced by a widespread belief that young men's participation in war would cure them of excessive selfishness and the attractions of effete urban life and thereby redeem their civic virtue. This cultural icon originated in the Revolution, appeared in the mythology of the frontiersman and Indian fighter, and resurfaced at the onset of every war. In a sense, young men's most active and significant form of citizenship throughout American history was not self-interested suffrage but preparation for self-sacrificing combat.

The nature of American citizen soldiering changed over time, but its connection with young men's civic virtue lasted across time. Early Americans honored the republican militia as an exercise in men's civic virtue; they detested standing armies as an invitation to corruption. But American men gradually consented to a national standing military, first the Continental Army, then the volunteer regular army, and eventually the modern conscript army. This shift in attitudes was partly a matter of military expediency, but it was also driven by common beliefs that impressionable young men needed an education in civic virtue and self-sacrificing patriotism to make them into trustworthy citizens.[33] At a time when materialism and the marketplace encouraged selfishness and greed, military service would teach young men to discipline their individualism, submit to authority, and honor the nation. Both symbolically and tangibly, honorable discharges certified young men's sobriety when they entered the marketplace, and combat medals attested to young men's patriotic credentials when they participated in politics.

Indeed, the significance of civic virtue for women and young men was especially conspicuous during national crises. American women were enculturated to be Spartan Mothers who willingly gave up their men to military service. They were expected to maintain the home front by managing families, cutting consumption, and producing war materials; by uplifting troop morale, courage, and effectiveness; and by honoring warriors, mourning the dead, welcoming home returning heroes, and retiring to prewar domesticity so veterans could resume prior employment.[34] Without women's civic virtue, men could not fight the country's wars. American men were taught to play the part of society's protectors. They were expected to volunteer for service or accede to conscription in order to defend their family hearths and local communities; submit to military discipline and cultivate ferocity for their women, children, and nation; and learn to die so that others might live.[35] Veterans were then to return to their families with a renewed sense of self-discipline, a commitment to sober breadwinning, and a merited sense of civic virtue that bound them together in patriotic civic organizations and challenged the next generation to demonstrate its military mettle. One may question whether American women and young men took their civics lessons to heart, but one can hardly doubt that they have exhibited remarkable self-sacrifice during the nation's many wars.

Individualism as a central value in American history was actually located on extremely narrow terrain. It was bordered on one side by the philosophical fear that men's passions and interests fostered social disorder, on the other by cultural expectations that women and young men practice civic virtue in the name of social order and national integrity. The only Americans who had a firm grasp on individual rights were middle-aged men whose appetites had been tamed by republican mothers and disciplined by martial masculinity if not actual military service. But even middle-aged men's hold on individual rights could be slippery. Liberalism in America was founded on such a deep disenchantment with people's ability to control their passions that it produced a misanthropic fear of individualism itself.

Liberal Misanthropy

Abstract individual rights flourished after the Revolution. States extended men's rights; the federal government added a Bill of Rights; Jacksonian America legitimated rugged individualism, entrepreneurship, and broader voting rights while being hospitable to movements for states' rights, minority rights, labor rights, and tenants' rights. Whig critics warned that extreme individualism would push American society to the brink of chaos. But compared to Western Europe, the United States seemed to be exceptionally tranquil. Class tensions, an influx of immigrants, regional conflict, and periodic wars did little to disturb national order until the Civil War. Thereafter, conflict persisted and intensified, but liberalism withstood episodic radicalism and reaction. Hartz explains domestic tranquility as a function of Lockean consensus. Wood points to Lockean conflict resolution. But neither adequately accounts for the conjunction of individualism and social order because both fail to recognize the full dimension of the problem.

Hartz argues that America's Lockean consensus was the link between the nation's "liberal bleakness" and its relatively placid history. Men's belief in private property and economic opportunity gave them a stake in social peace. Even discontented men were not particularly subversive. They blamed themselves for economic distress or sought modest reforms to enhance their prospects. Their discontents never congealed into significant class struggle. In retrospect, the Framers' fear of men's vices, irrationality, and factionalism was foolish. They failed to observe and understand men's devotion to property rights. They did not see that the "mob" actually consisted of individuals who anticipated ownership and identified with the property-owning classes. The Framers' complex constitutional restraints amounted to political overkill. Hartz puts it this way: "The American majority has been an amiable shepherd dog kept forever on a lion's leash." [36]

Was the majority of American men so amiable? Our history is replete with stories of men whose virtues and vices, desires and interests, ambitions and aggression drove them to self-destructive behavior and social pathology manifested in family violence, criminal activity, and senseless brutality. Numerous groups of men opposed liberal individualism, practiced racial, ethnic, religious, and nationalist aggression, and projected their own brand of communal exclusivity within, beside, and against the class-based movements that challenged men's stake in the capitalist marketplace and sought to restructure if not revolutionize government. Many individuals, groups, and movements were driven by a strong element of economic interest; but all were moved by considerable heterodoxy in appetites, values, perceptions of the market, social loyalties, and political aspirations that revealed significant cracks in Hartz's Lockean consensus.

To control heterodoxy, American elites responded with their own brand of lawlessness and aggression. Fear of the unruly masses, a sense of benign and malignant paternalism, and passionate prejudices, as much as any singular drive toward economic aggrandizement, explain elites' historical tendency to resort to violence as a priority cure for social unrest. Even those entrepreneurs and their political allies who neatly fit the billing of possessive individualists regularly broke their own economic and political rules to find quicker ways to wealth and power. Bribery, conspiracy, monopoly, thievery, patronage, corruption, small-scale coercion, large-scale private armies, and public violence made sense in their search for profits and privilege. Persisting inequalities and national dissension prompted elites to exercise tyranny in the name of stability.

Gordon Wood, far more attuned to social conflict than Hartz, does not believe the Framers were unduly fearful of social disorder. In his analysis, early America experienced substantial factional conflict between "the people" and "aristocrats." The Framers neutralized factionalism by instituting a complex system of checks and balances that fragmented authority. After 1787, discontented men were free to try their luck in the economic or political marketplace where their passions were exhausted and their interests tempered by institutionalized competition, compromise, reformism, and oversight by the "worthy" few. Extending Wood's logic, neo-Marxist scholars transform factionalism into class conflict and show how American institutions continued to neutralize it. For example, Howard Zinn argues that early farmer rebellions and urban riots were class conflicts that threatened upper-class interests. The Framers had the architectural foresight to place a constitutional buffer between the people and political power. Subsequently, elites used the federal government as a flexible instrument for engineering popular consent and upper-class hegemony. Conflict was not eliminated but, Zinn concludes, "these rebellions, so far, have been contained."[37]

Actually, much more than mechanical engineering was needed to contain popular rebellions. The Framers themselves recognized that institutional conflict resolution was contingent on a degree of self-restraint among the masses and some virtue among politicians.[38] Without these, citizens would elect representatives who injected social conflict into politics and government officials likely to abuse political authority and engage in conspiracies that undermined checks and balances. After all, that was the founding generation's view of what happened in late eighteenth-century England when British subjects selected a Parliament that conspired with king and court to produce the corruption that sparked the American Revolution. Hartz captures the necessity of a trusting relationship between individuals and institutions when he writes, "The Founding Fathers devised a scheme to deal with conflict that could only survive in a land of solidarity."[39] But how could America be a land of solidarity when it was populated by passionate and self-interested men?

The very absence of solidarity virtually guaranteed the failure of checks and balances to prevent political tyranny. The U.S. Constitution did fragment political authority, but, as anti-Federalists protested, it also centralized power over "the sword and the purse," the military and taxation. The federal government even had constitutional authority to suspend *habeas corpus* when it thought public safety imperiled. Henceforth, political elites confronting domestic disorders would always have a difficult time locating and exercising the unified political authority needed to orchestrate a package of reforms that might quiet rebellion. But they could readily call out the military, employ state violence, and force quiescence—a lesson fairly obvious to Indians, rebellious farmers, blacks and other minorities, labor organizers, and radicals throughout American history.

Hartz underestimates heterodoxy in American values, and Wood overestimates the effectiveness of institutional restraints. Equally important, both scholars neglect what may have been a deeper cultural threat posed by individualism: It was contagious. After the Revolution, individual freedom in families and in young men's relation to the military increased dramatically. Young people were freed from arranged marriages to choose their own mates, and women in particular won greater domestic and reproductive autonomy as their husbands were forced to seek work outside the home. To the extent that compulsory military service was recognized as legitimate and used as a source of acquiring manpower, it effectively disappeared as militia units were gradually replaced by volunteer companies and the regular army.[40] The growing individual freedom of women and young men was possibly more dangerous to domestic tranquility than either ideological heterodoxy or unresolved class conflict.

Reconsider Victorian womanhood for a moment. According to Diggins, Catharine Beecher's domestic piety "aimed at character formation in the name of 'conscience'" and thereby contributed to the apolitical individualism at the core of Hartz's Lockean consensus. But Diggins also reminds us that Beecher's belief in Christian character formation at home aimed at resolving "the chaos of democratic individualism" in the marketplace.[41] Similarly, Zinn argues that Victorian domesticity "made acceptance of the new [industrial] economy easier to . . . see . . . as only part of life, with the home as a haven." However, he also connects women's domesticity to women's struggle for empowerment and women's movements against amoral market priorities.[42] The implications for social order were ambiguous. On the one hand, it appears that women contributed to Hartz's Lockean consensus by creating islands of domesticity that prepared men to ride the waves of capitalism. On the other hand, one can argue that domesticity provided women free spaces for cultivating their own sense of historical agency that was manifested in movements protesting men's possessive individualism and market mentality. Conceivably, women constituted a vast reserve army against capitalist self-aggrandizement.

A related ambiguity can be drawn from historical accounts of men and the military. Diggins suggests that masculine virtues of courage, civic duty, and patriotism were anachronistic traces of an earlier republicanism. Yet these same martial virtues were essential for putting into practice the Lockean idea of industry as the sole basis for ownership, which, in turn, justified expansionism—the violent subjugation of the Indians and expropriation of their lands.[43] Likewise, Zinn portrays military service as an outlet for classical martial virtues and, sometimes, as complicity in the denial of workers' and minorities' rights. Still, he sees militarism as the preferred historical means for achieving Lockean ends such as opening up new markets, enhancing commercial opportunities, and spreading "the blessings of liberty" across the continent and globe.[44] The mixed message is, first, that martial masculinity subverted America's Lockean consensus by sustaining anti-individualist norms and suppressing individual rights; but, also, that martial masculinity was both just and necessary if American men were to defend individual rights and guarantee adequate land and resources for exercising them. It was therefore conceivable that young men would justify the cultivation of the strutting violence of martial masculinity as an affirmation of liberal individualism and, in the process, transform the right to self-defense into a license to wreak social havoc.

Women and young men rarely claimed individualism as an explicit basis for subverting social harmony. But when they did demand individual rights and autonomy, especially in the late nineteenth century, they provoked a deep-seated, misogynist and misanthropic fear that individualism was destroying the fundamental bonds of American society. For instance, working-class women who stood up for their own economic rights and material interests by organizing boycotts and strikes were consistently condemned as agents of disorder. Not only was their individualism considered subversive; their claim to individualism also recalled and reinforced the classical Western belief that women, by nature, were more passionate, more vicious, more evil, and more destructive than men.[45] When middle-class women fought to extend their domestic autonomy beyond the hearth and to share in individual rights, wealth, and power as well as to reform society and politics, antisuffragists were quick to proclaim that these selfish and self-interested females were undermining the integrity of family life by destroying the sanctity of self-sacrificing womanhood, pious mothering, and socially necessary man taming. These egotistic women, the critics said, were part of the social problem rather than the solution to it.[46]

Women were even considered dangerous when claiming that superior feminine virtues should serve as a significant moral force in social and political life. Just beneath the veneer of polite Victorian discourse was the specter of morally righteous women who emasculated their husbands and sons, robbed men of their autonomy, and seduced them away from reason and civility. Machiavelli called that specter *Fortuna*.[47] In Victorian America, *Fortuna* was masked in the ideology of "passionlessness," which portrayed middle-class women as meek, submissive, asexual beings who would moderate men's lusts and channel their passions into productive activity. But *Fortuna* was constantly unmasked, for example, by the misogynist medical profession. Barbara Ehrenreich and Deirdre English note, "Doctors themselves never seemed entirely convinced . . . that the uterus and ovaries had successfully stamped out female sexuality. Underneath the complacent denial of female sexual feelings, there lurked the age-old male fascination with women's 'unsatiable lust,' which, once awakened, might turn out to be uncontrollable."[48] Alas, the Victorian lady who dressed in moral purity was actually covering up her naked treachery.

Women's so-called treachery was unveiled by late nineteenth-century complaints about "Momism." Even within the domestic sphere, the argument went, women had an effeminating influence on their sons and thereby produced a new generation of emasculated boys lacking in manly character, ambition, and fortitude. Worse, women's malignant influence was reinforced in public schools and Sunday schools, where females shaped the morals of young men well into their adolescence. The champions of masculinity reacted by constructing and advocating a hypermasculinity symbolized by Teddy Roosevelt's Rough Riders, cultivated by the new Boy Scouts of America and sports culture, and justified by the preachers of Muscular Christianity.[49] When John Adams called women "a tribe more numerous and powerful than all the rest," he anticipated a battle of the sexes founded on the belief that women were an inherent menace to society.

However, hypermasculinity was also considered a social menace, which may explain why it was prescribed more as a remedial cure for boys' effeminacy than as a model for young manhood. Hypermasculinity hinted at the prospect of young men mixing claims to individualism and unrestrained martial ardor. If effeminacy suggested self-indulgence, youthful hypermasculinity connoted the unrestrained passions associated with bachelorhood—a period when young men were free from paternal authority but not yet subdued by marriage or a substantial economic stake in society. Worse, bachelorhood combined with the rhetoric of individualism fostered in youth the feeling that they could refuse military service and reject military discipline. Finally, the martial spirit in America invited selfish young men to cultivate hypermasculine aggression and vent their passions without much concern for victims or laws. For some, young men were loose cannons.

The subversive nature of youthful individualism began with boys fighting, adolescents dueling, frontiersmen enforcing might over right, and army enlistees rebelling against commanding officers. It often culminated in episodes of right-wing extremism and vigilantism, nativist and ethnic street wars, gang violence and urban crime, ominous class confrontations, and the failure of elites to mobilize military manpower or monopolize the means of coercion.[50] "Carefree youth" was viewed as licentiousness in the cause of making American life nasty, brutish, and short. In addition, young men's irresponsibility and bachelorhood were sometimes associated with socially destructive political subversion and sexual inversion. If Gilded Age reformers and radicals were attacked for their effeminacy, homosexuals were attacked as inherent threats to social order.[51]

Neither Hartz's consensus nor Wood's institutional conflict resolution can explain the possibility of controlling subversive women and young men. Women's economic status and opportunities deteriorated in early America, and the cult of female domesticity added a prejudice against women's labor outside the home or participation in conventional politics. At the same time, young men were leaving their families for the frontier or city, where temptations to youthful vice and violence were great and economic prospects irregular and uncertain. Those young men who enlisted in the regular army were generally too impoverished, ill-paid, uneducated, and mobile to set down political roots; and rank-and-file soldiers were cautioned against political participation lest they alienate civilians. Consequently, women and young men had limited economic opportunities and less political influence. They were poorly positioned to become quiescent in anticipation of ownership or by exhaustion in institutionalized political competition. They lived at the margins of the liberal consensus, where accessibility to pacifying reforms was negligible.

American thinkers had reason to despair and often did. Individualism and social order could be reconciled only if men voluntarily subdued their passions and interests, habitually obeyed the law, sustained a minimal sense of civic virtue, and transmitted an ethic of moderation to the next generation. But America was a fluid environment where individualism invited men to pursue their passions, the market eroded intergenerational continuity, and the cult of martial masculinity was a ready excuse for lawless violence. Men had to be transformed into sober, bourgeois individuals by self-sacrificing women and a military education in civic virtue. What was needed was a national consensus, not on possessive individualism but on the self-restraint and civic loyalty that would make peaceful conflict resolution possible. The problem was that men could not be trusted to subdue their passions and interests; women could not be trusted to tame men's passions without claiming a subversive individualism of their own; and young men could not be trusted to submit voluntarily to a restraining military education. How, then, were the differential freedoms of men, women, and youth reconciled to achieve relative domestic tranquility? The historical answer in America was "liberal patriarchy."

Liberal Patriarchy

The traditional bulwarks of patriarchal authority over women and young men were the church and state. Liberalism challenged both. John Locke condemned traditional patriarchy by defending religious toleration and attacking Sir Robert Filmer's monarchism, by affirming greater autonomy for women and denying the subordination of adult sons. But Locke did not eliminate patriarchy. He liberalized it.[52] His theories prefigured an American revision of patriarchy that fostered the consent of women and young men to the authority of middle-aged males and then saddled the middle-aged males with obligations that circumscribed their individualism.

When the traditional patriarchal authority of Protestant churches was eclipsed by post-Revolutionary disestablishment, American women became the informal caretakers of religious and civic morality, which they tended in families, schools, churches, communities, popular culture, and reform movements. The rise of companionate marriages, Victorian sexuality, and domestic autonomy afforded women the leverage necessary for managing morality. Women used popular recognition of their moral superiority along with norms of affection, passionlessness, and maternal prerogative to influence men's ideas and shape their behavior. Victorian prescriptive literature honored women for their piety and advised men to defer to them in spiritual matters. That way, virtuous women could make their men into sober breadwinners, and male society into a tempered community.[53] Marx was wrong: it was not religion per se but pious mothers, wives, and lovers who were to be the opiate of the male masses.

Women did not have to consent to feminine piety, and some women did not. As Karen Offen notes, the initial wave of scholarship on nineteenth-century feminism recovered women's early demands for equal rights, equal opportunities, and equal voting power.[54] Prominent activists argued that Lockean natural rights should be extended across gender lines, and various women's groups struggled for legal and political equality. That was the main thrust of the historic Seneca Falls Declaration of Sentiments and Resolutions. It is not surprising that nineteenth-century feminists employed individualist language and values. Subordinate groups usually adapt the established political discourse as a strategic means for furthering their cause. What is remarkable, however, is the extent to which American women ignored individualism and cooperated in the promotion of the Victorian cult of true womanhood.

Recent scholarship suggests that women had much to gain by consenting to true womanhood. Women's freedom to choose partners and influence them during marriage grew; their control over their own sexuality and reproductive capacities was enhanced; their influence over their children and households increased; their access to education improved; their moral stature in society soared; and their political influence through moral reform movements provided them a new and even powerful public voice. Ideals of womanhood evolved toward what Daniel Scott Smith calls a "domestic feminism" that anticipated the potential erosion of patriarchy and empowerment of women.[55]

We must remember, however, that domestic feminism exacted a price by restricting women's choices in private and public life. Women were free to choose their own marriage partners, but they were not free to opt out of marriage lest they suffer poverty and social sanctions. Women claimed greater control over sex, reproduction, children, and household, but they were expected to repress their own passions and devote themselves full-time to the details of professionalized motherhood and housekeeping. Women gained the authority to manage family and community morals, but they were also to exemplify the self-sacrifice, sobriety, and civic virtue they preached to men. In sum, domestic feminism required that women make a primary commitment to marriage, motherhood, and morality and, by extension, consent to exclusion from the politics of self-interest, materialism, and power. Meanwhile, men continued to control the social, economic, and political institutions that enabled them to use law and coercion to deny women's claims to individualism and public power.

When the American Revolution challenged the traditional patriarchal political authority that gave kings power over citizens, it simultaneously legitimated new freedoms for young men. They were increasingly able to choose their own mates and build marriages based on affection. They achieved economic mobility by leaving their fathers' farms and shops to strike out for the frontier, new industries, or the clerkships and professions on the new middle-class horizon. Moreover, these sons of liberty inherited the political rights established by the Founding Fathers. Young men could cultivate political influence and exercise citizenship by joining informal groups and participating in conventional political processes. But that did not mean that youthful impulsiveness and aggression were given free reign. Quite the contrary.

Young men's rights were enclosed in a cultural stronghold of adult responsibility. Parents were advised to teach their sons the self-discipline, sobriety, and fortitude that would accompany them on their journey away from home. Young men were to announce their maturity by assuming the responsibilities of marriage, fatherhood, and breadwinning. Matrimony was " 'a debt to society,' an 'indispensable duty,' that had to be fulfilled [for] the greater good." [56] That debt included moral deference to civilizing mothers, wives, and lovers as well as the provision of patrimony for sons. Young men who resisted marriage encountered a number of cultural stigmas attached to bachelorhood (and homosexuality) and also the economic sanctions of those who considered them poor credit risks and flawed hiring material. Young men who married but failed to fulfill their family obligations were subject to social penalties imposed by "good society" and legal sanctions enforced by neighbors and administered by local magistrates.

Young men's political rights were also circumscribed. They were free to participate in local politics without much risk to the social order. They could discuss local issues, join local organizations, and eventually even experiment with radical ideas reaching from anarchism to socialism. Should their radical politics overspill local boundaries, however, state and federal officials maintained the legal authority and coercive power to compel quiescence. As Gordon Wood notes, the Framers engineered the U.S. Constitution to ensure that federal officialdom would be composed of the few tested, trusted, and worthy men most suited to maintaining order. Among other things, that meant that young men with national political ambitions had little chance of having any influence unless they proved their worth and earned the trust of elder power brokers. George Washington, Andrew Jackson, Theodore Roosevelt, and others had taught that the proof of young men's public worth was their success in military service and courage in combat. Or, as Judith Stiehm observes, "Old men run governments; young men are used and tested by them especially through participation in the military."[57]

Did young American males consent to undergo political trial by military ordeal? More than a few refused. They claimed the freedom to stay with their families or ply the marketplace. They equated compulsory military service and subordination with political tyranny and unnatural aristocracy. That explains why military planners constantly worried about meeting even minimal recruitment quotas. They tried bounties and land incentives to entice young men, experimented with universal military training to integrate militarism into everyday life, and finally settled on massive conscription to meet wartime manpower needs. Not surprisingly, many young Americans evaded military service, resisted conscription, rioted against the draft, and deserted from the army. What is significant, however, is the extraordinary number of young men who heeded the call to arms, by voluntary enlistment or acquiescence to conscription, and then obediently served their time regardless of discomfort, disease, and danger.

Large numbers of American youth did demonstrate a willingness to die for their country. Why? The answer must include a widespread belief in the Aristotelian notion that youthful obedience is the basis for adult command. Many Americans believed that military service would tame young men's passions, counteract their subversive tendencies, and school them in the self-discipline, sobriety, and patriotism associated with upstanding bourgeois citizenship and community leadership. This cultural icon was affirmed by the middle-class men who served in Civil War volunteer companies, then joined veterans' organizations, and finally assumed positions of leadership in their localities. Labor leaders implicitly contributed to this chorus when they employed memories of self-sacrifice and wartime service to justify the cause of workers' rights.[58] "Good society" conspired to convey the message that youthful obedience would be rewarded by the trust of powerful men, and that trust was an asset that could be parlayed into social esteem, job preferments, recognized public voice, and eligibility for advancement in business and politics.

America's martial version of Aristotelian citizenship constituted a liberal revision of traditional patriarchy. The benign Lockean patriarch who taught his son the rationality necessary for adult independence was now replaced by the pedagogical state that was to rule in the interests of young men, guide them toward maturity by providing them an education in civic and martial virtue, foster intergenerational male bonding, and then set young men free with the expectation that they were prepared to act as responsible adults who could claim individual rights without sowing social disorder. The aggression and conflicts associated with youth would be neutralized, not by conventional political institutions, but by making young men accomplices in the state's coercive apparatus. Youth who refused to submit to military discipline and veterans who failed to heed their civics lessons could then be controlled by the state's coercive apparatus—as Pullman strikers discovered when 48,000 soldiers were mobilized against them.

The final piece of America's patriarchal puzzle concerned middle-aged men. Ostensibly tamed by pious mothers, subdued by moralizing wives, and tested according to the norms of masculinity and military service, middle-aged men were the one American minority free to claim individual right and even complain about authority without being accused of subversion. Nonetheless, even they could not be wholly trusted. Mankind's inherently passionate nature implied that there was always a chance of personal and political backsliding. Furthermore, it was not enough for men to *earn* their individualist stripes and simply enjoy their liberty. They were the ones encumbered with the duty to exercise patriarchal leadership. They bore the burden of securing women's domesticity and channeling young men into military service. They had responsibility for micromanaging women's and young men's behavior to protect social order. They had the obligation to serve as the guardians of the American Way who preached civic virtue and patriotic self-sacrifice to social subordinates in return for a lion's share of status, wealth, and power.

Being a liberal patriarch could be difficult and painful. Middle-aged men had to engineer popular consent rather than rely solely on brute force to maintain their hegemony. That required great prudence, patience, and self-restraint. Moreover, it was not particularly satisfying for middle-aged men to live with wives suffering from nineteenth-century "hysteria" or the twentieth-century "problem without a name." Nor was it gratifying for fathers who encouraged their sons to fight in war to greet their return in body bags. The costs of being on top of the gender heap, as the new men's studies literature details, were always quite high. What must be remembered, however, is that American men consistently consented to bear the costs of maintaining their hegemony.[59]

The Other Liberal Tradition in America

Diggins writes, "Classical [republican] philosophy aims to discipline man's desires and raise him far above his vulgar wants; liberalism promises to realize desires and satisfy wants. The first is more noble, the second more attainable."[60] Diggins is right in one sense. Republicanism demanded that men cultivate self-control and self-sacrifice in the cause of civic virtue and public good, whereas liberalism seemed to invite individual self-indulgence, self-interest, and self-satisfaction. Indeed, part of liberalism's historical appeal was that it combined the promise of individual freedom with the prospect of prosperity and progress. Even men weighed down by everyday woes could look forward to a better future. As Frances Fitzgerald observes, "That individuals could start over again, and if necessary reinvent themselves, was one of the great legends of American life. It was the stuff of self-improvement manuals."[61]

However, the American experiment with liberalism demonstrated that it was not necessarily more attainable than republicanism. Liberal individualism threatened to unleash men's passions and interests. And men could not conceivably escape Hobbesian conflict and chaos unless their appetites were subdued by a steady diet of republican civic virtue. In America, that diet was to be catered by selfless women, fortified by young men's martial spirit and military service, and managed by middle-aged men. What might be called "the other liberal tradition in America" was that aspect of our Lockean heritage that was much less intent on extending individualism, self-expression, and self-interest, and far more anguished over excessive individualism that begged restraint and suppression to secure social order. Manifested primarily in American culture, the other liberal tradition ennobled women for taming men, applauded the military for presiding over the rites of manhood, and, ultimately, justified and perpetuated liberal patriarchy. In America, individualism and civic virtue came wrapped in a single package.

Recognition of the other liberal tradition has two implications for the origins debate. First, each major contender tells a partial tale. Hartz's contention that Lockean liberalism pervaded early American thought, rhetoric, and culture forgets that ours was a Lockean liberalism that required and incorporated republican civic virtue according to an engendered division of labor. Wood's argument that republican discourse was central to early American thought neglects to specify that republicanism sought to restrain men's corrupt passions by relying on women to teach and young men to practice civic virtue. The third-wave scholars who locate both liberalism and republicanism at the origins of American thought fail to recognize that what they consider discrete intellectual paradigms were actually complementary components of a single-minded effort to make individualism conditional and compatible with social order.

Second, Hartz, Wood, and the others are wrong to assert the eventual triumph of individualism in America. The triumph of liberalism in America was not an unqualified victory for individualism. America's Lockean consensus and institutions prescribed a conditional individualism that combined individual rights and patriarchal responsibilities for tested middle-aged men. It also supported a selfless civic culture for women and for the young men who were not so much to inherit as to earn their individual rights. Were this tale of gender and generations enriched by including analyses of class and race, for example, one might conclude that individualism is no more than a whisper in the lives of most Americans.

Why then so much talk about individualism by its academic defenders and critics? Why so much concern with individualism expressed by right-wing and left-wing activists intent on finding correctives for it? After we locate the origins of the other liberal tradition in the intellectual ferment of Restoration England, analyze John Locke's articulation and anticipation of it, and trace its evolution in eighteenth- and nineteenth-century America, we shall see that even individualism for the few has become problematic. Hegel reminds us that the owl of Minerva spreads its wings with the fall of dusk.

Part One
English Origins

The fault is not in the government as

absolute, but in human nature which is not

often found sufficient.

—James Tyrrell

In the little experience I have had in the

world, I have observed most men to do as much

mischief as lay in their power.

—John Trenchard

The century following the English Civil War was a remarkable moment in political thought. Longstanding beliefs in the divine right of kings and the authority of the established church were challenged. Classical theories of liberty, commonwealth, and citizenship were resurrected and reformulated. Experiments with an ideology of individual rights, commerce, and limited government were initiated. English intellectuals sensed that they were leaving traditional patriarchal politics behind, saving the best of the past and pioneering new insights for the future. Still, they were not optimists. They deeply feared that enlightened thought raced ahead of people's ability to know it and live it. Human nature was flawed. People preferred mischief to civic virtue and rationality.

Everywhere, claims to liberty and rights produced the specter of chaos. Theorists associated common men with the mob and aristocrats with depravity. They accused commercial men of avarice and political officials of corruption. Male intellectuals were mostly horrified by protofeminist writers who disputed husbands' authority at home, promoted women's influence in society, mocked men's pretensions to civic virtue and rationality, and threatened to unleash female treachery on the nation. Social commentators constantly condemned the new generation of young men for effeminacy, lust, self-indulgence, stupidity, materialism, and reluctance to fulfill obligations to family and the state. Republicans and liberals converged on a "liberalism of fear" that was obsessed with the excessive individualism cutting across class, gender, and generation to subvert social order and destroy prospects for public good.

Part One locates the origins of liberalism in Restoration England's self-conscious fear of excessive individualism. It shows how early-modern views on gender and generation defined the nature and depth of that fear. And it analyzes the intellectual climate in which John Locke confronted that fear and developed an engendered response that conditioned individualism with civic virtue.

On the Man Question

There was cause for optimism in late seventeenth-
and early eighteenth-century England. Discontent,
protest, civil war, and revolution dealt fatal blows
to traditional patriarchal authority. Priests could
no longer impose morals; princes could not sustain
absolutism. A rigid system organized by coercion
could conceivably become an open society based
on consent. Men would reclaim ancient liberties
and proclaim natural rights, produce wealth and
procure prosperity, practice civic virtue and govern
themselves according to the dictates of reason. Rebellion against religious and political fathers invited
some talk of fraternal democracy. But intellectuals had reason for apprehension. The mob's mur-
murings, merchant greed, and aristocratic profligacy seemed to elevate licentiousness above liberty.
Women's call for freedom and young men's foppery
appeared to indicate widespread moral decadence.
So much good was possible; so much corruption
was evident.

Historians sort this intellectual ferment into distinctive republican and liberal paradigms. They tell
us that English republicans resurrected civic virtue
as a counterweight to the corrupt individualism,
commerce, and bureaucratic state that defined
modernity. English liberals, however, validated

modernity in social contracts that legitimated individual rights, market relations, and limited government. In brief, republicans wanted to conserve classical politics, liberals to free individuals from it. Historians then argue the relationship of each paradigm to politics. J. G. A. Pocock sees republicanism as a basis for democratic community, but Caroline Robbins views it as a justification for upper-class rule. Diggins links liberalism to Calvinist despair and democratic tyranny, while Appleby ties it to human perfectibility and democratic progress. Wood puts republicanism at the wheel of America's democratic revolution, but Hartz makes liberalism the driving force of America's democratic evolution.

"Republicanism" and "liberalism" are abstract constructs that partially distort the English political theory situated at the origins of later American political thought. English theorists did not recognize any paradigmatic divide between republicanism and liberalism. Their idea of a "Whig" swallowed James Harrington's republican fantasy and James Tyrrell's liberal contract in a single gulp. The republican Earl of Shaftesbury and his liberal protégé John Locke lived, wrote, and schemed together. Algernon Sidney joined liberal consent theory to republican values. John Trenchard and Thomas Gordon were republican writers who injected large doses of Hobbesian liberalism into *Cato's Letters*. The conflation, collaboration, and combination beg the possibility that concepts such as civic virtue and individualism were complementary components of a single discourse.

That discourse did not directly concern democracy. Whigs were far more obsessed with the issue of social order. They agreed that traditional patriarchal authority was responsible for the disorders of the age. Only in their search for arguments, allies, and audiences against absolute kingship and court corruption did they approach the borders of democratic politics and explore the terrain of popular sovereignty. But it was one thing to happen upon popular sovereignty as a protest strategy and quite another to invite men to unleash democratic passions. The overwhelming Whig view was that men's passions were destructive, their reason ineffectual, and their capacity for self-government weak. The Whig dilemma was to justify men's liberation from traditional patriarchalism without setting free men's destructive appetites and ignorance, or what I call "the man question": *How could impassioned men be granted republican liberty or liberal rights without fostering the twin evils of anarchy and tyranny?*[2]

The Age of Virtue

Republican theory presumed that men could live frugally and act virtuously, work industriously but accumulate modestly, contribute to collective good, and respect individuality. Ideally, men achieved personal fulfillment in politics, identified with the political community, and developed so strong a loyalty to it that they voluntarily risked liberty, livelihood, and life to protect it. Machiavelli, Harrington, Montesquieu, Rousseau, and other republican philosophers occasionally conceived so perfect a blending of individualism and community that they imagined that popular sovereignty and democratic fraternity could be viable foundations for political life.

The core of republicanism was the belief that men could renounce narrow self-interest and put moral thought in command of passion. In turn, thoughtful men would practice civic virtue, which "could signify devotion to the public good; . . . the practice, or the preconditions of the practice, of relations of equality between citizens engaged in ruling and being ruled; and lastly, since citizenship was above all a mode of action and practicing the active life, . . . that active ruling quality . . . which confronted *fortuna* and was known to Renaissance Italians as *virtu*."[3] Individual devotion to public good was demanding. Men had to rein in their selfishness, resist temptations to inequality, and tolerate disagreement, debate, and dissent while striving for consensus. They needed to master the irrational forces that existed within them as unruly passions and between them as domination, tyranny, and war. Citizenship was considered a difficult full-time job.

But it was a job promising a priceless reward. As Joyce Appleby notes, "Virtue and liberty were indissolubly linked in classical republican theory."[4] Men cultivated civic virtue to satisfy their political nature and also to establish and safeguard beloved liberty. Men who failed to discipline appetites or participate in public affairs would be enslaved by their passions and oppressed by their leaders. Men who lacked patriotic ardor or fell short of martial courage invited betrayal by mercenaries and conquest by enemies. Civic virtue was the bedrock of liberty. Conversely, liberty was the pillar of civic virtue. Men needed moral autonomy and political freedom to cultivate civic sentiment and fraternal feeling, harmonize private desire and public devotion. Ultimately, republican liberty meant the freedom to cultivate and practice the active civic life.[5]

Republican theorists were always alert to barriers in the path of civic virtue and liberty. Machiavelli's *Prince* outlined a political science that relied on a leader's "cunning assisted by fortune" to foster individual self-sacrifice and patriotism. The wise prince drew men to virtue and drove them from vice.[6] Machiavelli's *Discourses* stressed two other props for civic virtue. One was tradition. Machiavelli recalled the Roman Republic and its founding fathers as sources of historical continuity, community sentiment, and good citizenship guided by exemplary leadership. The other prop was political participation. Men's direct involvement in politics, especially in bearing arms for the state, would teach them to identify their personal prospects with the republic's prosperity and independence.[7]

English republicans resurrected Machiavelli in the seventeenth century with a special sensitivity to the fragility of civic virtue in an emerging commercial era. James Harrington hoped that civic virtue would be a buffer against modernity. He put traditional agrarian freeholding and militia service at the center of his *Commonwealth of Oceana*. Only independent landowners could raise themselves "out of the mire of private interest unto the contemplation of virtue." They alone had incentive and wherewithal to defend people against domestic tyrants and foreign enemies. By contrast, propertyless servants were "mere hirelings" and urban speculators acted as if "ambition [was] every man's trade."[8] Harrington's pastoral idyll provided a framework for a century of dissent. English republicans took turns condemning royal prerogative, court patronage, state bureaucracy, public credit, oppressive taxation, and the standing army as forces that robbed men of liberty, invited selfishness and greed, and empowered deceit.[9] The result was popular unrest, social strife, political factionalism, tyranny, and needless wars driven by the perverse spirit of commerce. Men's avarice, mobile property, stockjobbing, brokering, and profligacy conspired to elevate greed above public good and subordinate politics to private interest. Trenchard and Gordon blamed "the dirty race of money changers" for destroying virtue, attacking liberty, and corrupting politics.[10]

Republican writers did more than lament modernity. They wanted to redeem men's civic virtue. They recalled England's "ancient constitution" as the legitimate measure of a balanced political economy "in which the virtues of all may neutralize the vices from which none is free."[11] The ancient constitution was a complex of unwritten traditions. For some, it symbolized a golden age when rural aristocrats and their retainers kept royalty at bay. For others, it signified a historical agreement to balance liberty among the commons, nobility, and monarchy. For most, it was an instrument of expediency. For example, Algernon Sidney advocated the restoration of "ancient liberty, dignity, and happiness" and invoked Magna Carta as a "declaration of English liberties" to justify popular sovereignty and Parliament's authority. But Sidney was quite willing to condemn tradition and correct constitutional "errors" when necessary. He wrote, "There can be no greater mark of the most brutish stupidity than for men to continue in an evil way because their fathers had brought them into it." [12]

Nostalgia for the idyllic past was a convention that often masked a willingness to accommodate modernity. Montesquieu defined civic virtue as "a love for the republic . . . that may be felt by the meanest as well as by the highest person in the state." The modern dilemma was that, "when virtue is banished, ambition invades the hearts of those who are capable of receiving it and avarice possesses the whole community." To break this degenerate cycle, Montesquieu wanted to do more than restore the rhetoric of civic virtue. He thought that restrained commerce could be a bond of fraternal trust. He believed that private vice could be neutralized by state regulation and public vice by institutional engineering. In both cases, "Power should be a check on power." [13] His hope was to reconcile classical virtue with modern materialism and contain ancient vices with modern political technology.

Rousseau, however, had little confidence in Montesquieu's political science. He thought the likeliest cure for modernity was the appearance of a classical "Great Legislator" who, like Moses, would be a charismatic founding father able to urge men to set aside selfishness, participate in politics and war, and identify private interest with public good. The Great Legislator would force men to be free by habituating them to think and act in terms of a General Will. [14] Modern vice eradicated and ancient virtue restored, Rousseau's father figure would disappear, and thereby enable citizens to achieve freedom and equality in a democratic community. That is largely how Harrington ended his republican fantasy. Lord Archon, Oceana's founder, abdicated his authority to the people, who reacted "with tears in their eyes of children that had lost their father." [15] Men needed ancient fathers, but only modern orphans were free to govern themselves.

Republicans' overriding theme was that men could exercise civic virtue and secure liberty in a suitable environment. They might need leadership from founding fathers, foxy princes, and great legislators to create that environment; they may have to depend on freeholders and armed citizens to protect it; they certainly needed to participate in politics and install checks on corruption to sustain it; and they had to recall and resist the past while confronting and accommodating modernity. Even then, sustaining civic virtue was difficult because, as Montesquieu observed, "Virtue is self-renunciation which is always arduous and painful." [16] Still, republicans honored men's capacity for virtue and liberty because they thought that selflessness and sociality were essential to the human condition. Every age, even the most corrupt, was an immanent Age of Virtue.

That men can define their individuality in terms of public good may seem hopelessly naive in our Age of Skepticism. Judith Shklar thinks so. Hence she characterizes Rousseau as "the last of the classical utopists." John Diggins agrees, asserting that republicanism is more noble but less attainable than self-interested liberalism. [17] Before joining this chorus of skepticism, we should consider what George Orwell called "the overwhelming strength of patriotism [and] national loyalty" in our time. [18] Modern revolutions and wars indicate that many men are eager to forgo personal ease and comfort and identify subjective interests with national causes—and even die for them. Furthermore, the republican idea that men's civic virtue is the basis for personal fulfillment and liberty serves an important ideological function. It announces the distance between classical ideals and modernity and generates a discourse against established power. Along these lines, Pocock argues that republicanism persisted in America as an opposition ideology. [19] Finally, the republican merger of individualism and civic virtue was no more utopian than liberalism's reliance on men's rationality to unite self-interest and public good.

The Age of Reason

The straightforward baseline of English liberalism was that men sought self-preservation and shaped political life to secure it. However, the journey from self-preservation through consent and contract to limited government was circuitous. Liberal theorists expressed a remarkable philosophic faith in men's rational capacity to follow the route. They portrayed men as individuals who understood and obeyed natural law, accurately gauged current options against future consequences, placed intelligence and sobriety ahead of passion, and self-consciously adjusted private interests to public order. Liberal thinkers thereby evoked an Age of Reason where individual rights precipitated democratic politics.

Hobbes's pioneering theory required men to show a moment of incredible foresight and a lifetime of political fidelity. Naturally free and equal, all men were to follow a complex logic connecting individual self-preservation to prudential laws of nature. Next, men had to foresee that their consent to a social contract would end nature's war of each against each without producing a slavish submission to neighbors, sovereign authority, or enemies. Once having consented to the social contract, Hobbesian men were to exchange active intelligence for passive compliance. They not only had to honor contractual promises; they also needed to resist invoking individual rights whenever they felt inconvenienced by law or decree. The better part of Hobbesian wisdom was to cling to the belief that one's security was best safeguarded by habitual obedience to the Leviathan. Individual fidelity to the law and the sovereign was the key to personal safety and public good.[20]

Hobbes attributed to men a genius and sobriety that critics often consider fantastical. Carole Pateman argues that, for selfish and warring men in Hobbes' state of nature, "the prudential thing to do would be *to enter no covenants at all*" because individuals had no assurance that others shared their rationality or intended to honor the contract. Gordon Schochet adds that Hobbesian men lacked the organic bonds that made social agreement and political harmony thinkable. Leo Strauss warns that Hobbes's right to self-preservation amounted to "a natural right to folly" because it allowed individuals to determine what was necessary for self-preservation and thereby authorized them to contravene law and destroy order.[21] The critics clearly doubt that men's enlightened self-interest and rational self-control are sufficient sources for social peace.

Liberal contract theorists after Hobbes wanted to enhance popular sovereignty and limit kingship, a political project that demanded even greater faith in men's rationality. James Tyrrell and John Locke produced political schemes that required men to reconsider and renew rational consent in each generation, participate in periodic decisions regarding representation and the use of political power, and make economic choices with relatively few political restraints. The idea that men could make significant choices without generating anarchy or inviting tyranny presupposed an extraordinary if not utopian belief that men could master chaotic passions, cultivate reason, and demonstrate consistent wisdom.

Tyrrell's liberalism was predicated on men's ability to balance reason and desire. Fathers were to raise their sons to be free and equal adults. That meant fathers had to master powerful paternal affections and anxieties that might bind sons beyond their nonage; and adult sons were to balance the rights of manhood against obligations of filial loyalty, showing gratitude without inviting servitude. This domestic tightrope act prefigured liberal politics. Tyrrell's limited monarch was to respect men's natural rights despite impulses to dominate men; and his citizens were to claim individual rights while remaining loyal to the king.[22] The crucial test of men's balanced reason was their reaction to injustice. When a father abused his authority, for example, "the rules of right reason or prudence" counseled that paternal governance should be contested only when lives were imperiled. Otherwise, domestic order would be upset too easily. Likewise, when a limited monarch overstepped his authority, citizens had to determine whether the abuse was fundamental or frivolous. Tyrrell explained, "A mischief to some private men is better than an inconvenience in giving every private person power that thinks himself injured . . . to be his own judge and right himself by force; since that were contrary to the great duty of every good subject of endeavoring to preserve the common peace and happiness of his country, which ought to be preferred before any private man's interest." Not only did men have to be rational and sober enough to tolerate an unjust denial of their rights to preserve the greater good of "common peace and happiness"; they also had to adjust the calculus of self-denial to particular circumstances. For example, men might protest against a king who decided "to pull down a whole town for his diversion" in peacetime, but they were to obey a king who ordered "the suburbs of a city to be demolished . . . to make it serviceable" in wartime.[23]

Locke painted the most stunning portrait of men's rationality. His social contract required a minority of men to have sense enough to defer to majority rule. The majority was to make wise decisions in establishing civil society, framing lawful government, choosing worthy representatives, and entrusting authority to honorable political leaders. Political leaders had to recognize legislative primacy and resist temptations to abuse executive authority. In general, men needed the foresight to recognize that individual rights were best protected by support for impersonal procedures and law. However, Lockean men also had to understand that there were times when the better part of rationality was to ignore impersonal procedures and law. Locke defined government as an "express or tacit trust that it shall be employed for [men's] good and the preservation of their property." And there were times when men had to trust leaders who ignored or disobeyed law in exercising discretion for public good. John Dunn notes, "The reason [Lockean] government is a trust is precisely because discretion is intrinsic to the proper exercise of government." [24] Locke invested so much faith in men's rationality that his version of citizen–state relations approximated the degree of mutual understanding and loyalty usually associated with family life.

Locke also attributed to men an exceptional economic rationality. Once property rights were protected by social contract, law, and discretion, Lockean men were to understand and withstanding the pain of labor, tolerate the anxiety of seeking subsistence amidst scarcity, and recognize the necessity of industry and honesty. They needed to work hard, compete for life's necessities, and seek prosperity without becoming too upset, assertive, or violent over deprivation, failure, or perceived injustice. Locke presumed that men were rational enough to submit their property disputes to government adjudication and comply with official judgments, even adverse ones. Perhaps most challenging, Lockean men had to adjust their economic strategies to the long haul. The wise man entered the marketplace and played by its rules even when he had little hope for *immediate* gain. By Locke's logic, the marketplace unleashed men's industry, fostered general abundance, and enhanced all men's *future* prospects.[25] The enlightened entrepreneur suffered deprivation today to achieve prosperity tomorrow.

Nathan Tarcov summarizes liberalism's basic rationality rule: "Too firm an insistence on one's rights, whether expressed in a direct contest for mastery or in complaints to authority, makes civility impossible and some kind of conflict inevitable." [26] Liberalism required men whose reason counseled modesty regarding claims to individual rights, stoical acceptance of affronts, abuses, and injustices, and tolerance of personal, economic, and political self-denial in the cause of public peace and *eventual* freedom and prosperity. Judith Shklar thinks republicanism is utopian, but she also recognizes that liberalism makes extraordinary demands on men's intellect and self-control. She writes, "Liberalism is, in fact, extremely difficult and constraining, far too much so for those who cannot endure contradiction, complexity, diversity, and the risks of freedom." [27]

It is therefore not surprising that modern skeptics wheel out doubts about liberalism's viability. The theory promised a society where free and equal men could achieve individuality, prosperity, and peace; but, in fact, critics argue, it invited men to indulge acquisitiveness, submit to market priorities, and suffer the tyranny of monied interests. Other skeptics add that liberal rationality was so abstract, disembodied, instrumental, and materialistic that it neglected the mutual caring, nurturance, and bonding essential for peaceful order.[28] One could conclude that liberalism asked the impossible of men, promised more than it could deliver, and failed to reconcile individualism and order. But several qualifications require consideration. One is that liberalism was an effort to separate men from hierarchical traditions and promote an open society that *gradually* enabled men to cultivate reason, enlighten their self-interest, and choose social peace. Appleby highlights the face of liberalism that smiled on individual rights as a source of men's "initiative and creative intelligence" and civilization's "spiritual and material advances."[29] Another qualification is that liberalism was an effective, dissenting ideology. One can interpret social contract theory as a study in "hypothetical consent," or what abstract rational men would agree to under ideal circumstances. The result was a standard of justice and language of rights that were used to attack absolute monarchy and win popular support for the struggle against it.[30] In this sense, liberal utopianism was good opposition politics.

We can now identify two bridges across the ostensible republican–liberal divide. First, both theories contained an extraordinary if not utopian faith in men's capacities to reconcile private desires and public good. Republicanism placed individual self-sacrifice at the center of civic virtue, and liberalism put individual self-denial at the hub of enlightened self-interest. The common element was a shared sense of men's potential to identify their sense of self with the larger political community and then create and sustain a voluntary order that, sooner or later, involved experimentation with freedom and equality, popular sovereignty, and fraternal democracy. Second, republicanism and liberalism contributed to opposition ideology. One wanted to revive the Age of Virtue, while the other anticipated the Age of Reason, but both theories provided arguments that contributed to political movements against established political power. The two bridges were interconnected. Theorists' faith in men derived from their ideological opposition to traditional patriarchal authority.

Against Traditional Patriarchalism

Albert Hirschman writes, "A feeling arose in the Renaissance and became a firm conviction during the seventeenth century that moralizing philosophy and religious precept could no longer be trusted with restraining the destructive passions of men. New ways had to be found."[31] England's legitimation crisis in the seventeenth century was fueled by republican and liberal attacks on traditional patriarchal norms pervading religion and politics. Dissenting theorists converged on the Whig argument that neither church nor state could secure domestic peace because the passions of priests and princes exacerbated social anarchy and political tyranny. Whig opposition to traditional patriarchalism made it possible and expedient for theorists to ennoble men's capacities for civic virtue and rationality; but opposition did not necessarily prompt theorists to trust men to govern themselves.

Traditional patriarchalism in Stuart England had three facets. First, "anthropological patriarchalism" provided a historical account of political evolution from the original dominion of primitive fathers to the contemporary rule of kings. The usual story was that ancient fathers ruled their families, banded together to protect their families, and chose a military figure or king to lead defense efforts. Necessity gave birth to absolute monarchy. Second, "moral patriarchalism" called on the divine authority of God-the-Father and the natural authority of primitive fathers to legitimate absolute monarchy. Here, God authorized fathers to rule their families and ruling patriarchs gradually evolved into the political patriarchs of clans, communities, and nations. Necessity became a virtue. Third, "ideological patriarchalism" made family government a model for all human relations. Fathers' authority over families was the prototype for masters' rule of servants, ministers' leadership of flocks, and kings' dominion over subjects.[32] Traditional patriarchalism's overarching ideal was to establish, maintain, and enforce harmonious, hierarchical relations from family to kingdom. Priests and princes disseminated origin stories that announced the rule of fathers, a Fifth Commandment catechism that taught obligatory filial obedience, and a popular culture that diffused and reinforced "proper" hierarchical order.

Several post-Renaissance trends created a climate for disputing patriarchal church and state authority. The Reformation fostered religious conflict and provided theological support for religion-based dissent. Efforts to defend orthodoxy intensified but often backfired, fostering protest, zealotry, and armed resistance. The religious bulwarks of patriarchalism in disrepair, monarchs became more dependent on coercion to maintain social control. But coercion proved problematic. It hinted at political tyranny and encountered widespread resistance among the armed nobility. And as the means of coercion shifted from the longbow to the cannon and from the cavalry to the infantry, "the cost of [state coercion] increased, the number of men required rose, and the desirability of a standing army over ad hoc formations became ever more clear."[33] Royal reliance on coercion drove monarchs toward centralized bureaucracy, rising taxation, and forced conscription challenging the prerogatives of country aristocrats and fostering their rebellion. It was the fragility of absolute kingship that prompted Sir Robert Filmer's controversial defense of it.[34]

The Restoration following the English Civil War could not put the pieces of traditional patriarchalism back together again. Stable aristocratic ownership of landed estates kept intact by primogeniture and entail was assaulted by mobile property relations, commerce, credit, and complex government involvement in finance and trade that altered the economic landscape and produced uncertainty among freeholders. And more than a few propertied men suspected that the traditional balance of power between freeholders and the crown was tilting toward the corrupt court and its bureaucracy, placemen, agents in Parliament, and standing army.[35] With economy and politics in flux, republican and liberal thinkers began to question whether traditional patriarchalism was sufficient for sustaining civic order, stable property, social peace, and national integrity.

When posing these questions, English political theorists overstepped the conceptual boundaries between republican and liberal theory. For example, Harrington's commonwealth was founded on ancient prudence and natural rights, with civic virtue defined as "whatever [is] reason in

the contemplation of a man being brought forth by his will into action."
Trenchard and Gordon spoke of the ancient constitution and civic virtue
but also used the language of natural rights, rational consent, and social
contract. Conversely, Tyrrell strengthened his case for contractual limits
on kingship by recalling the ancient "liberties of the subjects." He argued
that limits on monarchy accorded with "the laws of nature and virtue."
Meanwhile, Locke dwelled on—and on—about the need for men to concern themselves with public good.[36] Whig thinkers could mix their republican and liberal metaphors because they were engaged in a common effort
to condemn the moral patriarchalism that justified absolute kingship.

In essence, republicanism and liberalism were alternative and overlap-
ping rhetorics that constituted the Whig argument that God, nature, history, and reason declared in a single voice that family fathers retained the
right to choose new forms of government for the public good.[37] The idea
that yesterday's fathers opted for traditional patriarchalism did not obli-
gate today's fathers to make the same choice, especially now that church
and state authority were viewed as disruptive forces. Thus, Harrington
attacked the "inexcrable custom" of Popish religion to foster war and
conflict. He warned that a commonwealth that did not rule its clergy
would "have neither quiet at home nor honor abroad." Whig fears of
religious intolerance intensified in the 1670s and 1680s with the prospect
of Charles II's brother installing Catholicism on the throne. In a notable
1675 tract, Shaftesbury and Locke collaborated to condemn Catholicism,
conformity, the court, the profligate aristocracy, and the standing army as
a seamless threat to English liberty, property, trade, and peace. Even after
the 1688–89 Revolution rid England of its Catholic king, Whigs still suffered anxiety over organized religion. Trenchard and Gordon noted that
"the Christian religion has not been able to tame the restless appetites of
men" but instead turned the Gospel into "a lasting warrant for contention,
severity, and rage."[38]

Blaming political patriarchalism for social disarray was a staple of Whig
tracts. Algernon Sidney's *Discourses* pointed the finger at absolute kingship for instigating a Hobbesian war of each against each. It caused factionalism over royal succession and further upset social peace by legitimating incompetent leadership, abusive authority, denials of rights, courtly
vice and venality, government violence, and national decay. Sidney contemplated the possibility of benign absolutism but quickly rejected it: "It

may be said that some princes are so full of virtue and goodness as not to desire more power than the laws allow. . . . That may be and sometime is. The nation is happy that has such a king but he is hard to find and more than a human power is required to keep him in so good a way." Arguing that "there is none more mutable or unstable than absolute monarchy," Sidney concluded that absolute monarchy would have to disappear before any semblance of political stability could reappear.[39]

The Whig attack on moral patriarchalism would have had a limited effect unless accompanied by a political theory that justified the attack and provided a replacement for absolute kingship. That was where talk about men's virtue and rationality fit in. Republicanism and liberalism argued that absolute monarchs were corrupt and ignorant, whereas English citizens, *by comparison,* were politically trustworthy. Still, most of the rhetoric regarding men's trustworthiness was purely instrumental. Whig propagandists used it to appeal to men's egos and aspirations in order to win popular support for opposition politics. As their commentary on anthropological and ideological patriarchalism revealed, Whig thinkers showed no serious urge to substitute men's freedom and equality for patriarchal restraints.

Whigs never contested anthropological patriarchalism. They adhered to the conventional belief that fathers had original dominion in their families and the right to represent their families in public life. For Harrington, "the derivation of power from fathers of families [is] the natural root of the commonwealth." Sidney's social contract was based on the principle that "every father of a family is free and exempt from the domination of any other." Tyrrell completed the thought, writing that "women, children, and servants . . . might be supposed as represented by their husbands, fathers, and masters."[40] This origin story legitimated fathers' sovereignty at home and in politics and thereby upheld fathers' right to challenge absolute monarchs. But the story also reinforced the conventional belief that individuals who were not male heads of households had no immediate claims on liberty and rights. Bachelors, husbands without sons, unpropertied men, and servants, in addition to women and children, were a subordinate majority. Family fathers alone were thought to have settled into the sobriety necessary for fulfilling patriarchal responsibilities.

Moreover, Whigs appeared to dispute ideological patriarchalism but actually revised their image of family patriarchy and then revived it as a model for social relations. Their overt message seemed to support hierarchy in the domestic realm and equality in the public arena. Sidney wrote that "What right soever a father may have over his family, it cannot relate to that which a king has over his people," and Locke added that the "two powers, political and paternal, are . . . perfectly distinct."[41] But this separation of spheres was not particularly neat. Whigs certainly thought that the demise of absolute kingship would foster the rise of individual fathers' authority. "Every man is a king till he divests himself of his right," stated Sidney.[42] But Whigs were not convinced that fathers could be trusted with the absolute domestic authority that enabled them to turn their little commonwealths into petty tyrannies. In general, Whigs supported a gradual shift in family norms from paternal absolutism to what Lawrence Stone calls "affective individualism."[43] Fathers' authority was limited by notions of marriage as a negotiable contract, moral prescriptions that husbands treat wives with warmth and respect, greater reliance on women's management of households and child rearing, and recognition that adult sons were free and equal men. Tyrrell and Locke, for example, espoused versions of fatherhood that obligated men to fulfill demanding familial duties while exercising limited authority. This was no easy task, and fathers would surely fail unless they showed the patience, prudence, and affection necessary for winning their families' consent and cooperation. Should fathers fail, it was possible that mothers would be justified in assuming family sovereignty.[44]

Whig political theory followed the same logic. Republican and liberal thinkers wanted to abolish *absolute* kingship but had no intention of abolishing monarchy itself. What they imagined was a new breed of monarchs obligated to serve citizens and public good while exercising limited political authority. To succeed, monarchs would have to demonstrate virtue, wisdom, restraint, and affection in order to engineer the consent and cooperation of the governed. Otherwise (Sidney and Tyrrell implying what Locke stated outright), citizens would have the revolutionary right to depose kings and assume political sovereignty for themselves. This parallel logic points to a revival of anthropological patriarchalism with limited fatherhood in families serving as a model for limited patriarchy in politics. It also points to Whig complicity in reinforcing royal authority. In the 1640s, Henry Parker argued that kings would be far more secure, effective, and powerful if they dumped disputed claims to absolute authority and affirmed the rhetoric of popular liberty and the reign of law. That way, kings would win people's affection and gratitude and thereby "magnify themselves by enfranchising their subjects." Some forty years later, Sidney made a similar argument: "They . . . who place kings within the power of the law and the law to be a guide to kings equally provide for the good of king and people, whereas they who admit no participants in power and acknowledge no rule but their own will set up an interest in themselves against that of their people, lose their affections, which is their most important treasure, and incur their hatred, from which results their greatest danger."[45] Whig common sense was that the wise king ruled with a velvet glove, and thereby reconstituted, reinforced, and continued his rule.

English theorists struck out on a very narrow path. They clearly opposed the *traditional* patriarchalism that rested on divine right, claimed absolute power, relied on coercion for social control, yet failed to restore domestic peace. But they also hesitated to forgo patriarchalism altogether. They continued to rely on the restraining influence of family fathers, political leaders, and even monarchs who were to establish their hegemony by parlaying limited authority into consent and compliance, anticipating what I shall call *liberal* patriarchy. Why did Whigs revise, revive, and liberalize patriarchalism rather than subvert it altogether? Why did they perpetuate the authority of fathers and rulers? The main reason was a deep-seated fear that most men, freed from patriarchal restraints, would destroy themselves and social order.

The Fear of Men

Republicans and liberals trusted men's capacity for virtue and reason just enough to experiment with men's liberty, rights, and sovereignty as alternatives to patriarchal kingship. Sidney summarized their hopes: "Liberty produces virtue, order, and stability," and "mixed and popular governments preserve peace and manage wars better than absolute monarchy."[46] Free men might restore stability and cut a path toward democracy. And progress along that path was possible as long as men demonstrated sufficient virtue and reason to avoid deftly or resolve peacefully their conflicts. The problem was that Whigs believed that the great mass of men suffered sinfulness, erratic and erotic appetites, foolish habits, and sheer ignorance manifested in everyday alcoholism, promiscuity, superstition, sloth, avarice, theft, deceit, aggression, and violence. The Whig consensus was that men's fidelity to civic virtue was weak, their claim to rationality anemic, and their capacity for democracy feeble.

Republicans regularly revisited the vices that toppled the Greek and Roman republics. They often recalled the rampant corruption of Renaissance city–states. History afforded abundant evidence of mankind's self-destructive tendencies and the failure of institutions to correct men's errant ways. Modernity made things worse, raising men's expectations and exposing them to new temptations. Stranded between distrust of traditional patriarchalism and doubts of modern men, republican theorists fantasized about the coming of a Messiah (a Moses, Lycurgus, Prince, Lord Archon, or Great Legislator) who would free men from self-destructive passions and lead them to a new commonwealth. But the philosophers knew that messiahs were rare, the decay of republics routine. Lamenting men's corruption, they offered remarkably little hope for men's redemption.

Republican laments had a class dimension. Harrington called for equality among men but looked to the nobility to control ignoble men. He explained, "Where there is not a nobility to bolt out the people, they are slothful, regardless of the world and the public interest of liberty." One reason that republicans opposed the standing army was that it put weapons "in the hands of ignorant, idle, needy persons." Trenchard stated, "I have observed most men to do as much mischief as lay in their power and therefore am for dealing with them as we do with children and mad men, that is, take away all weapons by which they may do either themselves or others an injury."[47] H. T. Dickinson's analysis concludes, "Commonwealthmen despised the masses as an ignorant and disorderly mob and as lacking in the necessary ability to resist bribery or to exercise independent political judgment."[48] The male masses were excused from republican citizenship.

This class dimension was complicated by Whigs' sense that the mob was no more corrupt than the idle, profligate aristocracy. Republicans bemoaned upper-class self-indulgence and luxury, and protofeminist pamphleteers took up the chant by accusing young dandies of addiction to alcohol, gambling, prostitution, effeminacy, and sodomy. Philosophers and pundits blamed the wealthy for squandering their patrimony, enslaving themselves to fad and fashion, and forsaking manly independence for materialism and moneychangers. "The men are so wickedly degenerated," according to one tract, "that learning, courage, and conduct seem to be unnecessary accomplishments." Without public-spiritedness and courage in defense of liberty, the young gentry were not "good commonwealth-men."[49]

Republicans also inveighed against aristocrats who abandoned landed estates to speculate in public credit and debt, stockjobbing, and wars of self-aggrandizement. Upper-class excesses added up to stupid, self-destructive greed. Profligacy wasted the nation's resources and robbed sober men of the incentive to be productive, honest, and law-abiding. The ultimate victim was civic virtue. Charles Davenant complained, "The little public spirit that remained among us is in a manner quite extinguished. Everyone is upon the scrape for himself, without any regard to his country; each cheating, raking, and plundering what he can, and in a more profligate degree than ever yet was known."[50] The spirit of commerce was said to have transformed the nobility from the stewards of social order into narrow economic specialists who preferred private interest to public good and used government as an instrument for private accumulation.

Pocock argues that "the most fundamental problem in eighteenth-century political and moral philosophy" was that "the conditions of life were such that virtue could never be fully realized."[51] No philosopher had a keener sense of men's corruption than Montesquieu, whose "misanthropy" made it plain "that mankind's moral powers were so inadequate that men were always in danger of mutual destruction."[52] *The Persian Letters* chronicled men's suicidal urge, best symbolized in the story of the Troglodyte people, who could resist no vice. Montesquieu told of "two extraordinary men" who rose above Troglodyte corruption and midwifed "the rebirth of virtue" into a republic. But the people could not keep it because virtue was too demanding. They sought a ruler who told them:

> I can see what is happening, O Troglodytes! Your virtue is beginning to weigh upon you. In the present state of affairs, with no chief, you must be virtuous in spite of yourselves. Otherwise you couldn't subsist and would fall into the misfortunes of your forefathers. But this yoke seems too hard to you. You prefer to be subjects of a prince and obey his laws, for they are less restrictive than your customs. You know that from now on, you can satisfy your ambition, acquire

riches, and languish in soft luxury, and that so long as you avoid falling into great crimes, you will have no need of virtue.[53]

Montesquieu's *Spirit of Laws* carried a sense of inevitable doom. Republics could not survive the world of men's passions, factions, and violence. Large republics fell victim to internal greed and jealousy, small republics to external aggression and war.[54]

Liberal theorists were equally despairing of men's chances to cultivate reason and master appetites. Henry Parker's precedent began with men's noxious passions: "Man being depraved by the fall of Adam grew so untame and uncivil a creature that the law of God written into his breast was not sufficient to restrain him from mischief, or to make him sociable." The challenge was "to regulate the motions of the people's moliminous body." The answer to men's "too excessive liberty" was absolute monarchy, but that promoted "the danger of unbounded prerogative." Parker's escape from mass anarchy and royal tyranny was to urge men's consent to a social contract that gave men *symbolic* sovereignty but gave a legislative assembly *tangible* authority to control the mob and limit kings.[55] Hobbes's fear of men's depravity involved men's tendency toward "competition, diffidence, and glory." He added, "the first makes man invade for gain; the second for safety; and the third, for reputation." Men's greed, insecurity, and pride fostered the aggression, violence, and war that drove men to the social contract but persisted after it. The Leviathan was to channel men's desires into habitual, productive, and placid activity.[56] Tyrrell's analysis was nearly as despairing. Most men lacked "that strength of mind, that they may know how in so great a liberty to govern their passions and lusts." Mankind was best known by its propensity toward "drunkenness, madness, or sudden rage." Men needed a bridle on their passions, which is why Tyrrell proclaimed, "I reverence monarchy above all other forms of government."[57] But sharing Parker's fear of absolute kingship, Tyrrell looked to Parliament to control common men and court excesses.

If Locke's philosophic faith in men's rationality was unequaled, his empirical skepticism regarding men's behavior was also unmatched. His writings dwelled on men's irrationality. His *Essay Concerning Human Understanding* portrayed sensate man as "a passive being, the plaything of external circumstances, weak, defenseless, helpless and dependent." Locke noted,

The ordinary necessities of our lives fill a great part of them with the uneasinesses of hunger, thirst, heat, cold, weariness, with labor and sleepiness, in their constant returns, etc. To which, if, besides accidental harms, we add the fantastical uneasiness (as itch after honor, power, or riches, etc.) which acquired habits, by fashion, example, and education, have settled in us, and a thousand other irregular desires, which custom has made natural to us, we shall find that a very little part of our life is so vacant from these uneasinesses, as to leave us free to the attraction of remoter absent good.

Even his political writings, which elevated men's rational potentials above history, kept returning to men's sins, passions, selfishness, foolishness, and prejudices overwhelming their reason.[58] Mankind's knowledge was flawed; man's lot constant toil, pain, and drudgery; and man's behavior a by-product of impulse, habit, and anxiety.

Lockean doubt encompassed upper-class legislators and voters. He warned against the king who acts "contrary to his trust when he either employs the force, treasury, and offices of society to corrupt the representatives and gain them to his purposes, or openly pre-engages the electors and prescribes to their choice such whom he has by solicitations, threats, promises, or otherwise won to his designs." The reason that the court could corrupt Parliament and voters was because even men of wealth and education failed to demonstrate adequate reason and self-control. Locke's education writings chronicled the ignorance of the upper class by cataloging the vices of its sons, appetitive creatures with an "inclination to riches, finery, or pleasing [the] palate." They loved liberty, but "they love something more; and that is dominion. . . . This love of power and dominion shows itself very early" in boys' craving to own, control, and monopolize property. Boys' power hunger largely derived from their fathers' example, encouragement, and "downright teaching them vice, and actually putting them out of the way of virtue." Locke lamented: "We shall have reason to wonder, in the great dissoluteness of manners which the world complains of, that there are any footsteps at all left of virtue."[59]

Locke's lament highlighted a spreading Whig fear that the landowning class was given to self-indulgence and self-destructive interest and could not be trusted to balance the commons and the king. He told the story

of an industrious farmer's heir who became "a fashionable young gentleman that cannot dine without champagne and burgundy, nor sleep but in
a damask bed. . . . He lives in splendor, 'tis true, but this unavoidably
carries away the money his father got, and he is every year . . . poorer. To
his expenses, beyond his income, add debauchery, idleness, and quarrels
amongst his servants." The result was predictable: "His manufactures are
disturbed, and his business neglected, and a general disorder and confu-
sion through his whole family and farm . . . will tumble him down the
hill the faster, and the stock, which the industry, frugality, and good order
of his father had laid up, will be quickly brought to an end, and he fast
in prison." The moral of the story had political consequences. Such vice
destroyed not only one's patrimony but also the nation, because "farm
and kingdom in this respect differ no more than as greater and less."[60]

English republicanism and liberalism converged on a fear of fratricide.
The male masses were anarchistic; monarchs practiced tyranny; and men
of property proved to be selfish and ignorant. *All* men shared destructive
passions and ineffectual reason, or, as Sidney stated, "Mankind is inclined
to vice."[61] Thus, while Whigs sought liberation from traditional patriarchalism in the name of liberty and rights, their fear of men's passions
and ignorance made them reticent to venture beyond "the liberalism of
fear" in politics.[62]

The Liberalism of Fear

In "On the Jewish Question," Karl Marx tried to
show how liberalism relied on men to tame their own passions and temper
their own irrationality. "To be *politically* emancipated from religion," he
wrote, "is not to be finally and completely emancipated from religion."
When priests and princes no longer enforced divine rules guiding men's
conduct, "religion not only continues to *exist* but is *fresh* and *vigorous*."
Similarly, Marx argued that political emancipation from property stimu-
lates men's drive to acquire and accumulate it.[63] By this logic, the eclipse
of traditional patriarchalism should have prompted men to harness their
passions to privatized religion and internalized codes of conduct; to sublimate their material desires into private acquisitiveness and economic

self-interest. Individual fear of God and hope for gain would make men compliant and industrious and politically free.

Republicans partially adapted but still doubted this logic. They generally supported religious toleration in lieu of church authority. But, following Machiavelli and Rousseau, they also proposed civil religions intended to ensure that men's private search for salvation aligned with public good. Montesquieu thought that religious toleration would encourage private belief, even errant belief. That was acceptable because "even a false religion is the best security we can have of the probity of men." Still, Montesquieu was wary of toleration lest it foster the "horror" of atheism that freed men from "the only rein which can restrain those who fear not human laws." Religious liberty ultimately required greater severity of law.[64]

English republicans, sensitized to religious violence during the Civil War and possible Catholic tyranny after it, saw toleration as a means to moderate religious tensions and conflict. They hoped that private conscience would gravitate to a Christian piety that would work against individual excess; unfortunately, private conscience would not ensure men's virtue or sobriety. Andrew Fletcher called on the militia to teach men lessons in "humility, modesty, charity, and the pardoning of private injuries." Sidney relied on "the good magistrate" to inculcate "youth in a love of virtue and truth." Trenchard and Gordon believed religion did little to "tie men's hands from wickedness," and argued that "the most certain security . . . against violence is the security of the laws."[65] The republican rule of thumb was that free thought had to be restrained by political guidance and legal regulation.

Liberalism covered the very same ground. At one extreme, Hobbes argued that individual judgment of good and evil was among the great "diseases" of a commonwealth. Private conscience and religion were prone to erroneous belief and set the individual in potential conflict with sovereign power. Hobbes eliminated conflict by authorizing the sovereign to define the words and attributes of God and thereby give public meaning to private belief. At the other extreme, Locke supported religious toleration as a pacifying but not an edifying social force. Toleration undermined zealotry without disturbing the "safety and security of the commonwealth." It even pointed toward a populist Christianity based on the Gospels. But even Locke's radical tolerance was limited. Atheism was a spur to anarchy, Catholicism a source of tyranny, and Lockean magistrates retained the authority to outlaw religious practices that offended public order.[66] Again, individual conscience was subversive and political restraint necessary.

Republicans and liberals were also convinced that giving men economic freedom from state control would not necessarily transform them into industrious producers and compliant citizens. On the one hand, English thinkers firmly believed that men's passions exceeded simple greed. Impiety, lust, adultery, whoring, gambling, drinking, idleness, ignorance, lying, hypocrisy, inconstancy, aggression, cruelty, fighting, dueling, pride, snobbery, waste, and luxury were embedded in men's nature and modern culture. These vices were perpetuated by upbringing and ubiquitous among the urban populace.[67] A common Whig complaint was that men were prone to squander inheritances and economic opportunities. On the other hand, republicans in particular were concerned with the disorders wrought by men's avarice. "Covetousness," wrote Harrington, "is the root of all evil."[68] Greedy men married for money, not love. They were easily bribed and corrupted. They often neglected virtue, foreswore citizenship, sought private power, and employed thugs to protect their wealth. They even imagined that money could buy immortality. Harrington marveled "that we should use our children as we do our puppies: take one, lay it in the lap, feed it with every good bit, and drown five. . . . [Primogeniture] is a flinty custom and all this for his cruel ambition, that would raise . . . a golden pillar for his monument . . . and a kind of immortality."[69]

The cure for avarice was stable property relations and a version of equality manifested in Gordon's eulogy of Trenchard: "He had a noble fortune . . . but though he was careful to preserve his estate, he was in no ways anxious to increase it."[70] But most Englishmen lacked noble fortunes, and the wealthy were ambitious to enlarge their estates. Redistribution was out of the question. It would fuel mob passions, rob the wealthy of their due, and further destabilize property relations. Without redistribution, however, propertyless men wanted economic independence, the rich monopolized ambition, and no one defended prudence and moderation. Theorists opted for what they considered the lesser evil. "Cobblers, tinkers, or fisherman were not people but *scum* to Whigs," writes Caroline Robbins. Whig ideologists wrote off the mob and devoted themselves to reforming the aristocracy. They promoted a rhetoric of civic virtue "to stiffen men's resistance to corruption and to unite them in defence of liberty." They cried "No Standing Army" to persuade the propertied to redeem their virtue through patriotic militia service. And they looked to government to enact policies to encourage economic stability and discourage commercial greed.[71]

An alternative was to contemplate a reconciliation of virtue and commerce.[72] Sober productivity, modest trade, and the search for comfort might foster social harmony, enhanced opportunity, general prosperity, and public good. But even Montesquieu, who married virtue to commerce, was reluctant to sanction men's economic freedom. He wrote, "The spirit of commerce is naturally attended with that of frugality, oeconomy, moderation, labor, prudence, tranquility, order, and rule," but he quickly added, "The mischief is when excessive wealth destroys this spirit of commerce." Economic freedom fueled the accumulation of excessive wealth which, in turn, militated against frugality, moderation, and equality, excited envy and jealousy, and caused major disorders. As such, government oversight was needed, especially to regulate "dowries, donations, successions, testamentary settlements, and all other forms of contracting" related to the growth of large fortunes.[73]

English liberals were not particularly optimistic that private acquisitiveness could be reconciled to public good. Hobbes saw individual greed as a major source of social chaos and "annexed to the sovereignty the whole power of prescribing the rules whereby every man may know what goods he may enjoy and what actions he may do." While Tyrrell upheld men's "absolute propriety in lands and goods," his aim was not to free property from state control but to enhance the Parliament's authority to protect and regulate property.[74] The main difference between Hobbes and Tyrrell involved the location of state regulatory authority. A more difficult question is whether Locke liberated possessive individualism, as C. B. Macpherson suggests. Certainly Locke was more willing than most to protect individual property rights against arbitrary state power, and he did believe that greater economic freedom would enhance industry and increase mankind's "common stock."[75] But Locke's commitment to property rights and economic freedom never involved freeing men's acquisitiveness from systematic state regulation.

The bulk of recent Locke scholarship stresses his consistent fears of men's passion for wealth. Peter Laslett states that Locke "profoundly mistrusted commerce and commercial men." Dunn notes that Locke had no enthusiasm for "the role of merchant or industrial producer." Neal

Wood interprets Locke as "the classic theorist of landed society and the landholder, not of commerce and mercantile interests." Richard Ashcraft argues that Locke incorporated "many features of a critical attack upon the private appropriation of property formulated within the framework of traditional Christianity."[76] Locke's dread of possessive individualism explains how he could echo Harrington when calling "propriety and possession . . . two roots of almost all the injustice and contention that so disturb human life."[77]

For Locke, it was men's avarice that originally disturbed the peace of nature. And the main reason for government was to establish an authority "to determine the rights and fence the properties of those that live under it." That authority required broad taxing powers to underwrite "the great art of government," which was to facilitate "the increase of lands and the right of employing them."[78] The state's role minimally included regulation of property relations, coinage, labor markets, poverty, shipping and navigation, imports and exports, and colonization.[79] In sum, Locke defended property rights and economic freedom but clearly expected to regulate men's excessive passions and greed with the visible hand of the state.

Whigs' liberalism of fear forced them to confront the man question. If traditional patriarchal norms and institutions were no longer to be trusted to maintain order, neither could men of conscience and appetite be given liberty and rights. The overwhelming Whig consensus, anticipating America's Lockean consensus, was that masculinity itself was a destructive social force, suggesting "an exceedingly somber outlook" for mankind. Individual men, the mob, merchants, freeholders, aristocrats, and monarchs shared the passions and ignorance that demanded political restraints, but no men could be trusted to administer those restraints. "Misanthropy's finest hour" tolled when Whig thought gravitated toward representative government as a political alchemy that ostensibly eliminated the rule of men by transforming it into the reign of impersonal laws.[80]

Away with All Men

The most striking theoretical difference between republicanism and liberalism involved participation. Republicans construed men's political activism as a mode of self-expression and stimulus to civic

virtue, but liberals devalued participation as a periodic exercise of political consent aimed at protecting individual rights. For one, politics was
primary; for the other, politics was derivative. In fact, this distinction between classical politics and modern individualism was mostly insignificant
for English thinkers because both republicans and liberals confined political participation within narrow boundaries and then subordinated it to
representative government and impersonal laws.

Whigs paused at the prospect of putting more than a cautious democratic element into government. Empowering a mass of flawed men would
be foolhardy. Republicans generally restricted citizenship to male freeholders and then shortened their political reach. Harrington divided government into a small senate composed of nobles who debated and framed
issues, and a larger assembly of freeholders that chose among prepackaged
options. Montesquieu thought most men unqualified to engage in political debate or choice. For "discussing affairs, the people collectively are
extremely unfit . . . [and] ought to have no hand in government but for the
choosing of representatives." And the pool of representatives was limited
to "people distinguished by their birth, riches, or honors" whose share in
the government "ought to be proportioned to the other advantages they
have in the state."[81] Republicans rarely wanted to extend participation
beyond either freeholders or the electoral choice of competing elites.

They did advocate secondary modes of participation. Engagement in
public discussion, debate, and local politics was to awaken, educate, and
refine men's commitment to public good as well as contribute to social
stability and political legitimacy. And participation in militia service was
to provide men an arena for cultivating and demonstrating civic virtue
while defending people's liberty and national independence. However, the
significance of such participation was not obvious. Did political discourse
serve to involve men in shaping decisions or function as a symbolic substitute for tangible influence? Did the militia muster provide men immediate
access to power or subordinate them to a hierarchical, disciplinary institution? One 1696 tract argued that men's political participation mostly
amounted to idle chatter and martial impertinence. The author belittled
the "Coffee House Politician" whose "constant application to the public takes him off all care for his private concern. He is always settling
the nation, yet could never manage his own family." Here, political talk
was an evasion of personal responsibility, not an exercise in citizenship.

The author also ridiculed militiamen as "terrible mimics of Mars" who gloried in masculine rhetoric but showed little civic courage, commitment, or discipline.[82] At best, the republican romance with participation invited men to vent their passions and aggression in harmless outlets with effective political power reserved for local power brokers and Parliament.

Social contract theorists affirmed popular consent to oppose traditional patriarchalism but not to promote democratic participation. Tyrrell excluded women, slaves, and servants from citizenship and limited freeholders' participation to choosing an elite assembly that would restrict the king's power.[83] Locke's major modification was to make explicit men's right to participate in revolution under appropriate circumstances. According to Richard Ashcraft, Locke intended this right to extend to the artisans, farmers, tradesmen, merchants, and small gentry who had a stake in overthrowing the Catholic king and his corrupt court in the 1680s. In fact, Locke may have been a radical democrat when it came to mounting opposition to traditional patriarchalism. But after the 1688 Revolution, Locke treated men's participation chiefly as an instrument for choosing an elite leadership. Ultimately, his rosiest hope was that "the hearty endeavours of a few good men guided by prudence" and "the labors of not many persons of understanding, diligence, and disinterestedness" would lead the legislature in securing domestic tranquility and the public good.[84]

The main ideological thrust of Whig political theory was to honor the people's sovereignty but legitimate the rule of the propertied elite, now viewed as first among equals. Algernon Sidney explained, "Valor, integrity, wisdom, industry, experience, and skill are required for the management of those military and civil affairs that necessarily fall under the care of chief magistrates. He or they may therefore reasonably be advanced above their equals who are most fit to perform the duties belonging to their stations in order to [foster] the public good for which they were instituted."[85] However, the advancement of individuals to representative officialdom posed two problems. One was whether the impassioned masses or a more select group of electors would recognize, choose, and obey suitable officials. The other problem was that even suitable representatives were flawed men vulnerable to pride and prejudice, emotion and stupidity.

The Whig solution was, in effect, to do away with all men by embedding representation in a system of impersonal laws. Their idea was that men were to resign their authority to the political community, which acted through a representative system of laws. Legal rules returned as disinterested acts of the community and accurate reflections of individual choices. The laws were thereby changed from coercive restrictions to expressions of men's liberty. This was the idea Harrington conveyed when he introduced his ideal as "the empire of laws and not of men." Liberal contract theory refined the legal mystique by ridding "authority of its personal elements" and legitimating a "system of laws designed to treat individuals indifferently."[86] Locke's separation of powers and Montesquieu's checks and balances ensured the reign of impersonal law by providing institutional guarantees that legal procedures were fair, and corrupt politicians were ferreted out.

A government that did not depend on men's personal authority was an elegant but inadequate answer to the man question. In theory, selfish men could be trusted with some individual liberty and rights if their participation was limited, their respect for law habitual, and their conflicts made into manageable legal cases submitted to impartial judges. In theory, corrupt men could be trusted with political office if they were periodically screened by voters, restricted in influence, and subjected to the laws and judicial conflict resolution. But as Shklar observes, "In spite of an enduring dream of 'a government of laws, not of man,' representative government involves highly personalized politics."[87] Men must demonstrate minimal virtue and wisdom to choose prudent lawmakers; legislators must win popular affection and trust to ensure legal compliance; citizens must have the will and self-mastery to resist illegal impulses; and politicians must possess enough honesty and sobriety to resist temptations to abuse public trust. Moreover, laws are blunt and inflexible instruments of order. They are notably poor in resolving intense personal conflicts or confronting the uncertainties that Machiavelli called *Fortuna*. English Whigs understood that even an empire of laws was vulnerable to men's passions and that men's passions were often beyond the scope of institutional conflict resolution. They continued to explore alternative ways to domesticate men.

2

On the Woman Question

Whigs thought modern men had grown "effeminate." One symptom was aversion to patriarchal family responsibility. Many men avoided marriage or indefinitely delayed it to indulge in licentious, bachelor lifestyles. Others married for money, neglected wives and children, and squandered family wealth. Still other men spoiled their wives and lovers with luxuries or played the part of petty tyrants and adulterers who fostered female rebelliousness. Their behavior threatened to undo patriarchal family life, unleash women's treachery, and unhinge social and political stability. The Whig remedy was to lure men back to patriarchal manhood, and the bait was biology and bliss. Intellectuals argued that men had a biological drive to sire and raise sons to become worthy heirs. This drive steered men into monogamous marriages that enabled fathers to identify their biological offspring, provide proper mothers for their children, and achieve a sense of personal fulfillment and immortality through their sons. Men's paternal responsibilities would serve as a strong incentive to restrain their own vices and to assert affectionate but competent control over their heirs' mothers.

The flaw in this portrait of renewed patriarchal family bliss was that men's devotion to family life would increase their dependence on women's reproductive capacities, parenting prerogatives, and affections. Writers feared that male dependence would enhance women's mysterious, dreadful powers to seduce men from civic virtue, reduce their fidelity to reason, and produce families dominated by irrational female desire. It was even possible that women's private passions would overspill public boundaries, wash away citizenship, and subvert political order. Some pamphleteers argued that women's treachery was already manifested in a protofeminist movement that antedated Abigail Adams's plea for women's independence and anticipated John Adams's rejoinder that women were the most fearsome tribe threatening civic peace.[2]

By calling men effeminate, Whigs wanted to shame them into redeeming their virtue and reason. That men might respond to shame implied hope; that they were sufficiently corrupt to deserve guilt by association with females implied despair. Men's capacity for self-government was in question; now their imputed effeminacy raised doubts about their ability to govern women's passions. Republicans and liberals joined modern misanthropy to ancient misogyny to produce the woman question: *How could corrupt men govern women's destructive powers?*

Dread of the Female

Traditional patriarchalism wore a mask of male superiority. Fathers were to rule families, represent dependents in public, and monopolize political power on the theory that men alone possessed the moral and intellectual attributes for creating, sustaining, and governing societies. Men might grant women some functional autonomy, but men were to regulate and restrict that autonomy to ensure public peace. However, beneath the mask of male superiority was the face of anxiety. Theorists not only doubted men's virtue and wisdom; they also worried about men's vulnerability to women's powers. Men's passions, especially their sexual appetites, made them easy marks for manipulative, seductive, and destructive women. In part, then, traditional patriarchalism sought to elevate and institutionalize male dominion to compensate for men's weakness and to limit women's influence.

Western tradition had it that women, by nature, were a tempestuous, whimsical, erratic, unpredictable, impassioned, irrational, mysterious, lusty, and powerful sex. Philosophers and artists ascribed to women elemental and omnivorous desires that fed on and fueled "dangerous, disorderly, and irrational forces" in the world.[3] Women were said to usurp men's powers, rob them of autonomy, lure them from labor, distract them from public life, and corrupt their courage. Women allegedly played on men's failings, toyed with their emotions, addled their thinking, and manipulated their actions. Women were identified with omnipresent desires that subverted the male search for order and enthroned the female love of chaos. In the battle of the sexes, women were considered the most treacherous combatants.

Gerda Lerner conjectures that this ancient "dread of the female" originated in women's prehistoric "magical" powers to reproduce life and monopolize "life-essential skills" related to birth, nurturance, and healing.[4] Always feared by men for their monopoly over birth and their management of death, women's powers became the target of the fifteenth- and sixteenth-century witch-hunts that spread across Germany, Italy, France, and then England. Barbara Ehrenreich and Deirdre English observe,

> The charges leveled against the "witches" included every misogynist fantasy harbored by the monks and priests who officiated over the witch hunts: witches copulated with the devil, rendered men impotent, . . . devoured newborn babies, poisoned livestock, etc. But again and again the "crimes" included what would now be recognized as legitimate medical acts—providing contraceptive measures, performing abortions, offering drugs to ease the pain of labor. In fact, in the peculiar legal theology of the witch hunters, healing, on the part of a woman, was itself a crime.[5]

Although women were not usually subjected to witch-hunts, male suspicions of their treachery always legitimated aggression and violence against them. Women were presumed to be malicious and dangerous if only because they were associated with nature and biology—mysterious, haphazard, and often lethal forces that men could barely understand and rarely control.

Western intellectuals commonly conjured up erotic and erratic female figures who symbolized the feminine evils that drove men to chaos, despair, and self-destruction. The Greek Furies, Nancy Hartsock argues, represented the "old religion" that elevated primitive, lawless, feminine powers of discord above the civic, legalistic, masculine forces that ordered the polis. Hanna Pitkin interprets Machiavelli's *Fortuna* as his "understanding the world as if it were run by a large senior, female person who holds men in her power." Other theorists condemned women directly. Carole Pateman observes that Rousseau's politics was predicated on the belief that women were a "source of disorder in the state."[6] And Montesquieu blamed women's uncontrollable desires for the ruin of republics, which explained why "all nations . . . agreed in fixing contempt and ignominy on the incontinence of women."[7] Western political theory was a cosmos where women destroyed men and performed postmortems on public good.

English Whigs adjusted traditional dread of the female to fit their own norms and rhetoric. Their common theology was a Protestant Ethic that replaced Catholicism's potentially benign Cult of the Virgin with a union of womankind and Grandmother Eve, "that fearful guilty ancestress" deemed responsible for Adam's fall and mankind's sins.[8] The English called women "the weaker vessel" to represent the idea that women were weaker than men when it came to disciplining their desires, but women's undisciplined desires were considered extremely potent. Intellectuals regularly blamed women's unlimited selfishness and greed for driving men from virtuous agriculture to corrupt commerce and speculation and then into the clutches of inconstant female figures such as the enchantress "Credit" who operated "malignantly and irrationally."[9]

Whigs saw the mark of malicious womankind wherever political problems appeared. For instance, Algernon Sidney believed that one of the greatest dangers of absolute monarchy was the possibility that a woman would ascend to the throne and project her private desires across the public spectrum. That is why he applauded the French custom of banning women from the crown. Equally terrifying, however, was the prospect that a king, his "lust unsubdued," would be manipulated and dominated by an ambitious wife or seductive mistress who was sure to bring untold miseries upon the people. For Sidney, attacking political patriarchalism was part of an orchestrated effort to avert the inevitable "distempers" that resulted whenever "woman, children, or such as are notoriously foolish or mad . . . advanced to the supreme power."[10]

If Sidney made women accomplices in tyranny, James Tyrrell made women accessories in anarchy. Sir Robert Filmer had argued that contract theory was an absurdity because it logically entailed political equality for women. As Peter Laslett notes, Tyrrell considered and dismissed the possibility that "there was no stopping place between the ground he and Locke occupied and logical individualism, final democracy, the sharing of political power with women."[11] His signal achievement was to cut the philosophic thread connecting consent to sexual equality by arguing that "woman, as the weaker vessel, is to be subject to the man, as the stronger, stouter, and commonly wiser creature." Not only were women "unfit for civil business,"—even worse, women were an uncontrollable and unpredictable force, a "promiscuous rabble." Granting them rights, like empowering the insane, the immature, the poor, the untutored, and others lacking the rudiments of civility, would surely produce social chaos. Thus, Tyrrell asserted that women should be "concluded by their husbands."[12]

Why did theorists dread women so consistently and deeply when, in fact, women's social, economic, political, and legal status was subordinate throughout recorded Western history? Why did they view women as powerful, dangerous creatures of desire when women had few outlets for their so-called treachery? In part, traditional dread of the female was functional. Intellectuals used women as symbolic representations of "the other," or the effeminate, that men were to escape, overcome, and conquer. Women's appetitive nature became a standard for knowing the forces that men had to master in themselves to achieve responsible manhood, social stability, and public good. Genevieve Lloyd puts it this way: "Femininity . . . has been constituted within the Western intellectual tradition to be what is left behind by ideals of masculinity, citizenship, and patriotism."[13]

Dread of the female was also related to tangible concerns. Since Aristotle, theorists had assumed that peaceful, patriarchal family life was an essential foundation for political life. If women's tempestuous nature threatened to corrode family harmony, it thereby imperiled citizenship and the state. The personal was political. Moreover, women were seen as powerful creatures because men seemed so weak. Women could be manipulative because men lacked the self-mastery, virtue, and rationality to control them; women could be temptresses because men were easily tempted; women could subvert order because men's desires disposed them to disorder. Dread of the female was largely based on despair of the male. Finally, despair of the male combined with doubts of men's redemption implied that men and women existed on a common plane of desire. What made women terrifying was that they mirrored men's own debased passions.

The Common Plane of Desire

King James I captured early seventeenth-century wisdom on women when he observed, "To make women learned and foxes tame had the same effect: to make them more cunning."[14] However, the English Civil War generated a different account of women's moral capacities. Women demonstrated their virtue by promoting piety amid slaughter, sustaining their families, maintaining the home front, nursing the wounded, engaging in heroic combat, and pleading their families' interests in postwar litigation. It was possible to imagine that educating and empowering women would elevate society and politics. The years of fraternal violence also provided men ample opportunity to testify to their moral depravity by reckless bloodshed and rapine, cowardice and covetousness, and postwar greed and dishonor, for example, manifested among young gentry who "married into the city for downright money" or squandered their patrimony in dissolute revelry.[15] Women's moral stock rose as men's moral failings were exposed.

The writings of Hobbes and Locke insinuated the possibility of women's moral uplift. Hobbes granted women full equality in the state of nature and even initial superiority when it came to parental prerogatives. However, Hobbes did uphold an implicit "sexual contract" that subordinated wives to husbands, excluded women from the social contract, and explained why "commonwealths have been erected by the fathers, not by the mothers of families."[16] Locke also hinted at a more benign view of women. Several scholars point out that Locke affirmed women's ability to reason, negotiate contracts, share parenting, own property, and, perhaps, exercise political power. Still, Locke's positive assessment of women was truncated. He saw "a foundation in nature" for wives' subjection to their husbands; he showed disdain for women by equating "effeminacy" with a weak will and uninformed mind; and he never explicitly included women in the public realm.[17] Hobbes and Locke only intimated a revisionist reading of women's capacities. Restoration pamphleteers openly debated it.

Robert Gould's 1682 *Love Given o'er or, a Satire against the Pride, Lust, and Inconstance, etc. of Woman*—like Filmer's *Patriarcha*—was an effort to reinforce tradition against adversity. Gould told an origin story that began with Grandmother Eve ushering in "plagues, woes, and death, and a new world of sin." Throughout history, men were victimized by women's "boundless lust," "treacherous wiles," and "ambition, luxury, and pride." Ultimately, men's attraction to women proved to be a seductive trap luring men into slavery. Gould advised men: "Avoid [women], as you would the pains of Hell" and thereby restore "ancient liberty."[18] Sarah Fige responded with a satire based on the premise that women were "more essentially good than men" when it came to piety, fidelity, honesty, honor, and virtue. Men's essence could be detected in their lust. They preyed on virgins, made honest women into whores, and seduced married ladies. Moreover, they fled virtue and turned "bully, hector, and human beast," practicing hypocrisy and delighting in debauchery. Only when men's vices were subdued by female virtues, Fige concluded, would men have "a share of that [goodness] which makes most females brave."[19] The defense of moral womanhood inspired a counterattack that admitted men's failings but blamed them on women. Richard Ames wrote, "There never was a plot or close design / That quiet of a state to undermine / Or private family to ruin brought / Wherein a woman was not in the plot." Ames fantasized a homosocial Eden ruled by male virtue liberated from women's corrupting influence: "There with a score of choice selected friends / Who know no private interests nor ends / We'd live and could we procreate like trees / And without woman's aid—promote and propagate our species."[20]

The debate expanded in the 1690s and early 1700s with a post-Revolutionary easing of censorship laws. More and more writers put pen to paper to demonstrate that men's degraded nature and vicious vices were responsible for modern corruption. Special scorn was heaped on the bachelor, who symbolized a rowdy man–child innocent of human decency and decent citizenship. The bachelor stood for excessive individualism. He personified self-indulgent greed, sin, profligacy, promiscuity, aggression, and violence. For example, Mary Astell wrote, "He who lives single that he may indulge licentiousness and give up himself to the conduct of wild and ungoverned desires . . . can never justify his own conduct nor clear it from the imputation of wickedness and folly."[21] The bachelor's fatal flaw was his refusal to assume the manly responsibilities of marriage, fatherhood, productive labor, and political duty. One satirist explained,

> A bachelor of age . . . has broken the laws of nature. . . . He ought not to have any protection from the laws of England. . . . Our forefathers purchased the liberties of the Magna Carta with the hazard of life and limb. . . . Now a bachelor contributes little or nothing to the support of our freedoms. The money he pays in taxes is inconsiderable to the supplies given by others in children, which are an addition to the native strength of the kingdom. . . . Indeed, my dear, a bachelor can, in no sense, be esteemed a good Englishman.[22]

Diatribes against bachelorhood both reinforced and reflected Whig criticisms of the single men who filled the ranks of the detested standing army.

Local militia were associated with sober family men. The standing army was generally considered a fraternity of dissolute bachelors, infamous Redcoats, who were dependent on government salaries, disrespectful of civic virtue, proud of their ignorance, and drilled in brutality.[23] Trenchard captured the flavor of the opposition by pointing out that the regular army rendered "so many men useless to labor and almost propagation, together with a much greater destruction of them, by taking them from a laborious way of living to a loose idle life; and besides this, the insolence of the officers and the debaucheries that are committed both by them and their soldiers in all the towns they come in, to the ruin of multitudes of women, dishonor of their families, and ill example to others; and a numerous train of mischiefs besides, almost endless to enumerate."[24] Bachelors and Redcoats were the enemies of family life. They sired no legitimate children and produced no value; but they did consume taxes and destroy domesticity.

Pamphleteers also reserved considerable venom for abusive husbands. Lady Mary Chudleigh, for instance, contrasted the "ingenious" woman "whom passions cannot nor interest tempt" to the "foolish, passionate, stingy, sottish husband" who thought himself "from all restraints, from all laws free." Mary Astell added that husbands' lawless impulses were unbounded, reaching from private to public life where men refused to render unto "civil and ecclesiastical governors the same submission which they themselves extract from their domestic subjects."[25] Authors accused married men of being anarchists who respected only their own base appetites (which is why Astell thought the wise woman would think twice before ever taking a husband). Writers also argued that husbands were tyrants who exercised arbitrary power over wives and children; and they protested men's sexual, emotional, material, and physical abuse of wives, echoing James Tyrrell's complaints about husbands' fits of "madness, drunkenness, or passion."[26] Married men were depraved. They needed to learn decency, respect, and affection for their wives, or, as a pamphlet entitled *The Duty of a Husband* concluded: "And man in duty is confined / By sacred laws to be more kind / And not like tyrant rule his wife / As if she was his slave for life."[27]

Astell saw a close connection between despotic husbands and political tyrants. Husbands who "will not be guided by their reason but by their appetites and do not what they ought but what they can" were the same as kings who exercised arbitrary power. The reason was that the male sex had an inclination and passionate self-interest in dominating women and also other men. But why was a husband's tyranny tolerable when a king's tyranny was intolerable? Or, Astell asked, "If absolute sovereignty be not necessary to a state, how comes it to be so in a family?"[28] Her writings implied that women should have the same rights within marriages as social contract theorists attributed to men in politics: freedom to consent, negotiate the contract, specify limits on governance, and revoke authority in cases of abuse. Though Astell herself was not ready to advocate sexual equality within marriage, the idea that women were moral agents with marital rights was widely discussed by the early eighteenth century.[29]

Pamphleteers were rarely optimistic about the likelihood of depraved bachelors, brutal Redcoats, and corrupt husbands redeeming themselves. Would education enhance men's virtue, reason, and sobriety? Writers insisted that men's intellectual life reflected rather than regulated men's selfish appetites, sinful pride, and material interests. One author grouped men into two categories: "learned and unlearned blockheads." Men who sought historical knowledge in the name of virtue were "superstitious, bigoted idolators of time past." Men with leisure enough for formal study learned mostly "to be fools." Only immense male vanity allowed self-proclaimed savants to declare themselves "oracles of reason" rather than face the truth that they were "ridiculous" and "trivial."[30] The heirs of Grandfather Adam, that guilty ancestor truly responsible for man's fall and mankind's woes, were inherently flawed creatures of selfish desire.

Several writers did argue that schooling would benefit women by endowing them with "greater propensions to virtue and a natural goodness of temper within, which duly managed, would raise them to the most eminent pitch of heroic virtue."[31] Antonia Fraser's study of Restoration writings reveals that "the notion of the 'softer sex,' 'the gentle sex,' which might actually be finer than its masculine opposite was growing in literature."[32] Even then, literary intimations of female virtue and rationality were chained to ideals of patriarchal family bliss. A good and learned woman was bearable if she became an asset to her husband. Daniel Defoe explained, "I cannot think that God Almighty ever made [women] . . . to be only stewards of our houses, cooks and slaves. . . . I would have men take women for companions, and educate them to be fit for it. A woman of sense and breeding will scorn as much to encroach upon the prerogative of the man, as a man of sense will scorn to oppress the weakness of the woman."[33] At best, refined women were considered superior companions, wives, and assets for men.

In fact, the rhetoric of refined womanhood was usually far more modest. Nearly all writers who defended women's educability and virtue were still haunted by traditional fears of women's treachery. They constantly dwelled on the everyday frivolousness, immodesty, hypocrisy, impiety, conceit, irrationality, avarice, profligacy, idleness, litigiousness, and immense self-love that most women shared with men. Taken together, the common passions of the two sexes engendered "debility, injustice, and . . . disorder."[34] Male corruption and ignorance were the primary barriers to social order, but female corruption and ignorance were nearly as dangerous because they aggravated private passions, exacerbated conflict, and doubled the difficulty of securing public good. The preponderant belief of English intellectuals was that men, though flawed, would have to reassert patriarchal authority over women; the perceived problem was that men, because they were flawed, had instead caused a crisis of the patriarchal family.

The Crisis of the Patriarchal Family

Richard Ames's fantasy of an Eden where men reproduced themselves without women was not unique. The idea of male fecundity was rooted in the biblical belief that men procreated by identifying with the masculine God who gave birth to the world, endowed males with an active seed to be "planted in the passive receptacle of women's womb," and promised men eternal dominion through the reproduction of sons.[35] A similar notion occurred in early Western culture as men downgraded the meaning of women's biological reproduction and upgraded the significance of poetic and philosophical production wherein great men, "pregnant in soul," gave birth to beauty and wisdom.[36] Male procreation also animated origin stories that told of founding fathers who created enduring political communities, which transcended individual mortality and served as mankind's eternal legacy. "The conventional understanding of the 'political,'" writes Carole Pateman, "is built upon the rejection of physical birth in favor of the masculine creation of (giving birth to) social and political order."[37]

The misogynist ideal of male procreation was an abstraction that existed alongside intellectuals' concrete view of women as functional adjuncts to private and public life.[38] Women satisfied men's sexual urges. They bore, nursed, nurtured, raised, and educated men's children. They managed men's households, servants, and slaves. They produced use–value and exchange–value, and sometimes served as valued commodities traded among men. Women were slave labor, cheap labor, and surplus labor. They could be useful for their therapeutic ability to soothe men's pains and their motivational ability to urge men on to labor, ambition, and patriotic glory. Women also served as convenient justifications for men's wars, participants in battles, and treasured spoils for conquerors. Montesquieu neatly captured women's functionalism when honoring this ancient Samnite custom:

> The young people were all convened in one place, and their conduct was examined. He that was declared the best of the whole assembly had leave given him to take which girl he pleased for his wife; the person that had been declared second best chose after him; and so on. Admirable institution . . . love, beauty, chastity, virtue, birth, and even wealth itself were all, in some measure, the dowry of virtue. A nobler, and grander recompense . . . could scarce be imagined.[39]

Women were traditionally seen as incentives to political manhood and rewards for it, means for consummating it, and factors for continuing it. They were functional "auxiliaries to the commonwealth."[40]

Women performed one unique, irreplaceable, and incontestable function. They reproduced the species. Women were needed to bear men's heirs, to reproduce generations of citizens to continue the commonwealth and generate new legions of soldiers to defend it. Neither expendable nor trustworthy, women were regarded as necessary evils who had to be subordinated and controlled by men. Thus, kings announced patriarchy and put the force of the state behind it; churches legitimated and adjudicated it; women were trained for it and family fathers administered it. Women safely could exercise their mystical powers over life as long as princes, priests, and fathers domesticated them. In seventeenth-century England, however, the authority of princes and priests was challenged and men seemed averse to fatherhood and family management. The result was an apparent crisis of the patriarchal family that threatened to unleash women's evil.

Customarily, Englishmen and women matured into adulthood by taking their marriage vows and producing offspring. God and the church enjoined men and women to marry and then increase and multiply the species. "Big-bellied" or "great-bellied" wives were judged the happy social norm—indicators of men's virtue, women's piety, and society's robust health.[41] Monarchs also considered marriage and birth essential to public good. Fathers were an extension of royal power in families, and pregnant wives provided a supply of young men for royal armies. One satirist proposed "an act for increasing the breed of Englishmen" because "you can have no navies, nor armies, without men, and, like prudent farmers, we ought always to keep our land well stocked."[42]

Whig attacks on church and state legitimacy had an important effect on family norms. On the one hand, religious injunction and reasons of state became secondary justifications for young men to undertake obligations of marriage, fatherhood, breadwinning, and the education of sons for compliant citizenship and obedient soldiering. On the other hand, the rhetoric of liberty and rights helped to undermine the practice of arranged marriages and strengthen young men's claims to choose if, when, and whom they might wed. The result was not necessarily a mass movement toward bachelorhood, as pamphleteers suggested, but an enlarged sense that young men no longer had a compelling moral duty to marry, to sire and rear children, or, in effect, to assume everyday management of women's passions. Domesticity was increasingly negotiable.

Englishmen did inherit traditional material motives for marriage and family life. Gerda Lerner's conjectural history of ancient patriarchy pinpoints the main economic factors that urged men to assume family obligations. Lerner argues that the emergence of labor-intensive agriculture simultaneously strengthened the influence of older males and enhanced the utility of child labor which, in turn, increased the functional value of childbearing females. Henceforth, men had an economic incentive to maximize the number of children who could labor in their vineyards, and that provided men an additional stake in controlling potential and actual mothers.[43] Over time, men's mechanism for controlling women took the form of family patriarchy. Husbands ruled the family economy and wives were perpetually pregnant; fathers commanded sons' labor, indoctrinated daughters for submissive motherhood, and profited by selling their children's productive and reproductive labor power.

In seventeenth-century England, however, men's economic incentives for family life diminished. The stability of agricultural property "capable of spanning the generations and permitting the living to succeed the dead in a real and natural order," as republican theorists complained, was upset by early modernity.[44] The gentry's ability to continue indefinite labor-intensive agriculture was uncertain. Merchants and traders had little need for child labor. Talk about enclosing the commons that kept marginal farmers afloat and concern for growing masses of propertyless men anticipated the moment when the cost of raising child labor would be more expensive than hiring wage labor. By extension, the falling value of child labor depressed the worth of reproductive women. Moreover, the contractual logic of the marketplace further devalued women's worth. To moral critics' dismay, many men satisfied their sexual lust most economically by commodifying women and making limited-liability contracts with prostitutes rather than by getting married.[45] The only residual material motive for marriage was for men to use it as a mechanism for getting their hands on other men's money. Marriage, it seemed, had become marketable.

Yet another traditional factor urging men into family life was their personal identification with enduring political communities. Mary O'Brien argues that men's inability to bear children deprives them of the sense of intergenerational continuity that attends female childbearing. Men alienate their seed, remain uncertain of their paternity, and stand apart from the "natural genetic continuity." Isolated from the flow of generations, men suffer an inherent sense of alienation and temporal discontinuity. Robert Jay Lifton suggests that men seek to overcome isolation by striving for "symbolic immortality" defined as a feeling of "human continuity" or "a larger human connectedness." Historically, men sought symbolic immortality through politics. They recaptured the past by identifying with founding fathers; they anticipated the future by promoting and performing heroic deeds that would become legendary; and they directly experienced intergenerational continuity by combining family, fatherhood, and citizenship to perpetuate the political community.[46] The political was personal.

But the political was in disarray in England. Civil war, regicide, restoration, and revolution estranged men from the political past. Economic change and social conflict made doubtful their connection to the political future. In that protean era eventually known as modernity, it made a certain amount of sense for men to travel lightly, and any long-term commitment to marriage, fatherhood, and citizenship might be considered excess baggage. There were alternatives. Men could return to religion as a guide to immortality; they could project meaning into self-interest and self-aggrandizement; they could identify with particular political factions promising national salvation; or, they could forsake immortality altogether and opt for profligacy. For Englishmen, traditional expectations of marriage and fatherhood were not only more negotiable and marketable but also carried considerable economic risk.

A 1690 pamphlet expressed the view that men's selfish and irrational neglect of marriage and family threatened to undermine domestic stability and English nationhood. With almost half the people of England dying single and a third marrying quite late, there was even talk of forcing twenty-one-year-old men to marry in the hope of restoring patriarchal family life, social stability, and political independence. Otherwise, bachelors would continue to forsake civic virtue and reason; and desperate women would fill the moral void with deceit and treachery. Another pamphlet lamented the "grievance of celibacy under which the nation groaneth," explaining the crisis of patriarchal family life as a function of "the lewd sort of men out of love with matrimony" whose sheer selfishness prevented the birth of "a race of heroes for the service of our country."[47] Unless men were persuaded to reprise their ancient role as family fathers, there would be no citizens to constitute the commonwealth and no patriarchs to control the women.

In Search of Family Fathers

"Considering the absence of legal coercion," writes Barbara Ehrenreich, "the surprising thing is that men have for so long, and, on the whole, so reliably, adhered to . . . 'the breadwinner ethic.' "[48] Restoration intellectuals did not assume men's reliability when it came to marriage, fatherhood, and provisioning. Some satirists toyed with making taxes a disincentive for bachelorhood and employing legal coercion to enforce a family breadwinner ethic. The more serious family-saving strategy was to reconceptualize men's motives for choosing family life. Thinkers de-emphasized men's religious duties and stressed what they believed was men's natural concern for biological posterity and happiness. They argued that men had an instinct to perpetuate their genetic lines, surnames, and estates that required they marry, sire offspring, provide suitable mothers, provisions, and protection, and educate sons to assume sober stewardship of family wealth. The message was that bachelors and abusive husbands indulged their appetites only to suffer alienation, whereas sober family fathers sacrificed for their families and achieved self-fulfillment.

Among the passions that overwhelmed men's virtue and reason, intellectuals highlighted one particular appetite that promised to draw men back to family life. That was men's innate desire for "transcendent" self-preservation. Men wanted not only to preserve their mortal lives; they also wanted to escape death and live eternally through their biological offspring. One pamphleteer noted, "Every creature desires to propagate its species. . . . We are, as it were, immortal on earth, in our surviving children."[49] Men's passion for immortality through fatherhood was considered so powerful that it forced selfish men to forgo immediate gratification and make sacrifices for their children's health, safety, and prosperity. John Toland wrote, "All men would live somewhere eternally if they could, and they affect to become immortal even here on earth. . . . This inclination never discovers itself so plainly as in the care men take of their posterity. Some are content to live beggars all their days that their children after them may be rich for they look upon these as their own persons multiplied by propagation."[50] In essence, instinctual fatherhood urged men to condition their individualism for the good of their children.

But which children? Historically, men could never be certain which particular children were their own biological offspring. They had to engage in "strenuous masculine activity to negate the uncertainty of fatherhood."[51] They made compacts with women who promised sexual fidelity in return for male provision and protection. But women were considered lustful creatures who could not be trusted to govern their own sexual appetites or keep promises of fidelity. Men also sought mutual guarantees from other men for exclusive access to particular women. However, this sexual contract required an inordinate degree of virtue, rationality, self-control, and trust among flawed men. Finally, men secluded particular women to shut off other men's access to women's bodies. The difficulty here, Restoration plays pointed out, was that true lust will out: women broke out of seclusion or other men sneaked in.[52]

Men's conventional efforts to negate the uncertainty of fatherhood were faltering without the support of a state that regulated sexuality and enforced women's fidelity, men's probity, and privileged access to female bodies. Judith Stiehm notes, "The energy and care given to providing men assurance of their paternity suggests the importance attached to parental ties. Indeed, these ties are apparently so important that men have used government, a created, forceful institution, to help guarantee them a relationship (that of parent) women have always been able to take for granted."[53] Virtually no one in Restoration England (or colonial America) advocated that magistrates or ministers or neighbors cease their sexual police work.[54] Still, dissent against the state, talk of liberty, and complaints about lewd men and licentious women urged intellectuals to revive popular belief in monogamy and reinforce public commitment to marital fidelity.

Sarah Fige believed that even men who hated marriage would support and participate in monogamy to secure themselves an heir: "Most mortally the name of wife [men] hate / Yet they will take on their proper fate / That they may have a child legitimate, to be their heir / If they have an estate, or else to bear their names."[55] Whig theorists contributed to family-saving by upholding the legitimacy of monogamy as a means to produce and nurture men's heirs. James Tyrrell declared, "It is evident that the power of fathers over their children can only take place in the state of wedlock; for as to children got out of marriage, it is uncertain who is their father. . . . The right of a father over his child commences by virtue of the marriage which is a mutual compact between a man and a woman for their cohabitation, the generation of children, and their joint care and provision for them."[56]

Montesquieu was to put particular emphasis on fathers' duty to nourish their offspring. He wrote, "The natural obligation of the father to provide for his children has established marriage, which makes known the person who ought to fulfill this obligation."[57] The underlying assumption was that men's passion for immortality and instinct for fatherhood made monogamous marriage tolerable and paternal self-sacrifice palatable.

Restoration writers posited an especially close relationship between fathers and sons. They argued that fathers felt a natural affection for their sons, who, after all, were an extension of themselves. They also argued that sons ought to feel natural gratitude toward the fathers who procreated and nourished them. Accordingly, Algernon Sidney described father–son relationships in terms of "love" on one side and "veneration" on the other.[58] The deep concern for homosocial, intergenerational bonding, one suspects, was partly a response to economic uncertainty. Fathers needed to forge strong bonds with sons in order to foster in them the character traits and skills necessary for preserving the family name and legacy in a fluctuating marketplace. Both Tyrrell and Locke insisted that authoritarian fatherhood was ineffective for rearing sober heirs. It taught a slavish obedience that ill prepared young men for adult decision making. It also tempted young men to dissemble filial obedience until they received, and likely squandered, their inheritances. Modern fatherhood entailed the use of paternal affection to foster filial consent, economic rationality, and sobriety.[59]

The emphasis on father–son affections reflected an emerging belief that individuals achieved self-fulfillment by cultivating familial bonds of love. Lady Mary Chudleigh suggested that marriages founded on mutual choice and affection were among "the joys of life."[60] Men should make lovers their wives and wives their lovers and all would achieve great happiness. Marital romance did have a practical side. "As Margaret Duchess of Newcastle put it, no one should marry 'against their own liking' because it led directly to adultery."[61] While ministers, magistrates, and neighbors continued to deter, detect, and punish wives' sexual promiscuity, marital affection was increasingly considered the main guarantee of wives' sexual fidelity. It was also argued that wives' affection for their husbands ensured wives' submission to their husbands. Lady Chudleigh wrote that men "need not doubt of their obedience; the desire to please will render the most difficult commands easy."[62] And modern men had a great need for obedient wives who, as mothers, were to cooperate and contribute to the upbringing of men's "own persons multiplied by propagation," their sons.

The idea that men's instincts and affections could revive patriarchal family life was a matter of great public consequence. Fatherhood was a potential source of men's civic virtue and sobriety. It forced men to forgo individual interest for family good. It motivated men to settle down into stable, monogamous marriages, husband family resources, and raise responsible, productive heirs. That fatherhood could be a crucial pillar of public order explains why John Toland advocated "that no man be obliged to go upon any foreign expedition during the year after his marriage; nor all the sons of any man at once; nor an only son ever, unless he's willing himself."[63] Young men needed time to become fathers, and fathers needed time to secure their posterity. Equally important, fatherhood brought men back into monogamous marriages where they could supervise and subdue women's passions. Married men had a compelling interest to oversee their wives' sexual fidelity to protect their paternity. It was to their advantage to enforce wives' frugality to preserve men's patrimony. Fathers had a stake in managing motherhood to ensure an appropriate upbringing for their sons and heirs. They even had reason to guard the modesty and marriageability of their daughters. As Mary Astell put it, "Though the son convey the name to posterity, yet certainly a great part of the honor of families depends on . . . daughters."[64] In sum, family men had strong incentives for reassuming patriarchal governance of women.

There was one serious problem with the Restoration revival of fatherhood. The more men invested themselves in it, the greater their dependence on reproductive women. The deeper men's concern for raising sober heirs, the more extensive their reliance on their sons' mothers. The stronger men's affectionate bonds with women, the more women acquired emotional leverage over them. The search for family fathers was part of Whigs' effort to secure social order and control women's passions; but the very importance of fatherhood hinted at male vulnerabilities that invited women's demands for greater freedom and equality.

Women's Freedom and Equality

Hanna Pitkin summarizes Machiavelli's classical view of women: "Contact with . . . feminine power is essential, but it can be safely achieved only under the most stringent masculine safeguards."[65] From the Code of Hammurabi and the Bible to Anglo-American coverture laws granting husbands legal dominion over wives, Western societies legitimated masculine safeguards that subordinated women within patriarchal families. Once enculturated and encapsulated in such families, women lost their most fearsome qualities. Grandmother Eve gave way to the Puritan "helpmeet," and one-time seductresses were transformed into Spartan Mothers. Still, intellectuals did not think contact with women was ever entirely safe. Women's treacherous nature may have been subdued temporarily, but it continued to lurk at the borders of civility. Thus, Restoration pamphleteers could not protest against corrupt bachelors and abusive husbands without being reminded that female sexual insatiability, wantonness, self-indulgence, seductiveness, greed, and arrogance were the root causes of men's failings.[66]

And men's constant failings seemed to provide new openings for women's treachery. Montesquieu's *Persian Letters* traced the logic of men's domestic dominion from enlightened patriarchy to self-destruction. The book told of a Persian man named Usbek who traveled to Europe, where he was exposed to modern thought and from where he sent letters home to ensure the proper governance of his harem. Usbek's rule was benign. He showed great affection and concern for his wives, especially Roxane. But Usbek's absolute power corrupted absolutely. The result was jealousy, violence, and tyranny on his part and then deception and anarchy among his wives. Slaughter and suicide in the harem followed. Usbek's last letter to his wives began, "May this letter be like unto the thunder that falls in the midst of storms and flashes of lightning! Solim is now your first eunuch—not to guard but to punish you." Roxane's final reply linked Usbek's tyranny to her own treachery: "Yes, I have deceived you. I seduced your eunuchs. I took advantage of your jealousy, and out of your horrible harem I managed to make a place of pleasure and delight. . . . I am dying."[67] Roxane's pleasure and delight were the sentiments of a corrupted spirit that could no longer tolerate life. The dilemma was this: Montesquieu believed that patriarchal power was absolutely necessary to control women's desires; but he also recognized that patriarchal power would "corrode and eventually destroy all traces of virtue, duty, or love."[68]

English Whigs appropriated Machiavelli's belief in patriarchal safeguards but anticipated Montesquieu's fear that patriarchal power would corrode family stability. Contractarians such as Tyrrell, Sidney, and Locke argued that women's place was in subordination to men in the home. But they betrayed a degree of skepticism. Filmer made them aware that their ideas on natural freedom and equality, consent, and contract conceivably generated claims for sexual equality. Tyrrell and Locke also recognized that patriarchal authority in families was often abused by drunken, ignorant, and greedy men who mistreated their dependents and sometimes drove women from distraction to rebellion. The suspicion that domestic patriarchy was neither warranted nor effective was the basis for some protofeminist writers to argue that social contract theory justified, and male corruption demanded, greater autonomy, educational opportunity, and even citizenship for women.

An outstanding example of Restoration protofeminism was an anonymous tract of 1696 entitled *An Essay in Defence of the Female Sex*. It began with a refutation of traditional arguments for women's subordination. God did not intend women to be men's slaves but men's companions. God did not simply enjoin women to propagate the species but also to participate in the wider sphere of societal affairs. An analysis of the animal kingdom and the human species revealed no essential differences of mind and soul between females and males. Historical research on lower-class English women and Dutch women of affairs demonstrated that women were as capable as men of physical toil, business management, and public life. The author's reading of God, nature, and history insisted on the truth that women were born to "primitive liberty and equality with men." Unfortunately, female liberty and equality had been forcibly denied by brutal men whose deepest fear was women's moral and intellectual superiority.[69]

Most protofeminist pamphleteers referred to women's natural freedom and equality when making a case for revising some of the rules of family life. They wanted greater recognition of men's responsibility to be sober husbands who worked for family good rather than consorted with gamblers, imbibers, and prostitutes. They advocated restraints on husbands' power to abuse their wives and children plus greater protection for abused dependents. They desired more affection among marital partners and more respect for women's contributions to family life. They also sought enhanced opportunities for women to develop their moral and intellectual potential through formal education and drew up detailed plans for the establishment of new women's schools. The Church of England preached that men had an obligation to wield patriarchal authority firmly yet lovingly; protofeminists proposed that husbands share a portion of their authority to secure family life on a more loving foundation.

Writers put forth two arguments to persuade audiences that greater female autonomy would secure rather than jeopardize domestic tranquility. One argument was that free and knowledgeable women made better wives. Women who were active and intelligent rather than frivolous and foolish were better helpmates. They were more likely to understand the need for a single family sovereign and to defer to husbands' authority. As such, Astell argued that educated women were "for the most part wise enough to love their chains, and to discern how very becomingly they set." [70] Moreover, pleas and plans for women's education mostly aimed at producing "good and careful housewives," not "manly" women. Antonia Fraser notes, "The girls tripped in dainty slippers down the ornamental paths of their education; so very different from the demanding course of classics and grammar set for their brothers. . . . The intellectual difference between the two sexes was becoming ever more sharply defined." [71] Liberated from enforced ignorance, women would elevate the household, not abandon it for society and politics.

A second protofeminist argument was that men in general and husbands in particular would benefit from the companionship of modern women. Men would learn to control excessive passions and practice complacency, exhibit good manners and perfect civility, by exposure to the modesty and wit of cultivated women. Astell put it this way:

> A good and prudent wife would wonderfully work on an ill man. He must be a brute indeed who could hold out against all those innocent arts, those gentle persuasives and obliging methods she would use to reclaim him. Piety is often offensive when it is accompanied with indiscretion; but she who is as wise as good possesses such charms as can hardly fail of prevailing. Doubtless her husband is a much hap-

pier man and more likely to abandon all his ill courses than he who has none to come home to but an ignorant, forward, and fantastic creature.[72]

What man could object to a modern wife who enchanted him, reclaimed his virtue, and guaranteed his happiness? What society could object to cultivated women who tamed men's excesses, diverted them from vice, and thereby fostered social order?

The protofeminist case was complemented by the historical trend toward companionate marriages in which husbands' arbitrary authority was weakened and women's claim to domestic autonomy was strengthened. Lawrence Stone describes the emerging ideal as follows:

> Marriage selection was determined more by free choice than by parental decision and was based as much on expectations of lasting mutual affection as on calculations of an increase in money, status or power. . . . The authority of husbands over wives and of parents over children declined as greater autonomy was granted to or assumed by all members of the family unit. There were the beginnings of a trend toward greater legal and educational equality between the sexes. . . . Although the economic dependence of these women on their husbands increased, they were granted greater status and decision-making power within the family.[73]

The companionate ideal proved to be a useful adaptation to modernity. Among other things, it facilitated a division of domestic labor that enabled wives to assume greater responsibility at home as more and more husbands devoted themselves to work in the marketplace. Women's consent to marriages, relative autonomy within them, and domestic education would help to secure wives' cooperation and contributions to household management and child rearing without the everyday supervision of their absent breadwinners.[74]

Contract theorists' suspicions, protofeminists' recommendations, and emerging companionate ideals seem quite innocent by twentieth-century standards. After all, few people actually recognized or advocated women's freedom and equality. Those who did asked for little more than greater respect, somewhat more autonomy for women within families, and greater access to domestic education. Meanwhile, men's patriarchal authority at home and their monopoly in society and politics were largely reaffirmed. And nearly a century would have to elapse before Mary Wollstonecraft sought to vindicate more extensive rights for women. Nevertheless, Restoration England saw no innocence in even modest images of semiautonomous women. Ancient misogyny declared, after all, that women would never be satisfied with small advances in liberty and equality because, by nature, they desired unlimited freedom and power.

A number of antifeminist writers articulated such masculinist fears. Given the opportunity, they argued, women would use their affections, and widows their money, to trap men into marriage. Brides would then negotiate marriage contracts to their own advantage and mothers use the children as a lever for controlling fathers. The traditional patriarchal family governed by the man's benign authority would be replaced by the matriarchal family dominated by what one writer called the "wanton wife." He explained, "Containing an unequal dividend / His business is to get and hers to spend / If he's unable to supply her lust / She'll take such care of that, another must." In addition, it was feared that the matriarchal family would provide women a staging area for extending their influence into public life. Effeminate sons would scout the terrain and armies of women feigning obedience and piety would invade the economy, usurp political power, and liberate women's destructive passions. What did women really want? According to another writer, women's ultimate goal was not greater respect, autonomy, or equality. Rather, women "not only dispute the superiority of men, but even pretend to the right of conquest over them."[75]

The misogynist's rule of thumb was to deny women small gains to prevent them from demanding larger ones. Patriarchal safeguards needed to be reaffirmed. But how? If men continued to evade marriage and mismanage families, there would be no competent governance of women's passions. If men bought into fatherhood and monogamy, they exposed themselves to matriarchal domination and emasculation. If men reasserted traditional patriarchalism, cries of tyranny would foster protofeminist dissent and rebellion. Who would rein women's destructive appetites? Who would prevent women from dragging men deeper into the world of private desire? Who would prevent women's passions from overwhelming public life? The danger, as Montesquieu suggested, was that disrespect for men's authority would prompt "wives, children, and slaves [to] shake off all subjection" and thereby destroy "such things as manners [and] order."[76]

Manners and Order

By the end of the seventeenth century, one could make the case that marriage, like politics, ought to be a contractual relationship founded on the voluntary agreements of free and equal individuals. As one tract put it in 1697, "The argument's good between the King and the people, why not between the husband and the wife?"[77] We have seen that efforts were made to persuade men to consent to marriage and act responsibly within it. Some writers suggested that women's consent, limited autonomy, and affections would help to stabilize family life. Why, then, was it so difficult for Whigs to grant even minimal recognition to women's freedom and equality within family life?

One reason was that virtually no one in Restoration England was willing to pursue contractual logic very far, in marriage or in politics. Whigs preferred to view marriage as a natural, patriarchal institution that authorized and enabled men to govern women's private passions. Even the proto-feminist writers who proclaimed women's natural freedom and equality almost always deferred to husbands' natural sovereignty in families and men's traditional monopoly in the public realm. Over the next few centuries, Anglo-American lawyers, legislators, and judges would continue to insist that marriage could not be a simple contract; it was also a status intended to protect public order and it had to be regulated to that effect.[78] In brief, the liberalism of fear that construed men's liberty and rights as threats to order was certainly not going to extend autonomy to women whose imputed treachery was considered a cause of disorder. Egalitarian marriage, like democratic politics, could be articulated but not condoned.

Whigs also resisted women's limited autonomy within families because they did not make a sharp distinction between the private and public realms. Women's domestic mischief was politically significant. Treacherous women who seduced, emasculated, and manipulated men undermined family sobriety, frugality, independence, and stability and thereby destroyed men's potential for civic virtue, rationality, productivity, citizenship, and patriotic loyalty. Within this context, selfish men had good reasons for choosing bachelorhood over marriage, but that only enhanced women's ability to do evil. And committed husbands had good reasons for reasserting patriarchal authority over wives, but that mostly steeled women's desire to resist and conspire against men. Just as English intellectuals feared that privatized religion and property were insufficient restraints on men's passions, so too they feared that privatized patriarchy administered by flawed men would fail to subdue women's passions or prevent women's private desires from corrupting public life.

Whigs' despair of men and dread of women created an intellectual atmosphere heavy with uncertainty. Their deep-seated misanthropy and misogyny implied that men's and women's manners would continue to fuel the forces of disorder. What they called "inconstancy" became "the archenemy that needs to be exorcised." [79] Inconstancy was in fact a hoary old enemy in Western political thought. Moses encountered it among those who worshiped the Golden Calf at the foot of Mount Sinai and Plato confronted it amid the tumult of ancient Athens. Their common strategy was to write off the adults as lost causes and look to the younger generation to revive virtue, reason, and predictability. America's English forebears also looked to youth only to rediscover the flaws of their parents.

3

On the Youth Question

We hear of few Spartans who did not willingly expose their lives for the service of their country; and the women themselves were so far inflamed with the same affection that they refused to mourn for their children and husbands who died in the defense of it.
—Algernon Sidney[1]

The Spartan story of patriotic parents who gladly gave their sons' lives for their country has long endured in the Western imagination. The tale honored fathers who sacrificed themselves and their sons to public good and praised mothers who bred courageous warriors and incited them to heroism. It applauded youth who sought their manhood on the battlefield only to die for the state and ennobled veterans who survived trial by military ordeal to attain full citizenship. The moral of the story was that out of the crucible of war came a new generation of males to participate in and perpetuate the polity. For Whigs, the message was to recognize the importance of confronting the youth question: *How were men to ensure that their sons acquired the self-discipline, skill, courage, and loyalty to protect the commonwealth and ensure political continuity?*

The youth question plagued English intellectuals. They feared that men's passions and women's treachery undermined the parental cooperation and commitment needed to rear patriotic sons. They worried that the new generation was made up of spoiled, malicious young men who loved self-indulgence far more than martial virtue. They were aggrieved by impoverished young thugs and disinherited aristocrats who joined the King's standing army and endangered liberty. Whigs were convinced that English youth did not measure up to Spartan standards. Could they be redeemed? One possibility was to revitalize and reform local militia as schools in civic virtue. Mandatory militia training would force all young men to take lessons in sobriety, obedience, civility, self-sacrifice, citizenship, and patriotic service, and, it was hoped, produce a new generation of citizen–soldiers dedicated to constitutional balance and national strength.

The problem was that few Englishmen wanted to enforce compulsory service and most youth seemed intent on evading it. The rhetoric of liberty and rights undermined young men's sense of obligation to the state, while the mobility of youth made it relatively easy to escape military service. Moreover, the militia appeared to be anachronistic. Modern war, national expansion, and colonization deflated the value of local defense forces and inflated the importance of professionally led standing armies. Whig misgivings about the popularity and effectiveness of the militia fostered an ambivalence that more often despaired of modern youth than invested hope in it. How useful was the Fifth Commandment when honoring one's parents entailed submission to adult passions and ignorance? What good was a militia that was neither compulsory nor functional? The corruption of English youth made talk of liberty and rights seem all the more dangerous.

The Corruption of English Youth

Greek philosophers were obsessed with youth. Socrates' capital crime was corrupting the morals of Athenian youth. Plato wanted older men to instill in young men a love of wisdom, courage, and justice. Aristotle stressed youthful obedience as the basis for adult citizenship. The issue was whether young men were adequately prepared for trustworthy citizenship. And the ultimate qualifying test was whether young men were willing and able to forsake private passions and demonstrate self-sacrificing military valor. Could young men resist the pleas of an Antigone or another woman who elevated family loyalty above the state? Could they achieve the Homeric ideal of the "warrior–hero" who mixed masculinity, daring, and patriotism on the battlefield to prove his selfless loyalty to the polis? If so, tested young soldiers returned from war as "men" of proved political worth. As Genevieve Lloyd points out, "The masculinity of war . . . consists in the capacity to rise above what female-ness symbolically represents: attachment to private concerns, to 'mere life.' In leaving all that behind, the soldier becomes a real man [and] emerges into the glories of selfhood, citizenship, and truly ethical, universal con-cerns."[2]

English thinkers were equally concerned with youth. No longer rely-ing on princes and priests to manage political education, they hoped that parents, especially fathers, would assume the obligation to school sons in civic virtue, rationality, sobriety, courage, and citizenship. That hope was compromised, however, by a liberalism of fear that accentuated fathers' selfish passions and mothers' dreadful effect on children. Blaming par-ents for young men's follies and failings was commonplace in England. James Harrington suggested that "innumerable children come to owe their utter perdition unto their own parents, in each of which the common-wealth loses a citizen." Avaricious fathers driven by desire and self-interest neglected their sons. Young boys were condemned to suffer de facto matri-archy or to follow freely their own chaotic impulses. At the other extreme, excessive parental affection translated into the overindulgence, especially among mothers, that reinforced filial selfishness. English parents appeared to be raising a generation of spoiled young men innocent of the rigors of civic virtue and the requirements of rational self-mastery. Harrington concluded that "the education of a man's children is not wholly to be committed or trusted unto himself."[3]

James Tyrrell infused Harrington's fears of parental neglect and indul-gence with apprehensions of parental cruelty and child abuse. The poten-tial of parents to terrorize their offspring was so great that Tyrrell took the drastic step of justifying filial disobedience. "It is a lesser evil," he wrote, "that the command of parents should be disobeyed, nay, sometimes their persons resisted, than that they should make a right to command or do unreasonable and unlawful things."[4] Some writers could not de-cide whether parental neglect, overindulgence, or cruelty had the worst effects. Others added to the Whig litany of parental failings by criticizing fathers' tendency to set poor examples for their sons, parents' propen-sity to exploit children's innocence, weakness, and labor, and, in general, adults' ignorance of proper child-rearing methods. Parents usually had good intentions, Whigs thought, but most did not devote adequate time, energy, resources, or intellect to molding the new generation.

No Whig thinker was more appalled by modern parenthood than John Locke, "the first great philosopher to devote an entire treatise to education."[5] Locke's philosophical and political writings commented on parental cruelty and overindulgence, but his *Some Thoughts Concerning Education* cataloged a lengthy, systematic, and detailed list of parental pitfalls common among the very best families. His understanding was that being a good parent, especially a virtuous father, required a remarkable degree of wisdom, foresight, and dedication to the management of young men's physical, moral, and intellectual development. There were no shortcuts. Sending boys to schools only exposed them to pernicious and unpredictable influences. Hiring a fine tutor was useful if not essential, but, even then, the tutor was no more than an aide in proper paternal pedagogy.

By Locke's logic, the most studious and dedicated father could easily fail his sons. Small paternal lapses during early childhood fostered vicious lifelong habits in boys. Worse, Locke believed that boys had powerful if not innate propensities toward vice. They had insatiable desires manifested in a self-indulgent laziness or a spirited selfishness. They loved dominion and power over people and property; they lied, cheated, and bullied; they resisted authority and reveled in licentiousness; and, as they grew older, they were subject to lust, gambling, violence, and the other sinful pastimes of modern city life. Unless parents confined their sons to the controlled environment of the home and carefully guarded them against temptation, boyish impulses would be worsened by the evils of society. For Locke, the combined effect of parental pitfalls, boyish propensities, and society's climate of temptation was that modern youth constantly complained about all restrictions, no matter how rational. Such complaining, he remarked, "weakens and effeminates their minds."[6]

Restoration literature implied that effeminacy was a social disease that had spread from corrupt fathers to impressionable sons. Its most virulent strain infected young bachelors who gravitated to large towns and cities where sheer numbers and mobility provided a sense of anonymity, a supportive subculture, and freedom from traditional family and community restraints. Pervasive wantonness and frivolity, warned one pamphleteer, were creating a nation of "unmanned" youth with "soft bodies" and narcissistic concerns for their self-images in "the looking-glass." Dandies who experimented with sodomy and hypereroticism, wasted their lives away in disease-ridden brothels, taverns, and gaming establishments, and emulated French manners and fashions were deemed positively treasonous. Another writer tried to capture young men's effeminacy in the symbol of the "compleat beau" who epitomized the self-indulgence and sexual lust that upset marriages and produced bastards only to spark vicious conflicts among former friends and neighbors.[7] The symptoms of effeminacy included slavery to passions, intemperance, and treachery.

Some pamphlets warned young girls to stay clear of licentious bachelors, fops, and beaus. Other tracts alerted young men to the perils that profligacy posed to their health and fortunes as well as to the nation's prospects. Many popular pieces carried a heavy load of nostalgia for the good old days when sons obeyed rather than usurped fathers' authority and young men respected the sanctity of monogamy and marital fidelity.[8] But there was more to these laments than nostalgia. Whig thinkers saw a close connection between the moral decay of modern youth and the regular resurgence of political tyranny.

The main characteristic of young men, wrote Harrington, was that, "though their wisdom be little, their courage is great." Young men's mindless daring was conceivably a basis for cultivating civic virtue among the new generation. Following Harrington's lead, John Trenchard argued that the "young nobility and gentry" who competed for self-glory and honors in military contests displayed a potential "noble ambition in making themselves serviceable to their country."[9] Properly directed and refined, the youthful quest for self-glory and public praise could be transformed into a mature patriotism. Unfortunately, Whigs feared, youthful courage without wisdom was following an ignoble course. Young men took mindless risks regardless of consequences. They ruined girls' chastity and wives' fidelity; they squandered inheritances and enriched moneylenders; they engaged in violent fights and lethal duels; and they practiced crime and encountered punishment. Dissolute young men did more than cause chaos around them. Their desire to avert the consequences of their acts—revenge, poverty, and imprisonment—provided them a powerful incentive to escape their troubles by enlisting in the king's standing army.

Troubled youth from all social classes were ripe for recruitment. The younger sons of the nobility, expecting minor portions of their fathers' estates and the prospect of downward mobility, often sought sinecures in the church, state bureaucracy, and standing army. From Whigs' vantage point, these upper-class youth were foolishly exchanging their liberty for slavery to the forces of tyranny. They became an army of mercenaries paid to carry out the conspiracies of churchmen, the court, and the military. Andrew Marvell expressed a special disdain for military officers who moonlighted in Parliament: "They and other 'placemen' would always support an increase in the standing army, or the levying of heavy taxes by illegal means, or indeed any bill the court desired." [10] Upper-class patronage reinforced court control of the sword and the purse and furthered the cause of political factionalism and royal tyranny.

Lower down the social scale, the middling sort of youth who gambled away their patrimony, lower-class youth who had none, rogues fleeing the wrath of cuckolded husbands and angry fathers, and criminals facing prosecution and imprisonment constituted a lumpenproletariat class-for-hire. When desperate, they sold themselves into the standing army to acquire food, clothing, and shelter, obtain liquor rations, elude enemies, and avoid jail. They became the thoroughly detested rank-and-file Redcoats whom Whigs considered mindless instruments of discord and despotism. Much of the time, the Redcoats constituted an idle mass of appetitive young men seeking diversions from boredom. William Prynne warned, "These lusty men spend their time eating, drinking, [and] whoring. . . . They make off with wives and daughters and leave 'not a few great bellies and bastards on the inhabitants of the countries' charge.' " All of the time, the Redcoats were a mass of "ignorant, idle, and needy persons" organized into a mercenary army "calculated to enslave a nation." Their trade and livelihood was the willingness to do violence at the king's command.[11]

The existence of the standing army posed a double-edged danger to the nation. First, it was intolerable in peacetime. John Trenchard argued that "a standing army in peace will grow more effeminate by living dissolutely in quarters." That effeminacy signified the presence of armed rogues roaming society and also the nation's preposterous reliance on an army that was too dissolute and ill disciplined to be effective. The Redcoats, after all, were noted for their insubordination, drunkenness, and high desertion rates. Second, the standing army was an invitation to war. Officers had an incentive to promote combat as a means to occupy and control their troops and to advance their own careers. And corrupt monarchs were almost certain to use the standing army as an extension of their own desire for power. Referring to Cromwell's reign and his New Model Army, Trenchard wrote,

> This is a true and lively example of a government with an army, an army that was raised in the cause and for the sake of liberty, composed for the most part of men of religion and sobriety. If this army could commit such violences . . . at home and abroad, at a time when the whole people were trained in arms and the pulse of the nation beat big for liberty, what are we to expect if . . . an ambitious prince should arise with a dissolute and debauched army, a flattering clergy, a prostitute ministry, a bankrupt House of Lords, a pensioner House of Commons, and a slavish and corrupted nation?[12]

What most Whigs expected was the loss of liberty, the rise of tyranny, and perpetual war.

Could young men be saved from effeminacy? Could the nation be freed from chaos and violence? Whigs certainly did not trust the church and state to teach young men anything other than dogmatic obedience to tradition and tyranny. Nor were Whigs optimistic that parents could overcome their own passions and ignorance—much less devote themselves to raising virtuous, rational sons. They were convinced, however, that the urban youth subculture and the debauched standing army promised more pandemonium and oppression in the future. If there was any hope that the new generation would contribute to political order and perpetuate the constitution, Whigs located it in the classical image of the citizen–soldier whose participation in local militia would ostensibly reinforce national security and revive civic virtue.

Reviving Civic Virtue

Machiavelli etched the ancient ideal of the Homeric warrior–hero into modern political thought. He argued that citizens' most noble virtue was their capacity to think and act as if war were imminent. Males were to be citizen–soldiers who devoted a good portion of their lives to anticipating war, preparing for it, and engaging in it to safeguard republican liberty from tyrants and national integrity from foreign enemies.

As Hanna Pitkin suggests, Machiavelli's men were obliged to cultivate "military fierceness" in "defense of civility."[13] There was no higher calling in an international climate marked by permanent insecurity and hostility. Only disciplined, organized citizen–soldiers could tend to the survival of the republic, and survival of the republic took precedence over all other matters. "Where the very safety of the country depends upon the resolution to be taken," Machiavelli wrote, "no considerations of justice or injustice, humanity or cruelty, nor of glory or of shame, should be allowed to prevail."[14]

Machiavelli's republic was a garrison state, and citizens' highest form of political participation was service in the state militia. Fathers and sons joined with neighbors to learn and excel at the art of war. If necessary, they left their families, friends, and estates at short notice, submitted to the orders of their military commanders, and risked their lives in defense of the republic. Machiavelli understood that such lethal loyalty was possible only if men gloried in martial self-sacrifice and aspired to a patriotism that demanded "warlike ardor with discipline" and the "true valor" that employed "its impetuousity at the right time and with moderation" in order to "sustain courage . . . and the hope of victory."[15] The education of citizen–soldiers was an immense challenge. Lust and avarice drew men toward particular interests instead of patriotic self-sacrifice, and ignorance fostered a false belief that mercenary soldiers could fight in the place of citizens. Corruption had to be overcome to avert national degeneration and disintegration.

Accordingly, Machiavelli urged that republics pledge peacetime to drilling citizens in disciplined ardor. Young men in particular had to be schooled in the virtues of martial self-sacrifice. The militia's responsibility was to teach skill in arms but also habitual courage, deference to orders, and a combat readiness that defined both masculinity and citizenship, "so that when fortune changes, she may find [citizen–soldiers] prepared to resist her blows, and to prevail in adversity."[16] While boys and men prepared for war in their militia musters, the republic's leaders were to gather military intelligence. Generals' task was to estimate potential and actual enemies' intentions, gauge their strengths and weaknesses, consider propitious moments for battle, and initiate preemptive strikes to surprise and defeat adversaries. That leaders might be too quick to make war and extend empire was problematic, but even ill-chosen combat had its advantages. It kept men's minds fixed on public good and provided patriotic outlets for ambitious individuals otherwise prone to self-aggrandizement and political factionalism.[17]

Machiavelli self-consciously recalled the martial virtues of classical Rome and highlighted the vices of modernity "so as to excite in the minds of the young men who may read my writings the desire to avoid the evils of the latter, and to prepare themselves to imitate the virtues of the former." [18] His seventeenth-century English heirs also wanted to excite youth to divert their energy from individualistic excesses to patriotic service as citizen–soldiers who divided their time between their freeholds and the local militia. Whigs' immediate concern was to rejuvenate the oft-neglected ideal of the citizen–soldier and the militia, also known as "the constitutional army," to provide an alternative to the standing army. Whigs believed that propertied men and their sons should be organized into an independent, armed force able to defend liberty and prevent court corruption, illegitimate taxation, and foreign aggression. They opposed court attempts to assert central control over local militia and resisted court efforts to enlarge the standing army. Whig opposition was especially intense in the 1670s and 1680s, when Shaftesbury, with Locke's help, spearheaded resistance to the anticipated coronation of a Catholic king who, they feared, would use the standing army to enforce religious intolerance, expropriate Protestant property, and install tyranny on the throne. While the 1688–89 revolution rid England of its Catholic king and installed restraints on the new king's military prerogatives, it failed to quiet Whig critics. They continued to defend the militia as the nation's only trustworthy army and kept up their attack on the standing army as an instrument of tyranny.[19]

Whig rhetoric honoring the militia and abhorring the standing army was somewhat deceptive. Most intellectuals recognized that England's decentralized, disorganized militia was not a sufficient military force for a modern nation. The militia could serve as a local police force and a useful home-defense force, but it was no match for the professional armies and advanced military technology of rival European powers. Some Whig theorists hoped to reform the militia to upgrade its military potency, but, even then, few Whigs were willing to enforce compulsory militia service or support the tax subsidies needed for a serious militia overhaul. Their reluctance to give priority to militia reform stemmed from several factors. They could not generate great enthusiasm for militia service among the propertied classes. When pressure to enlist in the militia was great, the wealthy often refused to leave their estates and hired substitutes to serve in their place. Also, Whig loathing for the standing army diminished after 1689 when Parliament weakened the king's ability to use the small standing army as an extension of his power. Historian Lois Schwoerer concludes, "The cry 'Reform the Militia,' like the cry 'No Standing Army,' had propagandist rather than substantive meaning. . . . The standing army menace had become a bogey which could be invoked to discredit the court while the demand to reform the militia could be served up to assure the politically conscious that the defense of the nation was not being neglected."[20]

However, the defense of the militia did have substantive meaning when it came to preparing youth for citizenship. Whigs reanimated the ideal of the citizen–soldier as a standard for measuring young men's masculinity and political maturity. They justified universal militia training as a means to educate, test, and reward youthful patriotism. Ideally, young men would be obligated to enroll in local militia units run by leading freeholders, gentry, and notables. Local youth would be schooled in civic virtue and molded by the exemplary influence of town fathers venerated for their commitment to public good. That way, parents' neglect and over-indulgence and youths' mindless daring could be corrected, freed of its impulsiveness, diverted from excessiveness, and firmly pointed toward civic-mindedness.

Whig theorists often used the rhetoric of the liberty-loving militia as a basis for advocating compulsory militia service for all young Englishmen. John Toland rehearsed the conventional argument that armed freeholders were the bastion of liberty and national independence as a prelude to arguing the political advantages of requiring all young men, eighteen years and older, to join the militia. He argued that militia training would turn young men away from vice and excite boys to emulate their fathers and older brothers: "Instead of tipling, gaming, and other diversions equally pernicious to their minds and bodies, [young men] learn the use of arms . . . [and] will be imitated by the very children who by that time their age obliges them to appear in the same place, will be superior to their fathers and need so little exhortation that they cannot be prevented from acquiring this art." Mandatory militia service would also contribute to the "education of youth," which, Toland lamented, "is shamefully neglected in this age." Militia trainees would be taught the obedience necessary for order and command, the self-discipline, sobriety, and industriousness required of good soldiers, and the civic pride that promoted public-spiritedness, love of community and country, and courageous sacrifice for public good. Toland suggested that only youth who had demonstrated martial virtue in the militia should be eligible for full citizenship. All others ought to be banned from holding "any post of honor or profit under the government." And "when young men (of all others the most ambitious of glory and honor) are once convinced that this is the only road to preferment, they will timely qualify themselves."[21]

Andrew Fletcher was even more insistent on the crucial place of militia service in the education of English youth. He blamed dissolute youth and the standing army for the "debauchery and wickedness" and the "frauds, oppressions, and cruelties" that pervaded Restoration England. Only the militia, which he called "the chief part of the constitution," could restore virtue and order. Fletcher wanted all twenty-two-year-old males to spend several years in militia training camps where they would learn skill at arms and also "Christian and moral duties, chiefly to humility, modesty, charity and the pardoning of private injuries." The camps would augment lessons in civility with efforts to identify future leaders by providing opportunities for youth to participate in patriotism. For instance, "Speeches exhorting to military and virtuous actions should be often composed and pronounced publicly by such of the youth as were by education and natural talents qualified for it." The potential impact of militia training was striking:

> Such a camp would be as great a school of virtue as of military discipline in which the youth would learn to stand in need of few things; to suffer as well as to act; to be modest as well as brave; to be as much ashamed of doing anything insolent or injurious as of turning their back upon an enemy; they would learn to forgive injuries done to themselves but to embrace with joy the occasions of dying to revenge those done to their country. And virtue imbibed in younger years would cast a flavor to the utmost periods of life.

Tutored in civility and military ferocity during their militia years, young men would return to their freeholds as mature men and capable citizens ready and able to participate responsibly in community politics and transmit civic virtue to their own sons.[22]

While social contract theorists were less emphatic about the benefits of a martial education, they were no less committed to it. They mostly presumed that the consent of the governed would be based on men's recognition of the need for mutual defense, willingness to cultivate the martial arts, and desire to rally to national defense. Algernon Sidney put it this way: "In a popular or mixed government, every man is concerned. . . . The body of the people is the public defense and every man is armed and disciplined. The advantages of good success are communicated to all, and everyone bears a part in the losses. This makes men generous and industrious, and fills their hearts with love to their country."[23] John Locke essentially agreed. His social contract required citizens to assist the executive in the defense of the nation, and his educational writings announced the importance of young men's military training. A young man "ought to be so bred as to be fitted to bear arms and be a soldier." Such training would teach "true fortitude," "courage in the field," and "contempt of life in the face of an enemy." Like so many others, Locke honored "the example of Sparta," which taught youth to withstand pain and practice self-denial, a sense of self-mastery that was "no small advance towards virtue."[24]

Whig idealization of the citizen–soldier and militia training echoed a number of related classical beliefs. Whig theorists presumed that young men had to be isolated from women's effeminate and dreaded influence while undergoing their militia rite of passage. Boys were to achieve adulthood and citizenship in a fraternal environment that encouraged martial bonding between the generations. Fletcher reinforced Machiavelli's misogyny by recommending that "No woman should be suffered to come within the camp."[25] Whigs also recalled the classical equation of martial virtue and civic virtue. Thus, Locke argued that the fundamental benefit of military training was to fortify youth against "dangers [that] attack us in other places, besides the fields of battle," for example, in "the warfare of life." Disciplined courage, bravery, and stoutness of heart were not only signs of good soldiering but also "marks of manliness" and requirements of citizenship.[26] Further, Whigs intended the redemptive effects of military training to be contagious. Spartan drills, parades, and competitions would be public displays orchestrated to inspire patriotism in children and civilians. The martial spirit, wrote Toland, "would excite our youth to pursue fame by noble and useful performances" and "merit the affection or applause of spectators."[27] Whigs' enduring message was that young men's excessive individualism could be cured by a strong dose of military discipline.

The idea of the militia as a school in civic virtue outlasted any serious attempts to revive and reform the institution. Whigs continued to view young men's militia service as a "means of moral regeneration" even as "the principle of obligatory personal service receded further and further into the background."[28] Young Englishmen did not want to suffer the restraints of militia service, pamphleteers argued, because they had become "soft, urbanized, and weak," and "forsaken their English birthright and their obligations as freeborn Englishmen."[29] Their fathers were not particularly helpful because they seemed to prefer material gain to martial excellence. J. R. Western observes, "The ideal of a citizen army, with men of property filling the ranks, had been made incapable of realization by the development of a capitalist economy. The middle class of businessmen and farmers-for-profit needed to devote their entire attention to business and could not take time off for fighting. . . . The upper class, likewise, no longer regarded war as its profession, and was not eager to sacrifice time and money to military pursuits."[30] It was as if the revitalization of the militia was a brilliant idea whose time had passed.

The difficulty of translating militia rhetoric into reality was part of the larger dilemma of recovering civic virtue at a time when men's individualistic and instrumental mentality seemed to command both private and public life. The chances for everyday civility were quite dim, one tract suggested, when "friendships (if they may be called so) . . . are always contracted with a tacit reserve to interest on both sides, and seldom last longer than the prosperity of either party."[31] The prospects for national security were even darker, Whigs feared, when England had to rely on young men's erratic and unenlightened calculations of self-interest as the basis for their service in defense of the nation. After all, why should impassioned young men seeking self-preservation consent to a social contract that obligated them to die for the state?

The Social Contract with Death

Social contract theorists made calculated consent the legitimate basis for political society, but they did not imagine that rational agreement could ever shape intercourse among nations. As they saw it, the natural and unchangeable state of international relations was lawlessness. One might posit divine and prudential norms that ought to guide nations and hope that mutual advantage and diplomacy might produce some harmony among nations. But the wise person never counted on perpetual peace. Men's erratic nature, nations' unpredictability, and global serendipity admitted no enduring common interests, no universal positive laws, no neutral referees, and no monopoly of coercive power to resolve international conflicts peacefully, justly, and consistently. Contractarians' liberalism of fear made international tension, violence, and war unavoidable. If primitive fathers made original social contracts to increase their military might, modern men banded together to protect their polities from ongoing aggression.

Thomas Hobbes made ubiquitous violence the centerpiece of political theory. His starting point was men's search for self-preservation in a world where the brutal struggle of individual against individual and nation against nation was the rule. Individuals' fear of being victimized by violence was their incentive to seek domestic peace by consenting to obey a sovereign power strong enough to order civil society, deter outside aggression, and conquer foreign enemies.[32] That meant that men had to be willing to put their own martial skills at the sovereign's disposal. While Hobbes's philosophical premise was that men were rational enough to accede to this arrangement, his empirical analysis cast doubt on the likelihood that men would recognize the connection between self-preservation and military service, obey their military commanders, endure the risks of war, and forgo opportunities to evade military service or desert their posts. To compensate for doubt, Hobbes advocated a mix of coercion and consent to overcome men's ignorance and subjectivity.

The Hobbesian state could use force to "urge" individuals to undertake military obligations just as the conqueror could use the threat of violence to "persuade" the vanquished to put away old loyalties and consent to a new sovereign power. The state's ability to muster superior power, instill fear, and force cooperation could be quite effective, in part, because it did not require much intelligence for men to choose compliance over resistance when confronted with the gallows. Nonetheless, Hobbes understood that coercion and consent formed an unstable compound. The threat of state coercion was not always sufficient for gaining men's consent and cooperation. For example, a vanquished people could refuse consent to a new sovereign, assume the status of involuntary slaves, and remain in a latent state of war with conquerors. Such a subjected people constituted a continuous source of social unrest. In addition, Hobbes recognized that men who were forced to consent did not make trustworthy citizens. "Without the sword" of the state hovering over them, their obedience was always questionable.[33] The inefficiency and uncertainty of "coerced consent" created a double bind. First, Hobbes could not be confident that state-generated fear would actually persuade young men to participate in the military or perform their military duties. Second, Hobbes could be fairly certain that the dormant discontents of coerced subjects, consenting citizens, and young soldiers caused considerable social instability. The prospect of military weakness and widespread discontent made the Leviathan vulnerable to external conquest and internal rebellion.

Hobbes not only recognized this vulnerability, he appeared to legitimate it. Still following the logic of self-preservation, Hobbes justified young men's resistance to military service and citizens' refusal to obey the sovereign's laws. He wrote that citizens were free "to defend their own bodies, even against them that lawfully invade them."[34] The right of self-preservation provided individuals a moral license to fend off robbers, defy threatening policemen, and refuse risky military service. Here is Hobbes's "engendered" legitimation of draft evasion and military desertion:

> A man that is commanded as a soldier to fight against the enemy, though his sovereign have right enough to punish his refusal with death, may nevertheless in many cases refuse without injustice. . . . There is allowance to be made for natural timorousness; not only to women, of whom no such dangerous duty is expected, but also to men of feminine courage. When armies fight, there is on one side, or both, a running away; yet when they do it not out of treachery, but fear, they are not esteemed to do it unjustly, but dishonorably. For the same reason, to avoid battle, is not injustice but cowardice.[35]

Young men obsessed with their own lives were free to evade military service and even desert their fellow soldiers. While the stigma of effeminacy, dishonor, and cowardice along with possible sanctions might persuade most young men to do their military duty, it still appeared that Hobbes's right to self-preservation was so absolute that it was to be honored even when it imperiled the state's ability to survive enemy assaults.

In fact, Hobbes performed a philosophical sleight of hand to solve the problem of national security. First, he implied that traditional misogyny was potentially more powerful than men's desire for biological survival. Hobbesian self-preservation referred to both masculinity and life, and young men were conceivably more concerned with preserving their manhood than with risking death on the battlefield. Second, Hobbes did spell out one explicit qualification to individuals' right to preserve their own bodies. "When the defense of the commonwealth requireth at once the help of all that are able to bear arms," he proclaimed, "every one is obliged because otherwise the institution of the commonwealth, which they have not the purpose or courage to preserve, was in vain."[36] In a single sentence, Hobbes authorized the sovereign to suspend individual rights, declare martial law, and require everyone to contribute to the war effort. Like Machiavelli's, Hobbes's rhetoric of liberty obscured a higher commitment to masculinity, militarism, and national security.

Was this a problem? In one sense, it was good politics. The Hobbesian state officially promised to recognize, guarantee, and protect men's absolute freedom to preserve themselves. The rhetoric of rights was a wonderful way to win men's loyalty. At the same time, the Hobbesian state informally reinforced a classical patriarchal prejudice that motivated young men to invest their freedom in martial ethics and military service to prove and preserve their masculinity. In a crisis, the sovereign who suspended individual rights, declared martial law, and enforced compulsory military service might be obeyed as a cultural power inviting youth to affirm their masculinity by disassociating themselves from the effeminacy, dishonor, and cowardice of evasion and desertion and staying home with the women, and as a political power employing expedience and discretion in defense of individual rights. A periodic national security crisis could be an opportunity to divert young men's attention from individualism and redirect their loyalty to the state.

In another sense, the gap between Hobbes's individualist rhetoric and statist priorities was problematic. Michael Walzer describes the core conundrum: "The very existence of the [Hobbesian] state seems to require some limit on the right of self-preservation, and yet the state is nothing more than an instrument designed to fulfill that right."[37] The Hobbesian state that limited or suspended individuals' right to self-preservation undermined its own moral foundations; but the Hobbesian state that respected individuals' right to self-preservation undermined its own existence. Either way, the state suffered an inherent legitimation crisis which increased the likelihood of resistance among the discontented and decreased the chances that young Englishmen would habitually honor their obligation to serve in the military. And if young Englishman were as effeminate as Restoration pamphleteers suggested, sovereign appeals to their masculinity could fall on deaf ears.

Ensuring national security was a more difficult challenge for Locke who specifically emphasized individuals' rights *against* state authority. As Walzer notes, "Any theory which, like Locke's, begins with the absolute independence of freely willing individuals and goes on to treat politics and the state as instrumental to the achievement of individual purposes would seem by its very nature incapable of describing ultimate obligation [to die for the state]."[38] Locke's rhetoric of natural rights and his instrumental view of politics implied that calculating young men could easily rationalize a refusal to serve in the military, insubordination to military officials, and escape from the dangers of the battlefield. A Lockean government that recognized youthful freedom would have difficulty defending its borders; but a Lockean government that suspended individual rights could provoke a revolution. The difficulty is all the greater because Locke explicitly justified both youthful freedom and revolution.

Unfortunately, Locke did not directly address this problem, and what we can glean from his writings is ambiguous. His collaboration with Shaftesbury during the Exclusion Crisis may have been indicative of his support for the militia tradition of compulsory service for freeholders as an alternative to the standing army. In the *Two Treatises*, however, Locke appeared to join the tradition of compulsory service to the court-controlled standing army. His version of the social contract obliged citizens "to assist the executive power of society . . . as the good, prosperity, and safety of society shall require." Locke's executive power was lodged in a national leader equipped with nearly unlimited prerogative and federative (that is, foreign policy) discretion, which included the authority to make military policy and declare war "for the public good."[39] One can infer that Locke's leadership had the prerogative to conscript young men into a central army.

And Locke overtly demanded that young soldiers submit "an absolute obedience to the command of every superior officer." Emphasizing his belief in absolute obedience to military orders, Locke added, "It is justly death to disobey or dispute the most dangerous and unreasonable of them." [40]

One can argue that Locke, like Hobbes, was quite willing to limit or suspend individual rights to force young men to play the part of martial patriots and national protectors in times of national crisis. Some scholars go further. M. Seliger suggests that Locke's liberalism contained the "presuppositions and conclusions that have become part and parcel of the rationale of modern nationalism." [41] Locke assumed a common descent, language, and culture among citizens that reflected and reinforced a common apprehension of outsiders. It was this deep-seated sense of community that fostered individuals' willingness to subordinate their private desires to public good. By extension, one would expect that young men would be raised to identify with the community and contribute to its defense. In turn, the chauvinistic, xenophobic community would provide broad public support for executive initiatives, including conscription and war, that promised national security and international conquest.

Richard Cox argues that "Locke's view of political society ultimately rests on the conception that foreign policy is decisive, or that it is the final determinate of the objectives and internal organization of the political society." [42] In essence, Locke's support for individual rights was a way to win the citizen loyalty needed to field a powerful army; and his mercantilism was meant to produce the massive national wealth needed to subsidize a powerful army. Further, Locke's opposition to absolute monarchy was based primarily on his understanding that patriarchal kings enslaved the very people they depended on for military manpower and productivity and thereby fostered internal dissension, economic waste, and military weakness instead of national strength. On this reading, Lockean individualism was subordinate and instrumental to the national security state. And the conscription of youth would be simply one manifestation of Locke's statist priorities.

One key implication of this interpretation is that Locke did not wholly rely on calculating, self-interested individualism to promote national security. If Hobbes put masculinity in the service of militarism, Locke harnessed cultural homogeneity and economic priorities to national power. Overall, however, this analysis of Locke is problematic. It not only underestimates Locke's devotion to individual rights but also ignores what might be called his business pacifism. Locke was no militarist. He wanted young men to cultivate martial virtues less to improve their fighting abilities and more to enhance their self-discipline, industry, productivity, and trade. On the one hand, he was horrified that "the honor and renown that is bestowed on conquerors (who for the most part are but the great butchers of mankind) . . . mislead youth, who by this means come to think slaughter the laudable business of mankind, and the most heroic of virtues." On the other hand, he hoped that economic prosperity would provide England so large an economic advantage that rival nations would be too poor to mount a serious assault.[43] Ideally, a distrust of war joined to a thriving commerce would eliminate the need for young men to die for the state.

But Locke was no idealist. Neither he nor other Whigs were confident that English trade advantages and prosperity would function as substitutes for war. Locke dwelled on the distinction between just and unjust war knowing that the international state of nature would continue to host bloody battles and destructive conflicts. He was also cognizant of common Whig sentiments that commerce could worsen international tensions and increase the likelihood of drawing England into a European war. Finally, there was no escaping the issue of young men's willingness to sacrifice and die for the state if only because Locke and his contemporaries were anxious about young men's participation in national expansion and empire.

National Expansion

Machiavelli was a classical hawk who believed that war was essential to the health of republics. Montesquieu was a modern dove who claimed that "peace and moderation" constituted the spirit of republics. However, the difference between the two viewpoints was not precise. Montesquieu believed that small republics were best suited to peace but expansive republics were least vulnerable to conquest. He thought that peaceful republics had to maintain vigilant armed forces to protect themselves but those forces necessarily imperiled peace. A part-time militia fostered domestic peace but invited external aggression; a standing army contributed to domestic tyranny but provided the most effective national defense. Ultimately, a small peaceful republic of citizen–soldiers invited war, war aimed at victory, and victory entailed conquest and expansion. The dove grew talons if it was to survive.[44]

Early-modern English theorists had one advantage over Continental thinkers. They could afford the luxury of pacifism because their nation was an island protected by an oceanic moat. Fortuitous geography allowed Whigs to imagine that national security was possible without a substantial military apparatus or an expansive military posture. They argued that a modest navy backed by a citizen militia would be sufficient for defending England against rivals. Few European states had the economic and military might to carry out an assault across the sea. And they could be deterred by a modest naval force. John Trenchard noted, "We have little reason to fear whilst we keep the seas well guarded."[45] Even if foreign troops evaded the navy and invaded England, Whigs were confident that enemies would be foiled by English militiamen forced to defend their own families, homes, farms, and communities. An added incentive to pacifism was that it promised to purchase liberty at a cut-rate price. The militia would defend liberty against court corruption while the navy would ill serve a corrupt king intent on tyranny. Moreover, the militia was mostly self-supporting and the navy was relatively inexpensive. Conceivably, England could be a small island republic that stayed clear of war, conquest, and expansion.

However, English pacifism was ambiguous. Harrington and other neo-Machiavellians preferred a more aggressive military posture. Harrington argued that a commonwealth had a duty "to put the world into a better condition than it was before," and his corresponding view of the militia was expansive. Older, experienced, and trustworthy citizen–soldiers were to man local garrisons and secure peace within the commonwealth. Courageous but foolish young militiamen were to form mobile armies to enlarge the commonwealth.[46] One problem with instituting Harrington's plan was that young freeholders were not only reluctant to join the militia but were also especially antagonistic to service that sent them far from their families, lovers, and material opportunities for long periods. When pressed into service, wealthy youth often purchased lower-class substitutes. As a result, the class origins of militiamen and Redcoats were increasingly similar.[47] The substantive issue that emerged was whether a mobile, standing army of lower-class youth could be trusted to put the world in a better condition.

Ironically, it was John Trenchard, England's most famous opponent of the standing army, who discovered that a mobile standing army could be tolerated. While surveying the destruction that standing armies had wrought in the world, Trenchard noticed that Venice and Holland had been able to maintain relatively safe standing armies because they garrisoned regular soldiers at a considerable distance from home. "The situation of these states make their armies, so posted, not dangerous to them." [48] Conceivably, a standing army could be a national asset if lower-class Redcoats were quickly shipped overseas where they could not disturb domestic order but could spread the blessings of English liberty. Whig support for a modest navy helped to provide the logistical means for transporting imperial armies around the world.

Would English armies improve the world? Whig pacifism and imperialism were fairly selective. Whigs could be exceedingly dovish when the issue was military confrontation on the European continent, where they found motivations for war questionable and the chances for victory uncertain. However, Whigs could be quite hawkish when it was a matter of sending soldiers into arenas where the chance of losses was minimal and the prospect for rewards was considerable. Thus, they debated among themselves whether England should unite the British Isles as their ruler or as a partner, but agreed that England had a moral, economic, and military stake in controlling the region. They disagreed among themselves whether colonization of the New World was more problematic than profitable but generally endorsed the idea that colonization was a legitimate moral endeavor worthy of consideration. In part, that consideration involved whether England could maintain consensual bonds with colonial settlers and elevate indigenous peoples by integrating them into the empire. [49]

Harrington's republicanism provided the impetus for empire, but liberal contract theory pointed empire toward colonialism. The English concept of the social contract divided the world into civil and uncivil peoples. Founded on Protestant theology, natural law theory, and consent of the governed, the social contract denominated those inside and outside civil society. English fathers of families were inside. Their wives, children, and servants were included as dependents. Neighboring European nations such as Holland and France might be considered inside parties to Christianity, natural law, and monetized, civilized society. Everyone else was clearly an outsider, and outsiders were dangerous. Thus, Algernon Sidney argued, "Peace is desirable by a state that is constituted for it, who contenting themselves with their own territories, have no desires of enlarging them. . . . It might simply deserve praise if mankind were so framed that a people intending to hurt none could preserve themselves. But the world being so far of another temper that no nation can be safe without valor and strength, those governments only deserve to be commended which by discipline and exercise increase both." Sidney counseled military preparedness as a minimal approach to outsiders. Then he added, "The best judges . . . have always given preference to those constitutions that principally intend war, and make use of trade as assisting to that end." Finally he concluded, "That is the best government which best provides for war." [50] If Sidney assumed a fear of foreigners that enhanced the wisdom of militarism and imperialism, Locke directed military and imperial expansion toward the colonization of ostensibly primitive peoples.

Locke argued that any place on Earth where land was underdeveloped and the economy was not yet monetized constituted a wasteland that was putatively unowned and subject to English colonization. He wrote, "There are still great tracts of ground to be found which—the inhabitants thereof not having joined with the rest of mankind in the consent of the use of their common money—lie waste, and are more than the people who dwell on it do or can make use of, and so still lie in common." [51] English settlers who mixed their labor with common land assumed ownership of it and acquired the right to exclude others from it. Like Harrington, Locke believed that the global expansion of English morality, economy, and politics improved the world by spreading Christian ethics, enhancing mankind's productivity and prosperity, and introducing barbarous people to civil society. However, where original inhabitants were foolish enough to resist colonization of their so-called wasteland, Locke's logic declared them to be unjust aggressors and authorized settlers to arm and defend themselves. That Locke recognized the possibility of resistance was evident in *The Fundamental Constitutions of Caroline*, where he and Shaftesbury required settlers to bear arms to defend their colony. [52]

Whigs' flirtation with colonialism simultaneously heightened the import of the youth question and promised to answer it. Expansion and maintenance of empire in a hostile world put a premium on youthful ambition and desire, courage and daring, imagination and action. Whigs did not doubt that young Englishmen had the necessary ardor—but they worried whether English youth could discipline their ardor. Would young soldiers submit to the military hierarchy necessary for claiming and retaining new lands? Would young settlers calm their passions and cooperate to found colonies, pioneer prosperity, govern and defend them? Would they demonstrate enough virtue and rationality to bring indigenous inhabitants into the civilized world? If the bachelors and Redcoats back home were representative of their generation, one could expect little other than mischief from the young soldiers and settlers shipped overseas.

Still, colonial mischief was not all bad. Young men who emigrated to overseas colonies would exhaust their passions, ignorance, and aggression far from the English crowds. They might harm themselves and "barbarous" peoples but not England proper. Moreover, the colonies could have a positive effect on the youth back home. Young men facing poverty might identify their aspirations with new opportunities in the colonies instead of turning to crime and rebellion at home. Dissolute youth seeking to escape the wrath of ruined women, their families, creditors, or prison could start over in the New World rather than add to social discord at home. As Americans would later discover, expansion and settlement could function as a safety valve that allowed the discontented and dissolute to let off steam without damaging social stability.

A more optimistic view of colonization was that it provided a pristine arena for English youth to play out possibilities for pioneering new commonwealths. Young men who faced the challenge of the wilderness were, in a sense, undergoing the classical test of the warrior–hero by participating in a modern-day moral equivalent of war. Young pioneers pitted their self-discipline and industry, sobriety and courage, fortitude and intelligence against wild nature and hostile populations. Distanced from European cities, moneylenders, courts, and corruption, young settlers could conceivably redeem their virtue, cultivate rationality, and mature into responsible adults and good citizens. There was even hope for young women in colonies where they would have to submit to men for reasons of survival but also have a calming influence on men who lived beyond the immediate grasp of English authority. Arthur Dobbs went further. He urged young women to go to America, marry Indians, and civilize them.[53]

Whether English colonies would become Never-Never Lands for lost boys or Edenic gardens for youthful redemption was unclear. Whether England would play the part of the affectionate but stern father and the nurturant but restrained mother that guided young colonies to maturity, independence, and equality was debatable. But Whigs were certain of one thing. English men, women, and youth would have to restrain their excessive individualism, tame erratic passions, and develop a self-sacrificial loyalty to public good to stop the social anarchy and political tyranny that amounted to national suicide.

Suicide Prevention

English republicanism and liberalism emphasized different epistemologies, rhetorics, and politics but nonetheless converged, first on a common opposition to traditional patriarchalism and then on a liberalism of fear. Republicans and liberals were all Whigs when it came to contesting absolute kingship, honoring ancient liberty and modern rights, doubting the sufficiency of human nature, and lamenting the propensity of men, women, and youth to do mischief in the world. They launched significant intellectual experiments regarding the possibility of making freedom and equality the voluntary foundation for social and political life. But they quickly aborted their experiments as the fearful results became evident.

Modernity seemed to bring out the worst in people. Modern men lacked the civic virtue and rationality necessary for fraternal self-government; their ideas and behavior would have to be regulated. Modern women were inherently treacherous and demanding; their education and activities would have to be closely confined. Modern young men preferred profligacy to frugality, industry, and sobriety; they would have to be disciplined. Faced with the prospect of liberty run to licentiousness, Whigs' primary response was to drift back toward truncated versions of traditional patriarchal authority. Men's individual desires, property, and participation would be restricted and regulated by political elites. Women's selfish passions were to be subordinated to husbands' sovereignty. Young men's licentiousness was to be cured by a strong dose of martial subordination to exemplary militia leaders.

As most Whigs recognized, however, the problem of social order was too complex to be settled by a half-hearted revival of patriarchalism. Whig thinkers were not confident that political elites, family fathers, and leading citizen–soldiers were any less corrupt than the dreaded court or the fearful mob. Nor were they confident that men, women, and youth exposed to the rhetoric of liberty and rights would readily submit to today's pale imitations of yesterday's discredited patriarchs. The best evidence of Whigs' fear that England was on a suicidal course was their fantasies. They imagined the messianic appearance of charismatic, superhuman father figures whose alchemy would reestablish order. Then they invented commonwealths where people and their flaws miraculously vanished: men were absorbed into a government of laws; women disappeared into domesticity; and youth evaporated across the seas. Ultimately, Whig intellectuals were far better at articulating the questions of modernity than at answering them.

John Locke contributed to Whigs' liberalism of fear but his contribution was not especially unique or noteworthy. One could attribute far greater significance to Harrington, Tyrrell, and Sidney, who challenged traditional patriarchalism, articulated the rhetoric of liberty and rights, and defined the problem of excessive individualism earlier and in some ways more clearly and completely than Locke. However, Locke's political theory was unique, noteworthy, enduring, and influential for a different reason. Locke was not only sensitive to the problem of excessive individualism; he also pioneered and anticipated an enduring solution to it. He showed how modern individualism could be conditioned by an engendered version of civic virtue; and his synthesis of individualism, civic virtue, and gender proved to be the original draft of what would become the other liberal tradition in America.

Part Two
Locke's Legacy

*I think it every man's indispensible
duty to do all the service he can to
his country.*
—John Locke

*Contract is far from being opposed
to patriarchy; contract is the means
through which modern patriarchy
is constituted.*
—Carole Pateman

John Locke gave greater prominence to men's individual rights and materialism than classical thinkers or contemporaries. He was also more adventuresome in exploring men's freedom and equality, political participation, and popular sovereignty. Thus, he anticipated Louis Hartz's early American consensus. At the same time, Locke doubted men's rationality, distrusted women's passions, feared youthful excesses, and suffered the disenchantment that Gordon Wood identified as the motivation behind the U.S. Constitution. Locke was a harbinger of hope and fear.

His hope was founded on a belief that men had a natural desire for fatherhood that restrained their passions and prompted their civic virtue, a willingness to elevate women's moral stature and recognize their potential contribution to public good, and a pacifism that enabled men to be both family protectors and patriots. Lockean men could be trusted to practice civic virtue, with the assistance of women and martial virtue, and they were therefore trusted to wield individual rights without sowing social disorder. Like republicans, however, Locke simultaneously sustained a fear that men, women, and youth would fail to curb their vices and fall short of civic virtue. He pioneered a theory of consent and coercion to enable fathers to ensure sons' deference, governors citizens' compliance, husbands wives' cooperation, and the state youth's obedience in war. The result was restrained democracy, protofeminism, and pacifism mixed with elitism, sexism, and militarism, or "liberal patriarchy."

Part Two explores elements of Locke's liberalism that were formulated to answer the engendered questions of the seventeenth century. It focuses on Locke's incorporation of civic virtue into families, citizenship, and the state as a means to condition individualism and reconcile it with domestic order and national security. It exposes the theoretical basis for "the other liberal tradition" that was essential to Locke's legacy to America.

4 Fathers and Sons

John Locke was Restoration England's staunchest defender of individualism. He endowed men with natural rights to life, liberty, and property. He asserted that men's rights preceded and superseded political authority. He made the defense of men's rights the foremost task of government. Further, Locke associated men's rights with democratic equality. He insisted that nearly all males were entitled to natural and political rights. Excepting a few lunatics and beastly souls, Locke argued that day laborers, artisans, farmers, merchants, and gentry had equal claims to rights and that young men automatically acquired rights on attaining adulthood. Remarkably, Locke's devotion to men's rights withstood both reservations about excessive individualism and a dim assessment of men's rationality. He imagined that impassioned, ignorant men could defend individual freedom and equality within a peaceful social order.

How was that possible? Locke's "individuals" were not isolated men who sought self-preservation, personal prosperity, and private happiness regardless of others. Nor were they rational men who self-consciously patterned their thought and action after a law of nature that reconciled individual rights and social order. Locke was a typical

Whig in his distrust of men's subjectivity and reason. But he was atypical because of the immense trust he invested in men's natural passion for fatherhood. This passion put men "under strong obligations of necessity, convenience, and inclination" to enter into conjugal and civil society. My thesis is that Locke's individualism incorporated patriarchal obligations and masculine virtues that promised to restrain men's excesses and bond them to society.

Rationality and Social Order

Locke was a radical individualist. He believed that "*all* men are . . . in a state of perfect freedom." Individuals entered into civil society only when "*every one* of the members hath quit his natural power [and] resigned it up into the hands of the community." By unanimous consent, "*every* man . . . puts himself under an obligation to *every one* of that society to submit to the determination of the majority." In turn, the majority limited political authority to the original "intention in *every one* the better to preserve himself, his liberty and property."[2] Locke's sweeping defense of individual rights was reflected in his political activism. He participated in a radical Whig movement that sought an alliance among "merchants, tradesmen, artisans, shopkeepers, *and* yeoman farmers and the gentry" against the crown. His *Two Treatises* served as "a radical manifesto" that advocated unprecedented freedoms for broad sectors of English society.[3]

How could individuals exercise their rights without abridging or destroying other men's rights? Locke's philosophical answer was, "We are born free as we are born rational."[4] Ideally, men secured their rights by thinking and acting rationally. They believed in God, honored His commandments, and tolerated sectarian differences. They understood and deferred to the law of nature that specified their rights and duties. And they cultivated sufficient self-mastery to overcome contrary habits, resist adverse temptations, and heed the voice of reason, which declared, "Being all equal and independent, no one ought to harm another in his life, liberty, and possessions." Rational men who heeded God, studied natural law, and mastered passion knew that the only way to protect their rights was to subordinate themselves voluntarily to civil society and limited government.[5]

Scholarly debate on Locke's political theory hinges on this conjunction of rights and rationality. Did Locke believe that most individuals were sufficiently rational to consent to be governed? If so, then men could be trusted with extensive individual rights and political participation in anticipation of modern liberal democracy. That is Louis Hartz's presumption. But suppose that Locke doubted men's rationality and commitment to voluntary subordination. Surely such irrational men would constitute a subversive mob that needed to be regulated by a superior authority. By this logic, Lockean politics seemed to reproduce Hobbes's authoritarianism and also anticipate the liberal elitism that Gordon Wood attributes to the American Framers.

Most Locke scholars recognize Locke's skepticism regarding men's rationality and reinterpret his political theory accordingly. One school argues that Locke sidestepped the issue of men's rationality. He was a philosopher of "hypothetical consent" who asserted men's rationality as a convenient means of justifying his version of political justice. All men, rational or not, were obliged to defer to political justice. A residual question concerned who was to judge political justice. If Locke believed that each individual was to judge, then he was an implicit political anarchist. But if Locke assumed men's tacit consent and empowered government to judge political justice, then he was guilty of elitist tendencies.[6] Another school of thought has it that Locke believed in differential rationality. He was a conventional Whig who saw the masses as irrational riffraff and the gentry as an educable, redeemable elite that must govern; or he was a pioneer in possessive individualism who reckoned propertyless men irrational and commercial men skilled in the accumulation that justified bourgeois rule.[7] Either way, Locke allegedly used rationality as a criterion for limiting men's rights and legitimating inequality.

These interpretations seriously underestimate Locke's radical individualism and his radical skepticism. Locke believed that men's natural rights to life, liberty, and property necessitated that men be endowed with political rights. These included consent of the governed, free public discussion, popular suffrage, majority rule, representative government, and, at the extreme, revolution.[8] The reason was quite simple. Only rights-bearing individuals could be trusted to protect their own rights against the political corruption that haunted republicans and the political tyranny feared by contractarians. Locke was not Hobbes because Locke insisted on men's political participation, their freedom to evaluate political decisions, their willingness to condemn abuses, and their essential political sovereignty. Locke was more than a philosopher of hypothetical consent because he was committed to enhancing men's natural and political rights, and he aspired to make individual voluntarism the foundation of social and political order.

At the same time, Locke was so skeptical about men's rational abilities that his effectual rule of thumb was to assume that no one followed the light of reason. He wrote in his journals, "The three great things that govern mankind are reason, passion, and superstition; the first governs a few, the two last share the bulk of mankind, and possess them in their turns."[9] His assessment was that mankind comprised appetitive, habitual creatures who rarely matured beyond adolescence. Very few men developed any intellectual sophistication, and nearly all men lacked sufficient intellectual rigor to deliberate morality. For the vast majority, Locke argued, "It is too hard a task for unassisted reason to establish morality in all its parts upon its true foundation with a clear and convincing light." Most men "never . . . made out an entire body of the 'law of nature.'" Their thinking was clouded by "necessities, passions, vices, and mistaken interests."[10]

Men mostly ignored reason. According to Locke, they were creatures of habit who "do and think according to the example of others." They submitted to mindless tradition, age-old superstition, and popular prejudice. They believed old falsehoods and bequeathed illusions to their children. Some men eluded the grasp of prejudice only to "put passion in the place of reason." Passionate men were enslaved by impulse and given over to immediate gratification regardless of the destructive consequences of their desire-driven behavior. Locke noted that a few men did "sincerely follow reason," but he warned that aspiring scholars usually lacked the "large, sound, round-about sense" needed for accurate insight into God, nature, and morality. Whether men's problem was poor education and miseducation or narrow-mindedness and parochialism, Locke's conclusion was that men's search for reason virtually always failed.[11]

Locke's conclusion left no room for differential rationality. From day laborers to leisured aristocrats, men were moved by passion and prejudice. The lower classes suffered "low and mean education" and "constant drudgery." The upper classes were tainted by "particular interests" and convenient "falsehoods." The commercial classes put avarice above rationality, for example, by hoarding the nation's wealth while "starving the laborer and impoverishing the landholder." [12] Locke conceded that all men had a capacity for rationality and some men even followed it, but he never suggested that the rational few were concentrated in any particular social class. More often, he expressed an unbounded loathing for men's ignorance and malice. He was upset that "barefaced bribery, corruption, and perjury never were so generally practised among us as lately." He felt that the modern Englishman was infected by "vain selfish imaginations that he may chance to thrive or escape, let what will become of the commonwealth, and that the public will take care of itself." And he feared that such selfish delusions produced a "pravity of mankind" that infected social order and crippled public good. [13]

Could men redeem their reason? Locke did not think an intellectual renaissance was imminent. He was resigned to mankind's perpetual adolescence. Thus, he did not insist that all men develop their rational capacities and become scholars of the law of nature. Nor did he suppose that scholarship would cure men's defective reason because even educated men were stirred by their passions, prejudices, and interests. He had no illusions that a messianic leader would arise to free men from supersition and liberate their reason. Nor did he conjure up a government of laws that magically circumvented men's flaws. Locke simply assumed that men would remain creatures of habit and passion.

In sum, Locke advocated extensive individual and political rights; his philosophical ideal was for men to exercise their rights with the rational self-restraint and voluntary subordination that would assure social order; but his practical assessment was that it was absurd to expect men to think and act rationally. An unsettling implication is that Locke advocated radical individualism for irrational men. Did this mean that his liberal theory was compromised by "an *internally incoherent* vision,"? [14] Locke did not think so. He saw no contradiction between individualism and irrationality. Indeed, he was confident of mankind's prospects despite its irrationality. His optimism originated in his sense that rationality was an ideal restraint on individuals and a certain source for social bonding among individuals, but it was not the only way to reconcile individual freedom and social order. Men's natural passion for fatherhood also provided individuals with powerful incentives to join with other men, voluntarily subordinate themselves to society, and act *as if* they were rational.

Fatherhood

Restoration Whigs were fixated on fatherhood. Their origin stories began with fathers' original liberty, moved to fathers' conditional support for absolute monarchy, and concluded with fathers' continuing right to limit political corruption and tyranny. While Whigs told these tales to contest the absolute authority of kings, they also enriched the moral significance of fatherhood. They reinforced the Royalist view that fathers were patriarchal authorities within their families, patriarchal families were the foundation for social order, and family patriarchs were the proper subjects of political discourse. Further, their attacks on *traditional* patriarchalism elevated the responsibilities of family patriarchs. If kings lost authority, then the "community of many fathers" became responsible for defending liberty. If church and state authority diminished, then individual fathers were no longer church and state agents in the home but autonomous patriarchs responsible for the moral and material welfare of their families.[15] Overall, Whig theorists generated an intellectual climate in which "individual" and "father" were synonymous terms.

Locke found this climate congenial. His *First Treatise*, for example, focused on *God the father,* political patriarchy, and family fathers. He countered Filmer's claim that God made Adam a "sole proprietor" who could bequeath authority to his sons with the argument that all fathers and adult sons shared proprietorship.[16] Locke's participation in patriarchal discourse went beyond convention. While he followed the lead of Harrington, Sidney, and Tyrrell in equating men, fathers, and citizens, he went beyond them by making men's passion for fatherhood the linchpin of his analysis. Consider Locke's modest "cure" for men's irrationality: he merely suggested that men be reasonable in their "daily employment," which was "no more to anyone than he has time for."[17] But he believed that men's most meaningful daily employment was fatherhood, and he considered reasonable fathers nearly as trustworthy and predictable as rational men.

Men's traditional duties, natural instincts, and self-interests produced in them a powerful passion for fatherhood. The traditional basis for fatherhood, reinforced by convention, was God's injunction that mankind propagate itself and preserve the species. Locke noted that God did not rely solely on divine revelation and human reason to achieve this end. "God in his infinite wisdom has put strong desires of copulation into the constitution of men, thereby to continue the race of mankind."[18] Men's sexual urges were no invitation to promiscuity. Popular religion, cultural taboos, and public opinion backed by common law limited legitimate sexual relations to the "security of the marriage-bed." Monogamy was crucial. It enabled individual fathers to identify their biological offspring and, therefore, to fulfill their natural "obligation to nourish, preserve, and bring up their offspring" as part of God's "great design of continuing the race of mankind."[19]

Locke insisted that most men wanted to fulfill this paternal obligation. On the one hand, fatherhood was a major source of personal meaning, satisfaction, and fulfillment in men's lives. On the other hand, fathers had a natural affection for their children. As a result, most fathers did whatever they thought necessary to house, feed, clothe, and protect their offspring. Locke went so far as to agree with John Toland that men's devotion to fatherhood was often the definitive characteristic and preeminent force in men's identities. Paternal affections even outweighed selfish appetites. Locke wrote that fathers "sometimes neglect their own private good . . . and seem to forget the general rule which nature teaches all things—of self-preservation." He then asserted that "the *strongest* principle" in men's nature was not a desire for self-preservation but a commitment to "the preservation of their young."[20] Even cowardly men ignored fears for their own safety and fortunes to become self-sacrificing, courageous defenders of their families.

Men's identification with fatherhood was reinforced by their interest in personal happiness and immortality. Locke observed that men generally sought to escape their fears of death by striving after eternal bliss. "Since nothing of pleasure and pain in this life can bear any proportion to the endless happiness or exquisite misery of an immortal soul hereafter," he wrote, "actions in [men's] power will have their preference . . . as they serve to secure that perfect durable happiness hereafter."[21] Men's desire for a joyous afterlife motivated them to devalue "the short pleasures and pains of this present state, and give attractions and encouragements to virtue."[22] Thus, men who followed God's injunction to sire and nurture children eased their fears of death and enhanced their personal prospects for salvation.

Locke also associated fatherhood with a sense of individual transcendence. Men's children were both extensions and reflections of themselves. Men could symbolically outlive their own mortality by transmitting their seeds (as well as their names and estates) to a new generation. When Locke wrote that God placed man "under strong obligations of necessity, convenience, and inclination to drive him into [conjugal] society," he was suggesting that it was men's nature to preserve themselves not simply by prolonging their own lives but by leaving an enduring, biological legacy in their children. Along these lines, John Dunn argues that Locke attributed to men a "biologically specified disposition" to found families and to identify their own well-being with the provision and perpetuation of their families.[23]

By Locke's reckoning, few men investigated, understood, or self-consciously obeyed the law of nature that obliged men to be responsible fathers. Nonetheless, most men identified with fatherhood and became fathers on the irrational grounds of convention and nature. Tradition validated fatherhood, culture reinforced it, and public opinion honored it, while men's instincts, affections, and interests drew them to it. Men's passion for fatherhood was so compelling, Locke believed, that Restoration jeremiads against spreading bachelorhood and abusive fatherhood could be safely ignored. Barren men and beastly fathers were aberrations. Yes, some avoided marriage and others failed as fathers, but the bulk of mankind desired marriage and fatherhood and also aspired to responsible parenthood. As such, Locke recommended no family-saving strategies. He assumed, quite correctly, that men would continue to flock to conjugal society and devote the better part of their manhood to fulfilling their children's needs.[24]

The vitality of fatherhood was central to Locke's social and political thought. It explained how irrational men could act *as if* they were rational by reproducing the species, nurturing their children, and thereby per-petuating humankind. It demonstrated that men could rise above their "vain, selfish imaginations" by identifying their individuality and self-interest with their families' welfare. Men's desire "to continue their *selves*" through their children effectively blurred any distinction between indi-vidual interest and family welfare.[25] Men's passion for fatherhood also prompted them to restrain immediate impulses and develop some regard for the future. If men were reasonable in their daily employment of father-hood, they would deny immediate gratification and deliberate economic strategies for securing family welfare over the several decades spanning infants' maturation to adulthood.

Family Welfare

The men who entered Locke's marketplace were not simply passionate, prejudiced, self-interested individuals prone to pos-sessiveness and acquisitiveness at any cost. They were family patriarchs whose instincts, affections, and interests urged them to strive after their children's welfare. That did not automatically prevent men from lying, cheating, stealing, or exploiting others in the name of family welfare. But Locke believed that men who were minimally reasonable fathers would hesitate to take such untoward risks. More was at stake than individuals' immediate pleasures and interests. Fathers bent on aggressive or illegal accumulation incurred the wrath of neighbors, the jealousy of competitors, and the concern of magistrates only to imperil their personal identities and aspirations for immortality as well as the bonds of family affection and preservation of their posterity.

God enjoined men to preserve themselves and provision their families through labor that, Locke asserted, was inherently unpleasant. Men were averse to labor. After all, it was "a curse upon mankind because of the Fall." And it demanded the "industry" associated with "the ploughman's pains, the reaper's and thresher's toil, and the baker's sweat."[26] Men's aversion to labor marked them with a tendency toward indolence and idle-ness, on the one hand; theft, exploitation, and profligacy, on the other. However, Locke thought that men's passion for fatherhood was sufficiently strong to overcome these vices. A dose of patriarchal responsibility was the best cure for laziness and luxury, and also a potent stimulus to productive labor.

Fathers committed to laboring for family subsistence immediately encountered a dilemma. In the modern marketplace, hard work was not always sufficient to support a family. Older mutual-aid networks among families and neighbors weakened, while mobile property relations, commercial activities, credit, and stockjobbing strengthened temptations to speculate. Like other Whigs, Locke worried about the vices and violence that attended modernity. But he was especially concerned that economic fluctuations and instability created an environment in which devoted fathers might falter and lose part or all of their family estates. It was rare, he noted, that "a thriving man turns his land into money to make the greater advantage." But if "there is scarce one in a hundred that thinks of selling his patrimony," the other ninety-nine had no choice when "mortgages have pretty well eaten into a freehold and the weight of growing debts force a man, whether he will or no, out of his possessions."[27] What could reasonable fathers do to secure their family estates?

Clearly, they needed to think ahead, to accumulate wealth beyond immediate need as a hedge against future loss. Minimally reasonable fathers had to cultivate a modest degree of economic rationality to insure their families against erratic market forces and unpredictable political abuses. In one sense, that entailed mastering irrational habits, resisting temptations to self-indulgence, alcohol, gambling, and other vices, restraining self-destructive aggression, and denying immediate consumption. In another sense, fathers had to deliberate and adapt their economic strategies to the requirements and rhythms of the modern marketplace. However, this did not mean that Locke expected fathers to enlist in the emerging bourgeoisie who, as C. B. Macpherson explains, "beget further capital by profitable investment."[28] Lockean fathers dared not become possessive individualists. They understood that "covetousness" was "the root of all evil," which drove men to waste, deceit, distrust, and mutual destruction.[29] They avoided "evil concupiscence," "ambition and luxury," and "the passionate heats of boundless extravagancy," which contributed to avaricious competition and the "very unsafe, very unsecure" enjoyment of property.[30] Instead, Lockean fathers sought access to necessities and conveniences that their families could enjoy without inciting other men's jealousy or aggression. They desired a peaceful, prosperous economy where the poor could labor and survive rather than an exploitative, erratic marketplace where immiserization might embolden the poor "to carve out their wants with armed force."[31]

Lockean fathers were producers and savers, not entrepreneurs or speculators. They were the small farmers, artisans, and shopkeepers whom Locke admired for their industry, honesty, and concern for good reputation. Their economic stratagies anticipated John Rawls's "maximin rule." They maximized the chance that the worst outcomes would be minimally acceptable to their families. Neal Wood puts it this way: "Prudent and self-disciplined, Locke's hero would never indulge in mere acquisitiveness or the insatiable chase after power and riches but would pursue self-interest in a reasonable, enlightened, and Christian manner."[32] Reasonable fathers pursued their family interests by seeking out the comfort of Main Street, not the tumult of Wall Street.

On Main Street, family fathers had undivided sovereignty in economic matters. Where husbands and wives disagreed, Locke wrote, it was "necessary that the last determination . . . should be placed somewhere" and "it naturally falls to the man's share, as the abler and the stronger."[33] In what sense were men abler and stronger? On the one hand, men's passion for fatherhood and concern for their families' welfare motivated them to cultivate some economic rationality. On the other hand, although Locke attributed to women an equal devotion to their children, he also associated maternal affection with economic irrationality. Mothers overindulged themselves and their children in luxury, waste, vanity, and erratic behavior that undermined their families' economic security. Further, Locke never questioned conventional Restoration expectations that men were primarily responsible for family support while women were subordinate "goodwifes." It is a safe inference that Locke authorized fathers to manage the household economy because, following Machiavelli, he considered *Fortuna* a woman.[34]

Locke also presumed that fathers necessarily ruled the economic roost in perilous times. He conjectured that primitive fathers united to protect their family property from aggressors. The union of family protectors then selected "the wisest and bravest man to conduct them in their wars and lead them out against their enemies."[35] Such wars in defense of family property were historically necessary and morally just. Still, Locke was fearful of the dangers of war to family survival. War entailed the death of fathers. Worse, conquerors often expropriated family property and enslaved noncombatant family members. Locke hoped that modern trade might create an international community of mutual economic interest that militated against war. But he also wanted to limit war's destructive consequences for family security and perpetuity. Thus, he argued that conquerors could put enemy soldiers to death, but they could not legitimately deprive enemies' families of their property and source of survival.[36] For Locke, fathers' lives were less dear than the economic well-being of their biological posterity.

If fathers' affection for their children urged them to overcome their aversion to labor and provide for their families, cultivate some economic rationality conditioned on restrained accumulation, and join with other men in defense of family property, fathers' identification of their individual interests with their children's future added further impetus to men's economic sobriety. Locke believed that fathers usually desired to produce material legacies as enduring monuments to themselves and lasting inheritances for their sons. They mixed their labor with nature and objectified themselves in estates that could last beyond their lifetimes; or they externalized their accomplishments and eternalized themselves.[37] Fathers' production was subject to spoilage, but the institution of money eliminated that problem. Goods could be converted into "gold and silver," which had the virtue of "not spoiling or decaying."[38] That enabled fathers to produce and accumulate surpluses, exchange perishables for hard currency, and build substantial estates that testified to their lifetime efforts and indemnified their children against future want.

Even then, fathers' estates were subject to waste. Their lifetime labor would go for naught if they were forced to bequeath the bulk of their estates to incompetent or profligate elder sons. Primogeniture endangered fathers' material monuments to themselves and the prosperity of their posterity. Locke argued that fathers should deliberate and possibly diversify their bequeathal strategies by leaving their estates, in due proportions, to those sons deemed most likely to be industrious, frugal, reasonable, and protective of their patrimony. While he did not prioritize men's natural rights, Locke was especially vehement in his defense of fathers' right "to bestow their estates on those [sons] who please them best" and a son's right "to inherit with his brethren his father's goods."[39] The stakes included fathers' immortality, sons' prospects, and also national health. Locke was convinced that family prosperity fostered social harmony and intergenerational stability that, in turn, encouraged nations to seek advantageous trade rather than accrue international debts or engage in destructive wars. For Locke, Richard Ashcraft argues, "Laboring activity . . . is never detached from its conjunction with the advancement of the public good." [40]

To recapitulate: Locke thought it unlikely that individuals' studious appreciation of natural law or their rational self-interest would drive them into society. But he did expect that the passion for fatherhood would provide the bulk of mankind sufficient incentive to be industrious but restrained and to secure family property and posterity by recognizing a stake in social stability, mutual self-defense, and national prosperity. If so, one could safely predict that fathers, despite their intellectual flaws, would act *as if* they had considered and consented to a social contract. Far less certain was whether men's sons were as likely to be reasonable and restrained in their economic and social relations. Consequently, Locke gave considerable thought to paternal strategies for raising responsible heirs.

Raising Heirs

Locke made three distinctions between paternal and political authority. First, fathers had limited access to coercive power. They did not possess *patria potestas*, the right to impose slavery or death on their children. However, governors could enslave wartime captives and exact capital punishment for heinous crimes. Second, fathers' authority over children was temporary, "the power of commanding [ending] with nonage." Political authority persisted indefinitely. Finally, fathers were presumed trustworthy because "God hath woven into the principles of human nature such a tenderness for their offspring that there is little fear that parents should use their power with too much rigor." In contrast, modern princes lacked natural tenderness as a curb on corruption and tyranny.[41] Accordingly, Locke's position was that fathers had limited power and time to apply natural tenderness and mold their sons into responsible heirs.

Why did Locke limit paternal authority when he assumed that fathers were trustworthy? One reason was that only God could be trusted with absolute authority. Locke added, "He that thinks absolute power purifies men's blood and corrects the baseness of human nature need read but the history of this or any other age to be convinced of the contrary." Locke's own reading uncovered tales of fathers who "cross the main intention of nature" by selling and castrating their sons and raising children "to fat and eat them."[42] Eliminating classical *patria potestas* meant eradicating the most unnatural acts of fatherhood. Moreover, Locke limited fathers' coercive power in the belief that corporal punishment was counterproductive. It instilled in children "a sort of slavish discipline [that] makes a slavish temper. The child submits and dissembles obedience, while the fear of the rod hangs over him; but when that is removed, and by being out of sight, he can promise himself impunity, he gives the greater scope to his natural inclination; which by this way is not at all altered, but on the contrary heightened and increased in him; and after such restraint, breaks out usually with more violence."[43] Coercive fathers exacted temporary filial obedience but also fueled filial deceit, license, and rebellion.

Lockean fathers could employ economic coercion to control their sons' behavior. A father could bestow family property "with a more sparing or liberal hand, according as the behavior of this or that child hath comported with his will and humor." Locke commented that 'this is no small tie on the obedience of children," in effect, announcing that the dead labor of the old should weigh heavily on the young. In turn, maturing sons who anticipated or received paternal largesse would defer to their fathers, show them due "esteem and reverence," and engage "in all actions of defence, relief, assistance, and comfort" for them.[44] Conceivably, the economic bonds joining fathers and sons would produce an informal network of mutual aid that would persist beyond young men's majority.

Still, Locke expressed grave doubts about the effectiveness and durability of paternal influence that accrued from dangling a legacy before sons. Youthful passions often got the best of economic interests; and sons could resist paternal rule regardless of inheritance prospects. Also, economic coercion invited filial deceit. Young men might feign obedience to their fathers to acquire their patrimony but, having obtained their share, would then be free to squander it on any number of vices. Locke advised fathers that "fear of having a scanty portion if they displease you may make [sons] slaves to your estate, but they will be never the less ill and wicked in private; and that restraint will not last always."[45] Reasonable fathers should be less interested in securing filial obedience than in making a lasting imprint on sons' predisposition and character, so that sons could be expected to preserve family estates after fathers' authority lapsed.

Locke's alternative to coercion was education, "the first part of paternal power."[46] He argued that fathers should habituate infants to obedience, win boys' affection and respect, use sons' emotional attachment as means to instill character and virtue, and then reinforce character and virtue by sensitizing young men to the importance of good reputation. Sons would not only obey their fathers; they would also identify with their fathers' values and incorporate them into their own identities. Locke summarized his strategy in this rhetorical question: "If the love of you make them not obedient and dutiful, if the love of virtue and reputation keep them not in laudable courses, I ask, what hold will you have upon them, to turn them to it?"[47] Locke limited formal paternal power, but he did not diminish paternal influence. To the contrary, he hoped to enlarge patriarchal hegemony by demonstrating that the bonds of paternal affection were more durable than Hobbesian relationships founded on fear.

Paternal affection was dangerous in one sense. Fathers were "ordained by nature to love their children," but their love was "very apt, if reason watch not that natural affection very warily, to run into fondness." Doting fathers could be enslaved by their children's wants and desires. However, reasonable fathers guarded against overfondness and budgeted their affections. They rewarded sons' good behavior with warmth and applause and they punished misbehavior with emotional withdrawal and censure. By cultivating sons' emotional dependence, fathers could take advantage of what Locke called "the great secret of education," to employ esteem and disgrace to mold boys' characters. Locke observed, "You have not that power you ought to have over him till he comes to be more afraid of offending so good a friend than of losing some part of his future expectation."[48] That fathers' influence could be magnified by the judicious use of smiles and frowns had two major implications. One was that reasonable fatherhood was not contingent on wealth. Lower-class fathers as well as freeholders could exercise paternal governance. The other was that sons' need for paternal approval could be generalized into young men's desire for good reputation in society.

Locke recommended that fathers teach sons "the love of praise and commendation." Boys should seek paternal praise and become habituated to courses of action likely to earn it. However, even devoted fathers were not omnipresent. Young men often made choices in circumstances where neither paternal commendation nor condemnation was expected. How could absentee fathers retain their influence? Locke suggested fathers teach their sons to cultivate good reputations and consult social opinion as "a proper guide and encouragement" to good behavior. Boys' desire for reputability would render them vulnerable to "the testimony and applause that other people's reason, as it were by a common consent, gives to virtuous and well-ordered actions."[49] Ideally, boys exhibited virtue to win public applause, and young adults continued to order their actions to secure good reputation.

At first glance, Locke's approval of reputation, social opinion, and public applause is perplexing. Recall that Locke believed the bulk of mankind was irrational because it adhered to popular superstitions and prejudices. In addition, Locke's warnings against the youthful vice and corruption often condoned in cities should have allied him with a healthy skepticism regarding social pressure. Nevertheless, Locke was convinced that fathers' benign influence would be reinforced by young men's dependence on public opinion. The reason was that Locke's individualism not only incorporated men's passion for fatherhood but also presumed select masculine virtues that were shared by fathers, sons, and male society speaking in the voice of public opinion.

Locke insisted that paternal education emphasize two particular masculine virtues. First, fathers were to teach sons what Nathan Tarcov characterizes as a "severe morality of self-denial" to ensure that they acquire a strong sense of manly "fortitude."[50] Locke considered fortitude a master virtue, "the guard and support of the other virtues." It referred to "the quiet possession of a man's self, and an undisturbed doing his duty, whatever evil besets, or danger lies in his way." Young men with fortitude stayed industrious despite indolent tendencies, acted honestly although deceit was profitable, and exhibited bravery when fear beckoned. They had the ability to practice Protestant self-denial and self-discipline, bourgeois sobriety and predictability, and courage against adversity. Indeed, fortitude was certification of male adulthood. It testified to young men's transcendence of an "effeminacy of spirit" associated with women's complaints and modern decadence; and it demonstrated "the character of a truly worthy man."[51]

Acquiring fortitude required exposure to physical hardship. Boys had to learn to endure pain and discomfort without complaint to become inured to life's inevitable temptations and dangers. Such fortitude prepared boys to resist self-indulgence, softness, luxury, spirits, avarice, deceit, lying, and other vices that robbed men of self-mastery. Fortitude also habituated youth to masculine self-denial, self-discipline, and self-control in the face of "dangers of all kinds," including the perils of "the field of battle." Ultimately, fortitude enabled boys to mature into men who remained "unmoved whatsoever evil it is that threatens."[52] Locke believed that a young man who exhibited self-possession and emotional toughness would win the respect of male society. He could be trusted to remain calm in the face of inconvenience, adversity, and peril.

Locke's second masculine virtue was "civility," which Thomas Pangle calls "the new star in the Lockean firmament."[53] Civility referred to "a disposition of the mind not to offend others." To master it, a young man had to resist common tendencies toward "natural roughness," "contempt," "censoriousness," and "captiousness." He also needed to condition his thoughts, words, and actions with a regard for others, a due respect for others, a refusal to elevate himself by degrading others, and a presumptive trust in others. For Locke, civility was a masculine virtue because it demanded the self-restraint that was notoriously lacking in women. Initially, boys were like their mothers. Both were given to constant complaining and petty bickering; both shared a love of self above others; and both were absorbed in their own power and possessions regardless of others. Devoted fathers rid their sons of effeminacy by teaching them self-restraint in the service of civility. That way, a boy could become "a good, a wise, and a virtuous man" who plied "the true art of living in the world," which was knowing how to be welcomed and valued in society.[54]

Responsible heirs needed civility and reputations for it. Young men who demonstrated regard for others were prepared to work, trade, and deal with other men. They could preserve their patrimony and provision new families by engaging in economic deliberations free from self-destructive narcissism, petty prejudices, and foolish jealousies. A major benefit of "good breeding," Locke wrote, was to "so soften men's tempers that they may bend to a compliance and accommodate themselves to those they have to do with." Moreover, young men known for civility would win other men's trust because he who "knows how to make those he converses with easy without debasing himself to low and servile flattery" will be sought out and respected.[55] Respectability was an economic asset that a young man could parlay into status and opportunity. Finally, young men with civility were likely to be compliant heirs. Sensitized to paternal expectations and social norms, they could be trusted to accept their inheritance "with the condition that it is under."[56] They would accept their patrimony, their fathers' commitment to industry, sobriety, and social stability, and the bonds of masculinity that constituted the organic basis for Locke's social contract.

The Bonds of Masculinity

Gordon Schochet suggests that Locke's social contract was "a consequence of something approximating an organic growth that emerges from and builds upon but remains conceptually and mechanistically separate from natural human associations."[57] For Locke, the most significant, natural human associations were father–son–male relationships. He thought that fathers' natural affection for their posterity was usually reciprocated by sons' gratitude and compliance. In turn, father–son bonding was generalized to society, with manly fortitude and civility serving as cultural criteria for good reputation and public applause. These bonds of masculinity cut across generations and social classes to form an organic seedbed of mutual respect, trust, and stability among flawed mankind.

Locke's vision of reasonable fatherhood invited intergenerational bonding. Fathers had to practice manly virtues to teach them. They demonstrated fortitude by resisting impulsive urges to apply corporal punishment, by controlling passion to budget affection, and by cultivating sufficient patience to observe and react properly to sons' behavior. They also had to exhibit civility. Lockean fathers were other-regarding in that they made family decisions based on what benefited their sons' eventual prospects and reputations in society. "I think it the worst sort of good husbandry," Locke noted, "for a father not to strain himself a little for his son's breeding which . . . is the best portion he can leave him."[58] A man's willingness to strain himself for his heirs combined fortitude and civility into an exemplary blend of masculinity that bound fathers and sons and, indeed, all worthy men. Locke's ideal was for the reasonable father to transform his son from his "obedient subject (as is fit) whilst he is a child" into his "affectionate friend when he is a man."[59]

The bonds of masculine friendship knew no class boundaries. Even lower-class men could be trusted as individuals who shared a passion for fatherhood and a commitment to masculine virtues. True, lower-class fathers did not have family estates to protect and bequeath. Nonetheless, they had property in themselves and their families, a natural affection for their offspring, a desire to continue their biological lines and surnames, a felt obligation to support their families, an ability to budget their affections, a wish to teach sons the industry, frugality, and honesty necessary for breadwinning, and also the manly fortitude and civility that would make them respected members of society. Restoration thinkers commonly assumed that lower-class men who headed their own families were more responsible, predictable, and fit for society than their social peers. Locke took another step. He identified individualism with fatherhood and masculinity instead of a freehold; therefore, he could view lower-class fathers and sons as restrained, respectable individuals capable of peaceful social interaction.[60]

Locke expected the bonds of masculinity to foster class cooperation. Gentlemen with civility exhibited "a gentle, courteous, affable carriage toward the lower ranks of men." Such civility instilled "love in inferiors" and thereby urged the lower classes to "share in their submission . . . [and] pay a more ready submission." Following the logic of fatherhood, Locke's message was that the upper classes should rely less on coercion and more on the bonds of affection and respect to encourage class harmony. Moreover, if fashionable gentlemen practiced due regard for inferiors, there was a good chance that the lower classes would develop a habitual compliance to superiors. After all, "the far greater part of mankind receive even those opinions and ceremonies they would die for rather from the fashions of their countries and the practice of those about them than from any conviction of their reasons."[61] For Locke, masculine civility trickled down the slippery slope of society and lubricated class relations.

In one sense, Locke's bonds of masculinity were a source of fraternal equality. The defeat of Filmer's supreme father would free men to act as brothers who trusted each other enough to legitimate and protect their rights by common consent to a social contract, joint participation in politics, and voluntary obedience to law. Locke's "brotherhood of men" could be read as a powerful albeit irrational basis for establishing a fraternal democracy that excluded women.[62] In another sense, however, Locke's version of male bonding was hierarchical. Fathers molded sons, set the criteria for admitting them to adulthood, and contributed to the public opinion that certified that a particular youth had earned acceptance in society. Similarly, upper-class gentlemen were superiors who shaped inter-class relations, while lower-class men were inferiors expected to consent to submission. Locke did not substitute fraternity for patriarchy. Rather, he modernized or liberalized patriarchy by insisting that family fathers and gentlemen rely less on force and more on affection to encourage the enduring consent of the governed.

Recall that Locke limited rather than eliminated patriarchs' coercive powers. Short of enslaving or causing a child's death, a Lockean father retained the prerogative to impose significant violence on children. Locke certainly advised against the regular use corporal punishment, but he also saw corporal punishment as a valuable reserve power. Coercion was available for use in cases of extreme misbehavior. Locke allowed that children could be beaten for obstinacy or rebelliousness and, as a last resort, for negligence or idleness.[63] Fathers' rare reliance on corporal punishment magnified its effect. When fathers actually beat their sons, "the shame of suffering" such extreme disgrace had greater impact on children "than the pain" itself.[64] When fathers kept corporal punishment in reserve, the sheer knowledge that they could resort to it created a psychological atmosphere conducive to filial compliance. Haunted by fathers' iron fists, boys were apt to be more receptive to fathers' velvet-glove tactics.

Lockean youth lived for their fathers' affection and approval. Thus, they were weighed down by the fear that errant behavior would result in a retreat of paternal love and a seige of filial shame. It was hard to escape that fear because Locke's pedagogy required boys to suffer overbearing patriarchal supervision while second-guessing their fathers' feelings. Lockean fathers gave "a constant attention and particular application to every single boy."[65] Like Orwell's Big Brother, devoted patriarchs were always watching. But they were not always commanding. Instead, they orchestrated progressively greater freedom for sons to make choices, participate in family affairs, and practice adult responsibilities. This was young men's initiation into adulthood. If adolescents used their freedom wisely, they were applauded and trusted with even greater freedom. But if adolescents failed, they faced their fathers' renewed restrictions and emotional lock-outs, self-doubts about their masculinity, and even ill repute in society. Knowing this, young men internalized their fathers' morality as a habitual monitor of their thoughts and deeds.

For example, Locke urged fathers to encourage older sons to keep ac-counts of their expenditures. The ostensible goal was not to regulate or criticize youthful expenditures but to encourage young men to learn a practical skill. Locke then related an anecdote that suggested that more was at stake than young men's ability to balance credits and debits:

> A noble Venetian, whose son wallowed in the plenty of his father's riches, finding his son's expenses grown very high and extravagant, ordered by his cashier to let him have for the future no more money than what he should count when he received it. This one would think no great restraint to a young gentleman's expenses who could freely have as much money as he would tell. But, yet this, to one who was used to nothing but the pursuit of his pleasures, proved a very great trouble which at last ended in this sober and advantageous reflection: If it be so much pains to me barely to count the money I would spend, what labor and pains did it cost my ancestors not only to count but to get it? This rational thought, suggested by this little pains imposed upon him, wrought so effectually upon his mind that it made him take up, and from that time forward, prove a good husband. This at least everybody must allow, that nothing is likelier to keep a man within compass than the having constantly before his eyes the state of his affairs in a regular course of account.[66]

Were the son's revelation and reform a matter of the son's free and ratio-nal choice? Not likely. Locke's noble Venetian knew that the required accounting procedure would alert his son not only to his profligacy but also to the fact that he had offended his father, contravened norms of masculine fortitude, and perhaps damaged his reputation. If that was not motivation enough to reform, the son should have recalled that his father could pursue a more extreme and coercive course, cutting off his allowance or cutting him out of patrimony.

According to Tarcov, Locke's fathers adhered to this axiom: "The best way to get men to do what is wanted . . . is not to terrify or force them but, in the language of our contemporary popular psychology and pedagogy, to 'motivate' them, to arouse and then rely on their desires, while letting them think . . . that they are acting for their own sakes and of their own free will." [67] Could Lockean sons really become free and equal adults? In one sense, yes. Locke expected all adult males to acquire formal rights to life, liberty, and property, to choose marriage and fatherhood, and to take their place as autonomous members of male society. In another sense, Locke preached patriarchal hierarchy. He believed that fathers should receive voluntary deference and consent from adult sons. Decades of paternal devotion demanded sons' enduring gratitude; decades of paternal affection fostered sons' continuing compliance. In the extreme, fathers could resort to economic coercion to ensure filial consent. For Locke, the predictable and desirable result was that adult sons would behave as if there were "no distinction betwixt minority and full age." It would be "almost natural" for them, "by a tacit and scarce avoidable consent," to submit freely to their fathers' governance. [68]

It is hard to imagine that Lockean patriarchs would settle for anything less than their sons' complete and continuing submission. After all, fathers invested tremendous personal meaning, effort, and self-sacrifice in their sons. They viewed male children as extensions and reflections of themselves and as means by which their lives, names, accomplishments, and estates could be perpetuated. They suffered the pains of labor, the uncertainties of the marketplace, and even the dangers of war for their sons. They devoted much of their lives to educating their sons and procuring for them "a good mind, well principled, tempered to virtue and usefulness, and adorned with civility and good breeding." [69] All told, Lockean patriarchs simply had too much at stake to "let go" when their sons turned twenty-one.

Locke's rendering of the bonds of masculinity drew on Thomas Hunt's and Algernon Sidney's earlier advice to monarchs and then anticipated Horatio Alger's reading of American society. First, patriarchs gained influence by refusing absolute authority, limiting coercion, cultivating the affections of subordinates, and controlling their motivations. That way, young men and citizens became complicit in their own subordination and voluntarily consented to it. Second, fathers and father figures were essential to reconciling individual liberty and social order. They sustained cultural continuity by preparing youth to exercise their rights in restrained and predictable ways; they transmitted values such as industry, sobriety, fortitude, and civility to transform unruly boys into self-possessed men; and they retained sufficient psychological authority to keep a rein on potential profligate young adults. Locke's youth, like Alger's redeemed street urchins, demonstrated their individual virtue, masculinity, reputability, and social acceptability by voluntarily assuming responsibility for siring, rearing, and educating the next generation.

Individual Virtue

Hanna Pitkin's basic criticism of Locke's theory is that it was founded on the mistaken image of the solitary, rational individual. She writes, "In truth, there is something profoundly wrong with the consent theorist's picture of man. Every free, separate, adult, consenting individual was first shaped and molded by his parents and (as we say) society. It is only as a result of their influence that he becomes the particular person he does become, with his particular interests, values, desires, language, and obligations. The only thing truly separate about us is our bodies; ourselves are manifestly social."[70] Pitkin's criticism may apply to Hobbes but certainly not to Locke, who believed that "individuals" were manifestly irrational, social beings. They were fathers, sons, and engendered males molded by family and society in ways that fostered patriarchal interests, values, desires, language, and obligations as well as masculine virtues that motivated them to act *as if* they were sufficiently rational to join their radical rights to a peaceful social order.

The distinguishing feature of Locke's liberal patriarchalism was that it downplayed Hobbesian fear and coercion to emphasize fatherly affections, filial loyalties, and masculine virtues as organic seeds of freedom and social order. For all practical purposes, Lockean individuals were born free to the extent that they were moved by patriarchal obligations, natural affections, and perceived interests to cultivate self-restraint, fortitude and civility, and the bonds of masculinity. Using Carol Gilligan's linguistic medium but reversing her message, one might say that Locke thought that men spoke "in a different voice." Men were caring, moral, family folks, whereas women were self-absorbed, erratic creatures.[71]

Men's special individual virtue was their devotion to their sons' well-being and to fitting into male society. Whether this individual virtue was an adequate substitute for rationality in politics, however, was not obvious. Locke believed that most men were reasonable in their daily employment of fatherhood, but he also recognized that few men were experts at it, most achieved varying degrees of success, and some failed miserably. Likewise, most men wanted to fit into society but many seemed ill suited to the true art of living in the world, and others were simply misfits. How could failed fathers, their sons, and social misfits be trusted, redeemed, or controlled lest they infuse anarchy into society and invite tyranny in politics?

Further, Locke's masculine virtues were *private* virtues. They may have had a sobering influence on family life and even class relations but not necessarily on *public* life. Greek philosophers argued that men's devotion to families diverted their loyalty away from the commonwealth. Joyce Appleby recalls this argument when she suggests that Lockean virtue "referred to a private quality, a man's capacity to look out for himself and his dependents—almost the opposite of classical virtue." And John Diggins adds that Locke's liberalism "stripped the traditional idea of virtue of its essential political content." [72] Did Locke expect individuals to be wonderful fathers and decent neighbors but uncaring citizens? Or did he have reason to believe that individuals' private virtues would stimulate them to acquire a sense of civic virtue?

5 Citizens and the State

The people's liberties are seldom lost but through negligence and the want of being taken care of in time, when a small matter will do it. How much easier, greater and more sudden, then, would the effect be, did all such as have yet pure hearts and clean hands among us set them seriously to understand and cultivate the public interest!
—*John Locke*[1]

John Locke generally used republican rhetoric in his education tracts and liberal language in his political works. His writings on paternal education touted the private virtues associated with fatherhood, filial gratitude, and masculinity. He also advised fathers to school their sons in civic virtue. "I think it every man's indispensible duty," Locke wrote, "to do all the service he can to his country." He added that a gentleman ought to study the "virtues and vices of civil society and the arts of government" in preparation for "service to his country."[2] However, Locke's political treatises honored religious toleration, individual rights, consent, and contract. Here, the author's concern for private virtue and civic virtue was subdued.

One explanation for Locke's "bilingualism" is that he supported separate ethics for separate spheres. His private sphere centered on deep bonds among families and friends whose natural affections and acquired virtues fostered civility and cooperation. By contrast, his public sphere was marked by contrived relations among self-interested individuals who associated on the basis of voluntary agreements meant to produce a mutually beneficial order.[3] Locke did suggest that young men learn civic virtue, but Thomas Pangle argues, his political theory attributed little significance to "patriotism or love of country."[4] Two implications follow. One is that Appleby and Diggins are correct to argue that Lockean liberalism reduced the idea of virtue to a private, familial concept. The other is that Pocock justifiably asserts that Locke's *political* theory was mostly irrelevant to the republican discourse on civic virtue and corruption.[5]

My analysis is different. Locke distinguished a natural private sphere from the contractual public sphere but drew a permeable border between them. Fathers' passions pervaded private and public life, shaped the family and the state, and served as the seedbed for civic virtue. Thus, it was "almost natural" for primitive fathers to consent to patriarchal kingships. The first major gap between the private and public spheres appeared with modernity. Men's private virtues continued to regenerate civic virtue, but corrupt kings betrayed their political obligations. The challenge of modern political theory, then, was not so much to reclaim virtue as to recognize natural rights, reconstitute civil society, and grant provisional consent to a new government dedicated to families' welfare.

My thesis is that Locke's political theory incorporated a republican commitment to men's private virtues as the source of civic virtue. Fathers had to cultivate "pure hearts and clean hands" to recognize their stake in and affection for "the public interest." The reason that Locke's political theory dwelled on liberal concepts such as natural rights, consent, and contract was that these constituted the ancient "liberties" that virtuous fathers had to reassert in order to secure their families' welfare against modern corruption and future betrayal. Locke not only retained the republican meaning of virtue; he enriched it by demonstrating that fathers' civic virtue was essential to individuals' civil and political rights.

Fathers and Kings

Restoration thinkers presumed "the intimacy of kinship and politics." Their origin stories transformed fathers of families into founders of governments, judged the suitability of governments by patriarchal norms, and debated the extent and limits of patriarchal authority. Their discourse emerged from a "world we have lost," one where patriarchal hierarchies were taken for granted. Fathers ruled their families, and women, children, and servants were expected to obey. Some fathers were educated and privileged, most were illiterate and subordinate. A few fathers resided in manor houses and forged kinship networks to achieve political power; the majority lived off the land and deferred to political authority. "It may begin to look strange," Peter Laslett observes, "that any one was ever bold enough to escape at all, impossible that ideas of individual rights, of the accountability of superiors, of contract as the basis of government could ever have occurred to the men of seventeenth-century England."[6]

It would have been quite strange if Locke had made a sudden break with patriarchal thought. In fact, he did not. Locke's idea of the "individual" incorporated men's predisposition to fatherhood, patriarchal authority, family obligations, and manly fortitude and civility. These natural or private virtues constituted the organic bonds of society. Gordon Schochet suggests that these virtues made it "possible for people to inhabit Locke's civil society." Schochet also indicates that Lockean men needed to cultivate private virtues or "they could not be citizens."[7] What was the link between men's private, patriarchal virtues and public life? Locke's conjectural history of the origin and evolution of government was premised on a belief that reasonable fathers necessarily became good citizens.

Locke argued that "government commonly began in the father." In particular, God endowed the primitive father with natural authority over minor sons. Paternal authority, in turn, engendered among youth a sense of juridical and emotional dependence. Boys looked to the father to settle sibling disputes and protect filial interests. If the father was reasonable, his sons came to respect him for his evenhanded justice and devotion to their good. Over time, filial dependence and respect turned habitual and endured into young men's adulthood. Accustomed to trusting and obeying the father, adult sons continued to submit their conflicts and problems to his judgment. "Thus it was easy and almost natural," Locke wrote, "for [adult] children, by a tacit and scarce avoidable consent, to make way for the father's authority." The change was "insensible" but significant. Consent transformed the primitive father from a natural patriarch into a political monarch.[8]

Locke's prehistorical world was populated by family polities governed by patriarchal monarchs. Alas, these family polities proved unstable. Their "simple, poor way of living . . . made few controversies," but their modest size made them vulnerable to external aggression and violence. The family monarch had little choice but to defend his family polity by joining together with other fathers, organizing for mutual protection, selecting the "wisest and bravest" father as leader, and, ultimately, consenting to obey the new leader as king. Locke offered two scenarios for the unification of family polities into small kingdoms. One was that small families grew and branched into extended families; a succession of eldest sons assumed political authority with the consent of brothers, uncles, nephews, and other male relatives. As Locke put it, "Fatherly authority continued on to the elder son, every one in his turn growing up under it tacitly submitting to it." In another scenario, Locke speculated that "several families, or the descendants of several families, whom chance, neighborhood, or business brought together, unit[ed] into society."[9] Here, extended family ties augmented by bonds of familiarity, proximity, and interest generated sufficient solidarity for fathers to consent to be governed by a common king.

Locke did not detail the evolution of early kingdoms into modern nation–states but he uncovered some seeds of political growth. His insistence that extended-family ties and "acquaintance and friendship together and some trust one in another" were crucial determinants of social bonding and political consent suggested that the extent of interpersonal relationships helped to determine possibilities for enlarging kingdoms.[10] Beyond that, men's shared sense of paternal obligations, filial deference, and masculine bonds regulated by reputation and public opinion might have generated enough surplus trust to support political growth beyond interpersonal relationships. Seliger takes Locke a step further. He argues that Locke relied on men's common descent, language, and culture, reinforced by shared apprehensions of outsiders, to produce a nascent nationalism that anticipated the consent of large multitudes in modern nation–states.[11]

Locke certainly believed that solidarity among fathers was necessary for political society, stability, and growth, but he also thought that political leadership was a crucial factor. Kings had to be wise and brave to lead men to military victory. They also needed to be "nursing fathers" who were "tender and careful of the public weal." Without "nursing fathers," Locke wrote, "all governments would have sunk under the weakness and infirmities of their infancy, and the prince and the people had soon perished together."[12] Monarchs' political obligations were modeled on fathers' private virtues. Kings were obligated to cultivate subjects' affections, win their habitual loyalty, mete out evenhanded justice, nurture public good, and thereby foster continuing compliance and lasting consent among the governed. The monarchies that survived early history were the ones led by beloved father figures supported by trusting family fathers.

Two features of Locke's conjectural history merit special comment. First, Locke made no *sharp* distinction between private life and public life. Sons' habitual deference motivated their consent to be ruled by the father's political authority; and fathers' concern for families' imperiled welfare necessitated their consent to be ruled by kings. In turn, kings maintained their legitimacy and power by assuming the role of "nursing fathers" who encouraged filial affection and gratitude, obedience, and consent among the governed. Patriarchy organized and pervaded private and public life. The main difference between the two spheres was that fathers' authority over minor children was natural, while monarchs' authority over subjects was based on consent. Still, that consent was "almost natural" and generally "tacit," and the actual changes wrought by it were "insensible."

Second, Locke treated men's private, patriarchal virtues as the source, justification, and model for early governments. The origin of government was father–son bonding. The reason for early kingdoms was fathers' concern for family welfare, their military fortitude in the face of external agression, and civility extended to relatives, friends, neighbors, and compatriots. Men's patriarchal devotion to their families mediated their identification with public good, fostered recognition of other men as equals ruled by a common sovereign, and urged their political consent and active participation in military service. In turn, political patriarchs transformed men's family loyalty into patriotic loyalty by becoming "nursing fathers" who capitalized on norms of filial deference to win men's affections and engineer their consent. For Locke, premodern history was the story of men's private virtues engendering civic virtue.

There were, however, germs of corruption infecting premodern polities. Men's private virtues could be neutralized by men's selfishness and ignorance. After all, it was because adult siblings could not settle their own disputes that they referred conflicts to the father; and it was because some fathers were beastly and others violent and warlike that most fathers were forced to unite into military kingdoms. Further, some early kingdoms did not survive because kings failed to be effective political leaders and beloved fathers. Looking back from the brink of modernity, Locke concluded that men's vices and kings' corruption had reached a breaking point. Men steadily lost trust in each another, feared their governors, and found traditional patriarchal kingship increasingly intolerable.

Against Traditional Patriarchal Kingship

Locke called the premodern combination of consenting fathers and patriarchal kings a "golden age" when men had "more virtue" and "better governors," and nations suffered "no contest betwixt rulers and the people about governors or government." [13] Fathers' virtues and kings' benign prerogative guaranteed men's liberty and satisfaction, civic virtue and social order, and public good. But the golden age was tarnished by the forces of modern commerce and covetousness. Fathers betrayed private, patriarchal virtues for "ambition and luxury." They flattered monarchs for personal gain and contributed to political "exorbitancies" and "abuses of power." Kings developed "distinct and separate interests from their people," seeking personal wealth and power at the expense of public good. The growth of political corruption and factionalism was nowhere more evident than in outrageous and unprecedented royal claims to "*jure divino.*" [14]

There was one striking difference between men's loss of virtue and monarchs' betrayal of public good: men were redeemable, but kings' affinity to public good was forever lost. Locke argued that modern men became self-conscious about destructive vices. They "found it necessary to examine more carefully the original rights of government, and to find out ways to restrain the exorbitancies and prevent the abuses of that power which . . . was made use of to hurt them." [15] By contrast, kings foolishly continued to cultivate corruption. They traded on men's greed, purchased allies in Parliament, put placemen in public office, and hired henchmen to secure their power and interests, even though their actions estranged the people, incited popular discontent, and invited rebellion. Just as Marx argued that the proletariat would become a revolutionary class-for-itself while the bourgeoisie pursued self-destruction, Locke indicated that self-conscious fathers would demand change while monarchs wallowed in corruption.

Locke was not explicit about what he meant by attributing this self-consciousness to modern men. One possibility was that he decided to put away the patriarchal past and adapt his politics to modern materialism. Perhaps fathers' private, patriarchal virtues were anachronistic; perhaps modern men's avarice was an immutable reality; perhaps modernity was an encounter between possessive individuals seeking expansive economic opportunities and traditional kings empowered by economic restraints such as primogeniture and entail. If so, then modern men's self-consciousness signified a new awareness of rational economic self-interest, a material stake in rejecting political absolutism, and the utility of limited government. Locke argued, after all, that men's desire for "the preservation of property" was the main incentive for them to shift their loyalties from Filmerian kings to a modern polity.[16]

The notion that Locke saw modernity as an invitation to possessive individualism has limited credibility. Locke never reconciled himself to modern avarice. As Richard Ashcraft observes, "For Locke, the Deity is the Great Property Owner" and men "are his productive tenants." God demanded "sobriety, frugality, and industry" and enshrouded property relations in a blanket of moral imperatives to limit acquisitiveness and encourage regard for public good.[17] On occasions when Locke supported a freer play of market forces, he was hoping to avert greater evils. He supported free-floating interest rates lest greedy bankers and brokers evade the law, make perjury fashionable, dissolve the bonds of trust, and render it "impossible for society . . . to subsist." Even then, he wanted to mitigate market damages, first by reminding men of "the virtue and provident way of living of our ancestors" and then by calling for legal restrictions on "money jobbers" who "prey upon the ignorance or necessity of borrowers." His rule of thumb was: "Private men's interests ought not . . . to be neglected, nor sacrificed to anything *but the manifest advantage of the public.*"[18] Given modern men's ambitions, he doubted that private interests regularly contributed to public advantage.

Even if we assume that modern Lockean men became sufficiently rational to sublimate their greed into predictable market channels, it does not automatically follow that possessive individualists would have found patriarchal kingship harmful. Locke understood that ambitious men found ways to flatter kings and profit from political corruption. He knew that those who suffered a long train of economic abuses were likely to propose political reform rather than oppose patriarchal kingship. After all, political reform was the agenda of moderate Whigs. It was consistent with Locke's mercantilist proclivities, which linked national prosperity to a powerful, unified central government able to regulate property, navigation, and trade.[19] And it was viable to the extent that kings could have loosened the reins of regulation to foster national prosperity and public satisfaction and thereby enhanced court coffers and royal legitimacy. In short, the logic of possessive individualism fails to account for Locke's belief that traditional patriarchal kingship was intolerable.

A more comprehensive interpretation is that Locke understood men's new self-consciousness as renewed awareness that individual avarice harmed families' welfare, while kings' corruption betrayed traditional norms of nursing fatherhood. Theresa Brennan and Carole Pateman remind us that "the 'individuals' who enter Locke's social contract and establish the liberal state are the fathers of families."[20] As fathers, their abiding sense of paternal obligations alerted them to the dangers that modern ambition and luxury posed to their families' welfare; and their abiding private virtues urged them to counteract modern avarice with self-restraint, industry, sobriety, and civility. Modern fathers certainly wanted to protect the "property which men have in their persons as well as goods," which meant they wanted to safeguard their biological posterity and family estates by restraining acquisitiveness and securing stability.[21] Modern men's vices were neither thorough nor irredeemable because men's instinctual devotion to fatherhood urged a constant return to private virtues.

The irreversible change wrought by modernity involved structural relations between family fathers and patriarchal kings. Originally, fathers relied on nature and consent to assure monarchs' fidelity to public good. They "put the rule into one man's hands and [chose] to be under the conduct of a single person, without so much as by express conditions limiting or regulating his power which they thought safe enough in his honesty and prudence."[22] Natural family affections, extended blood ties, and interpersonal male bonds were guarantees that the monarch would respect his obligation to protect men's liberties and families, seek popular affections, and nurse public good. Two factors destroyed the guarantee. First, the natural ties binding citizens to monarchs were extended, distended, and stretched thin as tiny kingdoms grew into nation–states. Now, impersonal relations, artificial affections, and contractual agreement proved to be an anemic basis for political cohesion. Second, monarchs were corrupted by modern commerce. The age of money and commerce allowed kings to choose status, wealth, and power for their private kinship and friendship networks—factions—at the expense of their public family. Feeling only weak ties to the public at large, kings gave preference to their own families and factions, stoked the fires of ambition and luxury that imperiled families' welfare, and thereby betrayed family fathers' trust.

The function of Locke's conjectural history was to specify sources of continuity and change in modernity. Men remained the same. They continued to honor the norms of fatherhood, gravitate to private, patriarchal virtues, and require that their kings be nursing fathers committed to family welfare, evenhanded justice, and public good. What changed was the structural foundation of political trust. Artificial affections and betrayed consent motivated fathers to doubt the honesty and prudence of any patriarchal king. The political ramifications were dramatic. Fathers' political affections were no longer habitual and their consent was no longer "almost natural." Henceforth, men's loyalty was contingent on the reconstitution of natural affections and contractual bonds between citizens and the state.

Reconstituted Citizenship

Modern fathers faced a complex challenge. They had to secure their rights, family estates, and sons' prospects in an environment marked by intolerance, growing temptation, and political corruption. They could not rely on other men's civility because the bonds of social affection were stretched thin. Nor could they trust governors to promote their families' good above factional interests. Fathers had no choice but to reassume individual responsibility for their families' fortunes, which was accomplished by overthrowing Filmerian kings. The problem was that individual fathers and their families were vulnerable to the destructive impact of fluctuating social, economic, and military forces. Like their forebears, then, modern fathers had to reestablish government. Their initial move was to strengthen the bonds of masculinity.

The first act of modern citizenship was for fathers to consent to a social contract that reconstituted civil society. Locke's call to consent was a reaffirmation of his version of the ancient constitution. It recalled a golden age when sons consented to the father's authority and fathers' consented to kingship. Patriarchal consent reinforced the natural truth that the "master of a family with all these subordinate relations of wife, children, servants, and slaves" was the sole source of political legitimacy.[23] It reclaimed the ancient experience of fathers as free and equal beings who submitted to no authority save by voluntary choice. In effect, Locke's consent was a plea to family fathers to rededicate themselves to deliberating their families' good in light of their newfound skepticism of patriarchal kingship.

Why did Locke urge fathers' consent to a social contract rather than to a particular government? He hoped to reconstitute the web of paternal obligations and filial deference, extended kinship and friendship ties, masculine virtues and cultural norms that were the original, organic basis for social solidarity. His social contract was a public declaration of male bonding. The declaration formalized men's commitment to fatherhood, fortitude, and civility to reinforce distended social ties. It was also a pledge of renewed trust, faith, and cooperation among men. And it was a sign of modern men's recognition of their common political need: fathers had to quit their natural power of familial protection, "resign it up into the hands of the community," and "put on the bonds of civil society" so that the community of fathers could pool its resources and mount a collective defense of social stability against vice, conflict, and corruption.[24]

Civil society could stabilize social relations in two ways. First, speaking through the voice of public opinion, it could pressure individuals to conform to the norms of masculinity. Men would have to restrain their destructive impulses lest they suffer ill repute if not social disgrace. That explains why Locke's reminder to entrepreneurs of "the provident way of living of our ancestors" was conceivably more than shallow sentimentalism or empty rhetoric. Second, civil society could grant or withhold political legitimacy. Locke argued that the community of fathers deliberated and expressed its preferences "by the will and determination of the majority."[25] Fathers' participation in formulating the majority's will and determination amounted to the rebirth of a political activism that announced the end of habitual political quiescence and the beginning of an ongoing reassessment of government's devotion to public good. In effect, civil society was fathers' mechanism for reasserting social and political control.

Locke expected civil society to be deliberative and sovereign, but he did not necessarily expect its deliberations and decisions to gravitate toward natural law and rationality. Civil society, after all, was an aggregation of impassioned fathers obsessed with their families' welfare. By what standard, then, would the modern community of fathers evaluate political legitimacy? If men's basic instincts were unchanged, then one would expect fathers to emulate their forefathers and support political leaders who appeared to be sufficiently wise and brave to protect families' welfare, settle disputes justly, and care for the public weal. But if men's faith in leaders' fidelity to the public good was severely shaken, then one would expect modern fathers to grant no more than conditional trust to political leaders. Thus, the first act of Lockean citizenship was for fathers to join the social contract that established civil society, and the second act was for the community of fathers to agree to no more than limited trust in any new government.

Locke modeled reconstituted citizenship on traditional filial deference that had two major features. It was provisional. Sons were obliged to obey their fathers only until reaching their majority. In addition, it was contingent. Sons' deference depended on their fathers' ability to fulfill paternal obligations, exemplify masculine virtues, and educate youth without constant resort to coercion. Adult sons would consent to the father's authority when he proved trustworthy, but sons would not consent should the father fail to cultivate, teach, and enrich filial respect, loyalty, and sobriety. Locke projected filial deference onto citizenship by employing the concept of "tacit consent."

Tacit consent meant that men who worked, owned property, resided, or simply traveled within the territorial boundaries of a state implicitly agreed to obey established political authority.[26] This concept troubles many scholars. It seems to suggest that men born into a society were automatically subordinated to government, that men could "unknowingly" consent to be governed, and, worse yet, that men potentially owed obedience to all governments, even criminal governments that broke the law of nature. J. P. Plamenatz argues, "If consent can be implied by some of the things that [Locke] maintains imply it, then there never existed any government but ruled with the unanimous and continuous consent of all its subjects."[27] Clearly, Locke did not intend to justify automatic, unthinking obedience to any government. He articulated natural law standards "to decide whether a government is acting legitimately."[28] And he urged contemporaries to rebel against James II and other political tyrants. What then did Locke intend by validating tacit consent?

Consider its main characteristics. Tacit consent was provisional consent, an "homage due to and from those who . . . come within the territories belonging to any government." Obligatory homage ended the moment that men left that jurisdiction. Even when men stayed put, their tacit consent generated no more than a weak political bond. Locke noted that tacit consent "no more makes a man a member of that society, a perpetual subject of that commonwealth, than it would make a man subject to another in whose family he found it convenient to abide for some time."[29] A tacit consenter's relation to government was the same as a son's relation to his father. Both were temporary subjects in another's jurisdiction; both implicitly agreed to defer to authority as a temporary convenience that was instrumental to civility and order.

Also, tacit consent was based on mutual expectations and produced a conditional political bond. In Locke's conjectural history, adult sons gave their tacit consent to the affectionate and just father; family fathers tacitly consented on the basis of rulers' wisdom and bravery; and extended families and neighbors gave tacit consent to elder sons and enlarged kingdoms on the condition that princes would nurse public good. In every instance, Locke's tacit consent was neither rational nor arbitrary. On the one hand, it was a by-product of family habits, social solidarity, and necessity rather than an exploration of natural law. For Locke, tacit consent was a useful concept precisely because it allowed men to establish political bonds despite their irrationality. On the other hand, premodern men did not give tacit consent to any government or recognize an obligation to obey any government. Acting *as if* they were rational, fathers submitted only to governors who were affectionate and dutiful political fathers who ruled in the interest of "public good and safety."[30]

Tacit consent was perfectly suited to fathers in the midst of a transition to modern government. Locke's civil society faced the dilemma of redirecting its political allegiances despite its distrust of political authority. Skeptical fathers who gave their tacit consent to a new government made no permanent commitment to it. Instead, they promised a temporary period of civility and order during which a new government would have to demonstrate its commitment to public good. Further, fathers' tacit consent put a new government on notice: fathers' continued acquiescence was contingent on proper political performance. Should a new government betray its fiduciary trust, civil society would withdraw its support, disobey, and possibly revolt. This warning was a strong incentive for leaders to avoid factionalism and coercion, to secure public affections in order to win the enduring consent of the governed. Tacit consent was the community's counterweight to modern political corruption.

It is tempting to suggest that Locke's third act of citizenship was for the community of fathers to formulate a new government, and a fourth act was for them to administer it. That would confirm Ashcraft's image of Locke as both radical individualist and radical democrat as well as support Louis Hartz's reading of the Lockean consensus on liberal democracy. However, textual and contextual evidence counsels caution here. Locke did not indicate that irrational family fathers, individually or collectively, could found or operate a new polity. Their tacit consent was passive, a matter of reacting rather than creating or governing. Moreover, Locke's support for and participation in the government of William III suggests that he was comfortable with government by the few. Indeed, Locke equated founding fathers and political leadership with an elite corps of nursing fathers.

Government by Nursing Fathers

Thomas Pangle remarks that Locke himself exhibited considerable "civic spirit" and "surreptitiously" expected it of others.[31] Locke was a lifelong bachelor who applauded the self-restraint and civic virtue of family fathers. He was a scholar devoted to rationality who honored the paternal instincts of irrational men. He was a political activist who risked his life and fortune and suffered exile for his opposition to absolute kingship. The most significant product of his civic spirit was his *Second Treatise*. Locke issued a plan for liberal government that he hoped would win men's tacit consent to an elite corps of political leaders whose survival depended on their ability to cultivate public affections and engineer the enduring consent of the governed. In essence, Locke was an aspiring founding father in search of government by nursing fathers.

Locke's *Second Treatise* reaffirmed primitive fathers' expectations that government should work toward "no other end but the peace, safety, and public good of the people." Did modern men suffer corruption in

Parliament? Locke responded that legislative authority "can never be supposed to extend farther than the common good." Had Englishmen been estranged from government by abuses of royal prerogative? Locke explained that executive prerogative could be nothing other than "discretion for the public good" so that political leaders could avoid the harm associated with the "inflexible rigor" of laws and act to "mitigate the severity of the law."[32] Locke's promise was that his plan for government would protect men's rights and families as well as secure public good by tempering justice with mercy. Like ancient kings, modern governors were to be competent, caring sources of public peace and goodness.

Locke equipped statesmen with the authority to carry out their charge and also to win citizens' affection and enduring consent. First, they had legislative authority. Their job was to translate the law of nature into positive laws that neutralized men's excessive passions and arbitrated disputes that men were too irrational to settle themselves. As Locke put it, "For though the law of nature be plain and intelligible to all rational creatures, yet men, being biased by their interest as well as ignorant for want of studying it, are not apt to allow of it as a law binding to them in the application of it to their particular cases."[33] Lockean legislators promulgated laws that articulated a common standard of right; they applied that standard to particular cases; and only as a last resort did they execute their decisions by the threat or use of state coercion. Like all Whigs, Locke thought that a system of just laws would counteract the prejudices and factionalism associated with the corrupted Parliament and court.

But Locke also believed that legislators had to do more than codify, adjudicate, and enforce men's rights. After all, if men were biased in their own cases, why would fathers comply with laws or judgments that they perceived as adverse to their families' good? The threat or use of state coercion was an insufficient motive. Modern legislators needed to understand what reasonable fathers knew and corrupt kings with their standing armies demonstrated: a ready resort to violence purchased temporary obedience at the cost of fostering suspicion, disenchantment, and rebelliousness. Ironfisted law enforcement undermined the cooperation and consent of the governed. As such, Lockean legislators not only had to enact just laws but also render the rod unnecessary by encouraging in men a habitual affection for "promulgated, standing laws" as an essential source of citizens' "united strength" and "the bonds of the society."[34]

Locke did not advocate an impersonal system of legal rationality, procedures, rules, or institutions administered by faceless state bureaucrats. He insisted that statesmen should not be inhibited by rigid rules, especially when they had to respond to the shifting tides of public opinion and the inevitable erratic events that shaped political life. Governing was an art, Locke argued, that involved striking a balance between citizens' habitual love of the laws and leaders' prerogative "to provide for the public good in such cases which, depending upon unforeseen and uncertain occurrences, certain and unalterable laws could not safely direct." Locke went so far as to equip statesmen with the discretion to act "without the prescription of law and sometimes even against it." [35] He clearly believed that political prerogative was the linchpin of good government because he enriched and legitimated it despite his historical attacks on kings' abuses of it.

In a remarkable tract entitled "Old England's Legal Constitution," Locke drew a distinction between wrong and right prerogative. "The wrong understanding of the word 'prerogative,'" he wrote, "has been the undoing of many kings and subjects. Flatterers and interested ministers seldom fail of screwing up this string till it cracks of itself." He accused the Stuart kings of treating prerogative as arbitrary, self-interested, unlimited, and, ultimately, self-defeating discretionary power that justified corruption only to generate "fear, hatred, and distrust" among the people. Rightly understood, however, political prerogative was akin to parental discretion; it was the exercise of leadership and initiative for the good and only the good of one's subjects. And it was virtually always rewarded with the "fond" gratitude, if not the open "love," of the people.

Locke memorialized the reign of Queen Elizabeth because it illustrated the true understanding, use, and effect of proper prerogative. He wrote that Elizabeth "was so wise as thoroughly to understand this truth and to determine the point after forty-two years' experience during which she happily governed this realm in most difficult times." Usually, Elizabeth exercised leadership initiative for public good and received the people's adoration for it. Occasionally, her discretionary actions appeared to be "irregular," but, even then, they were rooted in the public will and free from the taint of tyranny. "Her interest and that of her subjects was so much one and the same that they could scarce in any instance be separated." If she used prerogative "sometimes in a passion unjustly," she usually recognized her errors and made "large amends in kindness" to restore the bonds of public affection and support. Elizabeth, Locke concluded, was "a true mother of her people, not a stepmother." [36]

In effect, Locke translated his portrait of affectionate fatherhood into an androgynous theory of political leadership. His reasonable fathers were both rule makers who disciplined young sons and caretakers who nurtured older sons' affections, gratitude, and respect. Locke's fathers combined what Carol Gilligan has separated into male authority and female nurturance. When Locke called Elizabeth a true mother to her people and then indicated that "his present majesty" (William III) was a true father to his people, he was resurrecting and refining his ancient, golden age, androgynous image of "nursing fathers" who meted out justice and nurtured the public weal to win the lasting support and compliance of the people. [37]

In his *Second Treatise*, Locke defended proper prerogative as a manifestation of "nursing fatherhood." He argued that statesmen who used discretion for public good and thereby secured public acclaim were more influential and effective than those kings who ruled by fear, resorted to coercion, and reduced popular trust. Indeed, he explicitly linked wise leadership to reasonable fatherhood when writing that it was "impossible for a governor, if he really means the good of his people, and the preservation of them and their laws together, not to make them see and feel it, as it is for the father of a family not to let his children see he loves and takes care of them." [38] The Lockean art of governing men involved leaders' ability to mix legal discipline and flexible initiative in so subtle a way that family fathers would agree to a more stable commitment to be governed.

Unlike most Whigs, however, Locke did not believe that enhancing Parliament's power and enthroning more artful kings went far enough. Past betrayals had renewed fathers' awareness of their natural rights and produced in them a protective jealousy that militated against strong political loyalties, even to good government. Fathers' tacit consent symbolized the depth of their jealousy and also their abiding sense of having a provisional relationship with their political leaders. Further, the sheer distance separating subjects from rulers in modern nation–states afforded ample opportunity for men to reconfirm any doubts about leaders' prudence and honesty. If citizens had a habitual trust in their leaders during the Elizabethan era, an intervening century of political conflict and corruption had engendered widespread distrust by William's reign. To overcome such distrust, political leaders had to be artful governors *and* political educators who taught men to comply and identify with the state. As Locke put it, "A good government will make good subjects."[39]

Making Good Subjects

Locke was not explicit about the state's pedagogical role. He preferred family fathers to dispose their sons to civic virtue and consent.[40] But he knew that some fathers failed to fulfill paternal obligations, many youth were attracted by vice, and most modern men were loath to trust their governors. His writings tested a two-tiered strategy for binding citizens to the state. First, political leaders needed to secure the familial foundations of government to avoid serious challenges and ensure lasting political order. Second, public officials had to engineer men's limited participation in government to strengthen citizens' identification with the state. To the extent that Locke made governors responsible for making good citizens, he equipped them with sufficient authority to nurture civic virtue and nurse the public weal.

Locke empowered the state to regulate marriage and parenting. He believed that men had a natural desire for monogamous marriage, procreation, and provision of children. Beyond nature, he admitted great flexibility in family arrangements. Husbands and wives were free to make "voluntary compacts" regarding the distribution and execution of parental duties. And there was "no necessity in nature" that conjugal society continue beyond the years of child rearing. Locke noted, however, that public officials could enforce natural duties and use the "restraint of positive law" to regulate conjugal compacts.[41] "Unnatural" couplings should be legally banned. Fathers could be held liable for the proper care and education of children, and a father who "quits his care" of his children should "lose his power over them" to a "foster-father." Spouses who disputed "procreation and mutual support and assistance" were subject to state intervention. Further, "if the father die and fail to substitute a deputy in his trust" or "if he hath not provided a tutor to govern his son during his minority," Locke argued, "the law takes care to do it." The law could also ban divorce if marriage for life was thought beneficial to public good.[42]

Locke was particularly concerned with state authority over child care. He insisted that "the nourishment and education of their children is a charge so incumbent on parents for their children's good that nothing can absolve them from taking care of it." If men were reasonable about their children's good, the state should respect fathers' domestic rule. But if fathers crossed nature or proved to be inadequate parents, the state should intervene to ensure the productivity and loyalty of future citizens. Nowhere was state intervention more important than among the poor, Locke thought, where fathers so often lacked the morality, self-discipline, and resources to provide a suitable upbringing. A poor father was not inevitably a bad father. If necessary, he could fulfill his paternal duty by putting "the tuition of his son in other hands" or by making him "an apprentice to another."[43] By the 1690s, however, Locke questioned whether poor fathers could be proper parents. He agreed with "the commendable Oxford tutor" who wrote that "tinkers' and cobblers' children [exhibited] base, dirty qualities . . . of lying, filching, pailing, swearing, etc."[44]

Addressing the rise of pauperism, Locke drafted a "Report on the Poor" advocating reform of England's poor laws. He ascribed spreading poverty to "the relaxation of discipline and corruption of manners." Two forms of state intervention would cure the disease. First, political leaders should legislate a "restraint on . . . debauchery." Magistrates were to shut down brandy shops patronized by poor men, urge and assist them to find honest work, and, if necessary, force them to submit to hard labor in the navy. Officials should also eliminate the parish practice of providing a poor father with money for family support only to discover that "he not seldom spends [it] on himself in the alehouse whilst his children, for whose sake he had it, are left to suffer or perish under the want of necessaries." Second, the state should establish work schools for poor children. State schools would free poor mothers from daily child care and provide them "more liberty to work." They also would transfer parenting responsibilities from ill-bred adults to public officials committed to teaching virtue and industry as well as "religion and morality."[45] When poor fathers failed, political officials became surrogate fathers who schooled children in citizenship.

Locke's "Report on Irish Linen Manufacture" urged the state to become surrogate father to an entire people. English officials were to set up an industrial equivalent to the militia that would drill Irish men and women in weaving and spinning, respectively, sponsor yearly competitions, and grant special privileges to high achievers. The state should also create spinning schools "to which all persons that have not forty shillings a year estate shall be obliged to send all their children." Locke's implicit argument was that men who were Irish and poor could not possibly be proper fathers and, therefore, the state should assume responsibility to regulate Irish adults and provision, nurture, and educate their children.[46] In the case of Irish youth, however, Locke was more interested in fostering productivity and order than morality and citizenship.

Why would political leaders take on these onerous responsibilities? Their legitimacy was based on the consent of reasonable fathers; and inter-generational stability depended on the transmission of virtue to youth. Locke believed that poor fathers who were poor parents produced sons prone to idleness, drink, and crime. Together, they constituted an anar-chic element threatening class conflict and political upheaval. Thus, it was incumbent on state officials to rehabilitate (or regulate) the poor and in-culcate in their children both private and civic virtue. Many poor people might resent state intervention, others might invite it. But most citizens were likely to see state intervention as evidence that political leaders were indeed striving for family welfare. Locke anticipated what Michael Gross-berg calls "judicial patriarchy." In late nineteenth-century America, gov-ernors, legislators, and judges asserted authority to regulate family affairs and supervise children's upbringing in the twin cause of social control of the poor, immigrants, and minorities and civic education for future citizens.[47]

The problem of legitimacy and stability was also a function of men's distrust of the state. Lockean leaders had to woo public trust to be as-sured that laws and prerogative would command consistent compliance. And reasonable fatherhood provided a useful model for state efforts to promote civic virtue and secure men's enduring consent. In effect, Locke counseled political leaders to follow the example of the father of an adoles-cent who had internalized masculine virtues and was ready for initiation into adulthood. The father began the initiation by allowing his son the freedom to participate in decision making. If a youth demonstrated for-titude and civility, he could be given greater freedom to participate and earn paternal friendship and equality. But youthful maturation was not always so smooth. Recall Locke's story of the Venetian noble whose son took independence as an opportunity for profligacy.[48] The noble did not resort to coercion by suspending his son's allowance or threatening to disinherit him. Instead, the noble asserted the prerogative to put a minor restriction on his son's freedom, requiring the young man to account for his spending. As a result, the son became self-conscious about his profligacy, felt shame at offending his father, and voluntarily returned to the family's moral fold.

Locke thought most men were like the noble's son. They internalized masculine virtues and were ready to exercise the freedom to participate in politics. But their flaws made it predictable that they would abuse political independence. We can interpret Locke's political theory as an argument for political leaders to follow the Venetian noble's example. They should not force compliance to leadership by eliminating political rights. Rather, they should invite men to enjoy a restricted freedom to participate in politics. That would encourage men to feel *as if* they were friends and equals to political leaders and thereby prompt men to identify voluntarily with the state. In Lockean politics, participation produced patriotism.

Locke clearly did not support what he called "perfect democracy," the majority of men participating "in making the laws for the community from time to time."[49] His civil society was to entrust authority to governors, not become government. Nonetheless, Locke did suggest that men should have a restricted freedom to participate in the formation and administration of modern government. Men had the right to consent to and participate in the deliberations of the majority that entrusted authority to government. Men also had a political right to vote for representatives in periodic elections. In both cases, restricted participation was more important for its pedagogical value to leadership than for any impact it might have on public policy.

Men's participation in civil society contributed to the formulation of majority public opinion during two critical moments. The first was when the community of fathers recognized kings' betrayal and reconstituted itself to rethink its political commitments. This legitimation crisis shattered fathers' habitual loyalties and was an opportune moment for political theorists and aspiring founding fathers to appeal to nature and reason to educate men's self-conscious, political commitments. And to the degree that fathers helped to shape majority public opinion at a moment when it was a determining political factor, it was likely that men would experience a sense of personal identification with a new government. More than guests in another's political house, fathers who participated in building the structure would desire to be comfortable with it, ponder permanent residence in it, and feel some proprietorship of it. Locke's tacit consent was provisional and conditional, but participation infused it with a presumptive longevity.

Legitimation crises pass and men revert to quiescence, even as they retain their distrust of current political leaders. Such complacency was partly advantageous to leaders. It enabled them to exercise political prerogative without attracting much public attention and provided them an opportunity to cultivate public affections.[50] Still, officials could not be confident of their legitimacy until they confronted a second crucial moment. That was when their controversial use of prerogative cracked citizens' complacency and caused public unrest. At that point, Locke noted, "the people" would judge "when this power is made a right use of."[51] Embattled leaders had several choices. They could use coercion to shut down debate, which might produce temporary order. But it might foster increased public distrust and even a revolutionary "appeal to heaven." The alternative was to seize the moment to strengthen men's civic virtue. Following Queen Elizabeth, leaders could justify their "irregular" actions by schooling men in public good and shaming them for excessive doubt; or they could admit errors and make "large amends in kindness" to restore and reinforce public faith. In both cases, leaders should emulate the Venetian noble who engineered a restricted freedom to participate in order to win voluntary filial consent and sustained subordination.

For Locke, men's right to vote for representatives in periodic elections was an ideal form of political participation. It narrowed the distance separating citizens and leaders. Voters helped to select leaders and could remove corrupt politicians. Thus, they could feel confident that "freely chosen" officials would "freely act and advise as the necessity of the commonwealth and the public good should upon examination and mature debate be judged to require." Accomplices in leadership, voters would likely identify with public officials and comply with their policies. In addition, voting encouraged men to "hear the debate" among candidates and consider "the reasons on all sides" before casting their ballots. It habituated men to deliberating the connection between their families' good and public good on a regular basis and thereby fostered a more informed and lasting consent.[52] Indeed, Locke observed that a man who swore off idleness and participated in political discourse was apt to "consider himself as a piece of the public."[53]

Sheldon Wolin argues that Locke's restricted participation anticipated the American Framers' effort "to secure a steady and continuous flow of legitimacy *from* the people without promoting steady and continuous interference *by* the people."[54] By Locke's historical reckoning and political analysis, "a very few great men" were suitable as founding fathers and "not many persons of understanding, diligence, and disinterestedness" were needed as political fathers.[55] Restricted political participation helped to legitimate and secure political elitism. Still, the scope of elites' authority was limited by the very conditions that legitimated it. Political leaders had to resist a ready resort to violence and respect norms of nursing fatherhood. They had to care for poor families as well as control them, honor public opinion as well as educate it, and abide by political participation as well as restrict it. Like family fathers who exercised self-restraint to win sons' love and cooperation, political fathers had to show self-restraint to make good, loyal citizens. In short, Locke's political leaders were still patriarchs, but they were "liberal" patriarchs.

Locke's Liberal Patriarchy

Locke's political theory can be understood as the story of fathers securing family welfare amidst adversity. Recognizing the betrayal of traditional patriarchal kings, fathers reclaimed their individual right to secure their families' good, reconstituted civil society to reinforce the bonds of masculinity, and gave provisional consent to a new government likely to respect public opinion, allow restricted participation, and fulfill ancient political obligations associated with familial welfare. Because modern men's consent was not "almost natural" or habitual, leaders had to secure political legitimacy and stability by wielding authority with self-restraint. They had to limit state coercion, use laws and prerogative to foster public affections, and encourage men to identify with the state. Locke believed that wise leaders would teach civic virtue and attract explicit consent.

What was "liberal" about Locke's state? It was based on individual rights, founded on the consent of the governed, and governed by a combination of public opinion, male suffrage, and periodic elections, on the one hand, and an accountable leadership, on the other. However, the preeminent feature of Lockean liberalism was men's historical distrust of government that undercut their habitual loyalty to political leaders and urged them to condition consent on political leaders' performance. It was modern public skepticism, not what Gordon Wood judges to be the Lockean science of politics, that determined the reach of the Lockean state. What was "patriarchal" about Locke's state? It originated in the rights of individuals who incorporated norms of family fatherhood and masculine virtues. It was morally justified by the provisional consent of fathers bonded together in civil society and concerned to secure their families' good. Finally, it was modeled on patriarchal hierarchy. Citizens rendered a filial consent to government, governors honored nursing fatherhood and paternal pedagogy, and the gap between private and public life was finally reclosed.

Locke was a radical "individualist" who incorporated patriarchal obligations that generated civic virtue. He was a "democrat" who incorporated citizen deference to patriarchal political leaders. His mix of fatherhood, citizenship, and liberal patriarchy provided a compelling answer to the man question. *Individuals could be trusted with extensive rights because their passion for fatherhood and their filial deference to political elites subdued men's destructive passions, reinforced male bonds, and legitimated the rule of nursing political fathers.* However, Locke's answer to the man question was incomplete because the nature of fatherhood was evolving. Soon, fatherhood would become a secondary employment as men left their homes for separate workplaces; women would assume primary control of child rearing; and youth would have greater freedom to indulge its passions. Although no seer, Locke was prescient. He anticipated these trends and entertained ideas on augmenting men's self-restraint with women's civilizing influence and military training in civic virtue.

6   Women and Warriors

. . . and all this to be directed to no other end but the peace, safety, and public good of the people.
—*John Locke*[1]

Did John Locke pioneer liberal feminism and pacifism? Melissa Butler argues that Locke's support for greater marital give-and-take prefigured women's civil and political equality. Samuel Huntington thinks that Lockean liberalism validated individual rights, rationality, and peaceful conflict resolution to elevate diplomacy above war and produce in young men the expectation that they had a right to mature to adulthood without bearing arms for the state.[2] The historical drift of Locke's political theory, then, was toward the inclusion of women and young men as free and equal citizens who shared the same rights and responsibilities as all men.

Let me provide an alternative reading. Locke's overriding political concern was that men act as responsible fathers and citizens. Part of men's responsibility was to control their wives' and sons' excessive passions and acquisitive interests. But Locke went beyond traditional patriarchy. His version of the marriage contract fostered a liberal patriarchy that combined husbands' affectionate rule of wives with sufficient female autonomy to teach husbands and sons greater self-restraint and civility. Moreover, Locke's pacifist tendencies were compromised by his concern for masculine self-control and national expansion, which demanded that most young men undergo military training and some young men suffer martial discipline on ships and in colonies. Overall, Locke's political theory pointed toward later Victorian beliefs that women and youth should sacrifice their individuality to promote and practice civic virtue in the cause of "peace, safety, and public good."

Locke's Sexual Contract

Locke and Filmer presumed a "sexual contract" that legitimated men's supremacy over women. For both, Carole Pateman argues, "The original political right is a man's right to have sexual access to a woman's body so he can become a father."[3] Lockean men needed to control sexual access to ascertain biological fatherhood and also regulate female behavior to ensure proper mothers for their heirs. In turn, women were to accommodate men's demands for biological and social reproduction by voluntary service as obedient daughters, virtuous wives, and self-sacrificing mothers. In short, Locke subsumed women among fathers' "subordinate relations" and obliged them to exhibit fidelity, bear children, and nurture infants in return for male provision and protection.[4]

Unlike traditional patriarchalists, however, Locke attributed special significance to women as mothers to men's children. He viewed the child as a *tabula rasa* or a malleable creature that was formed or deformed by its early environment. He also believed that infant nurturing, child rearing, and education should be centered in the family home where the child could be molded in a controlled environment. Thus, he wanted boys kept away from public schools where they suffered the "waggeries or cheats," "roughness," and "plots of robbing" of unrefined youth and from cities where vices such as idleness, vanity, pride, luxury, liquor, gambling, dueling, opinionating, and other "unprofitable and dangerous *pastimes*" proliferated.[5] Unquestionably, Locke ceded to fathers the authority and obligation to manage parenting responsibilities; but he also recognized, for better or worse, that mothers' traditional role as infant nurturers and their mere presence in the home environment had a lasting effect on men's heirs.

Furthermore, mothers' influence over children was growing. Locke's era experienced the early phases of a rift between men's home life and work life. Fathers increasingly divided their time between the domestic sphere, where they devoted themselves to fatherhood, and the social, economic, and civic sphere, where they sought provision and protection for their families.[6] Zillah Eisenstein describes the emerging division of family labor this way: "The work done in the home . . . became separated and differentiated (from the market and male activity) and was increasingly defined as women's sphere."[7] Forced to leave home for work, men's daily employment shifted away from parenting to full-time breadwinning in the urban marketplace. This historical trend had two dramatic effects.

First, the rise in absentee fatherhood threatened to undermine men's motivation for self-restraint and sobriety. Spending little time with their families, men could more easily neglect their obligation to be self-sacrificing fathers and masculine exemplars. Worse, men's migration to cities revealed a downside to male bonding. According to Locke, cities were the places where men joined together for self-destructive gaiety and fraternal violence. Their brawling examples inevitably found their way back home, where their sons learned "to strike and laugh when they hurt or see harm come to others," delight in the "doing of mischief," and praise the "unnatural cruelty" that "custom reconciles and recommends to us, by laying it in the way to honor."[8] In sum, absentee fatherhood weakened masculine fortitude and civility, fostered male aggression and intolerance, and compromised public order.

Second, fathers' daily migration made it more difficult for them to manage their households and supervise their subordinates. Men could not keep a careful watch on wives' fidelity, mothers' nurturance, or sons' education. By default, women increasingly became household managers who exercised everyday discretion, assumed greater control of the family economy, and shaped the very home environment that had a lasting imprint on boys' development and education. The problem was that Locke did not trust women to manage family life. His version of "dread of the female" was that women tended toward self-indulgent profligacy, on the one hand, and overindulgent motherhood, on the other. They alternately neglected and coddled their children. If their major virtue was a "modesty" that militated against passionate excesses, Locke noted that women's modesty "cannot be kept" and was "often transgressed against."[9] Worse yet, women were blind to their errant ways. Their "reason" so often amounted to no more than "the superstition of a nurse, or the authority of an old woman."[10]

Men's gradual withdrawal from fatherhood and women's enlarged domestic responsibility threatened to breach the sexual contract. Fathers who neglected their familial duties were hardly more trustworthy than bachelors; they were not sufficient providers or protectors. Mothers who managed the home tended to squander family wealth and raise effeminate sons; they produced a generation of youth that was unfit for civil society. Locke was not particularly self-conscious about these trends, which were more immanent than actual in his time. Nonetheless, his political theory was rich enough to account for the trends and to anticipate an emerging reconstruction of gender relations. In effect, Locke salvaged the sexual contract, first by liberalizing the marriage contract and then by elevating women's moral status and responsibilities.

The Liberal Marriage Contract

Locke argued that God granted Adam and Eve joint dominion on Earth. Men had no divine authority over women. Fathers and mothers had "equal title" to authority over children. "Paternal power" was properly "parental power." Indeed, a man could not properly fulfill his paternal obligations without "a like carriage of the mother." [11] Locke indicated, however, that this grant of joint dominion was contingent because there was "a foundation in nature" for husbands' authority over wives. Husbands needed patriarchal authority not only to ascertain biological fatherhood and manage the family economy but also to compensate for wives' physiological and psychological deficiencies. Women were fated "to bring forth . . . children in pain and sorrow." Immersed in cycles of pregnancy, childbirth, and infant nurturance, they were bound to nature, physically disabled, and entrapped by maternal passions. They lacked the ability to sustain themselves and their children. Thus, "the laws of mankind and the customs of nations have ordered" husbands to assume responsibility for family provision and protection. [12]

But biology was only partly destiny. "If there could be found a remedy" for women's physical and emotional weakness, Locke noted, men's authority could be limited by a conjugal "contract" that exempted wives from strict subordination. [13] Extending this argument, Butler contends that Lockean "women were free to overcome their natural limitations [and] each woman was permitted to strike a better deal for herself wherever possible." Mary Lyndon Shanley adds that Locke "took the premises of natural freedom and equality of family members more seriously than had previous thinkers." Some Whigs wanted to shift the basis of marriage from scripture to consent while insisting that partners agree to a fixed, patriarchal marriage contract. Locke went further. He argued "that the parties themselves might not only agree to marry, but might set at least some of the terms of their relationship."[14] As such, he implicitly abetted proto-feminist pamphleteers who used the contract metaphor to support wives' greater freedom and equality against husbands' tyrannical tendencies.

But how flexible was Locke's liberal marriage contract? The chief end of marriage was to establish a "right in one another's bodies" for purposes of "procreation" and "continuation of the species." Spouses could best fulfill parenting responsibilities by cultivating "mutual support and assistance, and a communion of interests too, as necessary not only to unite their care and affection, but also necessary to their common offspring who have a right to be nourished and maintained." Overall, Locke's estimate was that husbands and wives joined by voluntary choice and mutual affection were likely to be superior parents. And within an affectionate relationship, marital partners were free to negotiate a division of rights and duties "as far as may consist with procreation and the bringing up of children."[15]

The negotiation process almost necessarily benefited women. On the one hand, men could not negotiate or reclaim the ancient right of *patria potestas*. The power of life and death was reserved for government. On the other hand, women could negotiate issues involving the "community of goods and the power over them, mutual assistance and maintenance, and other things belonging to conjugal society." Women could bring property into marriage and bargain for control over it. They could argue for greater autonomy and responsibility in the family division of labor. They could call in the magistrate or even threaten separation and divorce in instances of serious abuse.[16] Unquestionably, Locke's marriage contract invited limits on husbands' authority and extensions of wives' domestic freedom and equality.

However, less male authority and more female autonomy did not make the patriarchal husband obsolete or even erode domestic patriarchy. Pateman reminds us, "The question is not whether a husband is an absolute ruler, but whether he is a ruler at all."[17] Lockean husbands retained the last word in family matters as the "stronger and abler" partners responsible for provision and protection. Furthermore, to the extent that their domestic authority was limited, husbands had a strong motive to avoid coercion as a mechanism of domination and rely instead on mutual affection and concern for children to ensure their wives' fidelity, sober housewifery, and suitable mothering. Equally important, men's monopolistic control of public opinion, economic life, and political power supported husbands' efforts to control recalcitrant wives. Indeed, like reasonable fathers and nurturing statesmen, affectionate husbands could enhance their influence by putting aside the rod and cultivating the caress. Thus, women might "strike a better deal where possible," but only as accomplices in patriarchal rule.[18]

Locke's liberal marriage contract reflected the rise of "affective individualism" in England and prefigured the trend toward "companionate marriages" in Victorian America.[19] It implied that patriarchs should rule with a velvet glove to win women's cooperation as wives assumed greater autonomy within families. It also unveiled the possibility of revising traditional dread of the female. If husbands could exercise patriarchal hegemony through tenderness and make women act *as if* they were reasonable creatures, then men could leave home for the marketplace with some certainty that their wives would neither subvert the family economy nor spoil the children. Especially important, men might even be able to trust women to function as relatively autonomous, reasonable mothers.

Making Reasonable Mothers

Locke recognized that the mother was always an influential parent and sometimes the de facto parent, for example, when the father quit his care of children, abandoned his family, or died while offspring were young.[20] Unfortunately, women were emotional creatures with desires they could not master. Locke illustrated this with an anecdote about "two ladies of quality accidently seated on the opposite sides of a [crowded] room" who grew so heated in controversy that they edged their chairs forward and "were in a little time got up close to one another in the middle of the room where they for a good while managed the dispute as fiercely as two game-cocks in the pit." Female passions subverted good mothering and undermined sons' lessons in fortitude and civility. To make them into reasonable mothers, women would have to be schooled in proper "doctrine."[21]

Locke expected husbands to be affectionate schoolmasters. Confined to their homes, wives' only legitimate source of sexual and emotional fulfillment was their husbands' affections. Public opinion and law were particularly harsh on adulterous wives. Men had more options. They could seek emotional warmth from wives and even assert a conjugal right to wives' bodies. Moreover, Locke recognized that men enjoyed access to "adultery, fornication, uncleanliness, lasciviousness," and "whoredom" with minimal threat of stigma or punishment.[22] He was aware of the prevailing double standard that, as Mary Astell noted, allowed a husband "a hundred ways of relieving himself, but neither prudence nor duty will allow a woman to fly out, her business and entertainment at home."[23] The double standard enabled husbands to control wives in the same way fathers educated heirs: they budgeted affections to win wives' compliance, used praise and shame to secure it, and relied on reputation and public opinion to reinforce it. Thus, husbands could teach wives appropriate rules of motherhood.

Locke's educational writings hinted that husbands should require wives to become devoted and disciplined full-time mothers. For example, he advised fathers that boys' shoes should be thin enough to let water leak in and out to inure them to England's harsh climate. He added, "Here, I fear, I shall have the mistress . . . against me." Mothers were the ones likely to be pained by sons' exposure to the elements; they were the ones who washed sons' stockings and feet and tended to their wet shoes. Locke insisted this was not "too much pain" for mothers: "Truth will have it that [boys'] health is much more worth than all such considerations, and ten-times as much more."[24] In effect, fathers were to restrain mothers' tendency toward maternal overindulgence, require them to measure up to elevated standards of motherhood, and pressure them to sacrifice their own concerns to the minutiae of raising perfect little boys. Significantly, full-time motherhood would leave wives little time for infidelity and profligacy.

Locke also insinuated that daughters should be educated for reasonable motherhood. Girls were to receive the same schooling as boys, except "where the difference of sex requires different treatment."[25] Boys clearly needed to learn the self-mastery associated with masculine fortitude and civility. Locke's fragmentary writings on female education seemed to suggest that girls were to learn the self-mastery associated with feminine modesty and deference. Thus, he stated that he would not "go out of the ordinary road" to insist that girls (like boys) should be exposed to hardships to foster strength and courage. It was more important that girls learn to be accommodating than independent. Locke also noted that girls' education "properly belongs to the mother," who could teach little other than the virtues of spousal affection and reasonable motherhood. This was consistent with the conventional Restoration belief that daughters needed practical training in good housewifery and skilled mothering.[26]

Butler disagrees. She argues that, "Locke's thoughts on education clearly suggest a belief that men and women could be schooled in the use of reason." As such, "Women had intellectual potential which could be developed to a high level" and were potentially "capable of political activity."[27] Butler notes Locke's great respect for the intellect of his friend, Lady Damaris Cudworth Masham, and she may have noted Locke's praise for Queen Elizabeth. Still, this is questionable evidence. Locke had little faith in men's rationality and even less in women's intellectual powers. His deep concern for marriage and proper parenthood took priority over any conceivable interest in intellectual independence for women. His relationship with Lady Masham likely alerted him to the dangers of female intellectuals in that Masham's poetic forebears consistently attacked marriage. For example, Katherine Philips portrayed marriage in a way that Locke must have found subversive: "A married state affords but little ease / The best of husbands are so hard to please / This in wives' careful faces you may spell / Tho they dissemble their misfortunes well / A virgin state is crowned with much content / It's always happy as it's innocent / No blustering husbands to create your fears / No pangs of child birth to extort your tears / No children's cries to offend your ears / Few worldly crosses to distract your prayers / Thus are you freed from all the cares that do / Attend on matrimony and a husband too."[28] Finally, Locke's praise for the wisdom of Lady Masham and Queen Elizabeth meant little. "Throughout historical times," Gerda Lerner reminds us, "there have always been large loopholes for women of the elite classes, whose access to education was one of the major aspects of this class privilege."[29]

What meant a great deal was that female education in domesticity enabled men to invest greater trust in women than was once imaginable.

Husbands could admit their wives to greater freedom, equality, and friend-ship, entrust them with discretionary authority in the home, and rely on them to be restrained, skillful mothers to their heirs. To the extent that mothers participated in domesticity by schooling daughters in modesty and maternity to the applause of good society, men could indirectly ful-fill paternal obligations though they spent little time at home. Implicitly, and even inadvertently, Locke helped to pave the way for women's moral elevation into pious, educated, selfless mothers who wielded household authority that complemented fathers' breadwinning duties.

The price of women's moral elevation from Machiavelli's *Fortuna* to paragons of maternal virtue was high. Expectations that women should be full-time mothers made them increasingly reliant on male breadwinning. Lorenne Clark attributes such expectations to Locke, whose "argument is basically very simple. . . . Women who bear children are and must be de-pendent on men for their survival and for the survival of their offspring."[30] Yes, women might bring property into marriage and negotiate control over it, but most women had no property. And Locke assumed that fathers would bequeath family estates to sons, not daughters. Consequently, part of "the shame of the marriage contract" was that women were not free and equal parties to it; they bargained from a position of weakness and remained isolated in a domestic sphere "of privatized, irrational desire."[31]

This is not to say that women were passive victims of male domina-tion. The notion that women could be trusted to practice *private* maternal virtues was pregnant with *public* possibilities. Women's moral stewardship of the home would serve as a counterweight to men's selfish vices in the marketplace. Women's private virtues would authorize them to struggle against men's passionate excesses. Women's limited autonomy in the home would enable them to gain leverage over husbands and sons. And what be-came a widespread sense of women's moral superiority would legitimate female reform movements and political incursions. It would be another century before Mary Wollstonecraft parlayed maternal virtures into a jus-tification for women's guardianship of men's morals, social order, and political peace, but Locke and his contemporaries anticipated recognition of women's civic virtue.[32]

Women's Civic Virtue

The symbolic transformation of erratic females into reasonable mothers raised public expectations of women's virtue. Women would be praised as "angels of the house" but also held responsible for family-related failures. Meanwhile, men's migration to the marketplace increased the likelihood that male protection would become a protection racket.[33] Freed from the restraints of daily fatherhood but immersed in the pressures of a fluctuating economy, men were apt to vent repressed passions against their wives, engage in destructive social pastimes, and use breadwinning as an excuse for private and public vices. The emergence of separate spheres would make women more vulnerable to victimization and provide men a pretext to forgo reasonable fatherhood, civility, and citizenship.

Locke was vaguely aware that women could feel entrapped and victimized by their moral elevation. His long-term relationship with Lady Masham alerted him to the dis-ease of a privileged wife who disdained domesticity, claimed invalidism to avoid it, and sought meaning in the intellectual life. Lady Masham put her feelings into poetry: "And our weak sex I hope will then / disdain [the] stupid ignorance / which was at first imposed by men / their own high merits to enhance / and now pleads custom for pretence / to banish knowledge, wit, and sense."[34] Nonetheless, Locke remained largely insensitive to the potential costs of female domesticity. Nor did he imagine that women could assume historical agency to cushion or protest patriarchal subordination. He simply pleaded to Mrs. Clarke to be pardoned for "having more admired than considered your sex."[35] However, several of Locke's contemporaries did consider the plight of women. The Marquis of Halifax, for example, published a marital advice book in 1688 that counseled young wives on how to avoid victimization by their husbands.

Like Locke, Halifax supported the ideal of the voluntary, affectionate marriage. He explained to young women: "Your sex wants our reason for your conduct, and our strength for your protection; ours wants your gentleness to soften . . . us." Halifax noted that husbands' dependence on wives' softening affections was a subtle but significant source of female influence: "You have more strength in your looks, than we have in our law; and more power by your tears, than we have by our arguments." Ideally, wives' affections and piety would improve "the kindness and esteem" of good husbands. In reality, wives' moral influence was crucial when it came to living and dealing with irresponsible husbands.[36]

Halifax observed that women had to fine-tune their powers and use them with great skill to manage immoral men. When a husband was given to alcoholism, "the wife insensibly gets the right of governing . . . and that raises her character and credit in the family to a higher pitch than perhaps could be done under a sober husband." A governing wife was also needed in families where the husband was a weak, incompetent, and "dangerous beast." And in both instances, the wife "must be very dextrous, if when your husband shall resolve to be an ass, you do not take care he may be your ass." Wives' dexterity required the art of ruling without appearing to rule. Thus, Halifax advised, "Do like a wise minister to an easy prince; first give him the orders you afterwards receive from him."[37]

Halifax recognized that he was recruiting women to be man-tamers and family-savers. Women would have to sacrifice the joys promised by companionate marriages. Women would have to restrain their own affections and impulses, engineer a suitable environment for children, and use shrewdness to get their husbands to be, or at least appear to be, sober breadwinners and protectors. Could wives succeed? Halifax answered, "This power the world has lodged in you can hardly fail to restrain the severity of an ill husband." Would wives succeed? They had little choice. Separation and divorce were unlikely and also impractical because of women's economic dependence. However, Halifax provided women a positive incentive: "You are more than recompensed by having the honor of families in your keeping. The consideration so great a trust must give you makes full amends."[38]

In fact, there was more than honor at stake. The idea that virtuous wives within affectionate marriages could be man-tamers and family-savers made it possible to enrich justifications for women's education and reassess women's contributions to society. Mary Astell showed the way. Not only should women be educated to be reasonable mothers who give "form and season to the mind of the child as will show its good effects through all stages of his life" if only because "fathers find other business" and "have not such opportunities of observing a child's temper." But women should also be educated so that they could stir men "to be what they ought and not permit them to waste their time and abuse their faculties in the service of their irregular appetites and unreasonable desires." Astell intimated that women's moral guardianship of husbands and sons might be extended to "the largest sphere" and "the whole world." She concluded, "Perhaps the glory of reforming this prophane and profligate age is reserved for you ladies."[39]

Locke's liberal marriage contract and reasonable motherhood in combination with an emerging sense of women's historical agency prefigured an engendered version of civic virtue: *Women's patriotic duty was to reclaim fathers and sons from the immorality of the marketplace and renew in them the sense of family self-sacrifice and civility necessary for social order and political peace.* The performance of this duty was crucial to salvaging the sexual contract. If liberal patriarchs were to school wives in reasonable motherhood in answer to the woman question, virtuous matriarchs were to use their dexterity to domesticate husbands and sons to resolve the man question. Once this bargain was written into the habits of the hearts of men and women, it would become possible to imagine that both sexes could enjoy "individual" rights without causing grave disorders. Even the misogynist Montesquieu fancied that women could be "free by the laws and constrained by manners."[40]

Nonetheless, we should not overestimate the momentum toward women's engendered freedom. Theorists' dread of the female still compromised trust in women's virtues, while men's monopoly of power stood ready to enforce constraints on women's manners. There were times when the constraints were lifted, mostly when wartime necessity forced women to assert themselves to protect their families. With husbands off to war, wives assumed responsibility for breadwinning, child rearing, and defending family interests. Many women exhibited civic virtue by serving the nation as cheerleaders, fund-raisers, camp followers, spies, emissaries, nurses, and combatants. "During the [English] Civil Wars and after," observes Antonia Fraser, "it was axiomatic that women were enjoying a new kind of freedom and strength." But women's freedom was temporary: "An uneasy impression that women were 'stronger grown' was one of the many disquieting feelings produced in the masculine breast."[41] Free strong women threatened to subvert men's identity as "abler and stronger" partners and protectors.

Protection and Pacifism

That "stronger grown" women produced male disquiet highlighted the ambiguous relationship between families and war. Men who fought for the state abandoned their families and forced women to become protectors, but men who refused to go to war were readily accused of the cowardice and effeminacy that burst the bonds of masculinity and invited conquest. Recognizing that family life competed with patriotic loyalty, Plato solved the problem by abolishing families.[42] Locke hoped to avert conflict by limiting the prospects for English engagement in European wars.

Lockean fathers were life-givers responsible for siring and provisioning heirs. Lockean citizens were potential life-takers who participated in the polity's "right of making laws with penalties of death . . . and of employing the force of the community in the execution of such laws and in the defense of the commonwealth from foreign injury."[43] Locke appeared to settle any conflicts between life-giving and life-taking in favor of the state. Men who consented to the social contract resigned their right to enforce the law of nature and endowed the state with police powers. The consenter "has given a right to the commonwealth to employ his force for the execution of the judgments of the commonwealth whenever he shall be called to it." And the state's executive authority could determine when citizens would be called to arms, what Locke called "the power of war."[44] In effect, fathers ceded family self-protection to government and agreed to acquiesce to conscription.

Why would fathers consent to compulsory military service or heed the state's call to arms when their absence from home would upset domestic patriarchy, deprive families of breadwinners, expose wives and children to the uncertainties of war, and subordinate men's rights to the potentially corrupt rule of monarchs and military commanders? Locke's pacifist voice answered that men would rarely, if ever, be called on to abandon their families for war. If the origin of government was fathers uniting under a military commander for family self-defense, an early act of government was to seek peace and avoid combat. Thus, "several communities settled the bounds of their distinct territories" and "leagues . . . have been made between several states and kingdoms either expressly or tactily disowning all claim and right to the land in the others' possession." From the start,

Locke conjectured, state diplomacy resulted in "leagues and alliances" that contributed to peaceful international relations.[45]

Locke added that "a well-ordered trade" facilitated diplomacy. Men's labor added value to land and produced a surplus that would have been wasted were it not for the invention of money, which greased the wheels of trade. Money was a universal commodity that "men would take in exchange for the truly useful but perishable supports of life." Because men could produce and accumulate wealth "without injury to any one," exchange could be mutually beneficial and provide a foundation for peaceful trade among modern nations.[46] Locke noted that "trade . . . is a surer and shorter way to riches" than war. Further, "navigation and trade [are] more the interest of this kingdom than wars of conquest on the continent," in part, because commerce eliminated the need for costly expenditures on arms and armies.[47] Anticipating Montesquieu, Locke thought that trade profited everyone by encouraging productivity at home and peaceful ties abroad.

Locke's just-war theory also discouraged international violence. Legitimate violence was solely a matter of self-defense. A robber who put a knife to a man's throat and an aggressor nation that invaded another were both criminals under the law of nature. Their victims could do all that was necessary to protect themselves. But the victims could not go beyond self-protection by initiating further aggression or seeking a vengeance beyond reparations. Given England's superior defensive posture as an island nation, Locke mostly agreed with those Whigs who argued that a modest force composed of a citizen militia and small navy was sufficient for national self-defense.[48] Anything grander would promote injustice and butchery.

To reduce prospects for military engagement, Locke placed restrictions on armies and conquerors. He argued that soldiers owed absolute obedience to their officers but also enjoined officers from profiting from their rank: "Neither the sergeant that could command a soldier to march up to the mouth of a cannon or stand in a breach where he is almost sure to perish can command the soldier to give him one penny of his money; nor the general that can condemn him to death for deserting his post or for not obeying the most desperate orders can yet, with all his absolute power of life and death, dispose of one farthing of that soldier's estate or seize one jot of his goods."[49] In addition, Locke insisted that conquerors gained power over the lives of enemy soldiers but not over the enemy's civilian population or property. Conquerors could demand reparations limited by "the right of the innocent wife and children" to survive. If there was not sufficient wealth for both reparations and family subsistence, "preferable title" went to family members "who are in danger of perishing without it."[50] Thus, Locke hoped to take the profit out of war, depriving professional officers and standing armies of the material incentives for prosecuting it.

One can interpret the compulsory military service written into Locke's social contract as an abstract obligation suited to the exceptional occasion. For most of their lives, men could play the part of liberal patriarchs and rights-bearing individuals while their governors protected family property, practiced diplomacy, fostered trade, and discouraged war. Men would not be called away from their families and family property except in the most dire circumstances. In general, fathers' and sons' participation in national security would entail no more than periodic if not irregular attendance at a local militia muster. Nonetheless, Locke implicitly suggested that men's abstract obligation served three concrete functions: it discouraged invasions, reinforced bonds of masculinity, and promoted civic virtue.

Locke noted that citizens' martial fortitude made a nation appear dangerous to potential enemies while the absence of overt martial courage invited external aggression. He explained, "Debauchery sinks the courage of men. When dissoluteness has eaten out the sense of true honor, I think it impossible to find an instance of any nation . . . who ever kept their credit in arms or made themselves redoubtable among their neighbors after corruption had once broke through and dissolved the restraint of discipline."[51] Men were thus motivated to cultivate courage and honor, resist dissoluteness and corruption, maintain discipline and credit in arms, and broadcast a reputation for redoubtability, both in anticipation of actual military service and in an effort to avoid it. Following this logic, Locke advised fathers to teach sons to secure a "reputation of being brave and stout."[52] His message was that men who prepared for war would help to preserve the peace.

Moreover, Locke equated skill in the martial arts with the "manliness" that equipped individuals for "the warfare of life."[53] Those who heeded the mystique of martial masculinity were more likely to be disciplined fathers, sober producers, and good citizens. Those able to show courage in the face of danger were more likely to exercise self-restraint over their passions, budget their affections, and fulfill their family obligations. Those with a strong sense of martial honor were more likely to care for and protect reputations for fortitude and civility. Those who attended an occasional militia muster gave public testimony to their willingness to sacrifice their lives for the community good—without actually having to leave their family and put patriotism to the test. Ultimately, Locke's pacifism explained how to keep peace between families and the state, reinforce intergenerational male bonding, and provide men an undemanding, risk-free path to civic virtue.

However, Locke's pacifism was never more than partial. He could argue that boys should be taught martial courage to make them better men and also "an abhorrence of *killing*" to make "the world . . . much quieter and better natured than it is."[54] But he also recognized that diplomacy and trade often failed to produce peace, while breaches in the rules of war regularly made peacemaking problematic. Nations existed in a state of nature and agreed to no neutral arbiter to resolve their disputes and enforce international law. Peace was always precarious, and conflicts between men's family duties and military obligations could not always be avoided.

Families and War

Some men disregarded natural law and positive law; most preferred their own interests; and all feared unjust aggression. Locke advised individuals and nations to cultivate a psychology of fear. They should assume that men who overstepped the bounds of civility intended treachery. Locke argued that a man could kill a thief "who has not in the least hurt him" because there was "no reason to suppose that he who would take away my liberty would not, when he had me in his power, take away everything else."[55] Men reduced uncertainty by counting on others' immorality.

This was especially the case in foreign relations where men harbored little trust and appreciable "apprehensions of others."[56] The bonds of civility did not extend across national borders. Locke recognized no international social contract or global government, because nations had good reason to fear each other.[57] In the spirit of fear, Locke endowed his executive authority with nearly unchecked "federative" power over foreign policy, which, he noted, was "much less capable to be directed by antecedent, standing, positive laws . . . and so must be left to the prudence and wisdom of those whose hands it is in to be managed for the public good."[58] While not being explicit, Locke seemed to suggest that political prudence dictated the understanding that fathers would go to war to protect their families but would rebel against corrupt governors who recklessly endangered their families.

Recall that Locke attributed to men one instinct more powerful than self-preservation: the preservation of their offspring. He added, "When their young stand in need of it, the timorous become valiant."[59] Fathers' desire to preserve their families was a function of religion, biology, and self-interest. Their obligation to provision and defend their families was written into the marriage contract and supported by public norms of masculinity. The male bonds that united fathers would likely inspire a sense of mutual trust and national identification that urged men to link family good with state security. And because they were fathers-in-training, young males were also apt to take to heart Locke's notion that it was a man's "indispensible duty to do all the service he can to his country."[60] When men define themselves as family protectors, observes Judith Stiehm, they are able "to do (and justify) things they would not otherwise do," such as sacrificing their individual rights and demonstrating an untapped ferocity against enemies.[61]

As such, fathers and sons would heed the call to arms, submit to military discipline, and risk their lives if they believed that martial self-sacrifice was necessary to protect their families. That meant, first, that men had to be persuaded that a real peril to their families existed. Second, they needed to believe that governors and commanders would manage war in ways consistent with family protection. The best evidence of actual family peril and the defensive nature of war was that males were called to serve in militia units situated near their homes rather than required to subordinate themselves to a mobile standing army.[62] Should an executive be foolish enough to exceed his authority, for example, by prosecuting an unjust war across the sea, men's memory of past betrayals, combined with their provisional consent, would likely produce a legitimation crisis manifested in draft resistance and desertion. At the extreme, men's "appeal to heaven" could acquire subversive meaning. Richard Ashcraft notes that Locke's right to revolution was not intended to be an empty shell.[63] Rather, it was consistent with the republican notion that an armed citizenry was the best defense against government corruption and tyranny. As such, wise political leaders would try to win men's "hearts and minds," in part, by responding to familial concerns before issuing a call to arms.

How much Locke agreed with the republican analysis of local militia against the standing army is ambiguous because he wrote very little on the topic. Nonetheless, his political theory readily accommodated the idea that militia service was an important pillar of men's civic virtue. In peacetime, it offered fathers and sons an accessible forum for limited participation and reinforced their self-image as family protectors, promoted the mystique of martial masculinity, fostered private virtues associated with self-restraint and sobriety, and provided occasions for ritual exercises in masculinity and patriotism. In wartime, the militia mediated relations between families and the state by involving citizens in an organization constituted to defend families against external invasion and internal tyranny. Perhaps one reason that Locke wrote little about local militia was that he was more concerned with colonial expansion abroad.

Colonial Expansion

Locke made a sharp distinction between conquest and colonization. Conquest concerned victory against a modern nation–state with cultivated land, a monied economy, and a sovereign political power. It was what European nations did to each other. Colonization involved encounters between modern nation–states and premodern societies. It occurred when industrious Europeans migrated to a "wasteland," mixed their labor with it, enclosed it as private property, and put it under the jurisdiction of their government. "In the beginning all the world was America" and, Locke added, "There are still great tracts of ground to be found which . . . lie waste, and are more than the people who dwell on it do or can make use of, and so still lie in common."[64] In theory, then, colonization entailed Europeans appropriating the commons by migration, settlement, and productivity.

Locke was aware that encounters between European nations and premodern societies often resulted in violence. He attributed most of the conflict to "the heads and leaders of the church, moved by avarice and insatiable desire of dominion, making use of the immoderate ambition of magistrates and the credulous superstition of the giddy multitude." It was not Christian "friendship" or "kindness" that prompted European soldiers to "persecute, torment, destroy, and kill other men upon the pretense of religion." Rather, it was intolerance born of passion, ambition, and ignorance that drove them to unjust aggression. Locke prescribed two remedies. First, "Whosoever will list himself under the banner of Christ must . . . make war upon his own lusts and vices." Second, Christians should emulate the "Prince of Peace, who sent out His soldiers to the subduing of nations, and gathering them into His church, not armed with the sword or other instruments of force, but prepared with the Gospel of peace and with the exemplary holiness of their conversation." [65] Legitimate religious expansion required spreading the word, not wielding the sword.

Economic expansion was another matter. Locke more or less assumed that Europeans were fated to spread private property, money, and commerce across the globe to increase humankind's productivity, foster exchange of useful goods, and propagate the species. Ideally, economic imperialism would be peaceful. European settlers who enclosed wasteland would not compete with indigenous inhabitants because the latter had more land than they could or did use. Locke noted that occupying such "vacant places" as America would not "prejudice the rest of mankind or give them reason to complain or think themselves injured by this . . . encroachment." Also, industrious colonists potentially raised the local standard of living. Colonists would produce "greater plenty of the conveniences of life" which could benefit the "needy and wretched inhabitants," for example, of "the wild woods and uncultivated waste of America." [66] Still, it is not apparent that Locke was convinced that colonization would be entirely peaceful. In *The Fundamental Constitutions of Caroline*, he and Shaftesbury required colonists to bear arms, presumably against hostile Indians.

Locke might have foreseen several problems. One was that colonists' efforts at diplomacy, trade, and conversation with indigenous peoples were likely to fail. Lockean men harbored a psychology of fear that intensified apprehensions of outsiders. The likely course for colonists was to assume hostilities and take up arms against premodern peoples. Given men's passions, armed colonists could develop a frontier mentality that incited random acts of violence and caused disorders within settlements as well as war with indigenous inhabitants. Another predictable problem was that European nations would eventually compete for colonies. English settlers would square off against French settlers and struggle over jurisdictions. In both instances, colonists would develop a stake in posting a standing army to maintain order, fend off indigenous peoples, and defeat competing European powers. Many Whigs anticipated these problems and resisted colonial expansion. Locke showed no such concern. He believed that the benefits of colonies outweighed the costs, apparently because he considered economic prosperity the key to domestic peace and national security.

Colonization provided indigent, discontented, and youthful Englishmen access to abundant land, the possibility of becoming reasonable fathers and breadwinners, and even the potential to accumulate estates that could be bequeathed to heirs. On the other hand, the failure to acquire colonies was likely to endanger England. If other European powers invested in colonies as sources of abundance, England would find itself at a military disadvantage. Its neighbors could "maintain a greater force," "tempt away our people by greater wages to serve them by land or sea," "command the markets and thereby break our trade," and "ingross naval and warlike stores, and thereby endanger us." Thus, Richard Cox's analysis of Locke's writings on national security concludes that Locke was convinced that "economic and military power are the only effective bulwarks against external threats." [67]

Would English imperialism compromise the value of liberty at home? Locke's later writings showed little fear of regular armies or the corruption associated with them. For example, he advised that idle, indigent young men be put "on his majesty's ships . . . where they shall serve three years under strict discipline . . . and be punished as deserters if they go on shore without leave." [68] The implication was that a mobile standing military would not imperil English liberties by quartering soldiers in citizens' homes, setting profligate young soldiers loose in the towns, or providing the crown with an instrument of domestic oppression, because regular sailors and soldiers would be garrisoned at sea or abroad. Nor would Englishmen have to fear exploitation through taxation, because a mobile standing army would facilitate the colonization that produced economic abundance. Also, the military provided a partial answer to the youth question. Youth who failed to demonstrate economic sobriety, social civility, and good citizenship could be impressed into military service where they would be exposed to martial discipline, lessons in masculinity, and, conceivably, an education in civic virtue that prepared them to become responsible men and free citizens.

Would imperialism compromise liberty abroad? Arguing that England should refuse to allow Irish woolen manufacturing "to come in any way in competition with, or so much as threaten, that trade so necessary to the subsistence of England," Locke essentially wrote Irishmen out of the social contract and voided their claim to natural rights and national independence. Similarly, his disapproval of indigenous Americans who wasted the land, in tandem with his approval of American slavery, implied that he voided any Native American and African claims to rights or autonomy.[69] That Locke was a nativist, if not a racist, is clear. Still, the logic of Locke's liberalism was to link nativism to liberty. English colonizers would exercise affectionate authority, backed by force, over Irishmen, Native Americans, and Africans (as well as women and youth), so that "childlike" peoples could eventually learn the virtues that reconciled individual rights and public good. The English would be liberal patriarchs not only to Ireland and America but also to the world.

In summary, Locke's liberalism laid the groundwork for the legitimation, incorporation, and perpetuation of republican militarism. Fathers and sons would voluntarily assume the role of warriors to protect their families. They would protect the peace by honoring the masculine fortitude, martial skill, and civic virtue associated with local militia. They would also consent to actual military service, temporarily sacrificing rights and submitting to military discipline to defend their families against invaders and thereby secure public good. Conceivably, citizens would support a mobile standing army that absorbed and disciplined corrupt youth, founded and defended profitable colonies, and spread the "blessings" of English virtue and liberty across the globe.

Engendered Civic Virtue

Locke believed that liberal patriarchy within families was a powerful restraint on men's individualism, a source of men's sobriety, and a stimulus to the intergenerational male bonding that constituted civil society. It was a partial guarantee that men would exercise their rights without fostering chaos or causing class conflict. Still, Locke recognized the shortcomings of fathers and anticipated the time when they would leave their families for the marketplace. He limited men's political participation and justified government by liberal patriarchs who would engineer the consent of the governed, regulate men's passions, reinforce their sobriety, and teach them some civic virtue. Lockean liberalism was simultaneously an argument for more democracy and elite restraints on it.

Locke pioneered a liberal marriage contract that justified liberal patriarchy in the home but also legitimated an unprecedented degree of freedom and equality for women within families. He drew a family blueprint that recognized women's private virtues and implicitly abetted protofeminists who would link motherhood to women's civic virtue. However, Locke's liberal marriage contract was not a protofeminist document. Women might be virtuous wives who drove home men's stake in responsible fatherhood or republican mothers who taught sons to be good citizens; but women could not claim individual rights without society suffering serious repercussions. Lockean liberalism elevated women's virtue but affirmed their duty to be subordinate and self-sacrificing.

Finally, Locke promised pacifism to reconcile men's loyalty to families and consent to the state only to deliver an imperialism that recognized Englishman as liberal patriarchs to the world. Fathers and sons who participated in the cult of martial masculinity reaffirmed their self-image as family protectors and practiced patriotic self-sacrifice in preparation for occasions when they would be called on to suspend their rights and defend their families against aggressors and tyrants. Poor men and young men without much patrimony or civility could affirm their masculinity by serving in a mobile standing army and by founding colonies that promised abundance at home, new opportunities abroad, and even the chance to spread the Protestant ethic to non-European peoples. Lockean liberalism invited men to pursue peace, prepare for war, and redefine militarism as a legitimate defense against premodern waste and self-indulgence.

The driving force of Lockean liberalism was always a calculus of fear and trust. Were men, women, and youth to be more feared for their destructive passions than trusted for their familial fidelity to engendered versions of self-restraint and civic virtue? The most optimistic message that one can extract from Locke's liberalism of fear was a hope that traditional church and state authority could be replaced by a complex of civic virtues that prompted men, women, and youth to act *as if* they were rational enough to contribute voluntarily to public good with no more than the gentle guidance of affectionate, liberal patriarchs who ruled families, constituted civil society, and assumed national leadership. The firmer the cultural consensus linking gender to civic virtue, the greater the likelihood that adult males' individualism could be reconciled with public order.

Locke's legacy to America was more complex than either Louis Hartz or Gordon Wood imagines. Hartz's Lockean consensus included agreement on individual rights to life, liberty, and property, but those rights were reserved for adult males whose self-restraint and civic virtue were derived from fatherhood and masculinity, refined by self-sacrificing wives, reinforced in politics, and perhaps trained and tested by military service. Devoted mothers and exemplary warriors, along with fathers and father figures, each committed to civic virtue in her or his own way, were the unsung heroes who transform Horatio Alger's unruly boys into trustworthy men, neighbors, and citizens. Wood's Lockean science of politics involved institutional mechanisms to neutralize men's passions and resolve their conflicts, but Locke's science also encompassed liberal patriarchy as a source of male self-restraint, female subordination, and young men's complicity in state violence in the name of public good. In sum, Lockean liberalism incorporated significant aspects of republicanism, and the mix was clearly manifested in eighteenth- and nineteenth-century American discourses on gender and politics.

Part Three
Engendered Virtue

The only dead the Spartans "named"—their names were inscribed on tombstones—were men who had died in war and women who had succumbed in childbirth. . . . In death, a kind of symmetry of honor was summoned for those who have not crossed but instead fulfilled their culture's honored callings.

—Jean Bethke Elshtain

The rhetoric of liberal individualism in America beckoned the company of republican civic virtue to restrain men's selfishness, women's treachery, and young men's passions. Each generation hosted critics who worried that men's excessive individualism and materialism threatened to destroy family life, the bonds of society, public order, and national security. Each generation recalled images of Lockean fatherhood, political patriarchy, civic fraternity, companionate marriage, and the youthful struggle for manhood to redeem men's civic virtue and reduce women's vices. Middle America's Lockean consensus was that individualism wed to individual self-sacrifice for family, community, and nation promoted peace and prosperity.

Americans adopted an ideology that rejected traditional patriarchal authority but constantly sought liberal versions of it. They searched for father figures to order the family and unify the nation and for fraternities that resisted fragmentation and factionalism. Their liberalism of fear prompted them to recognize women's relative autonomy in families in exchange for women's willingness to tame men's vices and tend to civic virtue. Their liberalism of fear also motivated them to urge youth to cultivate martial virtue, submit to military discipline, and even risk their lives in war to achieve manhood, earn full citizenship, and safeguard the nation. America had a revolution every twenty years, one in which liberal patriarchs challenged men, women, and youth to revive the engendered virtue of revolutionary ancestors.

Part Three explores middle America's adaptation of Locke's liberalism in the eighteenth and nineteenth centuries. It traces the evolution of "the other liberal tradition" from colonialism to its climax during World War I, when America honored fathers and politicians who called for martial virtue, mothers and moralists who relinquished sons to military service, and young men who gave up their rights and lives in the cause of nationalism and imperialism.

7   In Search of Fathers

The Constitution set up a national authority, far from the work and daily lives of most Americans, to compensate for the experienced social weakness of the leading families. The natural aristocracy supported the Constitution "to defend the worthy against the licentious." It fell back upon that fatherhood supported by the state . . . which characterized colonial rule.
—Michael Rogin [1]

A combination of republicanism and liberalism marked the culture and politics of early America. Colonial fathers demonstrated civic virtue by taking up arms against tyranny but also deserted their families to prosecute the Revolution. The Sons of Liberty staged a successful filial rebellion to secure individual and political rights, but the Founding Fathers reestablished political authority to check individuals' tendency to abuse their rights. The Framers of the U.S. Constitution established formal limits on governmental authority, but citizens' informal deference to leading families and national leaders ensured a powerful state. For the next two centuries, American men both resisted political authority and relied on government prerogative to secure individual restraint, family welfare, social order, domestic peace, and national prosperity.

John Locke's political theory brought a measure of consistency to these ambiguities. Americans adopted Locke's presumption that "individuals" were fathers who sacrificed for their families, became temperate members of society, and practiced good citizenship. Ideally, the paternal self-sacrifice that mixed authority and affection generated filial attachment to masculine fortitude and civility to contribute to intergenerational continuity in a rapidly changing nation. In turn, liberal patriarchy in the home served as a source, foundation, and model for liberal patriarchy in politics. "Nursing fathers" like Washington, Jackson, Lincoln, and Roosevelt asserted political prerogative in the name of public good. Welfare reformers and domestic relations judges assumed patriarchal responsibility for fostering family stability, proper child rearing, social civility, and patriotism. As fears of men's licentiousness grew in the nineteenth century, the search for reasonable fathers and father figures became ever more desperate.

Paternal Self-Sacrifice

The ideal of paternal self-sacrifice is a constant theme in American family history. In the colonial era, fathers' daily employment required suppression of excessive passions and individual interests so that they could exercise fortitude against uncertainties and adversities that threatened their families. Fighting temptation was a religious obligation. Resisting idleness, greed, and self-indulgence was essential to family provisioning. And sober stewardship was fathers' main contribution to a seamless patriarchalism that linked family to society to state. Underlying the American ideal of paternal self-sacrifice was the Lockean belief that men generally sought symbolic immortality by devoting themselves to reasonable fatherhood.

Puritans certainly thought that men's quest for immortality drove them to self-sacrifice. Their Protestant God enjoined men to marry and produce legitimate offspring, not to emulate priestly chastity or honor a Catholic cult of virginity. Like women, men were considered lustful creatures whose passions were positive virtues if restricted to monogamous marriage and sublimated into managerial responsibility for the spiritual good of children who "came into the world 'stained' with sin." Indeed, men's salvation, community standing, and symbolic immortality were closely connected to their ability to rear proper sons. As John Demos notes, "Sons were seen as continuing a man's accomplishments, indeed his very character, into the future. Thus would a successful son reflect credit on his father—the credit of a 'good name' or 'good repute.'" Or as one Puritan moralist put it, "Natural fathers [are] willing to run all hazards to preserve [offspring and] to promote their welfare."[2]

The stakes were high, and so were the chances for failure. Fathers who doted on their sons were guilty of self-love and pride as well as the "effeminate" vice of overindulgence. The Reverend John Robinson argued that grandfathers were especially prone to this form of narcissism: "Grandfathers are more affectionate towards their children's children than to their immediates as seeing themselves further propagated in them, and by their means proceeding on to a further degree of eternity, which all desire naturally, if not in themselves, yet in their posterity. . . . Children brought up with their grandfathers . . . seldom do well, but are usually corrupted by their too great indulgence." Fathers were equally prone to child neglect and abuse. They sometimes ignored their sons and misguided them by setting poor examples, with "the sins of the fathers being found in the sons" and "drunkards, fornicators, and thieves . . . naturally reproduc[ing] themselves." Many failed to distinguish discipline from abuse. Stern corporal punishment was acceptable; maiming or permanently injuring youth was not. Popular manuals detailed the proper blend of "affections and duties, affection energizing duty, duty controlling affection," but fathers often strayed from the ideal. Thus, the 1641 Massachusetts *Body of Liberties* warned against child abuse, and neighbors, ministers, and magistrates punished it.[3]

Even where Puritan influence was absent, fatherhood and immortality were still knotted together. Colonial Americans inherited what Jay Fliegelman calls "the fundamental truth of Lockean pedagogy . . . [that] the parent who compels obedience by his parental example will be immortalized in his child, and that child though orphaned will never be parentless."[4] Popular literature suggested that reasonable fatherhood had great importance and fatherhood was sometimes considered men's highest calling. However, the best evidence of men's devotion to the paternal ideal may be their testamentary practices. Fathers consistently exhibited "dynastic" ambitions to ensure the survival and prosperity of their biological line.

A recent study concludes, "Colonial America produced an inheritance system designed to keep the family firm going for at least a generation." Between 85 and 90 percent of testators were male heads of household who owned mostly farmland, buildings, and personal property. They usually bequeathed a double share of property to eldest sons with the expectation (if not requirement) that the primary heir would buy out his brothers or work with them to keep the estate intact. Where land was cheap and abundant, younger sons often received more than a single share, enabling them to create new branches of the family firm. By contrast, testators provided for wives' and daughters' subsistence by making sons responsible for their ongoing welfare while leaving females modest shares of personal property.[5]

Men's testamentary behavior changed in the nineteenth century, but their dynastic ambitions did not. Fathers increasingly bequeathed liquid assets rather than land; sons and daughters received more nearly equal shares; and women eventually won independent property rights. These trends signified an adjustment in dynastic strategies as corporate family farming gave way to the modern market economy. Affluent men relied more on investment capital as the major source of family longevity. They sired fewer children and provided them more even shares, hinting at a diversification strategy that depended more on younger sons and sons-in-law to perpetuate family estates. In the fluctuating marketplace, wives' newfound property rights functioned to protect a portion of family assets from husbands' creditors, thus providing family heirs a degree of economic security. This pattern indicated that fathers were willing to put away tradition to perpetuate their line.[6]

Middle-class fathers' strategies aimed at ensuring that sons would prosper in the emerging white-collar world. Mary Ryan points out that "the making of the middle-class son entailed [family] effort, planning, and sacrifice." Farmers, artisans, and shopkeepers faced the individuating force of the marketplace and "small-business men . . . were particularly hard-pressed to put their progeny on a sound economic footing."[7] Middle-class fathers cooperated in reduced intercourse and coitus interruptus to limit family size.[8] New child-rearing ideals urged parents to devote more time to fewer children to ensure that sons internalized middle-class dispositions and skills. Fathers worked to generate small surpluses, mothers took in boarders, and daughters took on temporary jobs to free young men from labor and to finance their education for business and professions. In short, middle-class fathers sacrificed sexual fulfillment, labor, and status as sole family breadwinners to secure their sons' future. Thus, "the vaunted autonomy and egotism of the nineteenth-century male was not a monument to self-reliance [but] was conceived, cultivated, pampered, and protected within a revitalized American home." [9]

Immigrant and working-class fathers were also to pay a high price: they sacrificed authority over daughters to improve the lot of sons only to lose sons' respect. Immigrant fathers allowed daughters to work in factories to subsidize brothers' mobility. However, working daughters acquired a new sense of autonomy that freed them from paternal domination and invited them to test their independence in the dance halls, nickelodeons, and amusement parks that catered to the "new woman" of the late nineteenth century. Fathers who were rewarded by sons' rise into the middle class paid a surtax. One of "the hidden injuries" of upward mobility was that sons' successes attested to their fathers' backwardness and thereby produced a cultural generation gap. Nonetheless, paternal self-sacrifice remained routine.[10]

The persistence of the ideal and practice of paternal self-sacrifice in a nation that honored individualism and in an economy that individuated men is in part explained by the widespread belief that reasonable fatherhood restrained individual excesses, eased class distinctions, and provided most men with a stake in the future. The family man was likely to be a good neighbor and citizen who strengthened "the ligaments of society." [11]

The Family Man

Colonial administrators wanted settlers to marry to ensure that they settled down. For example, Sir Edwin Sandys attempted to lure English women to the colonies with matrimonial incentives. He "reasoned that the presence of women in Virginia 'would make the men more settled.'" Other colonial officials encouraged marriage by offering men additional property. And to make sure that women acquired husbands, "the Maryland legislature in 1634 introduced a bill threatening to repossess land from women who did not marry within seven years of receiving it." Also, colonial laws encouraged bachelors and spinsters to marry and widowed people to remarry.[12]

The emphasis on marriage was based on the assumption that family life subdued men's passions. Leaders wanted to contain men's lusts within monogamous marriage, or as a popular guide to reproductive lore put it, "nature has implanted in every creature a mutual desire of copulation for the increase and propagation of its kind." Most colonies enacted penalties to deter men from sex outside of marriage. Meanwhile, popular pressures urged family men to be exemplary ministers and magistrates in the home, represent community norms, and school subordinates in self-restraint. One seventeenth-century minister explained, "A family is a little church and a little commonwealth . . . whereby trial may be made of such as are fit for any place of authority, or of subjection, in church or commonwealth." [13] Thus, family men ruled the hearth and assumed the complex obligations of the family exemplar, community liaison, and political participant.

Family men had primary responsibility for breadwinning. Nancy Cott writes, "Marriage was seen as a relationship in which the husband agreed to provide food, clothing, and shelter for his wife, and she agreed to return frugal management and obedient service. To 'act like a man' meant to support one's wife." Colonial family life was framed by the English common-law tradition of "coverture" that gave husbands legal control of family property but also the legal duty of family provision, industry, thrift, and honesty. Men prone to idleness, deceit, luxury, and lawlessness risked their families' economic future as well as their own masculinity and social standing. Colonial culture and law intended that breadwinning responsibilities would encourage men to labor and "that fear of leaving behind penniless widows and children would dissuade men from crime." [14] Thus, he who failed "to act like a man" could expect pressure and punishment, even loss of custody of his children. One can hardly think of a harsher penalty. Fatherhood was so essential to American men's identity, aspirations, and standing that paternal custody rights received legal preference beyond the mid-nineteenth century. [15]

The family man was also thought the stuff of citizenship. During the Constitutional debates, for example, George Mason suggested that a husband and father, like a freeholder, might be qualified for suffrage because he had a long-term stake in social order and public good: "Does nothing beside property mark a permanent attachment? Ought the merchant, the married man, the parent of a number of children whose fortunes are to be pursued in their own [country] be viewed as suspicious characters and unworthy to be trusted with the common rights of their fellow citizens?" [16] In the early national period, democratic radicalism and diminishing community oversight gave rise to fears of subversive individualism; but the fears were eased somewhat by a general belief "that individual rights did have limits and that the [patriarchal] family was the natural place to establish them." [17] Thus, responsible family men were viewed as bulwarks against disorder as well as patriots for public good.

Plantation owners certainly thought that the family man was the most reliable slave. Thomas Jefferson believed that keeping slave families intact reduced male absenteeism and the discord that came with separations. Herbert Gutman notes that the slave economy did not demand intact families but "maintenance of labor discipline did." Owners considered married male slaves more restrained and obedient because they had to protect wives and children. While such slaves could develop a "pride of assertiveness" that reached "fearful proportions" when they tried to protect their families from owners' abuse, this danger was limited by masters' ability to punish or sell offenders. After Emancipation, Southern whites redoubled their support for black marriages based on "the prevailing belief that marriage civilized and controlled the brutish nature of all people." [18]

The social disorders produced by nineteenth-century urbanization and industrialization reinforced national reliance on the family man as a pacifying force. He would restrain his passions and dutifully "man" the workbenches, shops, factories, and offices where he would be subject to further discipline by large-scale industries and routinized bureaucracies. In 1829, the *New York Post* counseled, "The only way to make husbands sober and industrious was to keep women dependent on them." Married men with dependents were driven into the labor market and exposed to lessons aimed at what Anne Norton calls "unity in obedience to authority." Employers saw the "man of family" as a reliable employee and gave him preference in hiring, while bankers thought him a trustworthy risk and gave him preference in obtaining credit. And magazines advised enterprising young men, "If you are in business, get married, for the married man has his mind fixed on his business and his family and is more likely of success." [19]

German sociologist Werner Sombart was impressed by the pacifying effect that marriage had on American men and politics. Reflecting that "all socialist utopias came to nothing on roast beef and apple pie," Sombart added that American workers' relative prosperity and devotion to family life insulated them from radicalism. He calculated that American workers spent more of their income on family needs and less on personal vices such as alcohol than their German counterparts. Thus, Americans' family loyalties kept them from despairing of misfortunes and urged them to invest hope in their children's future. The Industrial Workers of the World essentially agreed with this analysis. The Wobblies argued that the family man was a poor recruit for class struggle; and they harbored great "contempt for the docile family man in contrast to the single man who was willing to fight."[20]

Early twentieth-century progressives, who feared that the poor, labor militants, immigrants, Catholics, and the lower classes with high birth rates were overwhelming the dominant order, looked to the family man and middle-class marital sobriety as a cure for subversion. Edward Bok of the *Ladies' Home Journal* encouraged readers to celebrate and promote mainstream matrimony, arguing that "if young men got married they would be more likely to get and hold a respectable job because any 'true woman would demand it.'" Ellen Richards, a leading figure in the domestic sciences, urged middle-class women to get their husbands more involved in family life, assume the responsibilities of home ownership and careers, resist profligacy and consumption, and raise virtuous sons able to assume the mantle of Anglo-Saxon citizenship so that "the nonimmigrant middle class, the family, and society [could] avoid the dangers of socialism, the communal pleasures of immigrants and workers, and the debilitating luxuries of new-found wealth." Or as Theodore Roosevelt succinctly stated, "No man can be a good citizen who is not a good husband and a good father."[21]

In sum, Americans concerned with reconciling individualism and social order saw the family man as a force for stability amidst flux. A patriotic warrior against *Fortuna*, he preserved the family foundations of social and political order by restraining his own passions, joining the work force and submitting to its discipline, respecting the law, and voicing the cause of public good against cultural and political radicals. He inherited individual rights but, more important, he passed the test of patriarchal self-sacrifice, social responsibility, and political sobriety. Consequently, he could be partly trusted to exercise individual rights and practice civic virtue without exciting America's liberalism of fear. That trust was reinforced by the perception that the family man transcended not only the "effeminate" vices of womanhood but also the subversion associated with bachelorhood.

Subversive Bachelorhood

Men's duty to marry was expressed by a Virginian who wrote, in 1779, "No man who had health, youth, and vigor on his side can when arrived to the age of manhood do without a woman."[22] Conversely, the man who did without a woman was suspect. Could he be trusted to restrain his passions or practice sober citizenship? Was he effeminate? Did he suffer from what the medical professionals would call inversion and what elites called subversion? Americans attached an enduring stigma to bachelorhood and thereby fostered a powerful, informal incentive for men to marry and stay married. Barbara Ehrenreich writes: "The ultimate reason why a man would not just 'walk out the door' was the taint of homosexuality which was likely to follow him."[23]

Early Americans believed that bachelorhood was unnatural and corrupt. Single men were selfish if not perverse for refusing to fulfill their manly duty to propagate the species and provision the new generation. Replaying Restoration fears of bachelors, colonists condemned unmarried men for their ostensible licentiousness: bachelors were notorious for siring bastards and refusing responsibility for them. Thus, colonial magistrates sought to establish paternity and force fathers to assume financial responsibility for illegitimate children lest bastards become town charges. Some colonies enacted sanctions against bachelorhood. For example, "Connecticut imposed a fine of one pound for each week a bachelor lived on his own while in Maryland the taxes on bachelors were almost punitive." Most towns "denied single persons the right to live alone without town approval"; local laws sometimes "required bachelors, spinsters, and other unmarried persons to live within an established household"; and local judges occasionally fined "single persons and couples living apart . . . for evading their civic responsibilities." Officials and unofficial overseers of morality felt that "people without ties lacked someone . . . to hold them within the bounds of order, and otherwise posed problems for social stability."[24]

Perhaps the starkest contrast to the family man was he who would later be labeled a "homosexual." Colonists believed that such a person lived at the extremes of anarchic passion and aristocratic corruption. Male–male sex represented the "potential in the lustful nature of all men—or indeed a potential for disorder in the cosmos." It was *Fortuna* in drag. At the same time, sodomy was perceived as passion "against the order of nature," both evidence of sin and an affront to "the peace, government, and dignity of the state." John Winthrop observed that acts such as sodomy and buggery were "dreadful" because they "tended to the frustrating of the ordinance of marriage and the hindering [of] the generation of mankind." And colonial administrators made what they understood as unrestrained sexuality and sexual corruption punishable by penalties ranging from ostracism and incarceration to castration and death.[25]

Antibachelor laws disappeared more quickly than antisodomy laws, but the stigma against single men persisted. For instance, a magazine article of 1848 stated, "The unmarried man is looked upon with distrust. He has no abiding place, no anchor to hold him fast, but is a mere piece of floatwood on the great tide of time." An 1850 novel, *Reveries of a Bachelor*, explored men's ambiguous longing for the perfect marriage but also their fear that actual marriage entailed burdensome emotional and financial obligations. Antebellum novels and magazines recognized that men were tempted by bachelorhood precisely because it meant freedom without responsibility, but they also deemed it men's duty to resist temptation and ensure social order.[26]

Efforts to strengthen marriage and orthodox sex became more vigorous after the Civil War. Immigrants "became scapegoats for the sexual anxieties of the native-born" as nativists and moralists championed the "social purity" of Victorian marriages against a middle-class association of social and political subversion with polygamy, prostitution, obscenity, intemperance, voluntary motherhood, abortion, women's suffrage, and juvenile delinquency.[27] For many would-be saviors of society, the issue was whether men would assert their masculinity, reassume the reigns of domestic patriarchy, and bring men of doubtful masculinity as well as wives and children under control. Thus, Gilded Age idealists who demanded more democracy and political reform to solve the social problem were accused of being "namby-pamby, goody-goody gentlemen" who "sip cold tea." They were labeled eunuchs and effeminates who were "impotent sissies at best, sexual mutations at worst." Such verbal assaults signified an escalation and politicization of the war against individuals who appeared to be neither "authentic" family men nor "manly males."[28]

During "the Masculine Century" that spanned the reckless daring of

Jacksonian expansionists and the aggressive competition required by Social Darwinists, many cultural critics promoted the view that men's masculine mettle had to be tested and validated. By itself, marriage did not
certify masculinity. Failed husbands and fathers became "stock figures of
domestic novels and stories." Meanwhile, middle-class clerks and bureaucrats were linked to effeminate dependence rather than manly independence. New tests of masculinity demanded evidence of fortitude. Did men
sweep aside domestic sentimentality and effeminate morality? Could they
conquer nature? Did they have the savvy and willpower to outdo the
competition? Could they contribute to America's manifest destiny and
celebrate war? Did they induct their sons into Theodore Roosevelt's cult
of hypermasculinity?[29]

In time, the medical profession established a new litmus test for masculinity in studies that mixed the authority of science with the ideology of
God, family, and country to suggest that effeminate males were infected by
sexual inversion and political subversion. Men who were single, sentimen-
tal, and/or gay were defined as biological males whose unbridled passions
and inverted sexual appetites made them like women but more dreadful
because they held male power and prerogative. Sexologists made "homosexuality" a distinct social category and associated it with "the 'bestial'
sexual practices of the outcast poor and 'lower orders.'" They thereby
legitimated antihomosexual crusades in cities and also stiffened military
prohibitions against homosexuality, "which was seen as subversive of
discipline and hierarchy in the armed forces." Conversely, reformers, radicals, and militants considered political subversives were stigmatized as
unmanly because, it was argued, subversion was a manifestation of inversion.[30]

Gary Kinsman argues that "queer baiting" served an important historical function. Taboos against homosexuality reinforced the idea that
masculine men were heterosexual family men, aggressive competitors,
and hyperpatriots. Put in Lockean terms, Americans elevated fortitude
above civility as the key marker of trustworthiness and citizenship. Fortitude cut across class lines. Whereas civility was a stylized disposition of
the upper class, manly fortitude was accessible to all classes. It could be
demonstrated on the farm and frontier, in the labor market and marketplace, through disciplined ardor and military service, and then on the
playing fields of the organized sports that both democratized competition

and ritualized aggression "to strengthen and extend male bonds between classes."[31]

Male Bonding and Liberal Society

Jay Fliegelman describes family evolution and political rebellion in eighteenth-century America as an "antipatriarchal revolt"; Carl Degler argues that the antipatriarchal revolt continued in the nineteenth century when "the typical husband in the middle-class family was hardly the patriarchal father"; and John Diggins contends that, "having overthrown political authority in the Revolution, American liberalism would *never again* be able to accept it."[32] The implication is that patriarchal society evolved into contractual society as family fathers lost control of sons and political fathers were subjected to institutional restraints and citizen oversight. This interpretation has some validity, but it fails to distinguish Filmer's traditional patriarchalism, which Americans did challenge, from Locke's liberal patriarchy, which Americans adopted and refined.

Early American fatherhood was patriarchal in a Filmerian sense. "At the beginning of U.S. history," writes Anthony Rotundo, "the father was a towering figure . . . chief of production . . . the family's unquestioned ruler." Conventional wisdom was traditional wisdom: only men had meaningful control of their passions; women and children rarely avoided excess. Fathers were to rule family subordinates, showing exemplary self-control and little visible emotion. Ideally, they expressed "approval or disapproval in place of affection or anger"; they governed through "persuasion and sympathy," backed by the threat of corporal punishment; and they directed the domestic economy, sons' education, and children's marriages to perpetuate the family line. Paternal power was not absolute, only dominant, because individual fathers had to answer to community fathers, who assumed that "good order in the home, sustained by a program of discipline that was educative as well as corrective" avoided the domestic chaos that "inevitably reduced the commonwealth itself to chaos."[33]

Three factors helped to redefine patriarchal authority in America. First, the Protestant father was seen as an extension of church authority, but

Protestant theology ennobled individual conscience and invited criticism of fathers' priestly powers. Protestantism devalued Old Testament authority and stressed New Testament benevolence, enabling youth to equate paternal domination with papist tyranny.[34] Second, fathers' economic leverage abated. Colonies became densely populated and fathers had diminishing access to surplus land for their heirs. They could "no longer control their sons by promising the gift of a farm later in life." In Dedham, Massachusetts, for example, population growth, intensified land use, family dispersion, and intergenerational diversity eroded fathers' authority. Mobile youth "wanted what only total independence would recognize, the right to shape their own communities." Youth who left family farms in winter for work or schooling widened the distance between generations and enhanced filial autonomy.[35] Third, colonists challenged ancient patriarchalism as unjust and ineffective, in part because they were influenced by the paternal ideals of Locke's *Some Thoughts Concerning Education*, according to Fliegelman, "perhaps the most significant text of the Anglo-American Enlightenment." Locke's influence was manifested in pedagogical works and best-selling novels. Its message was that "force and imperiousness be surrendered in favor of guidance."[36]

Recall that Locke's theory of education aimed to liberalize rather than eliminate patriarchal authority. It elevated fathers' discretionary affection over coercion and relied on the judicious use of shame and disgrace tied to social norms of masculinity and concern for reputation to shape sons' character. Having internalized patriarchal norms, independent young men would voluntarily act out their fathers' teachings. Although Fliegelman sees Lockean education as antipatriarchal, he admits that its goal "was not so much to create autonomous individuals as individuals who . . . are made independent so that they may become social and ultimately more truly filial." Rogin adds that Lockean pedagogy justified "paternal authority" and also "meshed with the structure of the colonial political order [wherein] leading families dominated . . . [and] colonial society promoted 'natural' deferential authority."[37]

Growing filial independence made the case for liberal patriarchy more compelling. The freedom of young men in nineteenth-century towns and cities regenerated the youth question. Thus, in 1828, Charles Loring Brace "warned that unattended ruffians would mature into a 'dangerous class' who might well threaten the value of property and the permanency of societal institutions." The solution proposed by Timothy Dwight in an 1835 manual for fathers was that "the child must be made his own disciplinarian." By extension, fathers who failed to mix authority and affection to instill proper self-discipline in sons were blameworthy for poverty, crime, and other social problems associated with youth. Commentators urged fathers to fulfill their obligation to eliminate the familial sources of "youthful misbehavior." [38]

It was no simple matter to adapt Lockean pedagogy to nineteenth-century America. Locke assumed that fathers managed boys' early education in a controlled home environment and that paternal lessons would be reinforced by public opinion. However, American diversity, dispersion, urbanization, and industrialization eroded fathers' control of the home environment and their ability to insulate sons from corrupting influences. John Demos notes that rapid change "reduced the capacity of the older generation to provide youth with leadership, with guidance, with assistance of traditional kinds" because youth confronted "new and difficult choices—to be made largely on their own." At best, fathers could instill some self-restraint, sobriety, fortitude, and civility while recognizing that youth would inevitably apply these norms with great latitude. The result was a reconceptualization of filial obedience that Fliegelman labels "the prodigal as pilgrim." [39] Model sons left home having internalized paternal norms but, rather than return on Lockean terms of equality and friendship, they adapted paternal priorities to the modern environment and explored new moral and economic terrain.

This refinement of Locke's liberal patriarchy suggested that intergenerational, male bonds could be stretched without snapping. The implicit agreement was that fathers would instill masculine virtues, gradually allow filial freedom, and then tolerate if not legitimate innovation. That way, fathers restrained young men's passions and conditioned their individualism but young men also claimed liberty and autonomy. A kindred agreement characterized American politics. The Founding Fathers, fearing that the Sons of Liberty were corrupted by rebellion at home and the French Revolution abroad, hoped to perpetuate patriarchal rule first by ratifying a U.S. Constitution that centralized political power and then by sealing off U.S. borders from corrupt European ideas with measures like the Alien and Sedition Acts (1798). They "turned from a discredited republican virtue to a strengthened paternal rule." [40] In the American environment, however, that patriarchal rule had to be liberalized, refined, and tied to conditional citizenship.

Patriarchal Rule and Conditional Citizenship

The U.S. Constitution contained bold prohibitions and institutional checks that deprived federal government of the *formal* authority to mold society. With the addition of the Bill of Rights, it established extensive individual rights and proclaimed citizens' freedom to work out the terms of social life. However, the Constitution did not abolish *informal* political powers. Deeply etched patterns of political hierarchy and presumptions in favor of political prerogative persisted. Indeed, for a people who had fought a revolution against tyranny, Americans demonstrated a remarkable willingness to defer to political patriarchs.

Consider the popular cult that honored George Washington. In the popular imagination, literature, and press, Washington was portrayed as self-sacrificing patriot and "nursing father" of a nation. He exemplified sobriety transcending passion and faction, masculine fortitude against adversity, immortality through courageous action, and civic virtue manifested in patriotic restraint. He was "father and friend of his country."[41] His legacy was virtuous leadership and his testament devotion to good citizenship—both liberal father and republican Cincinnatus. Washington's "charisma came from a prominently displayed eagerness to transcend itself; he gained power from his readiness to give it up." His influence had little to do with formal, legal authority. Like Locke's father, Washington asserted authority by attracting affection and respecting its limited, provisional nature. He made political authority safe and enduring. Like Cincinnatus, Washington was both citizen and patriot, a hero who was "heroically restrained." According to Garry Wills, the survival of the early republic was based on both popular equality and hero worship, the "social glue" that united Americans and produced popular deference to political leadership.[42]

A link between fatherhood and politics was apparent in early American consciousness. Fatherhood was the source of government. Noah Webster wrote, "All government originates in families, and if neglected there, it will hardly exist in society." Fatherhood was the basis for civil society. William Ellery Channing rejected Mary Wollstonecraft's feminism, arguing that her "principles respecting marriage would prove fatal to society, if they were reduced to practice"; and many Americans agreed that community fathers "who were property-owners . . . [should] rule also over lower-class males." Finally, fatherhood was a model for statesmanship. Early Americans upheld a "close identification of natural and political fathers," generally believing that the same union of limited authority, affection, masculinity, and reputation applied to family fathers and political leaders.[43]

In the colonial and early national periods, Americans often esteemed the patriarchs of leading families and supported men surnamed Adams, Livingston, Lee, Randolph, or Rutledge who dominated local political life.[44] In part, popular deference was paid to self-styled "natural aristocrats" who claimed superior self-restraint born of good breeding, classical education, and superior devotion to common good. Mason Weems, whose biography of Washington popularized the cult of Cincinnatus, joined others to project popular trust on to the leaders of the new republic. And that trust was magnified by constitutional prohibitions and institutional checks which promised to erase residual traces of political corruption and tyranny.

The debates of the 1790s followed by Jefferson's presidency quieted popular fears of national leadership. Federalists wanted "to remove politics from popular influence and restore the august majesty of government," curing social disorders with megadoses of elite prerogative. Jeffersonians disputed government "as the noblest activity" for the few and "celebrated the informal, voluntary political life open to all." Jefferson's presidency settled the debate. He invigorated the virtues of national leadership, or, as Rogin notes, "Jefferson defeated the Federalists, but he called upon their ghosts." Simultaneously, he wrapped political prerogative in the language of popular virtue and rights, anticipating democratic progress. But Jefferson was not an ideal liberal patriarch. Political leadership based on democratic rhetoric would not attract enduring consent until it was fortified by the bonds of public affection. Andrew Jackson recognized this and "infused politics with regenerated paternal authority."[45]

Jackson and the Jacksonians craved public affection. Thus, they endowed farmers and frontiersmen with divine grace and natural wisdom; they applauded the common man's natural fortitude, and praised America's amateur militiamen for defeating British professionals at New Orleans; they honored Americans' raw virtue and natural liberty as sources of national prosperity; and they parlayed the citizens' native genius into a populist bulwark against distinctions of birth, breeding, and education to foster an ideology of equal opportunity and political equality. In effect, the Jacksonians stripped Jeffersonian democracy of its elitist accent and intellectual trappings to solicit popular acclaim for what amounted to a powerful national leadership that claimed to rule for the people.

Powerful leadership was thought necessary because Jacksonian faith in the natural man was actually quite limited. Individuals who failed to tame nature suffered *Fortuna*'s whims and savagery, for example, in the murderous barbarism that Jackson attributed to the Creek Indians. They needed political help. Individuals who succeeded in taming the wilderness, pioneering civilization, and exploiting opportunity proved dangerous: they respected no law outside themselves, indulged their material urges, and imperiled the bonds of society. They needed restraint. "The problem the Americans faced," writes John William Ward, "was to reject savage nature, as embodied by the Indians, and decadent civilization, as embodied by Europe." [46] The solution was to fine-tune liberal patriarchy in politics.

Andrew Jackson was packaged as "nature's nobleman," a common but noble man. His image was that of an ordinary farmer and frontiersman, entrepreneur and soldier, friend to the people and one of them—quite the opposite of a cold, Eastern intellectual like John Quincy Adams. But the image-makers also portrayed him as a nobler version of the common man, the citizen with extraordinary instinct, will, experience, and civic virtue that marked him as the common man's leader. The challenge was to sustain a tension between the common and noble, the ordinary and extraordinary, the citizen and statesmen by tugging on American heartstrings. Jackson's affection for his mother and wife and his alleged love of children and Indians were publicized to demonstrate familial compassion and nursing leadership. His attachment to the land and devotion to the nation were proclaimed to make him into a second American Cincinnatus, the ordinary citizen called "from the plough to direct the destinies of his country." This blend of democracy and nobility refined by compassion and patriotism was an effective justification for presidential prerogative. Jackson acted "and let the legal rationalization catch up with the deed." His actions ran afoul of the Constitution but his use of prerogative won popular applause. Opponents criticized him for being a "military chieftain," but with little effect.[47]

The Jacksonian formula for legitimating patriarchal prerogative in politics reflected and reinforced the conditional character of American citizenship. The rhetoric of Jacksonian democracy resounded with echoes of Lockean masculinity rendered as freedom and equality, self-sacrifice and struggle, industry and fortitude, and conquest, expansion, and nationalism in the cause of extending the geography of white men's freedom. The *authentic* citizen was not simply the rights-bearing individual and family father but the man of manifest destiny who spoke with informal authority born of manifest masculinity. Moreover, the practice of Jacksonian patriarchy revealed an ongoing Lockean liberalism of fear that constricted the boundaries of citizenship. Engineered public affection provided leaders with a reservoir of trust that enabled them to disregard law, extend prerogative, and propel society to its national destiny in spite of common men's tendency toward effeminate cowardice and self-indulgence. The authentic citizen was not so much the rational voter or political participant as the loyal son and tested patriot who identified with political fathers, internalized their vision, and applauded their initiative. Ultimately, Locke's understanding that men's liberal rights and limited participation strengthened the bonds between political fathers and filial citizens gave substance to Jackson's presupposition that America was a national family.

The National Family

Louis Hartz argues that a crucial historical moment in American liberalism occurred in 1840 when the Whigs appropriated Jacksonian rhetoric for William Henry Harrison's presidential campaign. Hartz writes: "We think of the Whigs in the age of Harrison as stealing the egalitarian thunder of the Democrats, but actually they . . . transformed it. For if they gave up Hamilton's hatred of the people, they retained his grandiose capitalist dream, and this they combined with the Jeffersonian concept of equal opportunity. The result was to electrify the democratic individual with a passion for great achievement and to produce a personality type that was . . . the hero of Horatio Alger."[48] Did elites give up their liberalism of fear and support a familial consensus against claims to political hierarchy and prerogative? Or did they join patriarchal politics to liberalism?

The answer became evident when Jackson's national family was rent by civil war. Anne Norton argues that the North entered the conflict harboring traditional fears that men's passions threatened to destroy civil society. By mid-century, this liberalism of fear had been exacerbated by rising materialism, industrialism, and factionalism and also a persisting Puritanic belief that Southern planters were a sensuous, self-indulgent, and corrupt people.[49] When the Union came apart in 1861, Abraham Lincoln donned the mantle of the liberal patriarch in two senses. First, he played the part of the stern but affectionate father who resanctified the national family, the civic virtue of filial sacrifice, and the redemption of the South's prodigal sons.[50] Second, Lincoln became the Jacksonian man of action who confronted *Fortuna* with little regard for formal restraints and legal niceties. He declared martial law, suspended *habeas corpus,* centralized military power, used soldiers to suppress dissent, and authorized generals such as Sherman and Grant to ignore international conventions and wage total war against enemy soldiers and civilians.

Norton suggests that Lincoln's disregard for formal restraints and civil rights constituted a "Filmerian reaction" to liberalism.[51] Not at all. Lincoln claimed divine assistance, not divine authority. He exercised Lockean prerogative, sometimes without law and sometimes against it, to secure what he considered the public good. In the process, he hoped to educate citizens in civic virtue, reminding them that self-sacrifice and moral redemption were the foundation for liberty, unity, and peace. And he certainly expected to win consent, if not at the time, then after the fact. Like Jackson, Lincoln understood that the victor would be celebrated.

Norton also argues that the South entered the war with a republican respect for nature and natural men, civil liberties and voluntarism, and decentralized government. Southern men cultivated rather than repressed their passions, and the Confederacy honored (white) men's rights by recognizing the authority of state legislatures and relying on local militia units to wage war. The implication is that Southern men rejected patriarchy for fraternity, echoing the Founders' antipatriarchal revolt.[52] Let me suggest that Norton exaggerates the cultural differences between North and

South. Patriarchalism was particularly strong in Southern families. Beginning in the colonial era, planters showed exceptionally strong dynastic ambitions, practicing primogeniture far longer than others. They also saw themselves as the fathers and masters of extended families that included women, slaves, and the lower classes.[53] And like Puritanic Northerners, Southerners also repressed their passions if only to provision and protect their families.

Gerald Linderman's social history of Civil War soldiering demonstrates that expediency drove both North and South to increasing reliance on political hierarchy and prerogative. The early war was "Courage's War," fought on both sides by volunteers in locally based units. Soldiers equated courage with manliness, viewed war as a test of courage, and deferred to officers who exemplified courage. Unit cohesion, discipline, and efficiency had little to do with rank, hierarchy, or formal codes of conduct.[54] The war outlasted courage, however, and new military strategies and technology unraveled soldiers' sense of willpower. As a result, both armies tightened discipline, resorted to conscription, rationalized hierarchy, and employed terror tactics. By 1864, blue and gray soldiering had become less a test of courage than forced submission to patriarchal prerogative.[55]

Was Civil War politics exceptional? Sheldon Wolin observes, "The Civil War and the constitutional crisis provoked by the challenge to national authority led to a renewed interest in the idea of the state."[56] If postbellum America temporarily eased regional conflict, it quickly found itself in the throes of racial, cultural, sexual, and economic conflict. Reconstruction raised the question of whether emancipated slaves could join the national family. Waves of immigrants condemned for papism, alcoholism, and high birth rates generated fears that middle America would be inundated. Postwar feminism heralded a battle of the sexes that would become a war of attrition. And early unions boasting republican virtues in the Jacksonian era gave rise to the militant unions and socialist militants seeking justice in the Gilded Age. Widespread doubts that the national family could survive domestic diversity and internecine conflict transformed the Civil War model of the union-saving patriarchal state into a permanent fixture of American political thought. The stage was set for scholar–statesmen Woodrow Wilson to applaud individual rights, devalue political participation, and demand a positive, progressive, patriarchal state to govern for the people's good. Before that could happen, however, American elites had to test an alternative means of social control.

Following Herbert Spencer and William Graham Sumner, Social Darwinists urged men to cultivate Jacksonian action, will, and self-reliance to conquer nature and succeed in the marketplace. But as business leaders' fear of excessive individualism grew, they began to promote a "cultural change of direction from uncontrolled expansiveness to retrenchment, from unbounded optimism to cynicism."[57] On the one hand, elites worried that discontented workers sowed disorders subversive of capitalism while governors all too often coddled the restless. On the other hand, elites seeded the growth of big business and bureaucracy and demanded disciplined employees amenable to scientific management. A possible solution to the problem of excessive individualism was to privatize liberal patriarchy, with owners playing the part of surrogate fathers to their corporate families.

The prototype of private patriarchy was built in the first American universities, where the administration and faculty saw themselves as substitute parents to students, but it was first tested on an industrial scale in New England textile mills, where paternalistic owners provided segregated dormitory homes for male and female workers, preached Christian morality, sponsored cultural uplift, and espoused traditional republican virtues. In theory, the authoritative but affectionate owners won workers' filial respect and loyalty. The mature model of private patriarchy was constructed in later company towns such as Pullman, Illinois, where George Pullman was the patriarch who provided his workers and their families with a city, housing, shops, jobs, and lessons in morality and citizenship. The owner who acted *in loco parentis* was aided by Robber Baron philosophers, like Andrew Carnegie, who affirmed doctrines of Christian stewardship, philanthropy, and moral reform to legitimate private patriarchy.[58]

Nonetheless, private patriarchy for the most part failed. Workers saw it as a transparent attempt to control, if not enslave, freeborn citizens; and they rebelled against it, both in the Lowell mills and the Pullman factory. When confronted by labor militancy, owners shed their fatherly image and hired private police forces to maintain labor discipline. As Locke had predicted, the ready use of corporal coercion invited rebellion. Confronted by mass strikes, owners sought access to state coercion. During the 1894 railroad strikes, for example, owners persuaded politicians to call into action 32,000 militiamen and 16,000 regular troops (two-thirds of the regular army).[59] The problem for business elites was that they could not claim the same affection and trust accessible to political fathers. If the sheer size of corporations made any affection between owners and workers difficult, the explicit element of economic self-interest heightened worker fears of tyranny. Moreover, private patriarchy lacked a convincing element of consent and participation that might have induced workers to identify with owners. Capitalists lacked the legitimacy of government officials who claimed electoral authority and the political prerogative to do public good.

To Do Public Good

In the nineteenth century, many social functions once associated with families were diverted to state institutions such as poorhouses, hospitals, orphanages, asylums, and prisons. Nativist fears of immigrants, Catholics, and workers, the middle-class search for marketable skills, and business desires for a disciplined work force generated a strong impetus toward state education. Lyman Beecher announced the challenge in this way: "The danger from the uneducated mind is augmented daily by the rapid influx of foreign immigrants unacquainted with our institutions, unaccustomed to self-government, inaccessible to education and easily accessible to prepossessions, and inveterate cruelty and intrigue, and easily embodied and wielded by sinister design." The evocative symbol that tied men's drinking to subversion was the working-class saloon where activists plotted unions and planned strikes. The remedy, said Horace Mann, was public schools where "we shall teach mankind to moderate their passions and develop their virtues."[60] Locke's idea that the state might assume responsibility for civic education was echoed in calls for public schooling and universal military training (which is discussed in Chapter 10) and also in America's evolving welfare policies and domestic relations law.

Colonial welfare policies were framed by municipal laws meant to ensure that fathers managed the proper provisioning and education of youth. Where fathers failed, children could be removed from their homes, placed with relatives or neighbors, or indentured to solid citizens who would teach them virtue. As the numbers of neglected, abandoned, abused, and uneducated youth increased, antebellum reformers argued that "outdoor relief" was inadequate and state action was necessary. Reformers pioneered state institutions meant to serve as patriarchal surrogates for paternal pedagogy. Public almshouses, orphanages, reformatories, houses of refuge, asylums, and penitentiaries were established to manage "rehabilitative regimens of order, industry, and proper family life." The goal of these state institutions was to transform corrupt youth into "practical men of business and good citizens in the middle class of society." Welfare administrators added that their institutions were "the chief, if not the last barrier between the proper citizen and the life of vice and crime, between the nation and rampant disorder."[61]

Public pressure to enhance state regulation of families that did not conform to Victorian ideals grew stronger after the Civil War. Temperance advocates, feminists, and social purity activists attacked corrupt husbands and fathers given to alcoholism, gambling, sexual abuse, whoring, obscenity, idleness, and self-indulgence. In general, they hoped that informal pressure and public embarrassment would be sufficient to rehabilitate men. But the limited success of such tactics persuaded many activists to rely on state regulation. Most dramatically, the 1880s witnessed the beginning of a two-decade legislative campaign to bring back the public whipping post as suitable punishment for corrupt men. Elizabeth Pleck observes, "the image that appealed to these legislators was that of the state as moral father punishing a brutish son-in-law." Or as President Theodore Roosevelt told Congress in 1904, "The wife-beater . . . is inadequately punished by imprisonment. . . . Some form of corporal punishment would be the most adequate way of meeting this crime."[62] However, just as use of military force against workers undermined private patriarchy, the use of corporal punishment against brutish males eroded the legitimacy of state supervision. The whipping post campaign failed.

What did succeed, however, was the notion that compassionate judges could and should serve as "public custodians of the family." The evolution of domestic relations law and the eventual establishment of family courts in late-nineteenth-century America pointed toward increasing judicial regulation of sexuality, courtship, marriage, parental and reproductive rights, child care, divorce, and custody disputes. Sociologist George Eliot

Howard articulated the rationale for such judicial oversight: "In no part of the whole range of human activity is there such imperative need of state interference and control as in the sphere of matrimonial relations. . . . The highest individual liberty can be secured only when it is subordinated to the highest social good." Michael Grossberg argues that domestic relations judges became "new kinds of patriarchs" who designated "troubled homes as diseased" and construed "the state and the helping professions as agents of therapy." Like Lockean patriarchs, the judges were "stern but just fathers," agents of "the state, as the protector and promoter of the peace and prosperity of organized society . . . interested in the proper education and maintenance of the child to the end that it may become a useful instead of vicious citizen."[63]

Strong class, ethnic, and racial prejudices propelled the drive toward public education, state regulation, and judicial patriarchy. Patrician and professional reformers certainly saw men's anarchic passions at the root of social vice but they also saw social vice magnified by the moral and cultural inferiority of the poor, immigrants, and minorities who did not understand or practice the self-sacrifice required by fatherhood and citizenship. In addition, the reformers regularly blamed "individualistic tendencies" for destroying families, corrupting youth, imperiling order, and subverting the national family. The "progressive" solution, they argued, was to mix public authority with professional expertise to enable the state to exercise patriarchal prerogative and do public good. Still, the rise of state patriarchy was more than a by-product of prejudices linked to elite efforts at social control. Linda Gordon notes that it was also a response to pleas, demands, and activism by women who suffered the consequences of men's vices.[64]

Between colonization and the twentieth century, the American search for fathers resulted in "the increasing depersonalization of patriarchal power."[65] Early American culture required men to become fathers who honored patriarchal obligations that tamed their own passions, forged bonds with other men, secured control of women, ensured sobriety and civic virtue in youth, and provided a measure of intergenerational continuity in a rapidly changing environment. While an emphasis on family fatherhood persisted in culture and law, elites' confidence in the subduing force of family fatherhood diminished. Men's devotion to fatherhood, self-restraint, masculine fortitude and civility, and civic virtue had difficulty withstanding the individuating force of the marketplace. Meanwhile, the social diversity and conflict that imperiled the national family generated the complex of forces that urged the state to assume impersonal, patriarchal responsibility to keep men to their family duties and also to serve as surrogate father. Theodore Roosevelt reminded Americans, "The life of duty, not the life of mere ease or mere pleasure, is the kind of life which makes the great man as it makes the great nation"; and then he promoted political prerogative and state patriarchy to rein in men's excessive individualism.[66]

Locke Revisited and Revised

In one sense, American history outperformed republican and liberal expectations. Caroline Robbins observes,

> In the constitutions of the several United States many of the ideas of the Real Whigs found practical expression. A supreme court, rotation in office, a separation of powers, and a complete independence . . . of church and state fulfilled many a so-called utopian dream. The endless opportunities of the New World brought about a considerable degree of social equality. . . . The democratical element in the state was much extended . . . [and] nearly all the other aspirations of the classical republicans . . . found a measure of fulfillment.[67]

In addition, Lockean civil and political rights were etched into the nation's founding, guaranteed by constitutional arrangements and amendments, and then enriched by the end to slavery, a free press, extended manhood suffrage, and expanded opportunities for citizen participation in politics. But formal limits on government authority and legal legitimation of individual rights did not eliminate patriarchalism. Instead, they contributed to the liberalization of patriarchy, first by enabling citizens to see the state as benign and then by inviting citizens' complicity in it.

The subtext of American history followed Locke's idea that men's desire for immortality compelled them to sacrifice for their families, restrain their passions, cultivate sobriety, and practice good citizenship. Fathers who taught their sons to internalize masculine norms assured intergenerational bonding despite the freedom and equality of independent, mobile sons. Family patriarchy was also a source, stimulus, and model for liberal patriarchy in politics. It was an organic foundation for civil society, an incentive for popular consent to liberal institutions, and a familiar prototype for heroically restrained leadership, presidential prerogative, and the state regulatory apparatus. Precisely because republican restraints circumscribed government authority and liberal rights invited limited citizen participation in politics, mainstream fears of state tyranny waned as the state's patriarchal power waxed.

All the while, this adaptation of Locke's liberal patriarchy to America was riddled with tensions magnified by rapid change. Family fathers who sacrificed for sons could not be certain that their legacies would be appropriate to fluctuating market conditions. Even prescient fathers who armed youth with manly predispositions suitable to a changing environment could not foresee the individual challenges and social conflicts on the horizon. Indeed, fathers intent on provisioning and protecting their families discovered that they would have to leave their families to fulfill their duties. Men who applauded powerful presidents periodically discovered that they had legitimated the power of freewheeling leaders who abused and denied rights. And men who supported state patriarchy sometimes suspected that they had tacitly consented to agencies that fostered men's dependence. America did not entertain much of an antipatriarchal revolt, but it did sustain traditional doubts of patriarchal authority that gave rise to what Rogin calls "paranoid images of paternal oppression" as well as efforts to improvise liberal fraternity.[68]

8   In Search of Fraternity

Support for liberal patriarchy as a constraint on individual excess was accompanied by doubts of its sufficiency. Men's absence from their homes made fatherhood a part-time employment and an economic specialty. The locus of masculinity shifted to the marketplace where, many feared, the forces of individualism, materialism, and competition invited the male self-indulgence and conflicts that threatened civility. Meanwhile, ongoing fears of political tyranny continued to compromise the bond between citizens and the state. Many Americans heeded Walt Whitman's dictum to resist much and obey little, provoking middle-class and elite apprehensions that most men were ungovernable. The defenders of social order still believed and invested in the pacifying powers of liberal patriarchy, but they also experimented with a fraternal ethic of mutual self-help, voluntary organization, and communal association to reconcile individualism and civic virtue.

Following Benjamin Franklin's example and advice, American men built civic organizations such as volunteer fire brigades and volunteer military companies that wed the joys of male friendship and fellowship to the bonds of public service and common good. Men who joined these groups freely assumed the responsibilities of membership, identified their individual and family interests with community well-being, and participated in attempts to improve the quality and prosperity of everyday life. Tocqueville was duly impressed by the energy that American men put into associations and the ways in which their participation gave them a stake in public good. However, Tocqueville failed to appreciate how much the rhetoric of liberal fraternity masked significant sources of fraternal discord. Group life in America was often instrumental and exclusive, motivated by passions and interests that eroded civility and a clannishness that exacerbated social tensions and violence. Early-twentieth-century thinkers tried to ease fraternal conflict, first by refining Madisonian pluralism and then by regulating it with an updated version of Hamiltonian statism.

Part-Time Fatherhood

Richard Vetterli and Gary Bryner argue that when the Founders "wed virtue and self-interest . . . a new republican philosophy emerged." The American adaptation stressed "voluntary self-restraint, a commitment to a moral social order, honesty and obedience to law, benevolence, and a willingness to respect the unwritten norms of social life." The main sources of voluntary self-restraint were "family, school, [and] church." Ideally, restrained individuals pursued liberal self-interest, "properly understood," balancing personal liberty and public authority to ensure social peace.[2] The problem with this argument, however, is that American families, schools, and churches mostly reflected the gradual separation of virtue and the self-interest, however understood, associated with the rise of market capitalism. This problem was especially manifested in Americans' reconceptualization of fatherhood.

The colonial economy was built on a family capitalism in which husbands, wives, and children lived and worked together on the farm or in the shop. But a division of men's home life and work life was apparent by the Revolution and widespread by the Jacksonian era.[3] Domestic labor was replaced by factory production, and local bartering gave way to mass marketing. Farmers gave up subsistence agriculture for cash crops and became dependent on distant markets, banks, and transport companies, while land scarcity drove many fathers and sons to opportunities on the frontier or jobs in the city. Many married men went alone, and enterprising youth sought an economic foothold before establishing their own families. It is of signal import that vast numbers of men began a daily commute from their homes to separate workplaces.

The division of home and work life was an uneven process. Early capitalism made halting efforts to integrate families into factories. Wage laborers often lived and worked in family units. Some factories provided "the heads of these working households . . . some leeway in organizing and allocating the labor time of their kin." Industrial ownership was mostly a function of family economies. The first textile mills were "monuments to entrepreneurial kin networks" that aggregated resources to amass capital and labor for large-scale projects. Nonetheless, the ties between corporate families and industrial capitalism were steadily unraveled by the individuating forces of the urban marketplace.[4]

American men did not surrender family capitalism graciously or quietly. Northern farmers and artisans defended the old order by articulating classical republican virtues, such as freeholder independence, social cooperation, and animated community life. They tried to keep the new industrial order at bay by protesting against modern vices such as worker dependence, class conflict, and owner corruption. In addition, Southern planters defended a civic culture and sociology that honored the agrarian freeholder, the patriarchal family, and owner autonomy. They praised the virtuous Cavalier as an ideal father and citizen but attacked the malicious Yankee trader as a tyrant who commodified family life and politics. Much of this resistance was genuine, but some was ambivalent and self-serving. Artisans split over whether virtue inhered in craft autonomy or the prosperity promised by commerce. Patrician intellectuals defended the virtue of breeding over the materialistic mob and the *nouveaux riches*.[5] American men replayed old English debates regarding the relationship of virtue to commerce, but the fall of the republican freeholder was evident in men's commuting from home to jobs in new factories, emporia, and offices.

The fall of the freeholder engendered the rise of part-time fatherhood. "Now, for the first time," writes John Demos, "the central activity of fatherhood was sited outside one's immediate household." Commuter fathers had a reduced role in child rearing and filial education. They still "taught most of the lessons about the ethics of work, property, and money," issued warnings "against laziness, theft, extravagance," and served as the "ultimate disciplinarian." But part-time fathers also "stood outside the strongest currents of feeling that flowed between the generations in a family."[6] They were powerful visitors from outside, more apt to attract filial awe than affection. They issued orders and gave advice in the voice of distant authority because they devoted relatively little time to their families when becoming outside specialists in family breadwinning.

American practice did not quite mesh with Locke's reasonable fatherhood. Fathers' daily absence and emotional distance precluded effective management of praise and shame to form sons' characters. Their work life beyond the home made it difficult for fathers to be accessible exemplars of masculine fortitude and civility. And their practical advice, drawn from the business world, was likely to be received with some filial skepticism. Paternal wisdom was now based on abstractions culled from an environment distant from sons' immediate experience, reducing it to a cold rationalism apt to have minimal effect on boys' passions and prejudices. Also, fathers' immersion in city and business life weakened their credibility because, "The [business] world seemed deeply suspect from a moral standpoint. . . . The men who lived and worked in this environment were necessarily imperiled, and maleness itself seemed to carry a certain odor of contamination."[7] That odor was concentrated in the smell of alcohol, the symbol of intemperance that signified the idleness, immorality, and sensuality of men beyond the family hearth, the aggression and violence of bachelors on the frontier, and the ambition, greed, dishonesty, and deceit of men in the marketplace. As Peter Filene notes, nineteenth-century temperance crusaders essentially waged "a battle against men" outside the family circle.[8]

Commuter fathers faced a difficult situation. If they preached manly self-restraint at home while being tainted by vice outside it, they were vulnerable to filial suspicions of what Judith Shklar calls the master vice of modern liberalism: hypocrisy. We have already encountered this accusation in Diggins' argument that the Founding Fathers spoke the language of civic virtue but pursued the logic of possessive individualism.[9] However, if fathers downplayed virtue and initiated their sons into commerce, they faced two other problems. First, wives and mothers along with ministers and moralists could legitimately protest fathers' immorality and irresponsibility. Second, fathers gradually "lost the ability to teach work" to young men who confronted the rapidly changing dynamics of "trade, business, or the west." [10] Thus, liberal patriarchy suffered a lack of intergenerational continuity.

These problems were partly resolved by recasting the meaning of reasonable fatherhood. It was increasingly shorn of domestic duties. Mothers took greater responsibility for children's education so that fathers would be free to negotiate the marketplace and devise dynastic strategies for a dynamic economy. Men's dispensation from paternal pedagogy was reinforced by the emerging cult of the self-made man that honored the orphan—symbolic and actual—whose success was a function of sheer individual determination. If Andrew Jackson personified the entrepreneurial incarnation of the cult, a more sober version advised "that the way for a young person to move ahead was to leave the world of his parents and strike out on his own. . . . Getting *ahead* meant getting *away* from one's parents." [11]

The implications of part-time fatherhood and self-made youth for social order were potentially grave. The link between reasonable fatherhood and male self-restraint weakened. Stiehm explains that "men are probably more able [than women] to rationalize away [parental] obligations, especially if physically separated from the children." Part-time fathers did not surrender all family duties; rather, they focused on breadwinning. That meant that men could be less concerned with economic sobriety if only because their work and business were beyond their families' daily inspection. Indeed, the ethic of the self-made man, later wed to Social Darwinists' "tooth-and-claw version of natural selection," invited the younger generation to reject sobriety for an instrumental morality in which the appearance of virtue was more profitable than its practice. Eventually, masculine virtue itself was closely identified with "power, money, and status" justified by the "the common good" redefined as aggregate "public interest." [12] Certainly, some Americans sang hymns to possessive individualism, but many feared that undomesticated men and wild orphans posed a lethal threat to social order. They looked to church and state to redeem men from materialism.

Church and State Redemption

David Shi argues that "the simple life" and the virtue of economic moderation have been consistent, enduring threads running through American culture. He writes, "Americans remain ambivalent about the meaning of the good life, as they have since the seventeenth century. From colonial days, the image of America as a spiritual commonwealth and a republic of virtue has survived alongside the more tantalizing vision of America as a cornucopia of economic opportunities and consumer delights."[13] The Founders surely hoped that men's religious commitments would prevent individual liberty from running to avaricious license; and they favored the disestablishment of churches in the expectation that "virtue and religion would flourish in an ecology of freedom of conscience" and promote "unity, harmony, and cooperation in the American community."[14] But the Founders did not foresee that disestablished churches would underplay the vices of materialism when competing for congregants.

American Protestantism often overlooked possessive individualism. Revolutionary ministers who sought redemption from profligacy, luxury, and corruption were soon replaced by clergymen who devoted their time to "the Sunday School, the parlor, and the library, among women and those who flattered and resembled them." Preachers praised self-denial and frugality but mainly to audiences of women concerned with "family morals" and to new urban migrants seeking stability amid uncertainty. Piety was more personal and familial, "associated with feminine influence and disassociated from masculine activity." Women congregants took the lead in Jacksonian revivals and moral reforms, allying God to domesticity, motherhood, child rearing, and, later, the "social purity" movements that sought to inject Victorian morality into male manners.[15]

Simultaneously, Protestantism engendered a "manly" Christianity suited to the economic and political spheres. Jacksonians called on God and Providence to justify their conquest of nature, Indians, and the marketplace and to affirm their visions of nationalism and manifest destiny.[16] The ministry was also on hand to support abolitionists and anti-abolitionists, succor soldiers on both sides of the Civil War, and abet all classes party to industrial conflict. By the late nineteenth century, the image of "Christ as He-Man" surfaced as part of an effort to instill in young boys a Muscular

Christianity that would fortify them for manhood, the marketplace, and a world inhabited by threatening, heathen races.[17] In general, Protestantism was as likely to liberate men's acquisitive and aggressive impulses as resist them.

One consequence of Protestantism's adaptability was that it provided a theological foundation for social fragmentation, economic competition, and nativist violence in America. Denominational differences mirrored the segmentation of community life in that "churches, no longer made up of the whole community but only of the like-minded, became not so much pillars of public order as 'protected and withdrawn islands of piety.'" Sermons increasingly emphasized familial benevolence and service rather than authoritative commands to sacrifice for public good. To an extent, "Religion . . . [became] a place of love and acceptance in an otherwise harsh and competitive society."[18] Protestant love and acceptance sometimes reached beyond families but often stopped short of social tolerance. Churches promoted the idea that "the Protestant religion bottomed American republican institutions, and was an essential component of national character," thereby justifying nativist prejudices and brutality, in particular, against Irish Catholic immigrants.[19]

Churches also adapted to regional prejudices. Northern Protestants retained some rhetorical fidelity to Puritanic notions of law and covenant, spirituality, and self-denial. Many ministers continued to urge men to restrain acquisitiveness. Transcendental critics, Quakers, and other sects invoked the deity to attack avarice. Meanwhile, Boston Brahmins referred to spirituality and cultural refinement to condemn mass profligacy, and many politicians claimed the mantle of Protestant asceticism and republican simplicity to allege their opponents' corruption. The North's residual Puritanism helped it to legitimate attacks on the South, where Protestantism displayed what Anne Norton calls a "maternalist" tendency. Southern denominations often tied religious devotion to nature, family, and nurturance, not abstract precept or self-sacrifice. Thus, Northern critics could condemn Southerners as "irreligious, playful, indulgent in eating, drinking, and sex, passionate, and undisciplined"—and in great need of discipline.[20]

To the extent that paternal and religious education did not generate a sufficient, organic basis for social order, the main alternative was public schooling in civic virtue. Benjamin Rush, an early advocate of public education, feared that fathers and ministers could not be trusted to prepare boys for citizenship in the new republic. He planned a scheme for public education intended to augment if not replace family and church teachings. Rush argued that the schoolboy should certainly be taught "to love his family," but he should also learn "that he must forsake and even forget them when the welfare of his country requires it." Rush added provisions for inculcating precepts from the Gospels that encouraged self-restraint. Boys were to honor and practice "those degrees of humility, self-denial, and brotherly kindness that are directly opposed to the pride of monarchy and the pageantry of a court." And he insisted that schools give lessons in self-sacrifice and patriotism so that every American boy would know "that his life 'is not his own' when the safety of his country requires it." [21]

Rush's plea for public education followed from the widespread belief that civic virtue was essential to survival of the republic. He recalled the classical argument that "Every member of the community is interested in the propagation of virtue and knowledge in the state." Good schooling meant good citizenship. Particularly important, it would counteract the vice, greed, and corruption that seemed to spread after the Revolution. At all times, Rush wrote, "Man is naturally an ungovernable animal" who must practice self-denial if his neighbor is "to sleep with fewer bolts and locks to his doors." But especially after a revolution that freed men from traditional authority and invited acquisitiveness, it was mandatory that youth be insulated from the "company of every low-bred, drunken, unmoral character" and then "taught . . . industry and economy" to ensure that they "contribute to the wants and demands of that state." [22]

Here is a useful rule of thumb: The more American men claimed liberty and democracy, the louder the arguments for public schooling and state rehabilitation of men's morals. For example, Jacksonian reformers advocated the extension of men's civil and political rights but also warned that men's freedoms unleashed "terrible propensities" to social anarchy.[23] Thus, the reformers renewed old pleas for public education and pioneered new arguments for the state orphanages, asylums, and prisons that would redeem immoral boys and men. Later in the nineteenth century, middle-class concern about the integrity of families and urban decay gave rise to movements that attacked intemperance, supported purity, and spurred the growth of judicial patriarchy, government social agencies, and both punitive and protective legislation to restrain men's base impulses.[24] American reformers consistently launched campaigns for voluntary self-restraint and informal community sanctions only to turn to state authority to teach, manage, and enforce public morals.

From the start, the state's ability to function as an *adequate* surrogate for Lockean fathers and Puritanic ministers was problematic. Locke believed that the most effective means to inculcate proper moral dispositions in boys and forge strong intergenerational bonds involved affection and trust augmented by appropriate public opinion. To be sure, promoters of public education and state rehabilitation spoke the language of family affection and solicited public support. In reality, however, they built impersonal, bureaucratic, and even militaristic public institutions that relied on "force and strict confinement to maintain order."[25] Also, American public opinion failed to provide unified reinforcement of lessons in humility, self-denial, and civic virtue. The cult of the self-made man contradicted humility and sobriety by elevating acquisitiveness and aggression; it also contradicted liberal patriarchy in politics because it "failed to attach men to new institutions with powerful emotional bonds."[26]

By the early twentieth century, state education and welfare institutions suffered the stigma of effeminacy. Middle-class women professionalized motherhood, filled the teaching ranks, created and ran social agencies, operated settlement houses, and lobbied for welfare reform. Meanwhile, the women's club and suffrage movements along with the rise of the career-minded "new woman" suggested that "the housekeepers of the world" were intent on building a "maternal commonwealth." Male critics warned against the feminization of America and the effeminization of boys. They expressed a strong desire to remasculinize society by "dislodging women from their monopoly over socialization."[27] Antifemale prejudices intensified by the equation of masculinity with self-reliance contributed to a devaluation (and underfunding) of state education and welfare institutions in America.

Filial Freedom and Fraternity

Part-time fatherhood, fragmented religion, and impersonal education made uncertain the transmission of virtue from one generation to the next. If foreign travelers thought the permissiveness of

American families was remarkable, American family-savers feared that filial freedom engendered too much youthful vice. The man question recurred in this form: Could filial freedom be the basis for a stable liberal society? Locke provided a clue in his argument that fathers should recognize adult sons' independence, equality, and friendship and that male bonding might promote cohesion in the fraternity called civil society. Many Americans favored filial freedom. Steven Mintz and Susan Kellogg observe, "Fathers increasingly were expected to acquiesce in the early independence of their sons, and child-rearing experts openly criticized those who persisted in meddling in their children's lives after they had grown up." [28] But adult applause was accompanied by common expectations that young men would demonstrate manly fortitude disciplined by civility to gain full standing in civil society.

Popular literature counseled fathers to inculcate in sons the virtue of manly "character" in the pursuit of a calling. This emphasis grew stronger as nineteenth-century refugees from family farms confronted the uncertainties of the frontier, city, and marketplace. Joe Dubbert states, "Guidebooks often depicted life as a 'great battle,' not only against external forces but against internal temptations of the flesh as well. Since every successful man needed to be armed with 'patience, fortitude, energy and intense thought,' he could never afford to indulge in alcohol or tobacco, which would weaken the perceptive powers of his manhood upon which he relied to capitalize on opportunity." [29] Horatio Alger's novels infused manly character with an added sense of religious devotion, moral restraint, and mutual concern. Ideally, American "men of character" sufficiently recognized, respected, and trusted one another to forge fraternal bonds that functioned as the organic basis of the liberal social order.

But a man's reputation for good character was never secure. It had to be tested continuously if the individual were to acquire and maintain fraternal standing. In Puritan communities, for example, elderly men were honored for past records of good character and good works. Ministers and magistrates praised them for their age, wisdom, experience, piety, and proximity to God. Nonetheless, older men's physical frailties made them suspect. In "The Four Ages of Man," Anne Bradstreet articulated the self-doubts of the older male: "My hands and arms, once strong, have lost their might / I cannot labor, nor can I fight / My comely legs, as nimble as the roe / Now stiff and numb, can hardly creep or go." The stigma attached to old age centered on men's "loss of capacities and skills." [30] Weak arms and feeble legs implied that elderly men no longer contributed to the farm economy or local militia. Like women and children, they were dependents, the protected rather than protectors. Their lack of manliness was symbolized by their intemperance. As Cotton Mather commented, "To see an old man reeling, spewing, stinking with the excesses of the tavern, 'tis too loathsome a thing to be mentioned without a very zealous detestation." [31]

In the nineteenth century, the test of manly character moved away from familial and community service to individual fortitude in confrontation with *Fortuna*. Young men needed to become skilled in new survival techniques. Pioneers on the frontier encountered disputed land titles, shady speculation schemes, and the violence endemic to a lawless, hostile environment. The more savvy frontiersmen engaged in mutual self-help. They created or joined fraternal associations such as the Masons; they forged "wilderness compacts" to achieve greater stability and predictability in property rights and personal safety. Similarly, streetwise urban migrants came together to enhance their chances to survive and thrive amid the fluctuations of market capitalism. Enterprising youth aspiring to middle-class status joined young men's associations that functioned as makeshift families and also forums for "perfecting their skills," making "informal business contacts," discussing "self-improvement," and enhancing "career prospects." [32] In general, mobile youth pioneered numerous self-help fraternities that exchanged traditional, familial bonds for modern contractual ones.

They also altered the meaning of masculinity to accommodate a growing generation gap. Demos writes, "Success was measured in terms of the distance from the starting point to the finish in any given life, and the starting point was the position of the father. Here lay an inducement to competition between the generations, powerful and pervasive—however covert— and uniquely American." [33] Fatherhood became associated with built-in obsolescence. Fathers still preached manly virtues, but sons adapted to an innovative market morality. Wilson Carey McWilliams summarizes the structural imperative driving young men's moral metamorphosis: "Under conditions of rapid change, the experience of parents rapidly becomes irrelevant as a guide for the young." [34]

The substance of masculinity became more fluid and materialistic. If traditional fathers stressed self-denial and self-sacrifice, their enterprising sons gravitated to a more aggressive and daring morality that might be described as the "Jacksonian mystique."[35] Achieving manhood involved the conquest of nature and the frontier, the subjugation of Indians and Mexicans, the struggle against old wealth and new competition. After the Civil War, the rhetoric of aggressive masculinity focused more explicitly on the market. "With its rapid expansion, its exploitative methods, its desperate competition, and its peremptory rejection of failure," writes Hofstadter, "postbellum America was like a vast caricature of the Darwinian struggle for existence and survival of the fittest."[36] As the frontier closed down and the international marketplace opened up at the century's end, the test of masculine fitness centered mostly on the individual's battle to overcome any and all obstacles to accumulation, production, commerce, and prosperity.

Unquestionably, Hartz and Diggins are correct when they argue that America provided fertile soil for the growth of possessive individualism. What they forget, however, is that American men rarely went into economic battle alone. Individual competitors quickly learned that it was useful and usually necessary to seek allies and make alliances if they were to prosper in capitalist America. Fraternal alliances proliferated in nineteenth-century America. Millions of men bonded together in self-help groups, ethnic and religious associations, service clubs and social clubs, civic organizations and veterans groups, brotherhoods and trade unions, professional societies, and also business partnerships, combinations, and trusts. McWilliams reminds us that the Gilded Age "was a great age of fraternal orders."[37]

The search for fraternal alliances was especially difficult for a mobile, diversified population. As traditional sources of mutual trust eroded, men had to cultivate the rhetoric of male bravado and demonstrate manly self-reliance to develop the reputation necessary to win other men's trust. In many cases, the individual's willingness to engage in violence and his courage in seeking group goals proved to be an effective means "for testing one's friends and proving one's self."[38] But fraternal solidarity demanded more than aggressive individualism. Members had to discipline masculine ardor to fit in among fraternity brothers. Men had to submit to formal and informal codes of civility that harmonized members' relationships. Thus, fraternal rituals portrayed initiates as childlike and effeminate, took them through a series of ordeals that resulted in symbolic death and then symbolic rebirth, and ultimately validated their rebirth as true men and brothers. The result, states Mary Ann Clawson, was "institutionalized male solidarity."[39] And in the emerging corporate world, fraternal civility often depended on members' ability to submerge claims to individualism in recognition that "great management signified great prowess."[40]

Fraternal orders self-consciously fostered male bonding by reinforcing the rhetoric of masculinity while conditioning conventional relations among men. Fraternities provided their members some extra-familial space in which to cultivate male affection, friendship, loyalty, and solidarity. They articulated standards of honor and ethics that fostered greater mutual trust, secured strong alliances, ensured predictability among members, and promised action in behalf of both individual interest and public good while balancing members' claims to self-interest and fellowship. Freemasonry, for example, "affirmed the basic worth of productive activity" but also "attempted to check the growth of an unrestricted pursuit of individual self-interest."[41] Most fraternities joined manly character to collective discipline, and many routinized hierarchical relations by subjecting individuals to intricate bureaucratic imperatives. Efforts to strengthen male bonds were especially refined among middle-class professionals who participated in occupations and associations that claimed to reunite masculine virtues and commercial interests.

The Reunion of Virtue and Commerce

If most fraternities were predominantly middle class, the most sophisticated middle-class fraternities were occupational and associational organizations of "the professional-managerial class" that emerged in the 1880s and matured by World War I.[42] Scientists, engineers, technicians, physicians, lawyers, accountants, businessmen, writers and journalists, social workers, teachers, military officers, private managers and public administrators, and other "mental workers" filled new roles in the corporate economy and founded fraternities that promised to empower middle-class expertise to pursue public good. Professionals painted self-portraits that conveyed the image that they were dispassionate, self-sacrificing citizens dedicated to solving the nation's problems.

Meanwhile, their professional associations freed them from the taint of the marketplace while ensuring their advantage in it. Moreover, professional fraternities secured self-discipline within the middle class and legitimated social control of the lower classes, immigrants, and minorities as well as women.

The professionalization of municipal police forces in the early twentieth century is an excellent example of middle-class refinements of fraternity.[43] Progressive reformers hoped to eradicate notorious police corruption in cities by overhauling the culture and institutions of local state coercion. Police officers, they argued, should be hired for their sober characters and high intelligence, not their crude brutality or political connections. They should be trained in "police science," learning advanced techniques in crime prevention and enforcement specialization. They should dedicate themselves to obeying a professional code of ethics that elevated emotional detachment and objectivity above individual passion, prejudice, and interest. In addition, reformers wanted police departments to be centralized, rationalized, specialized, differentiated, and managed, stripped of frivolous functions, based on a meritocracy, and equipped with the latest technology in crime prevention and law enforcement. Reformers predicted that professionalization would result in greater discipline within police ranks and greater police efficiency in communities.

The class dimension of professionalization involved transforming police work from a job associated with working-class thugs and corrupt, ethnic politicians into a respectable middle-class career. Working-class applicants and officers would have to anticipate and conform to the rules and rituals of professional sobriety to get, keep, or advance in their careers. Educated middle-class men would move into the management ranks of police departments and oversee the conduct and continued education of rank-and-file officers. And all professional policemen would leave behind their individual, class, and ethnic differences to behave according to the inscribed and circumscribed professional norms articulated by fraternal police orders and journals and then enforced by police supervisors. Henceforth, police officers' primary loyalty would be to fellow professionals, not to individual or family interests, personal friends, or class and ethnic biases.

Police professionalization also had a gender dimension. It reflected and reinforced the next step in the evolution of masculinity. Professionalism disassociated manly fortitude from the sheer and reckless physical force, brute conquest, and aggression honored in the Jacksonian mystique, and also from the naked self-interest and greed that Social Darwinists praised as fitness. Instead, professionalism embedded masculinity in intelligence and intelligent restraint in the use of coercion. A professional policeman exercised rational self-discipline, demonstrated emotional detachment and objectivity, cultivated education and expertise, excelled at efficient problem solving, and relied on legal force only when other options failed. In Lockean terms, professionalism suggested that manly fortitude was respectable only if disciplined by civility; and state coercion was legitimate only as a last resort likely to win the consent of the governed.

Reformers' efforts to overcome the barriers to professionalization highlighted its promise as a form of fraternal bonding. One barrier was winning popular consent. Local police forces were often seen as standing armies, instruments of city bosses who built personal power by patronage, violence, and exorbitant taxes. Reformers had to persuade skeptics that the new professionals would be "peace" officers who fostered justice, harmony, and public good. August Vollmer articulated the challenge: "The public must drop its childish attitude of hostility and learn to appreciate this friendly, reassuring helpfulness, unceasing vigilance, and other services that the professionally trained policeman stands ready to give to all the people, high and low, rich and poor."[44] To educate the public to the advantages of police professionalism, reformers packaged trained officers as experts dedicated to eradicating corruption and brutality, public servants contributing to community cohesion and prosperity, and trustworthy friends to troubled youth, good families, local schools and churches, and civic organizations. Public education also had an experiential component. Some municipalities experimented with "Junior Police" programs that invited working-class youth to participate in police work; many police fraternal orders cooperated with community groups to cosponsor such patriotic activities as Fourth of July parades and Founders' Day picnics. Ideally, professional policemen joined the ranks of city fathers, expounding civic virtue and excelling at public problem solving.

Pleas for professionalism attracted considerable middle-class support. Professionalism promised middle-class men an opportunity to claim civic virtue and pursue self-interest simultaneously. Professional ethics stressed experts' contributions to clients, communities, and the nation. Thus, the police professional was a self-sacrificing patriot who risked life and limb for his community, a dedicated citizen who volunteered time and energy to enhance civic life. Likewise, the professional manager was a selfless expert who organized labor for productivity, enhanced opportunity, and national prosperity. Because middle-class professionals were ostensibly dedicated to public good, not individual avarice, they could be trusted by the public. And the main reason that professionals could avoid the stigma of self-ishness and greediness was that they relied on their fraternal associations to guarantee them substantial incomes. Professional societies legitimated expertise, supported professional autonomy, regulated supply and upped demand in professional markets, and promoted lofty salaries and benefits for members.

Professionalism also captured middle-class consent because it promoted a vision of a familiar, benign, and homogeneous, if not republican, social order. Professionalism "civilized" masculinity by attaching it to education, codes of ethics, and bureaucratic management. It universalized bourgeois sobriety by supporting equal opportunity for those individuals willing and able to shed individuality and adhere to standards of emotional detach-ment and scientific objectivity. It pledged practical solutions to social prob-lems and discord linked to poverty, cultural diversity, atrophied family life, and juvenile delinquency.[45] Professionalism in police work, criminology, and social work promised to make the nation safe for white middle-class families by making the virtues of advanced education a requirement for positions of informal and formal authority and then by persuading people that filial deference to professional authority was for their own good. In effect, all professions were sold as helping professions.

However, the potential of professionalism as a source of cross-cultural, cross-class, nationwide, fraternal bonding managed by a highly educated elite was partly betrayed by the practice of professional domination. To a degree, professionalization was a refined version of the social control of one class over others. Clearly, progressive reformers wanted to join police fraternities and city fathers to increase the efficiency of liberal patri-archy over those Vollmer considered "childish" citizens, a category that usually encompassed workers, ethnic enclaves, and minorities. But rather than win filial deference among these groups, professionalism often exac-erbated distrust between the police and local citizens because professional loyalties and specialization diminished officers' familiarity with and concern for neighborhood residents.[46] Related to this, the rise of professional management caused a loss of labor autonomy; the emergence of helping professions atrophied self-help traditions; and the empowerment of the American medical fraternity nearly destroyed female midwifery. Sometimes, the inroads of professions into private and public life solidified workers, neighbors, and women in opposition to what they perceived as patriarchal domination.[47]

Professional ethics also conflicted with older but enduring meanings of masculinity. In a corporate society managed by professionals, men's liberty and independence were compromised by bureaucratic imperatives that vitiated an abiding ethic of masculine willpower, self-discipline, and conquest. Thus, the growth of professional fraternities was accompanied by the rise of fraternities honoring hypermasculinity. Social fraternities once cast in the image of "the artisan as virtuous republican" gave rise to military branches linked to "concerns about social instability and perceptions of the need for both a military spirit and a military capacity." A variety of sports enthusiasts, educators, religious thinkers, and political officials called on men to recapture the heroic past, redeem themselves and their sons, organize a return to nature, competition, physical struggle, and "soldierly manhood" rather than to silently suffer the "effeminacy" of white-collar work.[48] The power of professionalism virtually assured the strength of the "Bull Moose mentality." This explains why modern professionals continue to develop programs to eliminate police brutality, middle-class wife and child abuse, and the traditional male romance with legal and illegal violence.[49]

Finally, professionals never quite avoided the taint of avarice. It was big corporations and big government that created the demand for professionals able to control and manage big bureaucracies and work forces. In part, professionalism was originally associated with elites' material interest in social pacification. Professional associations tried to put distance between corporate elites and their members only to foster group conflict. For instance, turn-of-the-century corporate philanthropists and college professors clashed over faculty autonomy in universities. And the American Society for Mechanical Engineers campaigned for conversion to the metric system only to confront overwhelming opposition from capitalists who had invested in English-calibrated machinery.[50] Professional fraternities wanted to be considered crusaders for public good against special interests, but they were sometimes seen as "fraternities of battle," contending factions engaged in self-serving competition.[51]

Fraternities of Battle

Americans have rarely considered accumulation of wealth as sinful or selfish in itself. Individuals who engaged in sober industry, sought familial comfort short of profligacy, and participated in community life were usually thought good citizens. Still, America's liberalism of fear declared that even good citizens were suspect. They too were impassioned, self-interested creatures whose claims to civic virtue often masked individual avarice. One way that men allayed suspicion was by submission to fraternal norms and reliance on fraternal leadership to reconcile virtue and commerce. Rather than permit individuals to make what could be construed as self-serving claims to civic virtue, for example, early labor and capital spawned fraternal orders that used republican rhetoric to translate members' interests into the language of public good.[52] But when contending fraternities claimed civic virtue and accused competitors of corruption, competitors responded in kind, and all sides suffered the stigma of collective selfishness, or factionalism.

McWilliams defines fraternity as a bond forged from men's common affections, shared values, toleration of tensions, and loyalty to society at large.[53] This definition accords with the aspirations of many Franklin-esque fraternities wherein individuals joined together for mutual education or community service. But it also suggests the brittleness of fraternal bonds in America. Was it likely that men would develop sufficient fraternal affection to overcome tensions inherent in the cult of the self-made man? The frontiersman who proclaimed independence and demonstrated strength through conquest was not likely to sustain enduring loyalty to his fellows when economic opportunity put him in competition with them. Rogin comments, "The fluid social conditions which called forth Masonic bonds also made them fragile. Masonic loyalty no more prevented conflict among brother Masons than family connections prevent conflict within a clan. . . . Land hunger and title conflict set friend against friend, brother against brother." Nor was the entrepreneur apt to sustain fraternal bonds with fellow businessmen when self-interest counseled fratricide. John D. Rockefeller explained, "The American Beauty rose can be produced in the splendor and fragrance which bring cheer to its beholder only by sacrificing the early buds which grow up around it. This is not an evil tendency in business. It is merely the working-out of a law of nature and a law of God." The capitalist norm was Andrew Carnegie declaring devotion to brotherhood while his "doctrine had little impact on his conduct." [54]

American fraternities were often exclusive, instrumental, and temporary associations organized to conquer an enemy and rationalize the conquest as civic virtue. Pioneers united to conquer nature, Indians, slaves, and Mexicans, justifying violence as a necessary way to Christianize heathens and open up the wilderness to industrious whites. Middle-class men joined educational, professional, and civic organizations to enhance their economic edge over competitors, ensure their autonomy against employers, and subdue lower-class disorders, all in the name of rationality, social harmony, and public good. And populist farmers and radical workers created fraternities to destroy the injustices of the old patrician caste and the new corporate establishment. In many instances, men participated in exclusionary, clannish enclaves built out of passionate racial, ethnic, religious, and nativist prejudices that justified ridding the nation of a self-destructive diversity that seemed to threaten moral goodness. These fraternities fostered mutual affection, shared interests, and internal tolerance among members, but they often organized and intensified hatred, conflict, and violence against nonmembers.

Fraternities had an ambiguous effect on politics. In one sense, passionate fraternal conflicts and efforts to legitimate competing values as manifestations of social loyalty and political justice encouraged a rich national dialogue over the meaning of civic virtue and public good. For example, consider the Anti-Renter Movement that occupied residents of New York's Hudson River Valley in the 1840s and 1850s. Long-standing tenants created mass organizations that engaged in guerrilla warfare, lobbying, and electioneering in an effort to gain title to land that was being appropriated and monopolized by landlords who, in turn, created counterorganizations. Descendents of Revolutionary soldiers, tenants argued that they were fulfilling the promise of their ancestors by exhibiting civic virtue in a struggle against landlords' aristocratic tyranny. Landlords made the case that stable property rights protected by law were the basis for public good. The state legislature eventually passed a compromise bill that provided relief for distressed tenants and raised taxes in a way that gave landlords an incentive to sell land to tenants at reasonable prices.[55] This was one of many instances when fraternal conflicts urged citizens and politicians to reassess and debate the common foundations of public life.

In another sense, fraternities offered an escape from politics. They sometimes functioned as surrogate families, so-called havens in a heartless world. Middle-class fraternal orders occasionally created an artificial "world of pure affection, a momentary place of romance" that offered like-minded men a momentary respite from competition and partisanship. They provided settings where men could escape individual, family, and citizen responsibilities, enjoy self-indulgence and male bravado, and find acceptance uncompromised by the fear of failure. Middle-class volunteer military companies were often bourgeois social clubs, "exclusive little societies" in which men played and paraded together, acted out aristocratic chivalry, and proclaimed patriotism without having to sacrifice for it. Cunliffe suggests that volunteer companies were "forerunners of the Elks, Red Men, Lions, and Rotarians."[56] Also, working-class taverns and fire companies as well as patrician private clubs were temporary shelters from the public life, though they could be drawn into partisanship in some circumstances.

The ambiguous relationship between fraternities and politics was especially evident in groups that forged solidarity through combat. Frontier violence, urban and ethnic riots, racial and regional confrontations, and various class conflicts were fraternal battles in which mutual reliance and self-sacrifice created powerful and sometimes enduring bonds. In effect, warfare was "the primary setting for the drama of male friendship."[57] And the Civil War was the greatest fraternal drama of the century. Young men joined with neighbors, left parochial communities, tested courage in battle, and developed deep loyalties to comrades and even respect for enemy soldiers. In war, they shed the selfishness of everyday life, learned the major issues of citizenship and nationhood, and exhibited lethal civic virtue.

But the Civil War experience also demonstrated why fraternities were a defective foundation for liberal politics. On both sides, soldiers failed to sustain fraternal bonds over the long haul. Group loyalty gave way to individual survivalism, mass desertions, conscription, public protests, and draconian discipline. If initial respect for adversaries and anticipation of postwar healing limited the scope of violence, men's passionate desire for survival and politicians' hunger for victory led to the brutal efficiency of total war tactics. In the war's aftermath, veterans' associations found it difficult to enlist members. Many ex-soldiers felt betrayed by the anarchic individualism of deserters, draft dodgers, and profiteers and also by the corrupt efficiency ethic manifested in total war tactics and reproduced in the postbellum "business pacifism" that portrayed war as barbarism and productivity as progress.[58] For the next decade, veterans and cultured society displayed a preference for social amnesia rather than civic engagement.

Indeed, the postwar efficiency ethic spread throughout national life to begin the process of subduing men's fraternal impulse. The efficiency ethic demanded that individuality and masculinity be subordinated to the new bureaucratic, corporate order. Men confronted huge, complex forces they could not hope to control. As always, they created fraternities in an effort to reclaim independence and manhood; but now, fraternities were as likely to accommodate as contest the efficiency ethic. Though populist farmers felt victimized by "innovations" justified by productivity, they were sufficiently ensnared in economic modernity that they "had great difficulty finding language that could convey their . . . disenchantment." And while organized labor often protested against managerial prerogatives aimed at efficiency, union leaders often "adopted an official posture of encouragement, accommodation and acceptance" of modern technique and organization.[59] Socialists also bought into the efficiency ethic. Edward Bellamy envisioned a streamlined industrial army organized by a socialist leadership, and Daniel De Leon thought the best way to beat capitalism was to organize a socialist vanguard that maximized workers' capacity to "storm the breastworks and capture the fort" of capitalism. If Eugene Debs was unique because he resisted the imperatives of martial hierarchy and strategy, the center of the Socialist Party accommodated hierarchical organization and leadership.[60]

The world we lost in the late nineteenth century was one where masculinity disciplined by fraternity bore the banner of civic virtue and stimulated discussion of public good. Lest we forget, it was also a world where men bonded into clannish enclaves, battled one another, justified bondage for outsiders, and often thrived on violence. Tocqueville was half right. Men's associational life did bind individuals to larger collectivities, but those collectivities reproduced on a larger scale the male passions and interests that subverted social order. The world we inherited in the early twentieth century was one where fraternity was feared because it meant factionalism and discord. American defenders of social order seemingly had two alternatives for subduing fraternal excesses. Minding Madison, they could recognize factionalism as reality, neutralize it, and institutionalize it as interest-group pluralism. Or, heeding Hamilton, they could rely on state authority to join factions to national destiny.

Pluralism and Statism

Between the Spanish-American War and World War I, the prospects for reconciling virtue and commerce seemed remote. National elites feared that America's self-interested, class-divided, ethnically diverse, materialistic men were unable to redeem themselves from selfishness or demonstrate sufficient civic virtue to restore social harmony and support the nation's international aspirations.[61] Still worse, individualism's excesses were magnified by fraternal factionalism. Organized farmers squared off against banks, railroads, and agribusiness, while militant workers confronted capitalism. The frontier, officially closed in 1890, was less a safety valve for men's discontents than an extended arena for class conflict as Wobbly miners and Western mineowners entered the fraternal fray. Even diehard defenders of capitalism began to realize that men's interests did not tame their passions. Hirschman writes, "The experience with capitalism had been such that the arguments about the benign effects of *le doux commerce* on human nature had totally changed . . . property was now seen as a wild, boundless, and revolutionary force."[62] Where were the sources of self-restraint and civic virtue that would moderate men's passions and interests, reforge social bonds, and foster national loyalty?

Some social scientists resurrected and refined James Madison's arguments for recognition, acceptance, and neutralization of factionalism. Arthur Bentley, Herbert Croly, and John Dewey explored ideas on group life to produce theories of pluralism that defined politics as a matter of organized interests seeking their own advantage.[63] The pluralist standpoint had significant implications. Pluralists announced the integration of individual rights and collective duties by linking individualism to group affiliations and relocating citizenship from freeholding to group affiliation. Moreover, pluralists devalued radicals' claims to articulate the voice of "the people" and their efforts to enlist the state in the cause of social justice; the group focus denied the notion of a coherent people or state. Individuals, owners, the people, and the state disappeared into "a welter of groups contending against each other, balancing, forcing compromises, overcoming resistance, a 'limitless criss-cross' of forces and counterforces" that created "equilibrium"—the social scientist's euphemism for order.[64]

Like Madison, modern pluralists encountered some basic dilemmas. First, group life did not necessarily foster social order. We have seen that it often generated fraternal domination, factionalism, and violence. Second, the pluralist standpoint undercut the foundations of political legitimacy. If individual rights were devalued, the will of people disaggregated, and the Constitution redefined as rules to facilitate peaceful group competition, it was no longer clear why groups should obey the law when their interests conflicted with it. Third, even if pluralism neutralized factional excess and secured social order, it was questionable whether passive citizens would show sufficient civic commitment to tolerate sacrifice to overcome national crises or achieve national destiny. For pluralism to be pragmatic, it had to be accompanied by some individual self-restraint and civic virtue and also some group fidelity to the good of community and nation.

Wolin's argument that "Madisonian politics virtually makes the Hamiltonian state necessary" is particularly applicable to early twentieth-century America.[65] Because group life provided a setting for class conflict, contending factions regularly turned to the state to resolve the conflict in their favor. Because group conflict often seemed excessive, middle-class moderates looked to the state to control or eradicate factions that failed to respect the tempering norms of interest-group competition. And because individuals' loyalty to local communities or fraternal organizations sometimes superseded their devotion to the larger community and nation, a

growing array of corporate, political, and military elites wanted to enhance the power of the state to guide individual actions and group factions
in the direction of their version of American destiny.

Thus, the same generation that sired the modern pluralist standpoint
also led a "neo-Hamiltonian" revival committed to empowering the federal government and its leadership to contain, regulate, and incorporate
group competition into what Theodore Roosevelt and Elihu Root called
the "New Nationalism," a version of patriotism that glorified America's
hegemony in the international marketplace and its territorial expansion
throughout the world. In theory, all fraternities were to be subordinated
to one national fraternity of battle that would enroll citizens and groups
in a communitywide effort to participate actively in competition, struggle,
and war in all parts of the globe, the official aim being the progressive
improvement of mankind. To this end, the neo-Hamiltonians systematically attacked individual selfishness and fraternal factionalism as failures
of will, courage, and duty. They pleaded for American men to redeem
their civic virtue, glory in making sacrifices for public good, and identify
with an increasingly powerful, aggressive state and national leadership.

As R. Jeffrey Lustig points out, the statists' problem was that their
ideology contained "no ideas of a principle or process that could *evoke*
[national] community voluntarily." American men's residual loyalties to
families, religion, and education, their enduring concern for individual
rights and fraternal bonds, and their long-standing suspicions of betrayal
by corrupt governors meant that their consent to a Leviathan state would
be difficult to win and, even then, never more than provisional. Until men
demonstrate significant civic virtue and devotion to public good, as Wolin
remarks, "the Hamiltonian state has *insufficient* legitimacy." [66]

Both pluralist and statist solutions to social disorder assumed a questionable degree of male self-restraint and patriotic self-sacrifice. They did
not reconcile individualism and civic virtue so much as reproduce long-
standing doubts about whether rights-bearing men could be trusted to be
self-governing and also familiar fears that liberal society continued to generate tendencies toward anarchy and tyranny. But neither liberal doubts
nor fears were decisive. The self-restraints of fatherhood may have atrophied and the bonds of fraternity may have fueled social conflict, but it
was still conceivable that men could learn to discipline their passions and

interests without massive state intervention. Victorian America elevated the possibility that wives, mothers, and women's groups could domesticate men's passions, moderate their interests, and urge husbands, sons, and lovers to practice some civic virtue in the name of God, family, and nation.

Breadwinners and Breadgivers

It was a short step from men's self-identification as specialized breadwinners to intense economic conflict and political partisanship. But the unleashing of possessive individualism and fraternal factionalism in America did not result in constant mob anarchy. Nor did the efforts of neo-Hamiltonians to enforce domestic order with republican rhetoric, patriarchal state regulation, and national expansion amount to domestic tyranny. To be sure, significant social conflict and oppressive state control were ever present threats and periodic realities but, by and large, discontented men and national leadership demonstrated remarkable self-restraint. Indeed, citizens, fraternities, and governors showed sufficient self-restraint to make possible the rise of an interest-group liberalism that routinized conflict and a welfare state that tamed dissent.

If Lockean fatherhood, Protestant morality, and state schooling and rehabilitation were limited sources of men's voluntary self-restraint, and if men's fraternal life mostly fostered factionalism, what were the forces that reconciled men's passions and interests to social order? Locke's first preference was that individuals exercise the manly self-discipline that translated into everyday sobriety, social harmony, and public good. But Locke also anticipated other means to encourage men to act as if they were rational. One was that women, bearing the relative autonomy written into the liberal marriage contract, might exercise enough affectionate and moral influence over males to foster greater self-sacrifice, sobriety, and civic virtue among them.

American analysts constantly dwelled on the question of whether domestic women could domesticate men. Many Victorian commentators worried that families, churches, and even state agencies were becoming feminized. Others saw these trends as an opportunity. Because American women played enlarged roles in families, participated in religious groups, and organized moral reform movements, they were well positioned to take on the function of subduing men's passions and interests. For this to be thinkable, the traditional Western view of females as wild, erratic creatures had to be modified. Locke's contract theory, adopted and refined in America, helped to elevate women's status as moral "breadgivers" who catered to liberalism's hunger for social order and public good. As Sylvester Judd stated in 1839, "The habits of men are too commercial. . . . Women are the bonds of society." [67]

The Keepers of Civic Virtue

A woman may live a whole life of sacrifice, and at her death meekly says, "I die a woman." But a man passes a few years in experiments of self-denial . . . and he says, "Behold I am a God."
—Abigail Alcott[1]

Men's migration from household to workplace created a domestic vacuum that women quickly filled. Traditional dread of the female persisted, and women were still disciplined by patriarchy, but men's misogynist distrust eased to accommodate a liberal marriage contract that recognized women's new functions as household manager and primary parent. The ideal of middle-class womanhood became the pious, affectionate wife and nurturing mother whose virtues included making sacrifices for her family and providing a peaceful haven for her men. A Victorian cult of domesticity proclaimed that women perpetuated "private" virtue in the nation's increasingly corrupt commercial society.

If American men imagined that the middle-class home was a republican retreat from the marketplace, American women "exposed the profoundly political nature of domestic life" by asserting their historical agency.[2] They reconstituted the home as a school for teaching males sufficient self-restraint to ensure social order. They sought to defend domestic virtue, redeem husbands from immorality and intemperance, and train sons in family obligations, sobriety, and patriotism. Women then moved beyond the home in an effort to rehabilitate society.

They parlayed private virtue into a public justification for female reform movements that spanned the major moral, socioeconomic, and political issues of the day. Moreover, in every war, women assumed the mantle of exemplary self-sacrifice on the home front to shame self-centered men into serving the nation on the battlefront.

Women's elevated domestic status legitimated their informal social and political power, which received the applause of clergymen, industrialists, politicians, and military leaders hoping that women's man-taming mission would reconcile individualism and social order. From the Revolution onward, women were duly honored as keepers of civic virtue in liberal America. But male applause and female honor were always contingent. When women's agency appeared to be dysfunctional, hinting at sexual equality if not matriarchal domination, male critics reinvoked traditional dread of the female and reinvigorated modern patriarchal prerogative. As Abigail Alcott recognized, women's self-sacrifice did not transcend men's misogynist illusions of immortality.

Fortuna and Functionalism

The idea that women were passionate, destructive beings pervaded early America. English judges sent "lewd women" from London prisons to the colonies, where Puritans confirmed that females were "especially sexual" creatures with weak "rational powers."[3] Dread of the female facilitated witchcraft trials, justified common-law patriarchy, and informed the Revolution. American men fought for liberty but could not imagine giving women the freedom to rob men of their self-control and reason. In 1775, John Gregory's *A Father's Legacy to His Daughters* warned young women against abusing their power "over the hearts of men," while the *Pennsylvania Magazine* alerted new husbands to "bad wives [who] flatter and tyrannize over men of sense." American men associated femininity with "caprice," "fickle dispositions," and "effeminizing luxury," and projected that image onto "the mother country," which they personified as an old hag preventing young colonists from achieving "manhood." *The Federalist* cast women as scheming courtesans and duplicitous mistresses; later, Federalists condemned Jeffersonians for their "womanish resentment" against England and "womanish attachment to France."[4]

Nationhood fueled distrust of women. Republican rhetoric made civic virtue essential to national survival but "equated female passion, trickery, and extravagance with the corruption ever threatening civic virtue." Male fears of female treachery were manifested among judges and juries that blamed the victims of rape and a public that accused women of sapping men's patriotism. Charges of female malice joined to "irrationality" were a common argument for removing young men's education in civic virtue from mothers' influence to state institutions.[5] Jacksonians and Social Darwinists likened women and Nature to cold, cruel mistresses who threatened civilization, while Victorian men equated passionate women with intemperate Catholics, immigrants, Indians, blacks, and the poor. Eventually, dread of the female was put on a medical footing. One doctor symbolized his profession in a metaphor of male domination: "I liked to follow the workings of another [physician] through these minute, teasing investigations to see a relentless observer get hold of nature and squeeze her until the sweat broke out all over her and sphincters loosened." Most doctors preferred a technical name for women's essence: "hysteria."[6]

Throughout American history, the male public presumed women to be inherently passionate, unruly beings. Judges treated "fallen women" as "unsalvageable victims of their own degeneracy." Social commentators denounced women who sued men for breach of promise as "mercenaries" seeking "lifetime sinecures," or "fortune hunters" subverting marriage and family. Even early-twentieth-century laws and programs developed to protect women and children functioned to stigmatize single, working, and divorced mothers as selfish, corrupt, and dangerous to their own children. Professional social workers recast daughters who were victimized by incestuous fathers in the role of sexual delinquents guilty of seduction. And civic leaders portrayed city girls free of family supervision as "villains" who spread venereal disease among the patriotic young soldiers and sailors preparing to embark for World War I.[7]

Fortuna was still a woman in America. She stripped men of their senses and seduced them from virtue, robbed them of reason and plundered their wealth, enslaved and emasculated them, and thereby deprived the nation of a worthy citizenry. As in England, the first line of defense against *Fortuna* was marriage. Guidebooks suggested that subordination to husbands was the cure for "difficult girls." A proper husband would "subdue even the most restless spirits." Moreover, spiritual and political leaders advised women to avoid selfishness and cultivate "female selflessness," to " 'lay aside all consideration of themselves' and to make their 'joys . . . the results of the gratification of others.' " [8] Unfortunately, men feared, such advice was insufficient. As long as women were functional to civil society, they would exercise informal and potentially treacherous powers.

"One image of women reverberated through Puritan sermons," writes Mary Ryan, "that of the 'helpmeet,' an industrious partner in the colonial family economy." Women reproduced men's heirs, farm laborers, and future citizens. They nursed infants, educated children, cooked, healed, manufactured, managed servants, apprentices, and hired help, grew food, tended livestock, and plied the local marketplace. They worked in husbands' shops and businesses, took in boarders, and took on paid employment. In general, women occupied the same sphere as men and were advised to practice the same virtues as men: "prayerfulness, industry, charity, modesty, serious reading, and godly writing." Colonial men relied on women's industry and "intellectual capacity to judge and advise" them on all family matters.[9] The main distinction between the sexes was not morality, productivity, or intelligence but the formal authority that men monopolized.

Even then, colonial women's usefulness enabled them to wield considerable influence. Most women had their own economic identities, while young women and widows sometimes claimed economic independence. Many women played a significant role in community life. Their exemplary piety was occasionally transformed into religious leadership. Their domesticity included operating informal social welfare programs, including responsibility for the care of orphans, sick relatives, poor neighbors, and even local criminals. Women also had political power. They used public morality and the courts to control abusive men and built family and neighbor networks to influence town meetings. Demos suggests that women's "influence was exerted, was *felt,* in countless informal ways." In effect, the perceived danger was that women were just like men because "the love of power, congenial to the human breast, reveals itself in the two sexes . . . with equal force." Men were thought as likely to be seduced by women's passions as to control them, which may explain why men patronized prostitution even as they railed against it.[10]

A set of unspoken but ubiquitous assumptions about gender framed the American Revolution. Women were not born with natural rights. Nor could they be granted rights until their passions were subdued and their informal powers were constrained. Women had to earn their liberty by demonstrating their sobriety, civility, and patriotism. Only then would the idea of female rights and citizenship be a topic worthy of discussion. In fact, women's notable self-sacrifices during the Revolution did engender a brief discourse on female rights and citizenship by revealing the possibility that "female emotionality, regarded as a source of disorder," could be changed into "affection, nurture, and piety" in the cause of nationhood. Conceivably, patriotic women could function as "the social glue" of the new republic.[11]

The Social Glue of the Republic

Women's place in public life was debated and modified during the Revolution. With men off to war, many women assumed de facto control of families and estates and participated in politics and war. "Liberty's Daughters" boycotted English goods, brewed herbal teas, wore homespun, protested against hoarding merchants, and petitioned leaders for redress of grievances. They also fed, clothed, housed, accompanied, nursed, and fought beside patriots and Loyalists. Mary Beth Norton argues that women's wartime initiatives were unprecedented: "Never before had female Americans formally shouldered the responsibility of a public role, never before had they claimed a voice—even a compliant one—in public policy." [12] While some male critics insisted that women should exit the public stage, patriots such as Esther DeBerdt Reed of the Ladies Association responded that no woman could be a "good citizen" unless she contributed to "our efforts for the relief of the armies which defend our lives, our possessions, our liberty." [13]

After the Revolution, women did not retain the independence born of exigency. Nor were their patriotic sacrifices rewarded with any sort of equality. Certainly, the idea of sexual equality was in the air. In the 1760s, James Otis raised the possibility that women as well as men were born free and equal and subjected only by their own consent. Over the next two decades, university students debated "Whether women ought to be admitted to partake in civil government dominions and sovereignty." [14] Soon, Mary Wollstonecraft's *Vindication of the Rights of Woman* attracted a wide

American audience and some radical Democratic Clubs rallied to women's rights. But patriarchal attitudes and coverture laws subordinating wives to husbands persisted. Women even lost some of their informal influence as they were stripped of prior functions. The rise of industry initiated the fall of female household production, and fears of instability prompted the state to assume and institutionalize many of women's welfare activities. The trend was for the "lady" to become a consumer of manufactured goods and the "mill girl" an expendable item on owners' balance sheets. Meanwhile, women's local networks lost their clout as political power was centralized in the distant reaches of the new federal government.[15]

The early American discourse on citizenship was masculinist. Only men were property owners with the independent judgment that qualified them to vote; females were dependents unfit for suffrage. Only men were soldiers who participated in politics through military service; women's wartime heroics were devalued as apolitical. Only men manifested fortitude in search of fame, honor, and public good; women cultivated an effeminacy associated with cowardice, dishonor, and selfishness among soldiers. Linda Kerber observes that "formulations of citizenship and civic relations in a republic were tightly linked to men and manhood," and a new language of female citizenship had to be "freshly devised" for women's citizenship to be contemplated. However, the Revolution provided ample ammunition for male critics desiring to keep women at home. They recalled the women who emptied pisspots on stamp tax collectors, rioted against merchants, and acted as spies; they remembered the women who kept men from military service, opposed the Revolution, and abetted Loyalists. Such "disorderly women" reconfirmed female treachery. "To honor or mythologize them," concludes Kerber, "would have been to honor and to mythologize the most disconcerting and threatening aspects of the rebellion."[16]

As in the English Civil War and most wars, threatening images of disorderly, powerful women effeminizing demobilized soldiers gave impetus to American men's attempts to reaffirm postwar patriarchy. At the same time, these images were part of the cultural climate in which the Founders wrestled with the man question. The Revolution raised hope for men's redemption but also gave cause to doubt men's sobriety and virtue. The Sons of Liberty, for example, found more than a few occasions to "indulge in rum, rhetoric, and roast pig" rather than to do deeds of patriotism.[17] Hartz and Wood agree that postwar statesmen were preoccupied with men's passions, avarice, and factionalism. Thus, the Founders explored fatherhood, churches, schools, and fraternity as sources of men's moderation, self-sacrifice, and civic virtue, but their faith in men's morality proved limited. Shaysites convinced them that America's possessive individualists and fraternities of battle blindly converted liberty into license. How could women's citizenship be seriously debated when men's rights proved problematic? Drawing on Locke's prescience, the founding generation examined the potential of domestic women to domesticate men.

One benign trait attributed to colonial women was piety. "Notable housewives" were religious exemplars for families. Thus, Eliza Lucas Pinckney resolved "to be a good mother to my children, to pray for them, to set them good examples, to give them good advice, to be careful both of their souls and bodies, to watch over their tender minds, to carefully root out the first appearing and buddings of vice, and to install piety, virtue, and true religion in them; to spare no pains or trouble to do them good; to correct their errors whatever uneasiness it may give myself; and never omit to encourage every virtue I may see dawning in them." The Revolution demonstrated that self-sacrificing wives could be enlisted in the cause of public good. Broadsides honored them for managing families, helping needy soldiers, and assisting war widows and orphans. They were "emphatic patriots." [18] This union of domestic virtue and patriotism engendered an emerging consensus on "republican motherhood."

Revolutionary rhetoric fostered contempt for individual dependence, which "rendered one susceptible to all sorts of temptations and impositions." The ideal citizen was the person who volunteered to be a "soldier, politician, and patriot" and sacrificed to defend fragile liberty.[19] The rhetoric of independence and women's wartime sacrifices urged Liberty's Daughters to disdain traditional dependence and claim citizenship. But what sort of citizenship was possible in a republic that outlawed women's social, economic, and political autonomy? Misogynists wanted women confined to their families. Misanthropes wanted limits on men's rights and considered "the family . . . the natural place to establish them." Women could satisfy misogynists and misanthropes by weaving together their "familial commitments with their newly discovered sense of civic duty."

Women could tame men's passions and teach sons patriotism as their unique contribution to public good. In the process, republican mothers would alter "the very definition of 'politics' and 'public life.' "[20]

Motherhood became a civic calling. Pious mothers instilled in children a sense of self-restraint and sobriety. They taught civic virtue to young men anticipating citizenship and prepared daughters to teach citizenship to successive generations. They alone could save the republic from men's selfishness, factionalism, luxury, and corruption. Their contribution to social continuity and public good was so significant that motherhood was at times treated as a "fourth branch of government." In addition, mothers were also wives who employed *Fortuna*'s power over male affections. They refused "to countenance vice, crime, or lack of benevolence in their suitors and husbands" and thereby managed "the moral development of the male citizens." In short, the republican mother centered her existence in the family home, where she dedicated her life to "the service of civic virtue: she educated her sons for it, she condemned and corrected her husband's lapses from it."[21]

Few Americans objected to the image of women who spurned frivolity, modeled piety, and taught patriotism to families. But male critics were upset by those who suggested that republican women needed to cultivate autonomy and intelligence to fulfill their republican mission. For instance, Judith Sargent Murray argued that young women should claim "independence" and a formal education that "taught with precision the art economical . . . to procure for themselves the necessaries of life."[22] The critics worried that female independence and education would divert women from domesticity and lure them into masculine pursuits such as business and politics. Like Mary Astell, advocates of republican motherhood answered that free, intelligent women would make superior wives and mothers.

Benjamin Rush located a middle ground. He defended female schooling but with a decisive domestic orientation. On the one hand, educated women would have a benign effect on men: "The opinions and conduct of men are often regulated by the women in the most arduous enterprises of life, and their approbation is frequently the principal reward of the hero's dangers and the patriot's toils. . . . In a republic [women] should think justly upon the great subjects of liberty and government!" On the other hand, a domestic education ensured that women would use their intellectual tools to train their husbands and sons for civil society and republican government. Thus, "the obligations of gentlemen to . . . discharge the duties of benevolence would be increased by marriage; and patriots . . . would find the sweetest reward of their toils in the approbation and applause of their wives." Whereas Mercy Otis Warren and Judith Sargent Murray urged women's education as a means to self-development and public good, male writers were mainly interested in women's ability to tame men's passions and encourage their civic virtue.[23]

Republican motherhood reconciled dread of the female and women's functional powers while promising to answer the man question. If women specialized in domesticity, their passions remained proscribed by family patriarchs. They could then be trusted to function as "the custodians of civic morality" who restrain male excesses. The implication was that "the home in effect gained a function so political that the domestic sphere could influence the outcome of history."[24] But the politicization of domesticity was still quite crude. Why would women consent to domestic confinement? Why would family patriarchs cede sufficient domestic authority to enable their wives to become effective civic educators?

Women's Domestic Authority

America's nineteenth-century cult of domesticity was predicated on two axioms. One was that home life was more natural and desirable for women than marketplace or political activity. Mary Ryan notes, "Women's . . . assigned place [in the home] was deemed a far better one than the rough-and-tumble world of war, work, politics; and women's superior nature—pure, pious, and gentle—entitled her to reign there." Middle-class women were considered privileged to stay at home, cultivate a higher nature and nurture, and avoid the corruption associated with the male sphere of production. They could infuse religion into their homes, raise standards of motherhood, and perpetuate female craft traditions such as baking and needlework.[25] The second axiom was that women's sense of meaning and immortality was situated in the home. If men achieved transcendence in society, women identified self-fulfillment with reproduction and relinquishment. God enjoined men to replenish the earth, but women administered the injunction by enduring natural cycles of menstruation, pregnancy, lactation, and menopause. They were rewarded with a personal sense of continuity. Judith Stiehm observes that "women's investment in the persons of the next generation gives them something precious—a stake in the future."[26]

The cult of domesticity did not automatically give rise to Veblen's notion that an "idle" wife functioned as public testimony to a husband's success. Middle-class women who honored domesticity saw themselves as creating a more pious, natural, and meaningful world than the one occupied by avaricious men. Bonnie Smith's observations on the French middle class also apply to America: "The home became the exclusive focus for the legitimate procreation of the human race. . . . Women gave birth to children at home and nurtured them there in the hope that they would survive the perilous course of childhood; they nursed the sick and closed the eyes of the dead. Because women preserved the ties of blood within an encapsulated space, they tended to see the home as a microcosm, a holistic universe to which the industrial world was a subordinate support system."[27] Nor did the cult of domesticity necessarily produce an image of frail, foolish, and inept women. What Frances Cogan calls the ideal of "Real Womanhood" equated female sickness with selfishness, insisted on women's education, and urged women to develop job skills to augment the family economy. Women with "intelligence, physical fitness and health, economic self-reliance, and careful marriage" were best able to ensure the survival of their families.[28]

Domestic women were expected to lead a natural and active but constrained life. They would maintain, exemplify, transmit, and enforce rigorous standards of piety and virtue regardless of individual desire, self-interest, or circumstances. They would marry, obey, and tame men prone to idleness, intemperance, gambling, and adultery as well as sexual brutality. They would reproduce and mold children into moral adults in an immoral world. Increasingly, guidebooks on child rearing were directed to women and advised them to become full-time, professional mothers who studied experts' advice and applied it to child rearing.[29] While women who met elevated expectations were honored as "angels of the house," women who internalized Victorian norms tacitly consented to the stigmas and penalties attendant to failure. Henceforth, wives' faults became the alleged cause of husbands' vices, while mothers' foolishness ostensibly drove children from home to "houses of pollution, directly to the grog shop, the gambling house, or the brothel." Women forced by necessity to leave home for "the grinding pressures and dark temptations of the world at large" were blamed for a host of social disorders.[30]

Locke hinted that domesticity might provide women with a morally superior but confined life. The ethic of self-sacrifice would restrain female passions, and the minutiae of professional mothering would fill women's time. Americans added that domestic women were sufficiently predictable and trustworthy to assume authority over their households, child rearing, and man taming. Men's limited trust in women was manifested in the rise of the "modern family" in which love was the basis of courtship, choice the foundation for the marriage contract, an engendered division of labor the means of family survival, and cooperation a model for parenting. The modern family ideal that matured in the mid–nineteenth century was bound together by mutual affection and interest and married women gained greater "power and . . . autonomy."[31]

Marriages founded on love provided women some emotional leverage over men that was further enhanced by the "ideology of passionlessness."[32] Traditional fears of female sexual lust, seductiveness, and treachery were quieted by modern doubts about women's sexual drive. Victorian physicians argued that women had dull libidos and frail physiologies. Too much sex was harmful to women's health and also exhausted the men's energy for production. Theoretically, everyone was better off if wives could refuse sex and limit it to procreative purposes. Once spousal affection was joined to the ideology of passionlessness, wives were in a moral position to opt for marital chastity, avoid a lifetime of childbearing and rearing, and budget love and sex to control husbands' behavior. In effect, the new sexual contract enhanced women's leverage in the marriage contract.

The modern family also "placed limits on the power of the husband." If marriage was seen as a contractual relationship, women gained greater freedom to choose their spouses and negotiate the terms of marriage. Advice books warned the young woman to scrutinize her suitor's character and select her husband with great care lest she "end up with a gambler, a speculator, a drinker, or a slacker whose non-industrious habits would eventually put the very home she essentially married for into the hands of tax or rent collectors." Some prospective brides struck antenuptial agreements that predefined the terms of marriage; some wives bargained for control and management of separate property; and a few wives invoked "the ultimate sanction," threatening divorce to ensure husbands' civility, responsibility, and fidelity, or to prevent their abuse and tyranny.[33]

The modern family also validated women's role as the primary parent. With fathers away from home and mothers honored for domesticity, middle-class Americans adopted the belief that *"mothers alone had the power to transform malleable infants into moral, productive adults."* The ideal mother acquired an education to enhance her parenting skills, assumed management over family resources to shape a proper home environment, and demanded husbands' acquiescence to maternal child-rearing techniques. By mid-century, a New York court could rule that "all other things being equal, the mother is the most proper parent to be entrusted with the custody of a child."[34] Part of the reason for elevating maternal authority was the growing popularity of Locke's educational ideas in America. "Most childrearing writers of the antebellum period," writes Elizabeth Pleck, "accepted Locke's argument that corporal punishment should be resorted to only if other means had been exhausted." Parents were to rely mostly on praise, shame, and social reputation to instill in children a sense of self-discipline and orderliness.[35] Thus, proper parenting required constant parental presence, prudence, and patience. A relative consensus on mothers' new moral stature and men's avarice and brutality helped to legitimate matriarchal authority.

While the modern family continued to presume that women required men's provision and protection, wives' dependence sometimes became a source of power. Thomas Dew observed in 1835, "Woman we behold dependent and weak; but out of that very weakness springs an irresistible power." Stay-at-home mothers were well placed to mediate father–son relations because they raised the sons who matured into fathers' heirs. Smith notes, "The cult of the heir glorified the woman who reproduced the father's image, the receptacle of his capital, his eternal life in a mortal world." Mothers might demand reductions in family size to provide quality care for each heir, assume pedagogical sovereignty to inculcate proper character traits in sons, or assert control of the family purse to finance young men's education. They could also justify female wage labor to underwrite sons' entry into the new middle class.[36] Fathers could resist these demands but only at the cost of endangering their symbolic immortality.

Finally, Victorian wives played a crucial role in the family economy.

Certainly they provided husbands rest and recuperation from the market-place, as this writer suggested: "We go forth into the world amidst the scenes of business and of pleasure . . . and the delicacy of our moral sense is wounded . . . and we turn from such scenes with a painful sensation, almost believing that virtue has deserted the abodes of men; again, we look to the sanctuary of the home; there sympathy, honor, virtue are assembled; there the eye may kindle with intelligence, and receive an answering glance; there disinterested love is ready to sacrifice everything at the altar of affection." But wives did more than soothe husbands' egos. They also performed nonwage labor such as child care, cooking, and clothing and feeding their families which augmented husbands' insufficient incomes.[37] While this nonwage labor did not provide women an autonomous, economic identity in the marketplace, it was yet another source of influence within their families.

Women's authority within the modern family grew, but not to the extent that it heralded "the weakness of paternal power" or "implicitly denied patriarchy" or constituted a "domestic feminism."[38] Young women had greater freedom to select a spouse but usually had to choose a mate to secure their economic well-being. Conversely, young men could defer or refuse marriage, an option announced by "bachelor books" that "extolled the pleasures of . . . a life in which women could be distanced or controlled." Indeed, men occasionally construed women's idealized piety, passionlessness, and marital authority as elements in a female conspiracy to dominate men. Thus, Barbara Ehrenreich and Deirdre English argue, "Underneath the complacent denial of female sexual feelings, there lurked the age-old male fascination with women's 'insatiable lust,' which, once awakened, might turn out to be uncontrollable."[39] The economic bottom line was that young women needed men's provision more than young men needed loving wives.

Nor was the liberal marriage contract an agreement between equals. A "matrimonial republican" wrote in 1792 that "marriage ought never to be considered as a contract between a superior and an inferior, but a reciprocal union of interest." But legislators and judges continued to treat marriage as a mixture of contract and status. If partners were free to choose whom they married, marital roles and responsibilities were defined and regulated by public officials who acted under the assumption that a wife's status was that of a husband's dependent. Further, when husbands

failed to fulfill their assigned role, public officials used the state as a surrogate patriarch who assisted but also regulated women's lives. Michael
Grossberg explains, "Judges recast the law to aid wives and mothers who
successfully performed household responsibilities . . . while at the same
time invoking their authority to check radical alterations in the subordinate legal status of women." Carole Pateman concludes that the Victorian
sentimentalization of love, marriage, and family "maintained the fiction of
the marriage contract and obscured the reality of the patriarchal subjection
of wives." [40]

Following Locke, Americans liberalized patriarchy. Young women,
wives, and mothers who consented to domesticity won a "realm of their
own." Their chances for virtue, fulfillment, choice, and authority in the
home increased, but men's continuing monopoly of coercive and hege-
monic power in society guaranteed patriarchal limits to women's authority. The major curiosity is that American men did so little to deny
women's elevation. Indeed, male writers, politicians, and judges helped
to elevate their social status and legal rights. For example, Congress resolved in 1914: "Whereas the service rendered the United States by the
American mother is the greatest source of the country's strength and inspiration; and Whereas we honor ourselves and the mothers of America
when we do anything to give emphasis to the home as the fountain of the
State; and Whereas the American mother is doing so much for the home,
for moral uplift, and religion, hence so much for good government and
humanity," the second Sunday in May was set aside to honor her.[41] This
rhetoric highlighted a series of nineteenth- and early-twentieth-century reforms that recognized mothers' property, child custody, testamentary, and
welfare rights. If part of the explanation is that men had little choice other
than to trust women to run the home while they occupied themselves in
the marketplace, another element of explanation is that women with limited domestic autonomy were needed to perform a crucial public function:
redeeming men's virtue.

Redeeming Men's Virtue

Scholars often argue that nineteenth-century mar-
ket society "destroyed family-based society." Families lost primacy as

centers of production, prep schools for transmitting economic skills, and social service agencies for communities. Prior social functions were assumed by factories, offices, and specialized institutions such as private and public schools or state asylums, prisons, and hospitals. Demos writes, "The family . . . seemed to stand increasingly apart." Degler suggests that families actually stood against market society: "The very slogan of Communism—'from each according to his ability, to each according to his needs'—is not only the antithesis of the market economy's conception of human relations, but the central principle of family life." [42] In fact, family-based society became stronger precisely because it stood apart from and against market morality. Female domesticity preserved a republican ethic intended to tame men's passions and interests.

"What has been insufficiently recognized," writes Glenna Matthews, "is the extent to which men, too, entered into the ideology of domesticity, helping to create and perpetuate it. . . . They took the home beyond the boundaries of 'women's sphere' and into the national arena." The ideal home was the place where men suffering an excess of selfishness and materialism were to be redeemed by Victorian wives and mothers. Advice literature counseled the affectionate, intelligent wife to keep her husband from "rough companions, bars, or gambling halls" and to contribute to "softening and refining the society around her." Guidebooks told the nurturant mother to teach her sons "a strategy for resisting too complete a separation of home and work" so that they could sustain self-control and resist temptation in the marketplace. Often, such injunctions were affirmed by male elites. For example, judges assumed that men's sexual passions were "almost bestial," condemned "the base, heartless seducer," and used breach of promise suits as opportunities "to punish the sexual machinations and treachery of their brothers as well as present themselves in the appealing role as the defenders of womanhood." [43]

Catharine Beecher urged women to appreciate the fact that they wielded significant power over fathers, husbands, and sons. Women's moral stature and emotional leverage were forces "to which [men] will yield not only willingly but proudly." If "the mother writes the character of the future of men," then she also had the power to sway "the heart whose energies may turn for good and evil the destinies of a nation." This power made women responsible for the "intellectual and moral character of the mass of the people" who, in turn, determined the success or failure of the

American republic. In her books, articles, and schools, Beecher prodded women to use their power to tame men's passions, mediate male conflicts, and ensure social peace. Thus, domesticity was a heavy responsibility but also an "exalted privilege of extending over the world those blessed influences, which are to renovate degraded man." Other female authors took up the theme that wives' greatest service was to "elevate" husbands' "moral feelings" and overcome the deficiency in their "spiritual nature." And male writers such as Ralph Waldo Emerson, Nathaniel Hawthorne, Andrew Jackson Downing, Theodore Parker, and Samuel May agreed that domesticity was crucial to civilizing men who otherwise succumbed to modern vice.[44]

The domestic literature sometimes conveyed doubts whether men could be civilized. Mrs. Margaret Graves advised young women to beware of "drunkards, gigolos, and heartless businessmen" who may be irredeemable. Many men preferred idleness, gambling, and violence to sobriety; many men squandered family wealth on prostitutes, alcohol, or business schemes. Magazines counseled women married to men lacking in "good character" to assert female initiative to ensure family survival. Echoing Lord Halifax, for instance, Samuel Jennings advised, "The husband ought at least to *seem* to be the head. . . . Adopt the following plan. When any article of property is to be bought or sold, take him aside, teach him the price to be given or received, point out the kind of payment, the time when to be paid. . . . Let the poor fellow go forward and seem to act like a man."[45]

Women's greatest service to society was as mothers who reproduced and reared a better breed of males. If Victorian women created home environments marked by "republican simplicity," the home would be a source of moral regeneration, not a training ground for greed and luxury. It would elevate selflessness above selfishness, frugality over sensuality, cooperation in place of competition, and affection ahead of instrumentalism. Journalist Sara Josepha Hale maintained, "Our men are sufficiently money-making. Let us keep our women and children from the contagion as long as possible." The ideal mother taught her sons to discipline unruly passions and resist profligacy, to assume the traditional obligations of manhood, and to "prefer home and the companionship of pious women to the temptations of bachelor life." Knowing they had to relinquish their sons to the corrupt world, wise mothers adopted a matriarchal but Lockean pedagogy of consent: they cultivated bonds of affection with sons and schooled them in "self-control without external restraints" so that boys would become inner-directed adults who voluntarily assumed the obligations of fatherhood and stayed clear of the temptations of the city.[46] In middle-class families, liberal matriarchy augmented if not replaced atrophied liberal patriarchy.

An emerging nineteenth-century consensus on women's civilizing influence became a common justification for enhancing women's educational opportunities and admission to nurturing professions like teaching and nursing. After the Civil War, middle-class women created literary clubs premised on the belief that women's "maternal sensitivity, moral superiority, and domestic ability" should be refined and extended into "offices and market places."[47] More than a few male critics sounded an alarm against "Momism," arguing that women were becoming too powerful in American society. The critics alleged that women dominated husbands, emasculated sons, effeminized schoolboys, and made them unfit for the material world. The specter of a new generation of "effeminate" youth fueled a turn-of-the-century gender crisis comparable to Restoration England's crisis of masculinity.[48] However, American critics of Momism were relatively subdued compared to English and French critics, who condemned women's moralism, familialism, and limited autonomy as subversive of modernity.[49] In America, women's republican values and liberal society reached an accommodation manifested in female reform movements applauded by male elites.

American women parlayed cultural recognition of their "moral superiority" into an "epic style of domesticity" that blurred the lines separating private and public life.[50] Their struggle to tame husbands and sons reached beyond families to the local and national community. Throughout the nineteenth century, women organized and operated social movements for religious revivalism, social purity, Sabbath schools, child welfare, charity, and public education. They conducted protests against slavery, prostitution, gambling, and, most notably, male intemperance. Female reform was a continuous crusade to protect family virtue by redeeming corrupt male society. The announced goal of many movements was to protect the home from male social vices. According to Beecher, "In matters pertaining to the education of their children, in the selection and support of a clergyman, in all benevolent enterprises, and in all questions relating to morals and

262 | Engendered Virtue

manners, [women] have a superior influence." Thus the New York Female Reform Society of the 1830s hoped to extend women's superior influence to counterbalance "the lascivious and predatory nature of the American male" who threatened to destroy familial and social bonds.[51]

Later in the nineteenth century, the women's temperance movement, club movement, and settlement house movement sought to organize "well-trained mothers" to spread Christian morality, force men to be responsible husbands and fathers, extend maternal nurturance to slums and tenements, and ensure decent child welfare, housing, food, and sanitation. Many female activists "seemed more concerned with uplifting men than with raising the status of women," but others thought domestic morality was also a path to women's political influence. Domesticity became a justification for women's efforts at self-improvement, social reform, and political change. Clubwomen initiated the idea of a Women's Parliament to make authoritative decisions on all family issues and to secure women's right to vote and hold office on school boards. Karen Blair's analysis is that many middle-class clubwomen were "feminists under the skin." [52] The epic style of domesticity also had an impact on organized labor and populist politics. Women within the Knights of Labor argued that the women's elevated morality was the seedbed "for a more cooperative and moral public life—a maternal commonwealth." Women who campaigned for the Populist party used a rhetoric of "politicized domesticity" to blame men for the problems of industrial capitalism and "to place the mothers of this nation on an equality with the fathers." [53] The concept of "virtue" was never privatized in America; it was embedded in domesticity and then linked to domestic women's civic virtue as a significant source of social order and political salvation.

The most controversial female reform effort was the women's suffrage movement. Activists used Lockean natural rights to justify women's individualism and suffrage. Ellen Carol DuBois argues, "The right to vote raised the prospect of female autonomy in a way that other claims to equal rights could not." The specter of female suffrage raised male fears that women would exchange self-sacrificing morality for selfishness. Orestes Brownson argued that female selfishness would destroy domestic virtue and exacerbate the individualism, fragmentation, and conflict endemic in liberal America. Thus, "The conclusive objection to the political enfranchisement of women is that it would weaken and finally break up and destroy the Christian family. . . . We are rapidly becoming a nation of isolated individuals."[54] Suffragists replied by adding the claim that voting women would domesticate male politics and restore public good. Isabella Hooker affirmed women's natural rights, stated that male resistance was due to men's misconception of probable results, and reassured critics that women would enter voting precincts carrying "the God-given power of womanhood—of motherhood—with us." The argument for "maternal suffrage" integrated liberal rights and republican virtue.[55]

In one sense, "male and female cultures were in collision in the late nineteenth century." Domestic values potentially subverted the possessive individualism of the marketplace. However, domestic values also promised to subdue men's commercial excesses. Elites who feared that "male solutions to the problems of social order and self-control did not work" supported female reform movements that fostered "individual comportment, self-restraint, and social order" in line with industrial capitalism's "emphasis on discipline and sobriety." Women's reforms conformed to popular advice for workers to swear off "idleness, profanity, and intemperance" in order to "move up the ladder of success" and also to the strategy of the manufacturer who offered a reduced work load for men who "go regularly to church" but dismissal for the worker "who smokes Spanish cigars, uses liquor in any form, or frequents pool and public halls." In this sense "the [modern] family was not so much a refuge from the work world as a sanitized ideal of it" and an ally in "the repression of individualism."[56]

Women's movements were often allies in elites' search for class harmony. The temperance movement won the support of Carroll D. Wright of the Massachusetts Bureau of Labor Statistics, who observed, "Temperance induces frugal habits, and frugal habits prevent strikes." Owners, politicians, military leaders, and clergymen wanted sobriety to ensure hierarchical discipline and eradicate social disorders associated with alcohol. With somewhat more skepticism, they also supported female reformers who served as "the social charwomen" of the modern society. "They tidied up the man's world, removing the most unsightly evidence of corrupt politics, smoothing over the ugly clash between the rich and the poor."[57] Elites occasionally saw female reformers as fellow nativists. Clubwomen sponsored classes in homemaking, mothering, health care, and self-help to integrate immigrant girls into Victorian culture. Meanwhile, the domestic sciences and magazines preached lessons in family and frugality to strengthen white, middle-class Protestantism against the surging numbers of working-class, Catholic, immigrant, and minority Americans. Thus, elites honored female reformers for melting immigrant women into a republican pot and for protecting republican harmony against subversive aliens.[58]

For Aristotle, the family home provided necessary logistical support for men's participation in politics; for early-twentieth-century Americans, home economics provided insight into logistical constraints on men's political passions. Henrietta Goodrich explained, "Home economics aims to bring the home into harmony with industrial conditions and social ideals. . . . Men in general must admit consciously that the home is the social workshop for the making of men."[59] The ideal of self-sacrificing, virtuous, educated, middle-class women who presided over domestic and social morality, made men and boys into sober citizens, and mopped up men's political debris was a version of women's citizenship that became especially compelling during wartime.

Women and War

"Home," wrote Mrs. Graves, "is the cradle of the human race. . . . It is here [a woman] can best serve her country, by training up good citizens, just, humane, and enlightened legislators."[60] The republican mother did more than raise public-spirited sons; she relinquished them to the military to defend the nation. The Reverend Abbott stated, "When our land is filled with pious and patriotic mothers, then it will be filled with virtuous and patriotic men." Theodore Roosevelt added, "The good mother, the wise mother, . . . is more important to the community than even the ablest man; her career is more worthy of honor and is more useful to the community than the career of any man." And Grover Cleveland concluded that the "army of woman's constancy and love, whose yearning hearts make men brave and patriotic teach from afar lessons of patient fortitude, and transmit through mysterious agencies, to soldiers in the field, the spirit of endurance and devotion."[61] Women's signal civic virtue was to encourage young men to prepare for war, go to war, and demonstrate courage in war.

The patriotic ideal was for everyday motherhood to anticipate Spartan motherhood. Nancy Hartsock observes, "Helping another to develop, the gradual relinquishing of control, the experiencing of the human limits of one's actions—all these are important features of women's activities as mothers." With every national conflict, mothers were advised to relinquish their sons to war where they would grow into men, citizens, and patriots. Genevieve Lloyd explains, "In giving up their sons, women are supposed to allow them to become real men and immortal selves . . . an ideal of citizenship that finds its fullest expression in war." In practice, many American women not only sacrificed their sons to military service; they also "went beyond the *sacrificial* stance—a resigned preparedness to 'let go'—to a martial enthusiasm to 'push out.' "[62] Female bellicosity was particularly striking during the fraternal strife of the Civil War.

Both Union and Confederate women "urged enlistment," demanded "courageous behavior," and attacked "cowardice." A Richmond clerk noted that the "ladies are postponing all engagements until their lovers have fought the Yankees." The popular press urged women to use their influence to raise troop morale and efficiency. One soldier wrote of the power of letters from home: "Sometimes our expeditions and reconnaissances take us away from camp for a month at a time. . . . The men always become rough and somewhat demoralized. . . . We get back to camp and a big mail awaits us. All the men will have letters and papers from mothers, wives, sisters, and friends. . . . A great quietness falls on the men . . . and an indescribable softening and tenderness is felt." Women also infused meaning into death on the battlefield. An article by "The Women of the South" stated, "Every true woman who has husband, father, brother, or lover . . . had rather see him prostrate before her with death's signet on his noble brow . . . than have him forfeit his good name and disgrace his manhood by refusing to do his duty to his country." Adding material to moral support, women joined the Sanitary Commission and established twenty thousand aid societies to provision armies with food, clothing, and medical supplies and services.[63]

Southern women's ambiguous response to General Sherman's tactics revealed the depth of their commitment to the Spartan ideal. On the one hand, the burning, rape, and pillage by Union soldiers deconstructed the myth that women were the protected and men their protectors. "In this brave new world of total war," writes Jane Schultz, "women were neither revered as objects of protection nor immune to the enemy's destructive will." On the other hand, Southern women tended to save the myth of protection by treating beastly soldiers as "errant men." And they continued to spur Confederate soldiers on to victory during the despairing last years of the Civil War.[64] In effect, Spartan Mothers continued to play the part of self-sacrificing wives and daughters who excused their victimizers and continued to rely on their men for protection beyond the possibility of victory.

In turn, nineteenth-century leaders relied on women to serve as allies in the struggle to discipline unruly, selfish young soldiers. Military officers applauded women's religious revivals, war against intemperance, and support for Victorian sexual norms that enabled soldiers to satisfy basic passions without sacrificing their health or draining their martial energy. While some military thinkers felt that female camp followers were an encumbrance, others argued that women's proximity to the troops brought out the best in fighting men. Wives and daughters who lived in isolated frontier forts motivated men to be women's "protectors" against Indians, Mexicans, and frontiersmen. Meanwhile, children raised in garrisons were deemed a steady source of future officers, soldiers, and military mates.[65] Military planners regularly used women's proximity to battlefields to urge soldiers to heroics. They resurrected the ancient idea that enemy soldiers were animals lusting after "Beauty and Booty"—lovers, wives, and daughters as well as family property. Thus, Andrew Jackson portrayed the defense of New Orleans as an effort "to save the ladies of the city from being ravished by a victorious British army." And Confederate General Beauregard called on soldiers to exhibit courage against Union troops "bent on rape and theft." Women were what Judith Stiehm calls "*de facto* pacifists" lacking access to legitimate means of violence; men equated masculinity with the protection of women; and young soldiers were pressed to prefer chivalry and death to desertion or defeat.[66]

Women's wartime civic virtue also encompassed a willingness to exemplify patriotic self-sacrifice. During World War I, for instance, liberty's granddaughters were urged "to eliminate waste and extravagance." The Wilson administration called on "The Women's Land Army of America" to "Save a Loaf a Week—Help Win the War" and "Eat Less" because

"Food is Ammunition." The Women's Central Committee on Food Conservation published a cookbook with patriotic recipes that provided substitutes for the meat, wheat, fats, sugar, and milk needed by fighting men. As the authors wrote, "All the blood, all the heroism, all the money and munitions in the world will not win this war unless our [troops] . . . are fed." Political leaders and popular commentators also counseled women to sacrifice domestic virtue to assume a larger role in production, contribute labor and money to the war effort, and organize and participate in patriotic events. Women's exemplary patriotism functioned to shame selfish men to do their duty lest they suffer the stigma of "despicable effeminacy." [67]

Furthermore women's civic virtue included keeping alive "the flame of nonwarlike values" during war.[68] Spartan Mothers operated the Victorian home as an island of peace, health, and prosperity ostensibly insulated from the violence, disease, and suffering of the battlefield. The home was a source of strength and meaning for men confronting their mortality. Soldiers fought to protect it and made innumerable sacrifices for it. Gerald Linderman tells the extraordinary story of why 140,000 Union soldiers reenlisted in late 1863 and early 1864. Although volunteers, they gradually became obsessed with survival that increasingly seemed unlikely. Why reenlist and risk dying? It was not abstract patriotism or the $400 reenlistment bonus but the prospect of an immediate thirty- to thirty-five-day furlough home. "Given the likelihood of their deaths, a reenlistment furlough would at least allow them to see their families again." [69]

Wars gave American women an opportunity to show unmistakable patriotism, "to engage in deeds that partake of received notions of glory, honor, nobility, civic virtue." Many women hoped that their "actual or quasi-military participation" would elevate their social status, enhance their rights, and generate greater female autonomy. Did women's civic virtue in wartime persuade men to overcome traditional dread of the female or honor women's claims to a fuller equality? Not quite. Male critics denounced women whose civic virtue took a pacifist bent. Some republican mothers preferred the role of "life-givers" to aiding "life-takers" and inhibited men's recruitment, discipline, and martial courage. The critics also feared women who participated in combat and threatened to destroy the myth that "war is manly" and warriors are women's protectors.

In sum, American men were always ready to devalue women's sacrifices and point to their disorderliness, presuming that they would resume the mantle of liberal patriarchy after the war.[70]

The Dialectic of Womanhood

By the early twentieth century, American womanhood was the cultural stronghold of republican values. Women's domesticity, limited autonomy, reformism, and martial patriotism were to transform the home into a school for male restraint, sacrifice, civility, and public good. Women's selflessness and self-sacrifice, reproduction and parenting, affection and morality as well as encouragement and shame were a civic arsenal that enabled wives and mothers to create a sense of republican timelessness, continuity, and stability to counterbalance men's ideology of forward progress, commerce, and national violence. Few Americans doubted that women's contribution was essential to taming men's passions, securing domestic tranquility, supporting political moderation, and ensuring national survival.

However, the very significance of American womanhood was its partial undoing. The growth of women's status, autonomy, reformism, and civic virtue reinvigorated men's traditional dread of the female. Male critics accused wives of using passionlessness to manipulate men, attacked clubwomen and reformers for family neglect and selfishness, condemned working wives for weakening husbands' sense of responsibility, and blamed working mothers for causing juvenile delinquency and domineering mothers for emasculating their sons. If some commentators denounced the female-managed family as "illimitably selfish, psychologically egocentric, spiritually dwarfish, and decivilizing" as well as a "factory of feeble-mindedness and insanity," others worried that an upsurge in divorces, declining white, middle-class birthrates, the New Woman, and demands for female suffrage signified the emergence of a female individualism that would free men from familial obligations and add female subversion to social disorder.[71]

Many men considered the "crisis of the family" a political crisis, especially in wartime. Jacksonians believed that youth had "to reject maternal influence" as a brake on their masculinity and martial courage. Military leaders feared that women lured lovers, husbands, brothers, and sons away from Civil War battlefields. National leaders argued that it was American mothers' tendency to raise sons with "effeminate tendencies" that explained why enlistees in the Spanish–American War performed so poorly on physical exams. Theodore Roosevelt honored motherhood but also linked it to treason: "The woman who, whether from cowardice, from selfishness, from having a false and vacuous ideal, shirks her duty as a wife and mother, earns the right to our contempt, just as does the man who, from any motive, fears to do his duty in battle when his country calls him." At the outset of World War I, Secretary of War Newton Baker created the Committee on Training Camp Activities, which was to protect young soldiers from seductive young women. Machiavelli's belief that women emasculated boys and ruined young soldiers manifested itself in American military planners' perpetual question: "How can women be controlled so that . . . they cause no loss to military efficiency?"[72]

With remarkable success, American culture called on the republican norms inscribed in fatherhood, fraternity, and female virtue to restrain liberal individualism, infuse it with civic virtue, and thereby reconcile it with social order and public good. Still, the ultimate test of the other liberal tradition in America involved the politics of national defense, geographical expansion, and periodic war. Were families reliable when it came to volunteering young men for military service? And were young men trustworthy when it came to sacrificing individual rights, submitting to military discipline, and risking their lives for the nation?

10 Martial Virtue

Republican mothers were not complete citizens. They lacked formal political rights and were declared deficient in the manly strength, courage, and daring thought necessary to defend the nation in peace and war. Even after women won property and voting rights, they still lacked the informal authority to speak on major affairs of state. Nor were liberal fathers necessarily complete citizens. They might master passion, practice sobriety, consent, vote, and obey law, but equally important, they had to demonstrate a willingness to leave their families, suspend their rights, submit to military discipline, and risk their lives in wartime. Could American individualism accommodate martial virtue?

Fathers' loyalty to families, a citizen–soldier ethic, and a manly martial spirit legitimated local self-defense, amateur soldiering, and male fortitude as civic virtues that prevented domestic tyranny and deterred enemies. However, this republican loyalty was mostly rhetorical. America's militia tradition asked little of men, enabled most to avoid self-sacrifice, and encouraged all to speak the language of civic virtue. The result was a Lockean pacifism that combined bellicose masculinity with a preference for private interest and peace with European powers. Simultaneously, men's economic interest in colonizing the continent urged a Lockean tolerance for a small standing army that subjugated Indians, hosted a professional officer corps, eventually supported an aggressive nationalism, and ultimately legitimated selective conscription.

Would rights-bearing American men support the growth of a powerful military establishment? Would passionate youth enlist in Indian wars, defer to military professionals, acquiesce to conscription, and carry the American flag abroad? Military planners were obsessed with these questions. Their concern neared desperation in the early twentieth century, when American elites announced their imperial ambitions and promoted the ideal of universal military training. Bankers, businessmen, politicians, and professional officers provided what proved to be an enduring answer to the youth question. Young men's excessive individualism should be tamed by a mandatory military education in civic virtue that would discipline them and transform them into trustworthy citizens prepared to die for the flag, veterans who promoted patriotism in peace, and fathers who fostered martial virtue in the new generation.

The Family Front

For Locke, individual consent produced an obligation to participate in state violence. Likewise, George Washington told Congress "that every citizen who enjoys the protection of a free government owes . . . his personal services to the defense of it." A century later, General Hugh Scott stated, "It is fundamental with a free people that . . . each owes to the body politic his duty not only in civil affairs but also in the defense of the nation."[2] Locke, Washington, and Scott presumed that citizenship demanded civic virtue manifested in military service. And they relied on families to reconcile men's selfishness and selfless service to the nation.

American colonists inherited the republican belief that free men were obliged to defend liberty and prevent tyranny by serving in militia units. The 1641 "Massachusetts Body of Liberties" stressed that the militia were local, self-defense forces: "No man shall be compelled to go out of the limits of this plantation upon any offensive wars which this Commonwealth or any of our friends or confederates shall voluntarily undertake." The militia's citizen–soldiers were fathers and farmers, part-time amateurs who drilled irregularly and bore arms only when confronted by imminent threats to family, property, and community. They were not expected to participate in protracted skirmishes far from home; they "felt no inclination to take the field for extended campaigns that did not involve their own interests and aspirations in any direct ways that they could understand."[3] As a result, governors had difficulty raising the militia and preventing desertions during the imperial wars of the colonial era.

The close association of family defense, amateurism, and militia service explained why Washington doubted the militia could prosecute a continental war: "Men just dragged from the tender scenes of domestic life, unaccustomed to the din of arms, totally unacquainted with every kind of military skill . . . [are] timid, and ready to fly from their own shadows." The key to building an effective Continental Army was to satisfy men's family interests by paying soldiers and officers enough money to provide for their dependents. Washington told the Continental Congress that the man who feels that "his pay will not support him" will also feel that "he cannot ruin himself and family to serve his country." However, "a support that renders him independent" will enable him to fulfill both family and military obligations.[4] The family front shaped the battlefront.

From the Revolution onward, men's relation to their families mediated military manpower policy. Though the regular army was a small force, planners understood that meeting minimal troop quotas required concern for recruits' proximity to their families and their ability to safeguard their family interests. Soldiers were often allowed to take their wives and children to frontier garrisons and even war zones. Enlisted men's wives were camp cooks, provisioners, laundresses, and nurses; officers' wives performed social service functions. Occasionally their children attended garrison schools where boys were molded into future recruits. Having women and children in the military's "tail section" reduced men's isolation and boredom, making desertion less likely and courage more common. "As more than one officer has said," notes Judith Stiehm, "My wife and children represent my country for me. They are the concrete answer to the question '*why.*'"[5] Planners also provided soldiers an opportunity to protect and enhance their family property. Enlisted men aspired to acquire cheap Western land or gold; officers could return home to tend to family business; and some, like Andrew Jackson, were able to use soldiering as an occasion for real estate speculation.[6]

Planners also recognized that men could be lured into the army as an escape from family responsibilities. Young men could evade parental authority or impending marriages by enlisting in the one organization where the stigma of bachelorhood was overshadowed by the doing of manly deeds. Husbands and fathers might forgo family obligations by disappearing into a mobile organization that cared little about one's past. In turn, the military offered recruits a surrogate family and an alternate route to immortality. The army was a fraternity of battle reinforced by the bonds of occasional combat. It provided men intense moments of what Robert J. Lifton calls "experiential transcendence" or what J. Glenn Gray describes as "nothing less than the assurance of our immortality."[7] With the atrophy of father–son bonds, military life restored hope for male continuity, cooperation, and bonding.

The military could not be a satisfactory surrogate family without women, and military planners usually included women in their calculations. They encouraged soldiers to stay in touch with families back home and urged women to play "the role of wives, daughters, mothers, and 'sweethearts,' waving their men off to war, writing letters of encouragement and devotion in the field, reminding them that women's and children's safety depends on men's bravery." The brass often allowed young soldiers to have access to mistresses, prostitutes, and Indian and Mexican concubines in the hope that young recruits would satisfy their sexual desires without sapping their martial energies. While army doctors and chaplains continually ranted against sexual license in the ranks, officers generally tolerated it.[8]

Still, the military's ability to recruit men by promising to support, absorb, or substitute for their families was compromised by a liberalism that legitimated individual rights against the state and a republicanism that stigmatized the regular, standing army as a source of corruption and tyranny. Why should a man attend a local militia muster when he wanted to work the family farm? Why should an individual voluntarily submit to despotic military discipline when he could be the patriarch of his own family? The initial answer was an American military ethic that reconciled individual interest and martial virtue by elevating the rhetoric of manly self-sacrifice over the practice of soldiering.

Individual Interest and Martial Virtue

"Men accustomed to unbounded freedom and no control cannot brook the restraint which is indispensibly necessary to the good order and government of an army, without which licentiousness and every kind of disorder triumphantly reign." Washington's liberalism of fear asserted that individual passions unleashed in a climate of liberty caused chaos. Men's fickle nature explained the "outpouring of enlistments and material and moral support" at the onset of the Revolution but also the antipathy and anti-army sentiments that surfaced in the 1780s. Materialism prompted many to avoid military service because they usually had more to gain on the home front than the battlefront. Recognizing this, the superintendent of an ironworks complained in 1776 that farmers took factory jobs "solely to be clear of the militia and from no other reason."[9]

For the most part, Americans served the nation at their personal convenience. Militia service was compulsory in theory but largely voluntary in practice. State officials recruited less by patriotism and coercion than by offering money and land bounties, exempting men who found substitutes, and pardoning deserters who returned to service.[10] After the Revolution, states maintained militia units on a sporadic basis, and politicians hesitated to call out the militia lest they alienate the electorate. Even when militiamen were mobilized, as they were in the War of 1812, some state officials refused to force men to leave their farms for combat zones. And those who did actual militia service usually did remarkably little. They rarely attended muster, regularly resisted military discipline, and usually elected compliant officers. Their training consisted of a little drilling and a lot of parades, games, and amusements mixed with drinking. Similarly, middle-class volunteer companies were often social fraternities that favored fancy uniforms and bellicose rhetoric, emphasizing showy pomp but avoiding bloody circumstance. Precisely because the militia and volunteers were often considered "a joke, a bore, a nuisance," most men were free to fulfill their family obligations and play part-time citizen–soldiers on the side.[11]

This reconciliation of individual interest and martial virtue fueled an enduring myth of the citizen–soldier. Popular culture applauded farmers, merchants, and frontiersmen as men who plied family interests but stood ready to defend the commonwealth. Their lack of training and discipline was construed as a civic virtue: amateurism testified to Americans' *natural* love of liberty and *natural* savvy, courage, and ardor, which flourished in an environment free from aristocratic officers, standing armies, and tyrants.[12] Presumably the average citizen would rise to the occasion. He would volunteer for self-sacrificial service, exhibit martial courage, and defeat enemies. Thus, Andrew Jackson told his troops at New Orleans: "Inhabitants of an opulent and commercial town, you have by a spontaneous effort shaken off the habits which are created by wealth, and shown that you are resolved to deserve the blessings of fortune by bravely defending them."[13] Every American citizen was a Cincinnatus.

The myth of the citizen–soldier fueled men's bellicosity. Textbooks, novels, speeches, newspapers, and guidebooks honored Revolutionary War heroes, the American love of arms, the patriotic symbolism of uniforms, and the martial testing of manhood. Pacifist A. A. Livermore lamented men's martial spirit:

> It is by the wooden sword, and the tin drum of boyhood. It is by the training and annual muster. It is by the red uniform and the white plume, and the prancing steed. It is by the cannon's thunder, and the gleam of the bayonet. It is by ballads of Robin Hood, and histories of Napoleon, and "Tales of Crusaders." It is by the presentation of flags by the hands of the fair, and the huzzas for victory. It is by the example of the father and the consent of the mother. . . . By one and all, the heart of the community is educated for war, from the cradle to the coffin.[14]

The martial spirit was manifest in boys' tendency to emulate soldiers to prove their masculinity. A common belief was that "a weak, puny boy" who excelled at martial virtues would be transformed into "a robust, healthy, manly man." His masculinity was measured by a "sense of courage and gallantry" and a belief that "the risking of life [is] an everyday affair." The martial spirit was also manifest in widespread support for the virtues of gun ownership, frontier violence, dueling, lynching, vigilantism, and "enthusiasm for . . . paramilitary organization." [15] If men were con-demned for reckless violence, they were partly excused by their manhood and martial spirit.

Boys who played soldiers and men who were soldiers considered the ultimate test of masculinity to be military combat. In the Revolution, the War of 1812, the Mexican War, and especially the Civil War, "many young men who filled the ranks voluntarily did so enthusiastically." Combat as the test of manhood was the central theme of *The Red Badge of Courage*, where the protagonist dreams of manly deeds but confronts effeminate cowardice. Military planners and officers used young men's search for manhood as a lever to foster recruitment, discipline, and combat effective-ness and then used young men's fear of effeminacy to inhibit dereliction of duty. They taught that true manhood was courage in confronting danger, while cowardice was "the burial of manhood and self-respect." [16]

Even youthful disenchantment with the grim realities of combat fed the martial spirit. Soldiers rarely sustained martial enthusiasm in the face of prolonged absence from home, tedious drilling, military discipline, and exposure to camp disease, rotten corpses, and battlefield perils. As each American war dragged on, enlistments fell and desertions rose. For many Civil War volunteers, the bellicose rhetoric of the early years was replaced by a deep sense of estrangement and antimilitarism. While one could not accuse hardened veterans of effeminacy, both disenchanted veterans and critics were quick to question the manhood of those who did not fight and also the fortitude of a postwar generation that talked war without having been tested by it. In the postbellum years, for example, Francis Parkman condemned "emasculate" mediocrity in the North and praised what he believed was the South's constant emphasis on "military honor." [17] By the century's end, a resurrection of martial masculinity was in full swing. War was "a matter of sacrificing job or education, an arm, a leg, perhaps life itself, . . . [and] that was . . . precisely its value," because "through the cru-cible of combat a boy would emerge a man." Politicians and officers argued that "real" men were needed to "cleanse America's soul of its impurities and halt the disquieting growth of a crass economic individualism." [18]

In every generation, one could hear critics diagnose the American dis-ease as excessive individualism and then prescribe martial masculinity and military training as the cure. This strand of liberalism legitimated masculine fortitude, fostered male bonding, and sustained a belief that citizenship, martial rhetoric, and military service held together the tapestry of American life. Boys who practiced war games, men who paraded in uniforms, and veterans who told war stories gave public testimony to the value of individual self-sacrifice for the flag. They were implicit Lockean pedagogues who forged a domestic environment that honored manly self-control, sobriety, discipline, and civic virtue. Though few American men actually served as soldiers, and fewer saw combat, men's identification with the martial spirit and citizen soldiering helped to restrain male passions and interests, strengthen civic fraternity, and foster community loyalty. Don Higginbotham writes, "To deny the credibility of the militia was to deny the worthiness of the people collectively." [19] And to deny the martial spirit was to deny the worthiness of American manhood and citizenship.

The Worthiness of the People

Republicanism measured the worthiness of the people by the proliferation of independent freeholders drilled in civic virtue and jealous of liberty. A 1799 letter to the *New London Bee* explained that republican citizens refused to submit to "Prussian military discipline, or devote their valor to promote the views of ambition or to oppose their country and prosperity with a standing army." Conversely, only corrupt, dependent men would enlist in a standing army, subject themselves to brutal discipline, austere living conditions, and meager irregular pay, and serve as the instruments of tyranny. [20] If a republic's health depended on the degree to which citizens voiced antipathy to a standing military establishment, then the early American republic was hale and hardy.

Samuel Adams stated the obvious when he said that a "standing army . . . is always dangerous to the liberties of the people. Soldiers are apt to consider themselves as a body distinct from the rest of citizens. . . . Such a power should be watched with a jealous eye." [21] During the ratification debates, opponents to the Constitution warned against putting the purse and sword in federal hands. Jeffersonians praised the militia, played on fears of a standing army, and partially transformed the small regular army into a corps of engineers and road builders. Jacksonians preferred to attack the military establishment as a corrupt European-style aristocracy. Postbellum orators launched jeremiads against standing armies, and Joshua Logan codified the sermons in his *Volunteer Soldier of America*. Anti-army critics found new allies among Social Darwinists who condemned militarism as unproductive and also among labor organizers who confronted strike-breaking troops. Thus, Samuel Gompers restated John Trenchard's old argument: "Standing armies are always used to exercise tyranny over people, and are one of the prime causes of a rupture in the country."[22]

This attitude gave rise to an implicit Lockean pacifism. Citizens and politicians rarely approved more than minimal expenditures or troop quotas for the regular army. They tolerated enlarged budgets and quotas during major conflicts only to demand immediate shrinkage when the crisis abated. Regular soldiers could not be trusted: they pursued crude self-interest without redeeming civic value. Poor men enlisted to acquire clothing, food, lodging, and bounties. The adventurous joined to go West with the army to seek their fortunes. Immigrants saw the army as a means of survival. Alcoholics sought the army's daily liquor ration. Criminals joined to escape prosecution. Overall, "the [regular] army was an evasion, a bolthole, a last resort, a confession of failure. . . . In the ranks, hiding under assumed names where necessary, the misfits, bad hats, transgressors and broken men could sink out of sight, could sink down toward the mudsill of society."[23]

Regular army officers were equally suspect of avarice. A U.S. Military Academy appointment provided a free education in civil engineering; an assignment in the city offered possible entry into upper-class society; a frontier post created opportunity for speculation. At the same time, periodic expansion and contraction of the top-heavy officer corps made tenure uncertain, promotion unlikely, and corruption omnipresent. For academy graduates, the future was in the civilian sector. West Point Superintendent Robert E. Lee confided to a friend, "I can advise no young man to enter the army. The same application, the same self-denial, the same endurance, in any other profession will advance him faster and farther." Recruiters knew they had to appeal to men's crude self-interest, but officers constantly complained, "For our small army we go to the labor market for recruits. When the demand for labor is lax, the stipend of the soldier attracts; when the daily wage goes up, recruiting is at its lowest ebb. There is no appeal to patriotism, no appeal for the individual to obtain military training as the highest duty of his citizenship."[24] The regular soldier was a hired gun.

The pervasive myth of the citizen–soldier in the militia stymied national leaders' effort to build a professional army. Top military thinkers tried to demythify the militia by arguing: "That a well-organized militia is essential to the security of a free people is one of those fine sayings that . . . are often copied, but never acted upon." Emory Upton ranked "the employment of the militia and undisciplined troops commanded by generals and officers utterly ignorant of the military art" as the main reason for America's military weakness.[25] Leaders hoping to professionalize the army's officer corps were put off by amateurs' bellicosity. Samuel Huntington contrasts two views of war: "The military ethic . . . draws a sharp distinction between armed strength and bellicosity, the military state and the warlike state. The former embodies the military virtues of ordered power: discipline, hierarchy, restraint, steadfastness. The latter is characterized by will, irresponsible excitement and enthusiasm, and by the love of violence, glory, and adventure."[26] Military professionals distrusted amateur soldiers whose passions outran their reason, destroyed the chain of command, and, at best, generated a sunshine patriotism. But the professionals remained on the defensive into the twentieth century. Cultural icons from Minutemen to Rough Riders reinforced the popularity of citizen–soldiers, while ancient fears of selfish thugs and standing armies isolated military modernizers.

The national romance with amateurs meant that early American soldiering was conceived in defensive terms. Militiamen and volunteers stayed close to the family hearth, while the regular army had insufficient appropriations and troops to engage in action beyond continental borders. The American public showed little inclination to take military initiative against European powers. For most, the militia and volunteers were social clubs that occasionally assumed local police powers. The small federal army was a social agency that provided employment for the poor, assimilated immigrants, built roads and bridges, and taught men traits and skills transferable to the civilian economy. "Like the organization of the factory," remarks Anne Norton, "that of the army inculcated in men . . . discipline and self-control."[27] Regimental life was preparation for a regimented economy.

Following Locke, early Americans seemed convinced that the militia and volunteers backed by a small regular army and navy were sufficient for maintaining domestic order and national defense. Their martial spirit promoted male fortitude, bellicose rhetoric, and patriotic parades, but not a militarism that reached toward imperialism. Before the Spanish–American War, "The idea that the United States would ever raise major expeditionary forces to exert its military power on the world stage scarcely occurred to anyone."[28] The military drama enacted on the continental stage, however, was quite another story.

Colonizing the Continent

J. G. A. Pocock argues that the ideal of the armed citizenry thrived on the American frontier where pioneers were considered the nation's best hope "for an almost unlimited renewal of virtue in the fee-simple empire."[29] The irony was that the myth of the citizen–soldier joined to the ostensible security of a representative government made the federal army seem less worrisome. If the people were armed, they could defeat any federal army manipulated by a political tyrant; if legislators and presidents were elected by the people, politicians would ensure civilian control of the federal army. Early in the nineteenth century, the traditional fear of the regular army as a source of tyranny began to be transformed into the modern anxiety that the regular army was an extravagance. However, this anxiety was partly offset by men's desire to acquire inexpensive homesteads on the frontier. The profits of colonization would underwrite the costs of a federal army that subjugated and exterminated Indians.

Americans could be pragmatists about standing armies. When militia units proved unreliable in the colonial wars, several provinces created "semiprofessional" armies that recruited militiamen but paid and trained them for extended service. Even colonial hostility to the Redcoats was mixed with support for the British soldiers who provided provincial defense and stimulated the local economy. For Puritan New England in particular, "the New Model Army and Cromwellian tradition provided a historical referent for acceptance of, indeed insistence upon, a standing army of nonmonarchical origin."[30] American colonists accepted the idea that a standing army could be functional in the cause of liberty.

American revolutionaries understood that protection of individual rights was contingent on a standing army. The 1780 Massachusetts Bill of Rights reaffirmed the citizens' obligation to serve: "Each individual of the society has a right to be protected by it in the enjoyment of his life, liberty, and property, according to standing laws. He is obliged, consequently, to contribute his share to the expense of the protection; to give his personal service, or an equivalent, when necessary."[31] But military analysts questioned whether that obligation was adequately fulfilled by the native "genius or inclination" of militiamen. Washington preferred the trained, disciplined soldiers of the standing Continental Army. His aide, General Friedrich von Steuben, preferred predictable, self-interested enlistment to both compulsion and passionate patriotism.[32] To the extent that the Continental Army led by professional officers was perceived as the military bulwark of the Revolution, the idea that individual rights were best protected by a standing federal army was part of the Revolution's legacy.

Anti-Federalists, Jeffersonians, and Jacksonians continued to criticize standing armies—but often halfheartedly. While anti-Federalists won Constitutional amendments and a 1792 Militia Act that reinforced the citizen–soldier ethic, they also ceded to Federalists a peacetime standing army and presidential authority over local militia. Jefferson reflected Americans' grudging toleration of the regular army by establishing the U.S. Military Academy to provide formal education for regular army officers and by increasing regular troop quotas during an 1808 conflict with the British. Andrew Jackson symbolized the virtues of the citizen–soldier but also expressed disdain for amateurs, complaining that his Kentucky riflemen were poorly equipped, trained, and disciplined. He told his troops, "The relative situation of your General to you is that of a father to his family, and as such pledges himself to *his* duty. Your *moral duty*, then, is obedience . . . yielded without coercion."[33] Jackson attacked aristocracy but sought to impose liberal patriarchy and military discipline on his troops as well as civilians, as military governor of New Orleans and Florida and as president.

Of signal import, Jackson and his followers adopted a Lockean logic to justify efforts by the federal government and army to impose military "discipline" on native Americans. On the one hand, Jacksonians treated them as children who were enslaved by their own passions but potentially educable, independent, and able to assimilate to white Protestant culture. The U.S. government played the part of the Lockean father who mixed affection and shame to guide Indians toward sobriety, industry, and adulthood. Rogin explains, "If Indians were 'red children,' whites thought of themselves as parents. . . . [Indeed,] whites could not imagine Indians outside the parent-child context." Jackson shone as the ideal father who "promised to rescue his 'red children' from the advancing tide of white settlement in the east, protect them in the west, and help them advance to civilization." On the other hand, Jacksonians also viewed Indians as barbaric foreigners outside the social contract. Failing to follow God's injunction to be industrious, Indians thrived on waste and spoilage. Their land remained part of mankind's common stock. The Lockean ideal was for whites to enter into commerce and conversation with Indians, but this was difficult when Indians were cast as wildly passionate creatures.[34] The pragmatic solution was to execute the law of nature by using the regular army to subjugate and remove them from the commons.

White colonization was justified by men's divine duty to produce and to extend the blessings of liberty. Secretary of War Lewis Cass called continental expansion "the progress of civilization and improvement, the triumph of industry and art, by which these regions have been reclaimed, and over which freedom, religion, and science are extending their sway." Jackson viewed geographical expansion a way to "place a dense and civilized population in large tracts of country now occupied by a few savage hunters."[35] He encouraged whites to settle on Indian lands regardless of treaties and then claimed a Lockean right to self-defense to legitimate war: "Whites fought Indians in the name of self-defense . . . of frontier families against Indian attacks and . . . 'infant communities' against attacks which would annihilate the political body."[36] Jackson was a master colonizer, manipulator, and warmonger. Critics called him a tyrant, but Jackson deflected criticism by focusing his militarism on the distant frontier, where his small regular army seemed to be no threat to civil society.[37]

American men had much to gain by trusting colonizing presidents and federal soldiers who executed America's "manifest destiny." If Locke helped to legitimate white conquest of native Americans, his arguments could be revived to justify Anglo conquest of Mexican territories and

American freeholders' claims to huge tracts of Mexican land. One American naval officer told Californians of their new future: "We come to prepare this magnificent region for the use of other men . . . who will hereafter occupy and till the soil. But . . . we shall not displace you, if you act properly. . . . You can easily learn, but you are indolent. I hope you will alter your habits, and be industrious and frugal, and give up all the low vices which you practice. . . . We shall watch over you, and give you true liberty . . . but beware of sedition, lawlessness, and all other crimes, for the army which shields can assuredly punish."[38] The choice was clear: assimilation or extermination.

Tales of continental expansion and heroic combat provided regular army officers increasing political respectability. Washington was the nation's first military president. Three decades later, Jackson's presidency produced enough popularity to urge "the electorate . . . to find more appeal than menace in candidates who had been warriors."[39] And looking back from 1880, Emory Upton remarked on the rising political legitimacy of military figures: "Our own people, no less than the Romans, are fond of rewarding our military heroes. The Revolution made Washington President; . . . the war of 1812 elevated Jackson and Harrison; . . . the Mexican war raised Taylor and Pierce; . . . the Rebellion [Civil War] has already made Grant President for two terms, Hayes for one term, while . . . Garfield owes his high office as much to his fame as a soldier as to his reputation as a statesman."[40] A man's military service and especially his combat record were becoming evidence of his civic virtue and qualifications for public office.

Pocock's argument that the frontier sustained hope for a renewal of civic virtue in America should be qualified. First, the West was home to an armed citizenry but perhaps the most important armed citizens were the federal soldiers who rid the frontier of indigenous peoples, built roads and bridges, and opened vast land tracts to white settlement and ownership. The regular army stood behind the frontier freeholder. Second, if the West provided land for freeholders, it also hosted crass speculation, commercial corruption, and unrestrained violence. Moreover, the pristine image of virtuous pioneers saving the commonwealth implicitly justified disregard for virtue in Eastern markets and cities.[41] Finally, the West was a laboratory for militarism and nationalism. Americans' support for continental expansion enhanced the likelihood that Americans would be willing to bring "liberty" to "children" and "savages" across the sea. John William Ward explains: "In 1825, Americans were to save the world by example; in 1845, Americans were to save the world by absorbing it."[42]

Saving the World

For military planners, the beauty of colonization was that it allowed the majority of men to pursue private interests and speak the rhetoric of martial virtue without forcing them to serve in the army. A relative handful of regular soldiers was adequate for westward expansion. However, the Civil War experience in total war indicated that large numbers of men would be needed to fight future battles. As a result, planners had to persuade American men to go beyond toleration of the federal army so that they would participate in it when called. Only then could America make a serious attempt to "save the world" by absorbing it.

National leaders with global ambitions had to counteract three common arguments against federal military service. Pacifists' perspectives included religious, rationalist, and economic reasons that a citizen should go about his own business and resist growing state and military influence. This view was reinforced by a Gilded Age "business pacifism" that praised industrial progress as antithetical to militarism. Rugged individualists' argument was that bearing arms was manly but a real man "yielded no automatic obedience to those in command." Masculinity required a "martial but unmilitary" attitude.[43] Finally, democratic critics railed against the Chevalier, a stereotyped Military Academy graduate whose feudal code of honor threatened men's rights by upholding aristocratic privilege.[44]

Each argument won some support from Victorian wives and mothers who preached male piety against male war games, opposed breadwinners' enlistments, and defended marital fidelity against soldiers' sexual escapades. Women were disproportionately represented among American pacifists.[45] And while men were less likely to preach pacifism and more apt to praise martial masculinity, they too had strong reasons to avoid military service. Why sacrifice their rights, livelihood, or opportunities to fight the Seminoles in Florida's disease-ridden swamps? Why garrison the frontier when one could buy and sell it or own and farm it? Women's family commitments and men's individualism were obstacles to military growth. Even on the eve of World War I, when martial enthusiasm ran high, Chief of Staff Hugh Scott complained that the army could not amass enough troops to push Pancho Villa back into Mexico: "Public interest in the Army and Navy, and national defense generally, had been aroused to a comparatively high degree; yet, in what is considered by the Government a grave emergency, . . . recruiting is found so difficult that many of its organizations have not yet, over three months after the call, been raised to even minimum peace strength."[46] The rhetoric of citizen soldiering was matched by men's desire to avoid it. And in daily discourse, "soldiering" referred to workers who wasted time.

The gap between martial rhetoric and material reality became apparent in the Civil War. Immense slaughter and extraordinary desertion rates urged North and South to experiment with national conscription. On both sides, antidraft protests and riots challenged the legality of conscription and the fairness of exemptions favoring the wealthy.[47] Meanwhile, evidence accrued that amateur soldiers lacked the discipline for prolonged modern warfare. Generals Grant and Sherman sought "complete conquest"; Mosby's Raiders employed ambushes, night attacks, and burnings; and war spilled into civilian life. Martial virtue and discipline faltered as troops engaged in an orgy of looting, rape, and destruction. One victim of total war was the myth that men were women's protectors rather than insatiable beasts.[48]

Military planners and political allies believed that American men had grown too individualistic, citizen–soldiers too soft, and enemies had become devouring monsters. The idea that America was defenseless and its enemies were ruthless produced what Rogin calls an "American demonology" that redefined the meaning of national defense.[49] Men's families and estates were permanently threatened by alien forces that used overt and covert means of conquest. Henceforth, extreme measures could be justified to ensure national survival. Men could be forced to serve in an enlarged standing army managed by professional officers. The civilian economy could be mobilized for "gross national product" wars. Battles could be initiated abroad as necessary to prevent wars at home.

James A. Garfield expressed the emergent viewpoint in an 1878 *North American Review* article: "A republic, however free, requires the service of a certain number of men whose ambition is higher than mere private gains, whose lives are inseparable from the life of the nation, and whose labors and emoluments depend absolutely upon the honor and prosperity of the government, and who can advance themselves only by serving their country." [50] The trend was toward building a professional officer corps composed of a few good men who could manage a modest standing army in peacetime and selectively conscript citizens who were not essential to economic mobilization in wartime. The success of this effort depended on leaders' ability to get Americans to support a professional officer corps, train for war, consent to conscription, and see economic mobilization as a source of both national victory and individual economic opportunity.

A military revival of the 1880s prepared the way. Fiction and nonfiction books, fraternal orders, newspaper accounts of heroic Indian battles, plus the rise of military schools and military training in public schools and universities pointed toward a growing "militarization of thought, activity, and style." Writers nostalgically recalled Civil War armies as institutions that made boys into men while uniting farm and city as well as rich and poor. Veterans forgot postwar estrangement, proclaimed their civic pride, and flocked into local Grand Army of the Republic posts. The revival was as much a matter of national desperation as martial patriotism. The military seemed to be the only national organization able to restrain men's excessive individualism and materialism, quiet class conflict, and counteract cultural fragmentation. Gerald Linderman observes, "The revival of military spirit was in significant measure the result of [men's] resistance to a society that threatened to measure all things 'by dollar-mark standards' and their search for some alternative way by which they might define what it meant to be an American." [51] It was the liberalism of fear beckoning its republican mate.

The martial rhetoric of the 1880s and 1890s provided a congenial atmosphere for the development of a professional officer corps. Emory Upton's *Military Policy of the United States* blamed wasted American lives and property on amateur soldiers, short-term enlistments, local and state interference in military matters, overreliance on bounties and volunteers, want of military education, and especially the lack of officer training in the art and science of war. Lives, property, and resources could be saved by centralizing military power in the federal government and delegating it to a professional officer corps that rationalized manpower through selective conscription. Should Americans fear the centralization and militarization of power? Upton answered, "No soldier in battle ever witnessed the flight of an undisciplined army without wishing for a strong government. . . . Shall we find greater safety in one that is weaker?"[52] Professional soldiers were in fact more trustworthy than most men because they were members of the civilian family and the public family, and proved devoted to both: "Are not their fathers, mothers, and their own sons in civil life, and . . . are they not citizens of the same country enjoying the blessings of the same government? Nurtured by this government, taught to love and defend its flag, are they alone a large family connection most likely to prove false to the institutions which have placed us first among nations? Is death on the field of battle not evidence of love for one's country?"[53] Upton and others argued that it was time to put to rest Americans' false fear of standing armies.

Gradually, the pacifist was quieted by the professional soldier who promised to secure peace by quelling anarchist and socialist disorders and by preparing for war so that no enemy would dare initiate one. Rugged individualism dissipated as the frontier disappeared, and an emerging efficiency ethic supported the professional officer's devotion to hierarchy, discipline, and order. And the Chevalier shed his feudal image and joined forces with corporate interests anticipating internationalism. Corporate, political, and military elites increasingly agreed that men's individual rights had set loose passions that imperiled domestic order, that national prosperity and security required imperial expansion, and that only a professional officer corps could achieve success.

Theodore Roosevelt was America's top cheerleader for militarism. America, he said, had a "most regrettable but necessary international police duty" and it performed that duty "for the sake of the welfare of mankind."[54] Like Locke, Roosevelt stressed the benefits of international trade and diplomacy but asserted a divine duty to extend the Protestant ethic to "barbarous" and "semi-barbarous" peoples. To defend national integrity and perform the nation's global duty, the military had to grow. That meant, among other things, that the republican case for a small defensive navy made way for a large investment in battleships to secure American trade and acquisitions in the Caribbean, Central America, the Philippines, Hawaii, and Alaska. Roosevelt explained, "The only efficient use for the Navy is for offense."[55] The line between defense and offense blurred; *Fortuna* was relocated from the continent to the high seas; and American civic virtue increasingly approximated Machiavellian imperialism.

Elihu Root fortified American Machiavellianism by arguing that the function of a peacetime army was "to provide for war." Officers were to be systematically trained for all possible contingencies and promoted on the basis of "ability, intellectual activity, faithful performance of duty, and gallant conduct." Citizens were to do their part by developing proper martial virtues, training for war and anticipating it, and voluntarily deferring to the military's professional expertise. Americans must recognize, Root declared, that "it is really absurd that a nation which maintains but a small regular army and depends upon unprofessional citizen soldiery for its defense should run along as we have done for one hundred and ten years under a militia law which never worked satisfactorily in the beginning, and which was perfectly obsolete before any man now fit for military duty was born." [56] The myth of the militia had to die for a modern military to come alive.

Roosevelt and Root hoped to fend off charges of militarism by appealing to patriotism. Roosevelt proclaimed, "Declamation against militarism has no more serious place in an earnest and intelligent movement for righteousness in this country than declamation against the worship of Baal or Astaroth. It is declamation against a non-existent evil." [57] Root reminded Americans of the army's proud record: "The manifold services which have been rendered by officers . . . and the effective zeal and devotion which they have exhibited in succoring the distressed, teaching the ignorant, establishing and maintaining civil law, fighting against pestilence, introducing sanitary reforms, and promoting and aiding peaceful industry should be regarded as proof, if any were needed, that American soldiers do not cease to be American citizens, and that no danger is to be apprehended from a reasonable enlargement of the army which affords such evidence of its character and spirit." [58] The army was a social service institution and its greatest potential service was to imbue young Americans with civic virtue.

A School for Civic Virtue

Would impulsive, individualistic youth sacrifice their rights to serve in the military? Early in the twentieth century, national elites argued for universal military training to strengthen the bonds between youth and the state. The idea was that "every able-bodied young man when he reached nineteen would be required to spend six months to a year or more in military camp, trained by professional soldiers in obedience, sanitation, citizenship, and combat." [59] One goal was to expose young men to martial virtues and military training before they established their own families or economic footholds. Another goal was to produce a mass of trained youth that would be the army's reserve force, ready to heed the call to arms and submit to military discipline. Especially between 1915 and 1917, national leaders waged an intensive campaign to garner public support for mandated training. They founded model training camps for civilians, encouraged high schools and colleges to install military classes in curricula, and lobbied for federal subsidies and political support.

One of their crucial selling points was the argument that universal training was a panacea for America's domestic problems. Wall Street interests wanted universal training to foster "a meek and disciplined labor group that will make no trouble at home, and will fight obediently to defend the American dollar abroad." The military would teach youth the self-control and fortitude demanded in the factory and the office and make them more desirable commodities in the labor market. Young workers and immigrants, in particular, would be habituated to self-restraint, national loyalty, and conditioned citizenship, contributing to the restoration of "order and unity to the country." Peacetime training would turn the military into the premier national university of civil virtue. General Leonard Wood capsulized the pedagogical benefits: "[It] would give us a condition of real national preparedness, a much higher type of citizenship, a lower criminal rate, and an enormously improved economic efficiency." [60]

The campaign for universal military training was a bold attempt to settle the man question once and for all. Plato hoped to build an ideal republic by isolating and educating youth. Locke wanted reasonable fathers to teach sobriety and patriotism to sons. Now a small but powerful clique of Americans called on the military to isolate youth from family and social influences, tame their passions and subdue their interests, and play the part of liberal pedagogue administering a compulsory civic education. Wood explained that universal military training would produce "the moral organization of the people, the building up of that sense of individual obligation for service to the nation which is the basis of true patriotism, the teaching of our people to think in terms of the nation rather than those of a locality or of a personal interest." [61] Here was a republicanism turned upside down. If early republicans believed that the armed citizenry defending property and liberty would cultivate civic virtue, America's martial republicans argued that officers should inculcate civic virtue and teach youth the sobriety and civility that would prepare them for restrained liberty and acquisitiveness in the marketplace. Civic virtue was no longer a defense against state tyranny but a statist instrument for disciplining citizens.

The drive for universal military training met considerable public resistance, but what Huntington considers the failure of neo-Hamiltonianism underestimates its influence.[62] Proselytizers like Leonard Wood laid the groundwork for a selective conscription in World War I that was expected to have the same effect as universal training. If "the old social agencies of socialization and social control—the family, the church, the school—seemed to have become ineffective, and grubby self-interest, materialism, and pacifism appeared to sap the vitality of the nation," selective conscription would encourage all young men to anticipate military training and service, many to undergo a compulsory military education, and a few to protect American interests abroad.[63] Selective conscription would assure corporate planners that their essential work force remained intact in wartime; it would provide political elites a powerful instrument for managing the allocation of the national manpower in the preparation and prosecution of war; and finally, it would solve the military manpower problem by enabling officers to build an expandable army "with the capacity to exert superior military force in time to meet any given national emergency."[64] From the elites' vantage point, selective conscription was a fine formula for realizing the bifurcated Lockean dream of domestic peace and international power.

Elites marketed selective conscription in republican rhetoric and liberal language. General Scott recalled compulsory service as the "corner stone of every republic in the history of the world" and the legacy of "the makers of our Constitution and . . . our early laws."[65] In effect, he evoked America's "ancient constitution" to justify the innovative idea of attaching compulsory service to the standing federal army. Other conscription boosters spoke in neo-Lockean accents, emphasizing that men's commitment to individual rights entailed an obligation to defend liberty through military service, especially in a demonic age when "the safeguard of isolation no longer exists." Men who believed in "asserting their own rights and in respecting those of others" were told to understand that "these high ideals impose . . . duties that require something more than a policy of merely passive defense."[66] In the fragile international state of nature, America needed active citizens willing to defend liberty in all corners of the world.

While these arguments did not eliminate all opposition to the draft, they did reflect a significant shift in public discourse. The revival of the martial spirit, the impetus toward universal military training, and the case for selective conscription all strengthened the presumption that citizenship involved an active, martial contribution to public good. Increasingly, leaders saw the military as a means to forge "a grand civic identity" and "the army [as] the great engine of nationalization in America." It was a "university in khaki" that would establish formal programs to teach literacy, sobriety, and industry and also train immigrants and minorities in how "to speak American and think American."[67]

Even a pacifist such as William James could appreciate the functional appeal of military life. "Militarism," he wrote, "is the great preserver of our ideals of hardihood, and human life with no use for hardihood would be contemptible." Selfishness was a trap. It failed to bring self-fulfillment or foster national unity. Instead, "Martial virtues must be the enduring cement; intrepidity, contempt of softness, surrender of private interest, obedience to command, must still remain the rock upon which states are built." James's "moral equivalent of war" was to conscript "the whole youthful population to form for a certain number of years a part of the army enlisted against *Nature*" and thereby restore youthful "manliness." Most young Americans would comply with conscription into a prefigurative Peace Corps because "military feelings are too deeply grounded to abdicate their place among our ideals," while martial self-sacrifice was tolerable because "the duty is temporary and threatens not . . . to degrade the remainder of one's whole life." Once having paid their "blood-tax" in national service, youth "would tread the earth more proudly, the women would value them more highly, they would be better fathers and teachers of the following generations."[68] Born to passion and greed, young males would become responsible adults, reasonable fathers of families, and patriotic citizens with sufficient civic virtue to practice individual rights without causing chaos.

"A central aspect of patriarchy that feminists have neglected," writes Judith Stiehm, "is the oppression of young men by old men and the price young men are required to pay to acquire old men's privilege. The patriarch, the father, dominates young men as well as women, and demands enormous sacrifices, sometimes including life, from the former. Patriarchs brutalize young men."[69] The martial ethic in America was an enduring challenge to youth to prove their manhood, practice self-denial, demonstrate obedience, and exhibit the civic virtue that informally qualified them to assume manhood and citizenship in a society that treated masculinity, fatherhood, fraternity, and military service as necessary prerequisites to individualism. In the other liberal tradition in America, martial virtues were integral to men's claim to rights.

Engendered Citizenship

An oft-forgotten element of America's Lockean consensus was the requirement that young men speak martial rhetoric and prepare to make military sacrifices for family, community, and nation. A common problem with analyses of America's complex checks and balances is a failure to recognize men's complicity in the state's use of coercive force. And recollections of the liberalism and republicanism at the origins of American political thought tend to overlook the conventional expectation that youth must *earn* their rights by demonstrating martial virtues. The American males who participated in martial rhetoric, militia service, volunteer companies, the regular army, and combat simultaneously laid claim to the manhood and citizenship that warranted individual rights. The self-proclaimed backbone of the nation were veterans, "the peaceful, submissive, law-abiding, order-loving of the country, ready to join hands with all good men in every good work, and prove themselves as brave and good in peace as they were stubborn and unconquerable in war."[70]

Fears of the standing army persisted; pacifism had periodic revivals; rugged individualism eroded martial discipline; democratic norms challenged military hierarchy; and calls for universal training and conscription generated opposition and protest. All this notwithstanding, American men showed remarkable tolerance and support for militarism and also complicity in it. That the militia asked little of men helped to legitimate soldiering. So did the regular army's isolation on the frontier. As middle-class men shed traditional fears of a political tyranny administered by a federal army, they became convinced that a professional military would enhance economic opportunities, discipline the poor, provide jobs for the industrious, ensure social harmony and cultural homogeneity, foster national unity, and defend liberty at home and export it abroad. Middle-class males always had a good chance of being exempted from military service; but many of them joined in state violence to afford both the vocal patriot and the hardened veteran an earned right to speak and act with public authority. That right entailed responsibilities. Family fathers and town fathers joined with fighting fathers to pass the torch of patriotism to the next generation.

Women were precluded from earning their citizenship stripes. Republican mothers' self-denial, female reformers' social services, Spartan Mothers' self-sacrifices, and even women's suffrage were not sufficient to authorize women to speak and act with public authority. Women were "de facto pacifists" lacking the "crucial political weapon" of the credibility that came with the masculine enterprise of proclaiming one's willingness to fight for the nation and from having borne arms for the state.[71] It was one thing to recognize women's right to do some moralizing and municipal housekeeping but quite another to admit women into the manly discourse on foreign policy, national defense, imperialism, and war. Thus, an essential component of the American demonology was that women and children had to be the potential victims of devouring enemies so that men could be their valiant protectors. Otherwise, why would men fight?

The close association of masculinity, militarism, and political rights helped to undermine nonmilitary aspects of citizenship. Men's everyday interest in public affairs, engagement in interest-group and party politics, or willingness to vote, serve on juries, or run for office became relatively low-priority forms of political participation. Far more important to the American republic were men's civic virtue and patriotism measured by their martial enthusiasm and complicity in militarism. The American blend of liberalism and republicanism can be summarized as follows: men were free to pursue private interests and ignore politics as long as they announced their willingness to suspend private interests, risk life and limb in defense of liberty, encourage fortitude and courage among youth, and reinforce the bonds of civic fraternity by worshiping with other men at the altar of martial virtue.

Conclusion
Fortune Is a Man

Next to virtue as a general idea, nothing, I think,
is so beautiful as that of rights, and indeed the
two ideas are mingled.
—*Alexis de Tocqueville*

Men are certainly more under the influence of
their appetites than women; and their appetites are
more depraved by unbridled indulgence and
the fastidious contrivances of satiety.
—*Mary Wollstonecraft*

The other liberal tradition in America was firmly embedded in our culture by the early twentieth century. It supported the proposition that men, women, and youth had to earn individual rights and national citizenship by demonstrating engendered civic virtue. Men who were domesticated by their mothers, lovers, and wives, trained in the rhetoric of masculinity, practiced in martial virtue if not military service, and committed to responsible fatherhood earned a reputation for sobriety, reliability, and civic virtue. They could be trusted with individual rights and full political membership. Women in the home, society, and politics could expect relative autonomy, even public acclaim, if they devoted their lives to marriage, man taming, motherhood, social reform, municipal housekeeping, and the patriotic sacrifice of their men to war. Finally, young men who learned fortitude from fathers and morality from mothers, proved their civic worth in manly rhetoric and martial deed, and matured into marriage and fatherhood demonstrated sufficient control over their passions and interests to assume the rights and responsibilities of citizenship.

This set of cultural assumptions was mostly a middle-class response to the liberalism of fear that equated excessive individualism with social disorder. It was informed by misanthropic doubts that working-class, minority, and immigrant males would acquire sufficient sobriety to serve public good. It was a malestream understanding of the requisites of social order informed by misogynist suspicions that female moralism was a mask for age-old treachery. And it was a reflection of the older generation's apprehension that youth was more prone to profligacy than self-restraint or civic virtue. Taken to extremes, the implication was that only white, Protestant, middle-aged, middle-class men could claim uncontested individual rights and full citizenship.

Ironically, these men could not fully enjoy individualism. Yes, they were formally free to speak their minds, choose their values, and seek their goals, pursue their self-interests and enhance their wealth, participate in politics, and pronounce on public policy and foreign affairs. But they also suffered from the perception that their neighbors and countrymen were a threatening, impassioned, acquisitive population that claimed rights without having earned them. Consequently, middle-class men had to be liberal patriarchs who took responsibility for monitoring other men, all women, and new generations; they had to manage family, social, political, and military institutions; they had to cultivate affection to win subordinates' consent, police the boundaries of individual excess, and monopolize the means of coercion as a final resort for ensuring order. The costs of being on top were high. The duties of the dominant gender were burdensome. Powerful men became estranged from themselves and others. Competitive men suffered stress-related illnesses associated with success and failure. Aggressive men played war games and entrapped their heirs in what Hannah Arendt calls a "banality of evil" that fostered psychic numbing and collective violence. Nonetheless, following Machiavelli's prince and Locke's statesmen (or Hegel's master and Dostoyevski's Grand Inquisitor), American men sacrificed individual aspirations, asserted male prerogative, and endured the physical and emotional load associated with patriarchal domination.[2]

If Americans were "born equal," they were born equally liable to the pull of passions and interests that threatened to erode family obligations, social organization, civic order, and national integrity. The other liberal tradition sought to limit democratic liabilities by "the genius of sexual difference." Symbolic distinctions between manhood and womanhood reinforced civic bonds forged from marriage, paternalism, fraternal fidelity, maternal self-sacrifice, and filial obedience. Social differences that divided the sexes joined women's cultural influence to men's institutional power to legitimate conformity to middle-class moderation. Political expectations that charged women with peaceful management of the home front while men prosecuted violence on the battlefront conspired to promote sexual unity in national self-sacrifice. Individualism has infected the habits of our hearts, but engendered civic virtue has monitored the pulse of our passions.

Habits of Our Hearts

Louis Hartz associates America's Lockean consensus with "the democratic individual" who had "a passion for great achievement," but Hartz discounts that aspect of the consensus which included deep-seated fears of men's excessive passions. Gordon Wood links the Founders' disenchantment with men's civic virtue to their Lockean "science of politics," but he fails to note that Locke's science legitimated patriarchal control of women. Scholars who put both Lockean individualism and republican civic virtue at the origin of American liberalism enlarge the story only to narrow the possibility that individualism incorporated civic virtue. Susan Moller Okin tells us, "Behind the individualist rhetoric, it is clear that the family, and not the adult human individual, is the basic political unit of liberal . . . philosophers."[3]

Our English forebears understood this. Early republican and liberal writers put fathers of families at the center of political theory. They rejected the traditional patriarchalism associated with established churches and absolute monarchs but also doubted that men could be trusted with extensive liberty or individual rights. Restoration intellectuals were shaken by protofeminist rumblings that threatened to free women from traditional restraints and set loose their mischief on society. Worthy Englishmen were horrified at the prospect that a new generation claimed liberty only to practice the profligacy symbolized by licentious bachelors and brutal Redcoats. Prominent theorists such as Harrington and Tyrrell went on a fruitless search for charismatic father figures and impersonal legal norms that would ensure order regardless of people's fundamental flaws.

John Locke's genius was to synthesize the ancient constitution and the modern social contract. He looked back to fatherhood to restrain men's passions and interests, promote their virtue, and foster the fraternity known as civil society. He called on fathers to teach sons manly fortitude and civility in the cause of intergenerational continuity. He proposed a liberal marriage contract that anticipated sufficient autonomy for women to domesticate male passions and still harness female treachery. He projected family affections onto the public sphere, hoping to win men's consent to political father figures with sufficient prerogative to enforce order and protect national boundaries. While he wanted youthful passions to be channeled into martial virtues that supported family prosperity, he also relied on men's family ties to urge their military service and underwrite colonization. For Locke, the heart of England's ancient constitution was the habitual self-restraint and civic virtue that made the extension of individual rights conceivable.

Locke's political theory liberalized patriarchy by elevating consent above coercion. Lockean democracy invited more men to assume individual and political rights *and* also to grant provisional consent and broad prerogative to affectionate political father figures. It unveiled the possibility that middle-class women could increase their domestic autonomy and education *and* also concede private and public power to affectionate men. It justified domestic peace, pacifism, and national self-determination *and* martial virtues, military service, and imperialist aggression against "primitive" peoples. Locke pioneered a theoretical frontier where greater individualism and autonomy, consent and contract, political participation and representative government urged men, women, and youth to submit voluntarily to patriarchy, be complicit in it, and practice a version of civic virtue that sustained it.

Locke articulated the democratic hopes and liberal fears that eventually wed an American dream to an American demonology. Lockean fatherhood prefigured Americans' reconciliation of individual consent and patriarchal authority in families and politics. Lockean marriage anticipated Americans' version of a domestic feminism that enhanced women's opportunities and reinforced male domination. Lockean pacifism foreshadowed Americans' bellicosity in peace, self-righteousness in war, and demands for youthful self-sacrifice in the cause of liberty. Locke authored modern liberal hegemony, and his American heirs extended the copyright.

An investigation of liberal patriarchy and hegemony reveals two of liberalism's darkest secrets. First, individualism in America was neither intended for the many nor consistent with equal rights for all. Individualism was originally reserved for male freeholders whose nineteenth-century heirs were the married, middle-aged, middle-class men willing to serve as the cultural models, mentors, and monitors of bourgeois sobriety, civic fraternity, political order, and military ardor. Individual rights were not universal or natural rights. Women were excluded from them so that they could tame men's passions; and young men had to earn them so they could be trusted to act with restraint. Second, individualism in America was necessarily disappointing. Married, middle-aged, middle-class males were weighed down by delicate tasks and powerful pressures toward the self-sacrifice best epitomized by the good citizenship of fathers who sent their sons to war only to mourn their lost immortality at young soldiers' graves. Middle-class wives achieved degrees of domestic autonomy and social opportunity unimaginable to female ancestors but also encountered cultural expectations and institutional restraints that urged them to follow the path of self-sacrifice and dependence on male providers and protectors.

Individualism in America is mostly myth, a pervasive norm that gives meaning to people's lives even though most fear its consequences and few realize its promise. We honor it; we often claim it; and we occasionally approximate it. Since World War I, workers, women, minorities, students, seniors, gays, environmentalists, the disabled, and others have demanded their share of it and won some access to it. Each step of the way, however, the drive toward individualism was monitored by "liberal" men (and women) who worried that excessive passion and interest would destroy their families, disorder social life, and subvert political integrity and national security. The rise and fall of the Equal Rights Amendment (ERA) in the 1970s and early 1980s illustrates a patterned rhetoric and reaction.

Jane Mansbridge observes that "Americans can favor abstract rights even when they oppose substantive change." Decades ago, political scientists recognized that many Americans give vocal support to abstract rights involving free elections but then object to allowing an elected communist to take office. In the case of the ERA, polls testified to the fact that many Americans gave rhetorical support to equal rights but opposed the ERA because they thought its passage would give license to sexual liberation and homosexuality, expose women to conscription and combat, and destroy the delicate gender balance that ordered society. "Once the [ERA] debate shifted to its substantive effects," Mansbridge argues, "it was doomed."[4]

The STOP ERA forces were fueled by the frustrations of middle Americans who believed that they had earned their rights through moral behavior, hard work, and patriotic self-sacrifice but could not enjoy their rights because of others' selfish passions. They believed that America suffered a crisis in family life, widespread social pathology, pervasive political factionalism, and a national spinelessness rooted in modern men's propensity to neglect piety, avoid and escape marriage, practice profligacy, and suck up the resources of a welfare state that they often disobeyed and rarely respected. What Richard Nixon called "the silent majority" was composed of people who saw the American dilemma symbolized by blacks' demand for rights without individual restraints or civic responsibilities.

In the 1960s, many white Americans believed that black males had fled paternal responsibilities and forced black women to assume the unnatural role of family matriarchs. They thought that the "crisis" of the black family was a direct cause of black youth's license and aggression, manifest in teenage pregnancies and high unemployment rates, individual crimes and gang violence, plus ghetto riots, protests, and uprisings. Worse, middle Americans feared that black anarchy was being rewarded. Welfare state liberals were building a Great Society by throwing tax dollars at black indolents, criminals, and rioters. The silent majority spoke up, at least to pollsters. Its message was that while all citizens should have civil rights, the unwarranted demands of irresponsible black militants and the spendthrift welfare state that coddled them were intolerable.[5]

For many, the limits of liberal tolerance were again breached when privileged white college youth claimed individual rights without adult responsibilities. They demanded free speech to shout obscenities. They wanted student power to destroy discipline. They asserted citizenship but refused to obey law or serve the nation in war. Then the student movement generated a youth counterculture that opposed piety, restraint, sobriety, and self-sacrifice but applauded spontaneity, passion, sexuality, and drugs. Rebellious youth infiltrated picket-fenced neighborhoods, sending their message over the airwaves and through underground newspapers. For middle America, the feminists and politicians who pushed the ERA in the early 1970s continued a course to societal suicide. Standing first in line to inherit the other liberal tradition in America, fearful middle Americans joined forces with "conservatives" who wanted to redeem engendered civic virtue to save liberal society from its own excesses.

Saving Liberal Society

One reason Tocqueville is often considered the foremost analyst of early America is that he brought to his investigation a strong belief in the necessity and danger of democracy. Democracy was coming, he announced, but, so far, "Democracy has been left to its wild instincts; it has grown up like those children deprived of parental care who school themselves in our town streets and know nothing of society but its vices and wretchedness." Tocqueville was impressed by the parental care shown by Americans. He applauded fathers' authority, wives' voluntary submission, the combination of consent and coercion that bound spouses, the thick bonds between male generations, and also men's deference to women's virtue and practical intelligence.[6] He implied that family fathers restrained by pious women were the core of a stable citizenry that defended freedom of thought but showed little independence of mind, that participated in politics but deferred to political authority. For Tocqueville, domestic virtue reconciled individualism and social order.

George Gilder now echoes Tocqueville's analysis and uses it to explain the upheavals of the 1960s and the feminism of the early 1970s. He proclaims that, by nature, all males are savages. They are the prime offenders against family life, morality, and legal order. Indeed, "the chief perpetrators are *single* men," who constitute "our leading social problem." Fortunately, the "conspicuous and calculable power of males is counterbalanced by a deep and inexorable power of women." Men's uncontrolled lust is normally tamed by women's superior ability to restrain sexual impulse, unique capacity to bear men's children, and biologically inscribed concern for the future. "The essential pattern is clear. Women manipulate male sexual desire in order to teach them the long-term cycles of female sexuality and biology on which civilization is based. When men learn, their view of the woman as an object of their own sexuality succumbs to an image of her as . . . the keeper of social immortality."[7] Gilder essentially translates Locke's marriage contract into the story of male passion subdued by female civility. However, he adds, today's problem is that modern women are buying into sexual license and equal rights. They refuse to recognize that differences between the sexes are essential to fulfilling family life, civic order, and political unity. Women are failing in their civilizing mission.

Gilder's analysis rings true to Jerry Falwell's parishioners, who are mostly skilled workers, white-collar clericals and technicians, and entrepreneurs poised to achieve the American dream only to find it endangered by sexual liberation, pornography, teenage pregnancy, illegal drugs, homosexuality, rising divorce rates, and the spread of "secular humanism," including feminism. Falwell and his pastors argue that the solution to men's vices and women's selfishness is to restore engendered family virtues. Boys should play hard at manly sports as a "prescription for the sublimation of male violence and male sexual energies." Young males should mature into husbands and fathers who assume "the responsibility of leadership" and serve as "the loving heartbeat" of the home. Wives should submit to husbands' authority for two reasons. First, "Submission is learning to duck, so God can hit your husband!" Second, female submission forces husbands to take responsibility and thereby restores the balance between male prerogative and patriarchal obligation.[8]

In theory, the restoration of engendered family virtues will encourage economic sobriety and civic loyalty. Good fathers seek prosperity for their families. While their search appears to border on possessive individualism, it stops short of unconditional acquisitiveness. Gilder preaches supply-side economics but is careful to anchor capitalism in "giving" as the basis for voluntary exchange and risky investment. He notes that "giving" is "a spirit closely akin to altruism, a regard for the needs of others, a benevolent, outgoing, and courageous temper of mind." He also criticizes entrepreneurs who lack "the gift impulse."[9] Falwell advocates the virtue of individual industry in pursuit of material wealth, with the corollary that industrious men must invest a portion of their wealth in God's church and good works. And good works include men's efforts to protect their families from modern social pathologies, welfare state illusions, socialist ideologies, and godless communists who subvert American civic virtue.

Common usage justifies a "conservative" label here, but it is a serious mistake to classify these arguments as antiliberal, illiberal, or outside the Lockean consensus. People such as Gilder and Falwell support individual rights, consent of the governed, and limited, representative government. They argue that blacks, youth, and women should have rights. But they also believe that individuals must earn their rights by exhibiting self-restraint and civic virtue lest excessive individualism destroy the bonds of society. This combination of rights and virtue is most clearly manifested in Phyllis Schlafly's words and deeds. Schlafly is not a member of a *new* right; she promotes an *old* line of thought rooted in the ideas of John Locke and Mary Astell, adapted by Catharine Beecher and Theodore Roosevelt, and closely linked to traditional middle-class beliefs.

Schlafly applauds the Declaration of Independence as "the most perfect orientation of man to God and government outside of the Holy Scripture." She agrees that "each of us is created equal . . . and that government derives its just powers from the consent of the governed." She praises the American Revolution during which "government was reduced from master to servant." Ultimately, however, she believes that the success of the American experiment had less to do with male architects and citizens than with pious, practical women: "It is on women that civilization depends— on the inspiration they provide, on the moral fabric they weave, on the parameters of behavior they tolerate, and on the new generation they breathe life into and educate." American women consented to "marriage and motherhood" as their "number-one career choice." And the typical American wife knew how to "motivate [her husband], inspire him, encourage him, teach him, restrain him, reward him, and have power over him that he can never achieve over her with all his muscle." [10]

The result was that American women enjoyed the benefits of being relatively autonomous household managers and mothers free from the "repetitious, tiresome, and boring" tasks of the marketplace and "servitude to the boss." Schlafly is a functional advocate of the marketplace. She writes, "The real liberator of women in America is the free enterprise system, which has produced remarkable inventors who have lifted the drudgery of housekeeping from women's shoulders." Wives supported by husbands are capitalism's beneficiaries; they enjoy prosperity without suffering wage labor. Also, capitalism motivates otherwise idle men to work and then disciplines them by its routines. Schlafly's brand of "domestic feminism" is capsulized in this message to men: "After twenty years of diapers and dishes, a mother can see the result of her own handiwork in the good citizen she has produced and trained. After twenty years of faithful work in the business world, you are lucky if you have a good watch to show for your efforts." [11]

Still, American men are not sufficiently disciplined. Schlafly says that "Men are philosophers, women are practical." Men's abstract bent distorts reality. Men are prone to imagine impossible worlds and then use government to impose fantasy on recalcitrant reality. In the process, they undermine family stability, evade male responsibility, eliminate moral education from schools, indulge a bureaucratic welfare state, and sap the public's will to defend America against "every potential aggressor." Moreover, men seduce a few women from their practical sense and entice deluded feminists into joining their search for "a make-believe world." One result is the struggle for the ERA which, Schlafly believes, is actually a dangerous male fantasy about freedom from responsibility, women's loss of autonomy, and America's neglect of "freedom, independence, civilization." [12]

Schlafly's plan for saving liberal society from male individualism goes well beyond defeating the ERA. She argues that men are inherently weak creatures. They have muscle power and institutional power, but they are psychological dependents. Their "prime emotional need is passive." They want "to be appreciated or admired." [13] Practical women who appeal to male vanity can manipulate, domesticate, and civilize fathers and brothers. They can take full advantage of individual and political rights to engage in part-time volunteer work, grass-roots organizing, moral reform, and political lobbying. Joining eighteenth-century republican motherhood to nineteenth-century female reform, Schlafly insists that women are historical agents of female virtue, not innocent victims of male vice. They can achieve domestic happiness, teach men restraint and virtue, and clean up men's political mess; they can urge husbands to "work hours of overtime to pay premiums of life insurance policies to provide for their wives' comfort when they are widows" and teach sons "that the password of freedom is . . . 'Give me liberty or give me death'—not the plea of the handout hunter, 'Gimme, gimme, gimme.' " [14]

Schlafly's antipathy to male selfishness resonates in the writings of Samuel Huntington, who argues that excessive individualism has generated an "excess of democracy." Too many individuals and special-interest groups make demands on government; too few Americans defer to "the claims of expertise, seniority, experience, and special talents" in government. We must show "more self-restraint," a "measure of apathy and noninvolvement," and "a greater degree of moderation in democracy." Only then will our governors have "the authority to command the resources and sacrifices necessary to meet the threat" of enemies.[15] Huntington's argument for more political prerogative is not simply a reaction to protests, feminism, or political alienation. It reflects his long-standing fear that liberalism has failed to come to terms with national security. In his 1957 study, *The Soldier and the State*, he noted that "liberalism does not understand and is hostile to military institutions and the military function." Liberalism invites men to put individual rights above collective needs, commerce over civic virtue. The result is our foolish pacifism and bellicosity in foreign affairs; the solution is "the military mind" that gives priority to national security.[16]

Huntington's study is now a well-worn text for American military officers, but their adaptation of it is more sophisticated. They accept Huntington's version of the military mind and portray soldiers as armed republican citizens who practice civic virtue and patriotic self-sacrifice. For instance, a recent Army White Paper on "Values" states, "All who serve the nation must resist the temptation to pursue self-gain, personal advantage, and self-interest ahead of the collective good." Moreover, "self-advancement," "self-glorification," and "careerism" are condemned, while "selfless ambition" and "selfless service" are condoned, along with martial virtues like discipline, stamina, skill, loyalty, duty, courage, and male bonding—"the strong ties that develop between people who share adversity."[17] But the American military mind is loathe to accept a sharp contrast between liberalism and the military. Lieutenant Colonel Hugh A. Kelly's 1984 proposal for a "United States Army Ethic" points out that a soldier's duties are based on his voluntary consent, the "oath" that makes him "party to the contract." Kelly makes liberal choice the basis for republican service. Or as General John W. Vessey, Jr., told a U.S. Naval War College graduating class, "You have *chosen* to give up some of the benefits of your own personal liberty so that the citizens of the nation may enjoy those benefits in full."[18]

Modern military thinkers link choice to service even for conscripts. As the Vietnam War escalated in 1965, planners put together an orientation kit for new draft board members that explained that the eighteen-year-old who registers for the draft could choose military service or alternative service related to "skills needed for his country." Metaphorically, the potential draftee was "standing in a room which has been made uncomfortably warm. Several doors are open, but they all lead to various forms of recognized, patriotic service to the nation." Getting young men to practice civic virtue was a matter of "pressurized guidance." Indeed, "The psychology of granting wide choice under pressure to take action is the American or indirect way of achieving what is done by direction in foreign countries where choice is not allowed. Here, choice is limited but not denied, and it is fundamental that an individual generally applies himself better to something that he has decided to do rather than something that he has been told to do."[19] Here is Locke's Venetian noble speaking with a modern military accent.

Many middle Americans join Gilder, Falwell, Schlafly, Huntington, and military thinkers to participate in an ongoing public discourse that originated in the elitism, patriarchalism, and militarism of seventeenth-century England's liberalism of fear, Locke's synthesis of liberalism and republicanism, and America's adaptation of it. They want to conserve the other liberal tradition in America that both justifies and circumscribes individual rights, conditions democratic equality, supports liberal patriarchy, and regards filial obedience and martial discipline as evidence of civic virtue and earned citizenship. For conservatives, a liberalism that incorporates republicanism is a usable and reusable past.

However, the other liberal tradition in America is politically ambiguous. It is sufficiently flexible to inform the discourse of radical democrats, feminists, and peace activists who fear that excessive male individualism destroys community, devalues women's unique contributions to society, and deprives youth of the opportunity to find pacific routes to manhood. Modern radical thinkers also recall Locke's liberal incorporation of republicanism as a usable past that points the way to a better future, but they have in mind a more egalitarian family, social, and political order.

A World without Father

Mary Wollstonecraft "dared to take the liberal doctrine of inalienable human rights . . . and assume these rights for her own sex."[20] She argued that male tyranny was injurious to liberty. Patriarchal families, economic inequality, and political hierarchy promoted corruption among the powerful and servility in subordinates. The result was that men and women were "often only overgrown children" who indulged selfish appetites, worshiped Mammon, and fought "wild-goose chase" wars. Only equal rights would encourage the independence and reason to sustain a social contract, good citizenship, and legitimate government. Significantly, Wollstonecraft's liberal daring was matched by her republican sensibility. Individual rights, she thought, were instrumental to engendered virtues that fostered "public spirit." Equality in education, marriage, economy, and citizenship generated enlightened parenthood and spousal friendship, strong intergenerational bonds, industry and productivity, social harmony, sound politics, and recognition that individual lives were joined to a "general good" conducive to peace.[21] Wollstonecraft's cure for tyranny was equal rights, and her corrective for excessive individualism was civic virtue.

Wollstonecraft's mix of liberalism and republicanism informs Barbara Ehrenreich's inquiry into *The Hearts of Men*. Ehrenreich criticizes Gilder and Schlafly for supporting patriarchal families that reinforce tyranny and servility, but Ehrenreich also joins conservatives in their indictment of men's selfish individualism. After World War II, she observes, traditional sanctions against the male deviance symbolized by bachelorhood and homosexuality began to give way to a *Playboy* psychology that tempted men to escape marriage and practice acquisitiveness. In the 1970s, a men's liberation movement refined male excuses for avoiding commitment. It called on men to seek greater emotional self-fulfillment only to reinforce "all the old grievances and resentments" against females who allegedly rob men of their independence. Today's result is legitimation of a "consumerist personality for *men*" that degrades women and a brand of "mask-ulinity" or middle-class sensibility that reinforces stigmas against working-class males as moral retrogrades.[22]

Ehrenreich is convinced that excessive, middle-class male individualism cannot be corrected by restoring patriarchal marriages in which men are free to dominate and also neglect economic responsibility. "Short of a program to conscript men into marriage and (in recalcitrant cases) have male earnings deposited directly to their wives' accounts, women have no sure claim on the wages of men." Still, Ehrenreich would "like to think that a reconciliation of the sexes is possible." She imagines "a world without father" where men and women "learn to be brothers and sisters" and equality in personal life is the basis for "loyalty and trust" in public life. To this end, Ehrenreich advocates "a state committed to the welfare of its citizens and prepared to meet their needs—for financial assistance, medical care, education, child care, etc.—when they are unable to meet these needs themselves." The compelling question is whether the welfare state is "intrinsically paternalistic."[23]

Sheldon Wolin's answer is that democracy has been absorbed into the welfare state only to reemerge as subjection. The consequence is "dependent man, the rump remains of democratic man." Kathy Ferguson incorporates women in this story of modern dependence, arguing that welfare state administrators have a structural need to "regulate and control the behavior of clients" who are mostly women. Indeed, state bureaucrats promote a dependence tantamount to "the feminization of the client" and an "increasing feminization of the polity." She concludes that democracy and feminism are "not compatible with bureaucracy." Indeed, equality is "endangered by too-close contact with bureaucratic linguistic and institutional forms."[24]

Radicals who resurrect republicanism as a usable past usually recall classical notions of civic virtue, participation, and the active life as alternatives to excessive individualism in society and paternalism in politics. For instance, Benjamin Barber advocates a "strong democracy" constituted by "citizenship, participation, public goods, [and] civic virtue." He makes a case for civic education and an engaged citizenry which, in turn, "become an argument for universal citizen service . . . [which] would enlist every American citizen—male and female alike—in a service corps for one to two years of either military or nonmilitary training and service." Drawing on the Anglo-American militia tradition and William James's moral equivalent of war, Barber believes that universal citizen service will expose young Americans to a compelling civic education that encourages "many of the undisputed virtues of military service: fellowship and camaraderie, common activity, team work, service for and with others, and a sense of community." But he wants these martial virtues stripped of traditional hierarchical content and linked to civic equality and cooperation, what he calls "a sense of mutuality and national interdependence."[25]

The complement to Barber's vision of citizen service is Ehrenreich's image of a welfare state that encourages greater public voice and influence.

She states, "Publicly sponsored services do not have to be bureaucratically or professionally dominated but can be actually generative of participatory citizenship and self-help initiatives." A welfare state that truly seeks the commonweal and public good must nurture a free and independent citizenry and "call forth active citizen involvement." An "active, participatory citizenship," adds Ferguson, will have an especially powerful impact on women, who need to deconstruct traditional training in submissiveness and silence by articulating their unique experiences and femaleness "through the shared process of speaking, deliberating, and judging, ordering their collective lives through institutions they have designed and in a language they have made their own."[26]

The goal of today's radical republicans is not so much to oppose individualism as to condition and infuse it with civic virtue and redefine it in ways that reconcile the genius of sexual difference with feminist equality and public good. Robert Bellah and his collaborators call it an "experiment with our friends, our fellow citizens." Yet, radicals should not ignore Allan Bloom's suggestion that the notion "we should all get along" is a "saccharine moral."[27] Putting friendship at the center of citizenship is an ancient Greek ideal, but the ancients stressed that authentic friendship is demanding. It involves self-sacrifice and exclusivity, mutual tolerance and a willingness to do battle and even die for one's friends. That raises two difficult questions. Can we imagine American men sacrificing their patriarchal privileges to establish egalitarian relations with women? And can we imagine American women going to war to protect their male friends?

Since the early 1960s, radicals have argued that active, participatory citizenship enhances individuals' sense of personal satisfaction, political efficacy, and connectedness to the large community. In the early 1970s, feminists pioneered experiments aimed at overcoming isolation by encouraging participation in women's groups, collectives, and institutions. For men, the personal was political; for women, the personal was political. But for men and women together? An emerging men's studies literature proposed that men who treat women as friends and equals will simultaneously enhance their personal lives and political relations. For example, Warren Farrell listed twenty-one ways in which "liberated" men would benefit from egalitarian partnerships with liberated women. And the Berkeley Men's Center issued a manifesto calling for a "human liberation" founded on men's and women's shared individual needs and social goals.[28] Let me suggest, however, that the idea that joint participation in personal life would create bonds of mutual friendship and civic equality was doubtful from the start.

Consider Harry Brod's argument that pornography victimizes men and women. Pornography, he says, entraps men in an alienated, commercialized form of sexuality that fosters self-degradation. Thus, "in being asked to give up pornography, men are being asked to give up disadvantages, not advantages, of their position."[29] Brod's intention is to enlist men on the side of feminists fighting against male violence and female victimization. But his argument that pornography degrades men does not provide a compelling motive for male feminism. If pornography degrades women, then it contributes to men's familial, social, economic, and political hegemony. In turn, male hegemony carries with it the power, privilege, and ability to ameliorate the impact of alienation, commercialization, and self-degradation. Men can purchase distractions or therapy. Indeed, it seems to me that men's interests rarely coincide with opposition to patriarchy.

Fathers may find satisfaction in sharing the joys of parenting but not the sacrifices and pains of parenting. Men need money and leisure to seek self-fulfillment and fraternity, and their interest is to monopolize jobs that promise affluence and autonomy by denying women equal access to them. Men want freedom to carry out experiments in self-expression and political participation, so why commit themselves to feminist demands that reduce their social and political space? Carrigan, Connell, and Lee conclude, "The liberation of women must mean a *loss* of power for most men; and given the structuring of personality by power, also a great deal of personal pain."[30] In short, equal participatory citizenship for men and women is hard to foresee unless men adopt an ethic of self-sacrifice.

Our individualist rhetoric makes it difficult for us to imagine that men would engage in voluntary self-sacrifice. Yet we have seen that male self-sacrifice is central to the other liberal tradition in America. And American men have sacrificed the freedom of their passions, interests, rights, and lives for their families, communities, and nation. From Locke's time to our time, the meaning of masculinity has included private and public virtues such as reasonable fatherhood and family provisioning, fortitude and civility, sobriety and industry, civic devotion and citizen soldiering. In fact, men have routinely engaged in nearly all kinds of self-sacrifice *except* the self-sacrifice entailed by giving up the patriarchal power that supports their identity as protectors of other men, women, and children.

One major test of men's willingness to sacrifice their identity as patriarchal protectors is their willingness to allow women to share protection duties. "Historically," Judith Stiehm writes, "citizenship has been based on what one contributes to the state. The two principal contributions have been the payment of taxes and service in the military." As long as women are precluded from full military service, especially combat service, they lack the authority to speak on critical matters of foreign affairs and war. Stiehm suggests that "accepting liability to participate in the legitimate use of violence may be required of all who wish to be full-fledged citizens."[31] The ideal of civic equality may require that women assume official combat status and have the opportunity to risk their lives to protect men and the state.

This highlights some complex challenges for radical republicans. Legitimating women's combat status would shatter the enduring meaning of masculinity. Men's exclusive claim to the protector role would dissipate. The notion that youth should join the military, suffer its discipline, and risk their lives to test their manhood, cultivate fortitude, and become "men" would falter along with the myth that war is manly. And if military planners are right, combat equality would erode martial discipline and destroy combat effectiveness by depriving soldiers of the sense of fraternity necessary for effectiveness in battle.[32] Of course, many radicals welcome the shattering of conventional masculinity and the weakening of the American military. Feminists want masculinity to become problematic, and peace activists delight in the prospect of making men more reluctant to fight and elites less likely to wage war. However, radicals express several deep-seated doubts about women's initiation into combat.

First, women's official assumption of combat status promises to make women complicit in male elitism and violence. Radical democrats are opposed to the imposed discipline and hierarchy of military command structures. And quite often, they agree with the majority of Americans who are against exposing women to conscription and sending women draftees into combat. Moreover, pacifists and peace activists believe that equality in the military invites women's complicity in American imperialism and aggression. "Access to the use of legitimate force is important," writes Kathleen

Jones, "if one essentially agrees with the *purposes* of state power." If not, one must challenge "the authority of the state itself." For radical feminists who ennoble women's differences, virtues, caring, nurturance, and what Gilligan sees as a female identity of connectedness and an ethic of responsibility, women's official combat status signifies their submersion in a masculine ethic of rights, separation, hierarchy, competition, and violence.[33]

Second, the prospect of women's combat status is problematic for radicals who reject the traditional republican equation of citizenship and soldiering. Carole Pateman notes, "The image that accompanies, but lies in the shadow of, the citizen soldier is that of the citizen mother; women's ultimate duty is to give birth for the state." Americans mostly believe that sexual difference is relevant to political life, women's sacrifice should focus on mothering, and maternal sacrifice is honorable but secondary to soldiering. The result is "to obliterate any image of citizen as a woman; all that remains is the image of the soldier, and, more generally, the citizen as a masculine being." Pateman wants citizenship redefined to include women's experience with "private" virtues that put nurturance and sacrifice for others above men's "public" selfishness and violence. Indeed, "Feminine individuality and womanly activities provide examples of the relational, altruistic, social qualities which participatory democrats wish to see developed in the public realm." Therefore, we ought to investigate "differentiation within civic equality" and develop "a democratic theory that begins from sexual difference, and women's potentially distinctive contribution to political life."[34]

Does that mean that women's citizenship will somehow alter men's approach to politics? Not necessarily. Pateman writes, "It is not so much a question of whether men, as citizens, would also participate in fostering civic virtue in the young, as whether a now distinctively womanly practice (and, as far as I can see, one that is likely to remain so for some time) can itself become part of citizenship and enrich and transform our understanding of what it is to act and think politically." Pateman holds out the promise of a feminist republicanism that provides grounds for making "reasonable motherhood" and "maternal thinking" the center of family life, social relations, public action, and peace politics. However, maternal thinking is not a certain step toward participatory democracy, gender equality, and peace if it encompasses traditions of Spartan motherhood manifested among "American women, with countless feminists among them, [who] support a strong national military establishment."[35] Moreover, how can feminism enrich citizenship when men continue to mint masculinity in the coin of patriarchal power and military conquest?

The Pulse of Men's Passions

Traditional misanthropy persists. Ancient dread of the female endures. Classical masculinity and militarism march on. The seventeenth century's liberalism of fear remains a core feature of twentieth-century American liberalism. But opposition to the liberalism of fear is also a major factor in modern American discourse. Participatory democrats elevate men's ability to be virtuous fathers, neighbors, and citizens. Feminists struggle to transform subordinate images of women into exemplary emblems of virtuous citizenship. Peace activists hope to imbue young men with a sense of manhood that brightens prospects for human ecology and dims the specter of the mushroom cloud. Ultimately, today's obsession with individualism is less a debate over supporting or opposing it than a dialogue about how to restore it and reconcile it to civic virtue in order to foster stronger human bonding and greater political justice.

The subscript of that dialogue centers on the man question. A recent Los Angeles task force reports that discrimination against unmarried men is "a pervasive national problem." Landlords refuse to rent to singles, and insurers reduce rates for married folks, while many Americans see AIDS as divine retribution against gays, and finance corporations give credit preference to straight couples. A highly publicized poll of sixth- to ninth-graders reports that 65 percent of boys say that it is okay for a man to force sex on a woman he has been dating for six months; and 24 percent of boys agree that it is acceptable for a man to force sex on a woman after spending money on her. Overall, Americans still fear bachelors as impassioned, selfish, untrustworthy, untamed creatures; boys' attitudes tend to legitimate that fear; and Riane Eisler capsulizes it: men think "peace is unmanly" and male violence is a "normative ideal."[36]

In large part, the future of American democracy, feminism, and peace hinges on a direct encounter with the man question. Is it conceivable that men can be trusted to exercise individual rights, commit to civic virtue, and contribute to a harmonious society, just political order, and tranquil world? If so, we can imagine overcoming obstacles that guard liberal patriarchy in private and public life, ensure women's confinement to domestic duties, and secure young men's identification with aggression and violence. If not, we can expect a regular revival of the traditional liberal argument that men's excessive individualism must be conditioned by virtuous statesmen, self-sacrificing women, and martial discipline. Deeply embedded in America's Lockean consensus is the question of the mutability of men's passions and interests and, relatedly, the necessity of women's steadfast devotion to civilizing men.

Hanna Pitkin interprets Machiavelli to argue that *Fortune is a Woman*.[37] She is chance and conflict, seduction and domination, deceit and destruction. She is both necessary and evil. She lures men into selfish complacency, mindless resignation, and mutual violence but also challenges men to achieve liberty through civic virtue, community through participation, and meaning and immortality in public life. In fact, Machiavelli had it backwards. When Harrington revived him and Locke incorporated him and Americans adapted him, the result was a middle-class preoccupation with controlling men's fickle nature and foolish struggles, restless desires and acquisitive impulses, self-delusions and sustained brutality. There could be no flowering of individual liberty or democratic equality because the pulse of men's passions had to be monitored to prevent anarchy and tyranny. Women's tacit understanding of men's tendency toward destruction challenged the mothers of humankind to exhibit remarkable self-sacrifice and civic virtue in their struggles for liberty and equality, family survival and social justice. At the origin of the other liberal tradition in America was women's certain knowledge that Fortune is a man.

Notes

INTRODUCTION

1. Sheldon S. Wolin, *Politics and Vision* (Boston: Little Brown, 1960), pp. 293–294.
2. Louis Hartz, *The Liberal Tradition in America* (New York: Harcourt Brace & World, 1955), pp. 111–112.
3. Gordon S. Wood, *The Creation of the American Republic, 1776–1787* (New York: Norton, 1969); and Bernard Bailyn, *The Ideological Origins of the American Revolution* (Cambridge: Harvard University Press, 1967).
4. J. G. A. Pocock, *The Machiavellian Moment: Florentine Political Thought and the Atlantic Republican Tradition* (Princeton: Princeton University Press, 1975), chap. 15; Steven J. Ross, *Workers on the Edge: Work, Leisure, and Politics in Industrializing Cincinnati, 1788–1890* (New York: Columbia University Press, 1985); and Dorothy Ross, "The Liberal Tradition Revisited and the Republican Tradition Addressed," in *New Directions in American Intellectual History*, ed. John Higham and Paul K. Conkin (Baltimore: Johns Hopkins University Press, 1979), p. 119.
5. See Steven J. Ross, "The Transformation of Republican Ideology," a paper delivered at the Shear Symposium, Philadelphia, July 18, 1987.
6. Robert N. Bellah et al., *Habits of the Heart: Individualism and Commitment in American Life* (Berkeley: University of California Press, 1985); Richard M. Battistoni, *Public Schooling and the Education of Democratic Citizens* (Jackson: University of Mississippi Press, 1985); Sara Evans and Harry Boyte, *Free Spaces: The Sources of Democratic Change in America* (New York: Harper & Row, 1986). See also William M. Sullivan, *Reconstructing Public Philosophy* (Berkeley: University of California Press, 1986).
7. Caroline Robbins, *The Eighteenth-Century Commonwealthman: Studies in the Transmission, Development, and Circumstances of English Liberal Thought from the Restoration of Charles II until the War with the Thirteen Colonies* (Cambridge: Harvard University Press, 1961), p. 16; and H. T.

Dickinson, *Liberty and Property: Political Ideology in Eighteenth-Century Britain* (New York: Holmes & Meier, 1977), p. 59; Joyce Appleby, *Capitalism and a New Social Order: The Republican Vision of the 1790s* (New York: New York University Press, 1984), p. 9; and Rogers M. Smith, "The 'American Creed' and American Identity: The Limits of Liberal Citizenship in the United States," *Western Political Quarterly* 41 (June 1988): 225–251.

8. For example, see Richard Vetterli and Gary Bryner, *In Search of the Republic: Public Virtue and the Roots of American Government* (Totowa, N.J.: Rowman & Littlefield, 1987); and Allan Bloom, *The Closing of the American Mind* (New York: Simon & Schuster, 1987).

9. See Isaac Kramnick, "Republican Revisionism Revisited," *American Historical Review* 87 (June 1982): 637; John P. Diggins, *The Lost Soul of American Politics: Virtue, Self-Interest, and the Foundations of Liberalism* (New York: Basic Books, 1984), p. 12; Appleby, *Capitalism and a New Social Order*, p. 15; Sheldon S. Wolin, "The Idea of the State in America," in *The Problem of Authority in America*, ed. John P. Diggins and Mark E. Kann (Philadelphia: Temple University Press, 1981), pp. 41–58; and Mark E. Kann, "Challenging Lockean Liberalism in America: The Case of Debs and Hillquit," *Political Theory* 8 (May 1980); 203–222.

10. Gordon S. Wood, "Hellfire Politics," *New York Review of Books* 32 (February 28, 1985): 30; James T. Kloppenberg, "The Virtues of Liberalism: Christianity, Republicanism, and Ethics in Early American Discourse," *Journal of American History* 74 (June 1987): 11; Smith, "The 'American Creed' and American Identity," pp. 225–251; Vetterli and Bryner, *In Search of the Republic*, esp. chaps. 1, 8; Anne Norton, *Alternative Americas: A Reading of Antebellum Political Culture* (Chicago: University of Chicago Press, 1986); and Jean Bethke Elshtain, *Women and War* (New York: Basic Books, 1987), p. 249.

11. Wood, "Hellfire Politics," p. 29.

12. C. B. Macpherson, *The Political Theory of Possessive Individualism: Hobbes to Locke* (London: Oxford University Press, 1962), chap. 5; see also Leo Strauss, *Natural Right and History* (Chicago: University of Chicago Press, 1953), chap. 5. Appleby's work is exceptional. She sees in Jefferson's version of Lockean liberalism an impulse toward productivity, comfort, prosperity, and progress rather than an obsession with individual accumulation. See Joyce Appleby, "Republicanism in Old and New Contexts," *William and Mary Quarterly* 43 (January 1986): 20–34.

13. For example, see Richard Ashcraft, *Revolutionary Politics and Locke's Two Treatises of Government* (Princeton: Princeton University Press, 1986). This interpretation of Locke will be developed in detail in later chapters.

14. Hartz, *Liberal Tradition in America*, pp. 43, 80; Diggins, *Lost Soul of American Politics*, p. 7; and George Washington, quoted in Wood, *Creation of the American Republic*, p. 472.

15. Compare Carl Becker, *The Heavenly City of the Eighteenth-Century Philosophers* (New Haven: Yale University Press, 1932); and Henry F. May, *The Enlightenment in America* (Oxford: Oxford University Press, 1976).

16. Albert O. Hirschman, *The Passions and the Interests: Political Arguments for Capitalism before Its Triumph* (Princeton: Princeton University Press, 1977), p. 41.

17. Hartz, *Liberal Tradition in America*, p. 122.

18. Wood, *Creation of the American Republic*, p. 605.

19. Aileen S. Kraditor, *The Radical Persuasion: Aspects of the Intellectual History and the Historiography of Three American Radical Organizations* (Baton Rouge: Louisiana State University Press, 1981), p. 15. See also Kathy Peiss, *Cheap Amusements: Working Women and Leisure in Turn-of-the-Century New York* (Philadelphia: Temple University Press, 1985).

20. Hirschman, *Passions and the Interests*, pp. 123–128.

21. David Hume, "Of the Original Contract," in *Hume's Moral and Political Philosophy*, ed. Henry Aiken (New York: Hafner, 1948), pp. 364–365.

22. Ibid., p. 368. See also Carole Pateman, "The Shame of the Marriage Contract," in *Women's Views of the Political World of Men*, ed. Judith H. Stiehm (Dobbs Ferry, N.Y.: Transnational Publishers, 1984), pp. 67–97.

23. For example, see Horatio Alger, *Ragged Dick* and *Mark, the Matchboy* (New York: Collier Books, 1962).

24. Hartz, *Liberal Tradition in America*, p. 185; Wood, *Creation of the American Republic*, pp. 415–416 and chap. 12.

25. Michael Walzer, *Spheres of Justice: A Defense of Pluralism and Equality* (New York: Basic Books, 1983), p. 68.

26. See John Demos, *Past, Present, and Personal: The Family and the Life Course in American History* (New York: Oxford University Press, 1986); Wilson Carey McWilliams, *The Idea of Fraternity in America* (Berkeley: University of California Press, 1973); Appleby, *Capitalism and a New Social Order*, chap. 1; David E. Shi, *The Simple Life: Plain Living and High Thinking in American Culture* (New York: Oxford University Press, 1985), chap. 7; Richard Sennett, *Authority* (New York: Knopf, 1980), chaps. 1–2; Michael Paul Rogin, *Fathers and Children: Andrew Jackson and the Subjugation of the American Indian* (New York: Random House, 1975), "Introduction"; Sheldon S. Wolin, "Higher Education and the Politics of Knowledge," *democracy* (April 1981): 38–52; and Joe L. Dubbert, *A Man's Place: Masculinity in Transition* (Englewood Cliffs, N.J.: Prentice-Hall, 1979), chap. 2.

27. Robert Nisbet, *Twilight of Authority* (New York: Oxford University Press, 1975).

28. See Diggins, *Lost Soul of American Politics*, p. 169; Pocock, *Machiavellian Moment*, chap. 15; and Norton, *Alternative Americas*, chaps. 2, 4.

29. Linda K. Kerber, *Women of the Republic: Intellect and Ideology in Early America* (Chapel Hill: University of North Carolina Press, 1980), p. 235.

30. Mrs. A. J. Graves, "Woman in America," in *Roots of Bitterness: Documents of the Social History of American Women*, ed. Nancy F. Cott (New York: Dutton, 1972), p. 145.

31. See Glenna Matthews, *"Just a Housewife": The Rise and Fall of Domesticity in America* (New York: Oxford University Press, 1987), chap. 3.

32. See Marcus Cunliffe, *Soldiers and Civilians: The Martial Spirit in America, 1775–1865* (Boston: Little Brown, 1968), esp. chap. 3; and Peter Filene, *Him/Her/Self: Sex Roles in Modern America*, 2d ed. (Baltimore: Johns Hopkins University Press, 1986), chaps. 3–4.

33. See John W. Chambers, "Conscripting for Colossus: The Progressive Era and the Origin of the Modern Military Draft in the United States," in *The Military in America: From the Colonial Era to the Present*, rev. ed., ed. Peter Karsten (New York: Free Press, 1986), pp. 297–311.

34. See Cynthia Enloe, *Does Khaki Become You? The Militarization of Women's Lives* (Boston: South End Press, 1983), for an analysis of the complex relationship between women and soldiers.

35. See Judith H. Stiehm, "The Protected, the Protector, the Defender," in *Women and Men's Wars*, ed. Judith H. Stiehm (Oxford: Pergamon, 1983), pp. 367–376.

36. Hartz, *Liberal Tradition in America*, p. 129.

37. Howard Zinn, *A People's History of the United States* (New York: Harper & Row, 1980), chap. 5 and pp. 570–573.

38. See Garry Wills, *Explaining America: The Federalist* (New York: Penguin, 1981), p. 192.

39. Hartz, *Liberal Tradition in America*, pp. 85–86.

40. See Carl N. Degler, *At Odds: Woman and the Family in America from the Revolution to the Present* (New York: Oxford University Press, 1980), chap. 1; and Cunliffe, *Soldiers and Civilians*, esp. chap. 6.

41. Diggins, *Lost Soul of American Politics*, pp. 168–169.

42. Zinn, *A People's History of the United States*, p. 113 and chap. 6.

43. Diggins, *Lost Soul of American Politics*, pp. 149, 169.

44. Zinn, *A People's History*, pp. 125, 152, 158, 241–246, 277, 291–293.

45. See Gerda Lerner, *The Creation of Patriarchy* (New York: Oxford University Press, 1986), p. 182.

46. For example, see Orestes A. Brownson, "The Woman Question," in *Up from the Pedestal: Selected Writings in the History of American Feminism*, ed. Aileen S. Kraditor (Chicago: Quadrangle, 1968), pp. 192–194.

47. See Hanna Fenichel Pitkin, *Fortune Is a Woman: Gender and Politics in the Thought of Niccolò Machiavelli* (Berkeley: University of California Press, 1984).

48. Compare Nancy F. Cott, "Passionlessness: An Interpretation of Victorian Sexual Ideology, 1790–1850," in *A Heritage of Her Own: Toward a New*

Social History of American Women, ed. Nancy F. Cott and Elizabeth H. Pleck (New York: Simon & Schuster, 1979), pp. 162–181; and Barbara Ehrenreich and Deirdre English, *For Her Own Good: 150 Years of the Experts' Advice to Women* (Garden City, N.Y.: Anchor/Doubleday, 1978), p. 121.

49. See Michael S. Kimmel, "Men's Responses to Feminism at the Turn of the Century," *Gender and Society* 1 (September 1987): 269–272, and Filene, *Him/Her/Self*, chaps. 3–4.

50. For example, see Seymour Martin Lipset and Earl Rabb, *The Politics of Unreason: Right-Wing Extremism in America, 1790–1970* (New York: Harper & Row, 1970), chaps. 2–3; and Cunliffe, *Soldiers and Civilians*, chap. 3.

51. See David G. Pugh, *Sons of Liberty: The Masculine Mind in Nineteenth-Century America* (Westport, Conn.: Greenwood Press, 1983), pp. 101–104; and Gary Kinsman, "Men Loving Men: The Challenge of Gay Liberation," in *Beyond Patriarchy: Essays by Men on Pleasure, Power, and Change*, ed. Michael Kaufman (Toronto: Oxford University Press, 1987), pp. 109–111.

52. See Carole Pateman, *The Problem of Political Obligation: A Critique of Liberal Theory* (Berkeley: University of California Press, 1985), chap. 4; and *The Sexual Contract* (Stanford: Stanford University Press, 1988), esp. chap. 1; see also Zillah R. Eisenstein, *The Radical Future of Liberal Feminism* (New York: Longman, 1981), chap. 3.

53. See Ann Douglas, *The Feminization of American Culture* (New York: Knopf, 1977); and Degler, *At Odds*, chap. 1. An excellent study of women's role in the making of middle-class men is Mary P. Ryan's *Cradle of the Middle Class: The Family in Oneida County, New York, 1790–1865* (Cambridge: Cambridge University Press, 1981).

54. Karen Offen, "Defining Feminism: A Comparative Historical Approach," *Signs: Journal of Women in Culture and Society* 14, no. 1 (1988): 122–123.

55. See Daniel Scott Smith, "Family Limitation, Sexual Control, and Domestic Feminism in Victorian America," in *A Heritage of Her Own*, pp. 222–245.

56. Mary Beth Norton, *Liberty's Daughters: The Revolutionary Experience of American Women, 1750–1800* (Boston: Little, Brown, 1980), p. 43.

57. Stiehm, "The Protected, The Protector, The Defender," p. 374.

58. See Russell F. Weigley, *History of the United States Army*, enlarged ed. (Bloomington: Indiana University Press, 1984), chaps. 15–16; Gerald F. Linderman, *Embattled Courage: The Experience of Combat in the American Civil War* (New York: Free Press, 1987), epilogue; and Ross, *Workers on the Edge*, p. 197.

59. Compare Harry Brod, ed., *The Making of Masculinities: The New Men's Studies* (Boston: Allen & Unwin, 1987); and Mark E. Kann, "The Costs of Being on Top," *Journal of the National Association of Women Deans, Administrators, and Counselors* 49 (Summer 1986): 29–37, for discussion and criticism of the new men's studies.

60. Diggins, *Lost Soul of American Politics*, p. 16.
61. Frances Fitzgerald, *Cities on a Hill: A Journey through Contemporary American Cultures* (New York: Simon & Schuster, 1986), p. 23.

CHAPTER I

1. Hirschman, *Passions and the Interests*, p. 43.
2. I have adapted "the man question" from Judith H. Stiehm, "The Man Question," in *Women's Views of the Political World of Men*, ed. Judith H. Stiehm (Dobbs Ferry, N.Y.: Transnational Publishers, 1984), pp. 207–223.
3. See J. G. A. Pocock, *Virtue, Commerce, and History: Essays on Political Thought and History, Chiefly in the Eighteenth Century* (Cambridge: Cambridge University Press, 1985), pp. 41–42; see also S. M. Shumer, "Machiavelli: Republican Politics and Its Corruption," *Political Theory* 7 (February 1979): 5–34.
4. Appleby, *Capitalism and a New Social Order*, pp. 16–17.
5. See Pocock, *Virtue, Commerce, and History*, pp. 40–41, and *Politics, Language, and Time: Essays on Political Thought and History* (New York: Atheneum, 1973), pp. 85–86, 89.
6. Niccolò Machiavelli, *The Prince*, in *The Prince and The Discourses* (New York: Modern Library, 1950), chap. 9, p. 35; chap. 18, p. 64.
7. Niccolò Machiavelli, *Discourses on the First Ten Books of Titus Livius*, in *The Prince and The Discourses*, bk. 1, chap. 1 and chap. 58, p. 263; see also Pitkin, *Fortune Is a Woman*, pp. 50–51.
8. James Harrington, *The Commonwealth of Oceana* (London: J. Steater, 1656), pp. i–ii, 2–4, 10, 57–58, 217.
9. See Pocock, *Machiavellian Moment*, pt. 3; see also H. T. Dickinson, *Liberty and Property: Political Ideology in Eighteenth-Century Britain* (New York: Holmes & Meier, 1977), pp. 103, 107.
10. John Trenchard and Thomas Gordon, *Cato's Letters*, 4 vols. (London: Wilkins, Woodword, Walthoe, & Peele, 1724), 1:7.
11. Pocock, *Machiavellian Moment*, p. 365.
12. Algernon Sidney, *Discourses Concerning Government*, 2d ed. (London: J. Darby, 1704), chap. 3, sec. 37, p. 382; secs. 27–28, pp. 343–346; sec. 25, pp. 332–334.
13. Charles Louis de Secondat, Baron de la Brede and de Montesquieu, *The Spirit of Laws*, ed. David Wallace Carrithers (Berkeley: University of California Press, 1977), bk. 5, chap. 1, pp. 132–133; bk. 3, chap. 3, pp. 118–119; and bk. 11, chap. 4, p. 200.
14. See Jean Jacques Rousseau, *The Social Contract*, in *The Social Contract and Discourses*, ed. G. D. H. Cole (New York: Dutton, 1950), chaps. 7, 14; see

also Judith N. Shklar, *Men and Citizens: A Study of Rousseau's Social Theory* (London: Cambridge University Press, 1969), esp. chap. 1.

15. Harrington, *Commonwealth of Oceana*, p. 190.

16. Montesquieu, *Spirit of Laws*, bk. 4, chap. 5, p. 130.

17. Shklar, *Men and Citizens*, p. 1, and Diggins, *Lost Soul of American Politics*, p. 16; see also Judith N. Shklar, *After Utopia: The Decline of Political Faith* (Princeton: Princeton University Press, 1957), esp. chap. 6.

18. George Orwell, "The Lion and the Unicorn: Socialism and the English Genius," in *The Collected Essays, Journalism and Letters of George Orwell*, vol. 2, ed. Sonia Orwell and Ian Angus (New York: Harcourt Brace Jovanovich, 1968), p. 56.

19. Pocock, *Machiavellian Moment*, p. 548.

20. See Thomas Hobbes, *Leviathan: On the Matter, Forme and Power of a Commonwealth Ecclesiaticall and Civil*, ed. Michael Oakeshott (New York: Collier Books, 1962), esp. chaps. 17–18.

21. Pateman, *Problem of Political Obligation*, p. 42; Gordon J. Schochet, *The Authoritarian Family and Political Attitudes in Seventeenth-Century England: Patriarchalism in Political Thought* (New Brunswick, N.J.: Transaction Books, 1988), p. xx; and Strauss, *Natural Right and History*, pp. 181–182, 185–186.

22. See James Tyrrell, *Patriarcha non Monarcha: The Patriarch Unmonarched* (London: Richard Janeway, 1681), chap. 1, p. 19, and chap. 4, p. 134.

23. Ibid., chap. 1, pp. 28–30; chap. 6; pp. 212, 214–215, 218–219.

24. John Locke, *Two Treatises of Government*, ed. Thomas I. Cook (New York: Hafner, 1947), II, par. 171, p. 208; and John Dunn, *The Political Thought of John Locke: An Historical Account of the Argument of the "Two Treatises of Government"* (London: Cambridge University Press, 1969), p. 162.

25. See Locke, *Two Treatises*, II, par. 37, pp. 139–140.

26. Compare Nathan Tarcov, *Locke's Education for Liberty* (Chicago: University of Chicago Press, 1984), p. 140, and Samuel P. Huntington, "The United States," in Michel J. Crozier, Samuel P. Huntington, and Joji Watanuki, *The Crisis of Democracy: Report on the Governability of Democracies to the Trilateral Commission* (New York: New York University Press, 1975), esp. pp. 59–64.

27. Judith N. Shklar, *Ordinary Vices* (Cambridge: Harvard University Press, 1984), pp. 4–5, 7.

28. See Strauss, *Natural Right and History*, pp. 202–251; Macpherson, *Political Theory of Possessive Individualism*, chap. 5; Carol Gilligan, *In a Different Voice: Psychological Theory and Women's Development* (Cambridge: Harvard University Press, 1982), esp. chap. 3; and Carole Pateman, ed., *Feminist Challenges: Social and Political Theory* (Boston: Northeastern University Press, 1986).

29. Joyce Appleby, "Republicanism in Old and New Contexts," p. 25; see also Hirshman, *Passions and the Interests*, pp. 44–52.

30. See Hanna Fenichel Pitkin, "Obligation and Consent—I," *American Political Science Review* 59 (December 1965): 990–999; Pateman, *Problem of Political Obligation*, p. 163; and Ashcraft, *Revolutionary Politics*, chap. 11.

31. Hirschman, *Passions and the Interests*, pp. 14–15.

32. See Schochet, *Authoritarian Family*, pp. 11–15.

33. Immanuel Wallerstein, *The Modern World-System: Capitalist Agriculture and the Origins of the European World-Economy in the Sixteenth Century*, text ed. (New York: Academic Press, 1976), p. 23; see also John Keegan, *The Face of Battle: A Study of Agincourt, Waterloo, and the Somme* (London: Penguin Books, 1976), chaps. 2–3, for an analysis of how changes in the technology of violence altered the use of coercion.

34. See Schochet, *Authoritarian Family*, chap. 4; and Sir Robert Filmer, *Patriarcha*, appended to Locke, *Two Treatises*, pp. 249–308.

35. See Pocock, *Machiavellian Moment*, esp. chaps. 13–14.

36. See Harrington, *Commonwealth of Oceana*, p. 10; Trenchard and Gordon, *Cato's Letters*, 1:264; Tyrrell, *Patriarcha non Monarcha*, chap. 6, pp. 227, 240–241; and Locke, *Two Treatises*, II, par. 159, p. 203.

37. Compare Dickinson, *Liberty and Property*, pp. 61, 64, 72, 77, and Ashcraft, *Revolutionary Politics*, pp. 210–212.

38. Harrington, *Commonwealth of Oceana*, pp. 28, 224; *A Letter from a Person of Quality to His Friend in the Country* [1675] in *A Collection of Several Pieces of Mr. John Locke*, ed. P. Des Maizeaux (London: J. Bettenham, 1720), pp. 55–149; and Trenchard and Gordon, *Cato's Letters*, 1:xxxviii, 243.

39. Sidney, *Discourses*, chap. 1, secs. 17–19, pp. 35–47; chap. 2, sec. 11, p. 93; sec. 20, p. 131; sec. 21, p. 136.

40. See Harrington, *Commonwealth of Oceana*, p. 62; Sidney, *Discourses*, chap. 1, sec. 11, p. 20; and Tyrrell, *Patriarcha non Monarcha*, chap. 2., p. 78.

41. Sidney, *Discourses*, chap. 3, sec. 1, p. 227; and Locke, *Two Treatises*, II, par. 71, p. 155.

42. Sidney, *Discourses*, chap. 1, sec. 7, p. 15; see also R. W. K. Hinton, "Husbands, Fathers and Conquerors," *Political Studies* 15 (October 1967): 294.

43. See Lawrence Stone, *The Family, Sex and Marriage in England, 1500–1800* (New York: Harper & Row, 1977), chap. 6.

44. For the moment, see Tyrrell, *Patriarcha non Monarcha*, chap. 2., p. 109; and Locke, *Two Treatises*, II, pars. 81–82, pp. 160–161.

45. Henry Parker, *Observations on Some of His Majesties Late Answers and Expressions*, 2d ed. (London 1642), p. 2; and Sidney, *Discourses*, chap. 2, sec. 30, p. 219.

46. Sidney, *Discourses*, chap. 2, sec. 11, pp. 92–93, and sec. 21, p. 136.

47. Harrington, *Commonwealth of Oceana*, p. 25; John Toland, *The Militia Reformed: or an Easy Scheme of Furnishing England with a Constant Land Force Capable to Prevent and to Subdue Any Forein Power, and to Maintain Perpetual Quiet at Home without Endangering the Public Liberty* (London:

John Darby, 1698), pp. 17, 88–89; and John Trenchard, *An Argument Shewing That a Standing Army Is Inconsistent with a Free Government, and Absolutely Destructive to the Constitution of the English Monarchy* (London: 1697), pp. 17–18; see also J. R. Western, *The English Militia in the Eighteenth Century: The Story of a Political Issue, 1660–1802* (London: Rutledge & Kegan Paul, 1965), p. 116; and Lois G. Schwoerer, *"No Standing Armies!" The Antiarmy Ideology of Seventeenth-Century England* (Baltimore: Johns Hopkins University Press, 1974), p. 13.

48. Dickinson, *Liberty and Property*, p. 116.

49. *The Levellers: A Dialogue between two young Ladies, concerning Matrimony, Proposing an Act for Enforcing Marriage, for the Equality of Matches, and Taxing Single Persons. With the Danger of Celebacy to a Nation* [1703] reproduced in Michael S. Kimmel, ed., *Mundus Foppensis and The Levellers*, The Augustan Reprint Society No. 248 (Los Angeles: William Andrews Clark Memorial Library, 1988), pp. 420, 422.

50. Charles Davenant, quoted in Dickinson, *Liberty and Property*, p. 110.

51. Pocock, *Virtue, Commerce, and History*, pp. 78–79.

52. Shklar, *Ordinary Vices*, pp. 216–217.

53. Charles Louis de Secondat, Baron de la Brède et de Montesquieu, *The Persian Letters*, ed. and trans. J. Robert Loy (Cleveland: Meridian Books, 1961), Letters 11–14, pp. 59–66.

54. Montesquieu, *Spirit of Laws*, bk. 9, chap. 1, p. 183.

55. Parker, *Observations*, pp. 13–15, 41.

56. Hobbes, *Leviathan*, chap. 13, p. 99; and Wolin, *Politics and Vision*, chap. 8.

57. Tyrrell, *Patriarcha non Monarcha*, chap. 1, p. 23; chap. 6, p. 242; and p. iv.

58. Compare Shklar, *Men and Citizens*, pp. 70–71, and John Locke, *An Essay Concerning Human Understanding*, 2 vols., ed. Alexander C. Fraser (New York: Dover, 1959), vol. 1, p. 343; see also vol. 2, pp. 443–457; *Essays on the Law of Nature*, ed. W. Von Leyden (London: Oxford at Clarendon Press, 1954), p. 135; *On the Conduct of Understanding* (London: Bowdery & Kerby, 1829), p. 4; *Some Thoughts Concerning Education* in *The Educational Writings of John Locke*, ed. James Axtell (London: Cambridge University Press, 1968), pp. 140–141; *On the Reasonableness of Christianity*, ed. George W. Ewing (Chicago: Henry Regnery, 1965), pp. 178–179; *Letter Concerning Toleration* (New York: Liberal Arts Press, 1955), pp. 26–27; *Two Treatises*, II, par. 124, p. 184.

59. Locke, *Two Treatises*, II, par. 222, p. 234, and *Some Thoughts Concerning Education*, pp. 140, 152, 207–208.

60. John Locke, *Some Considerations on the Consequences of the Lowering of Interests, and Raising the Value of Money*, 2d ed. (London: Ansham & Churchil, 1696), pp. 27–28.

61. Sidney, *Discourses*, chap. 2, sec. 12, p. 100.

62. See Shklar, *Ordinary Vices*, p. 237.

63. Karl Marx, "On the Jewish Question," in *Early Writings*, trans. and ed. T. B. Bottomore (New York: McGraw-Hill, 1964), pp. 9–10, 29.

64. Montesquieu, *Spirit of Laws*, bk. 24, chap. 8, p. 326; chap. 2, p. 322; chap. 14, p. 328.

65. Andrew Fletcher of Saltoun, *A Discourse of Government with Relation to Militias* (Edinburgh, 1698), p. 54; Sidney, *Discourses Concerning Government*, chap. 3, sec. 19, p. 312; and Trenchard and Gordon, *Cato's Letters*, 1: 244.

66. See Hobbes, *Leviathan*, chap. 29, pp. 238–239 and chap. 31, p. 269; Locke, *A Letter Concerning Toleration*, pp. 18, 32, 45, 48; *On the Reasonableness of Christianity*, pp. 175, 193–194; and *The Fundamental Constitutions of Caroline*, in *A Collection of Several Pieces by Mr. John Locke*, pp. 41–42, where Locke and Shaftesbury advocate requiring all freeholders to acknowledge and publicly worship God.

67. For a tirade against men's vices, see Sarah Fige, *The Female Advocate: or, an Answer to a Late Satire against the Pride, Lust and Inconstancy of Woman* [1687], in *Satires on Women*, ed. Felicity A. Nussbaum, The Augustan Reprint Society, no. 180 (Los Angeles: William Andrews Clark Memorial Library, 1976), pp. 1–24.

68. Harrington, *Commonwealth of Oceana*, p. 107.

69. Ibid., p. 103.

70. Thomas Gordon, Preface, in *Cato's Letters*, 1: xliv.

71. See Robbins, *Eighteenth-Century Commonwealthman*, p. 16; Dickinson, *Liberty and Property*, pp. 170, 173–191; and Schwoerer, *"No Standing Armies!"* p. 170.

72. See Pocock, *Machiavellian Moment*, pp. 468–483.

73. Montesquieu, *Spirit of Laws*, bk. 5, chap. 5, p. 135; chap. 6, pp. 137–138.

74. Hobbes, *Leviathan*, chap. 18, p. 138, and Tyrrell, *Patriarcha non Monarcha*, chap. 6, pp. 227, 231, 242.

75. Locke, *Two Treatises*, II, par. 37, p. 139.

76. Peter Laslett, "Introduction," in John Locke, *Two Treatise of Government*, ed. Peter Laslett (London: Cambridge University Press, 1963), p. 43; Dunn, *Political Thought of John Locke*, p. 255; Neal Wood, *John Locke and Agrarian Capitalism* (Berkeley: University of California Press, 1984), p. 113; and Ashcraft, *Revolutionary Politics*, p. 258.

77. Locke, *Some Thoughts Concerning Education*, pp. 207–208.

78. Locke, *Two Treatises*, II, par. 136, p. 190, and par. 42, p. 142.

79. See Wood, *John Locke and Agrarian Capitalism*, p. 33.

80. See Shklar, *Ordinary Vices*, p. 197.

81. Harrington, *Commonwealth of Oceana*, pp. 14–15, and Montesquieu, *Spirit of Laws*, bk. 11, chap. 6, pp. 204–205.

82. *An Essay in Defense of the Female Sex* (London: A. Roper & E. Wilkinson, 1696), pp. 86–93. This is sometimes attributed to Mary Astell.

83. See Tyrrell, *Patriarcha non Monarcha*, chaps. 2, 6.
84. Compare Ashcraft, *Revolutionary Politics*, chap. 11, and John Locke, "Old England's Legal Constitution," in H. R. Fox Bourne, *The Life of John Locke*, 2 vols. (New York: Harper & Brothers, 1876), 2: 321.
85. Sidney, *Discourses*, chap. 1, sec. 16, p. 32.
86. Harrington, *Commonwealth of Oceana*, p. 2; and Wolin, *Politics and Vision*, p. 347.
87. Shklar, *Ordinary Vices*, pp. 220–221.

CHAPTER 2

1. Jean Bethke Elshtain, *Public Man, Private Woman: Women in Social and Political Thought* (Princeton: Princeton University Press, 1981), p. 119.
2. See Abigail Adams, "Letter to John Adams," and John Adams, "Letter to Abigail Adams," in *Feminism: The Essential Historical Writings*, ed. Miriam Schneir (New York: Random House, 1972), pp. 3–4.
3. See Nancy C. M. Hartsock, "The Barracks Community in Western Political Thought: Prolegomena to a Feminist Critique of War and Politics," in *Women and Men's Wars*, pp. 283–286.
4. Lerner, *Creation of Patriarchy*, pp. 44–45.
5. Ehrenreich and English, *For Her Own Good*, p. 35.
6. See Nancy C. M. Hartsock, *Money, Sex, and Power: Toward a Feminist Historical Materialism* (New York: Longman, 1983), p. 192; Pitkin, *Fortune Is a Woman*, p. 165; Carole Pateman, "The Disorder of Women: Women, Love and the Sense of Justice," a paper delivered at the annual meeting of the Western Political Science Association, San Francisco, March 27–29, 1980, and *The Sexual Contract* (Stanford: Stanford University Press, 1988), pp. 98–103.
7. Montesquieu, *Spirit of Laws*, bk. 7, chap. 8, p. 167, and bk. 16, chap. 12, p. 274.
8. Antonia Fraser, *The Weaker Vessel* (New York: Random Houses, 1984), p. 147.
9. Pocock, *Machiavellian Moment*, pp. 452–453.
10. See Sidney, *Discourses*, chap. 2, sec. 19, p. 131, and sec. 24, p. 178; chap. 3, sec. 18, p. 310, and sec. 46, p. 418.
11. Laslett, "Introduction," p. 69.
12. Tyrrell, *Patriarcha non Monarcha*, chap. 1, p. 14, and chap. 2, p. 84.
13. Genevieve Lloyd, "Selfhood, War, and Masculinity," in *Feminist Challenges*, p. 75.
14. King James I, quoted in Fraser, *Weaker Vessel*, p. 122.
15. Ibid., pp. 268–270.
16. See Hobbes, *Leviathan*, chap. 20, p. 152, and Pateman, *Sexual Contract*, pp. 48–49.

17. See Locke, *Two Treatises*, I, par. 47, p. 37, and II, par. 82, p. 161; *Some Thoughts Concerning Education*, pp. 116, 155, 213, 218, 252–253, 317; and *On the Reasonableness of Christianity*, p. 193. See also Melissa Butler, "Early Roots of Feminism: John Locke and the Attack on Patriarchy," *American Political Science Review* 72 (March 1978): 135–150; and Mary Lyndon Shanley, "Marriage Contract and Social Contract in Seventeenth-Century English Political Thought," *Western Political Quarterly* 32 (March 1979): 79–91.

18. Robert Gould, *Love Given o'er or, a Satire against the Pride, Lust, and Inconstance, &tc. of Woman* (London: Andrew Green, 1682), in *Satires on Women*, esp. p. 12.

19. Sarah Fige, *The Female Advocate*, reprinted in *Satires on Women*, esp. p. 24.

20. Richard Ames, *The Folly of Love; or, an Essay upon Satyr against Woman* (London: E. Hawkins, 1691), reprinted in *Satires on Women*, esp. pp. 24–26.

21. Mary Astell, *Reflections upon Marriage*, in *The First English Feminist: Reflections upon Marriage and Other Writings by Mary Astell*, ed. Bridget Hill (New York: St. Martin's, 1986), p. 94.

22. *The Levellers* [1703], pp. 422–423.

23. See Western, *English Militia*, p. 269.

24. Trenchard, *An Argument*, pp. 28–29.

25. Lady Mary Chudleigh, *The Ladies Defence, or, the Bride-Woman's Counsellor Answer'd* (London: John Deeve, 1701), esp. p. 3, and Astell, *Reflections upon Marriage*, p. 70.

26. Tyrrell, *Patriarcha non Monarcha*, chap. 1, p. 24.

27. *The Duty of a Husband* [1706], cited in Michael Kimmel, "The Contemporary 'Crisis' of Masculinity in Historical Perspective," in *Making of Masculinities*, p. 128.

28. Astell, *Reflections upon Marriage*, pp. 75–76; see also Carole Pateman, "Women and Democratic Citizenship," The Jefferson Memorial Lectures delivered at the University of California, Berkeley, February 1985, pt. 1, p. 8.

29. See Lawrence Stone, *Family, Sex, and Marriage*, p. 240.

30. *An Essay in Defence of the Female Sex* (London: A. Roper & E. Wilkinson, 1696), esp. pp. 28–35.

31. Mary Astell, *A Serious Proposal to the Ladies for the Advancement of Their True and Greatest Interest*, in *First English Feminist*, pp. 142–143.

32. Fraser, *Weaker Vessel*, pp. 465–466.

33. Daniel Defoe, "An Academy for Women," in Daniel Defoe, *An Essay upon Projects* (London: Thos. Cockerill, 1697), pp. 302–303.

34. See *A Farther Essay Relating to the Female Sex* (London: A. Roper & E. Wilkinson, 1696), esp. pt. 2.

35. Lerner, *Creation of Patriarchy*, p. 201.

36. Hartsock, *Money, Sex, and Power*, p. 196.

37. Carole Pateman, "Introduction: The Theoretical Subversiveness of Feminism," in *Feminist Challenges*, p. 7; see also Pateman, *Sexual Contract*, p. 36.
38. See Susan Moller Okin, *Women in Western Political Thought* (Princeton: Princeton University Press, 1979), esp. pt. 5.
39. Montesquieu, *Spirit of Laws*, bk. 7, chap. 16, pp. 168–169.
40. See Teresa Brennan and Carole Pateman, " 'Mere Auxiliaries to the Commonwealth': Women and the Origins of Liberalism," *Political Studies* 27 (June 1979): 183–200.
41. Fraser, *Weaker Vessel*, pp. 60, 148.
42. *The Levellers*, p. 416.
43. See Lerner, *Creation of Patriarchy*, pp. 49–50.
44. Pocock, *Machiavellian Moment*, p. 463.
45. Compare Pateman, *Sexual Contract*, chap. 7, and Michael S. Kimmel, "Introduction," in *Mundus Foppensis* and *The Levellers*, pp. v–vi.
46. See Mary O'Brien, *The Politics of Reproduction* (Boston: Routledge & Kegan Paul, 1981), p. 53; Robert Jay Lifton, "The Future of Immortality," in Robert Jay Lifton, *The Future of Immortality and Other Essays for a Nuclear Age* (New York: Basic Books, 1987), pp. 10–14; and Hartsock, *Money, Sex, and Power*, chap. 8.
47. See *Marriage Promoted in a Discourse of Its Ancient and Modern Practice* [1690], cited in Fraser, *Weaker Vessel*, p. 270; and *The Levellers*, p. 419.
48. Barbara Ehrenreich, *The Hearts of Men: American Dreams and the Flight from Commitment* (Garden City, N.Y.: Anchor/Doubleday, 1983), p. 11.
49. *The Levellers*, p. 417; see also Thomas Hunt cited in Schochet, *Authoritarian Family*, p. 198.
50. John Toland, *Militia Reform'd*, pp. 7–8.
51. O'Brien, *Politics of Reproduction*, p. 49.
52. See Fraser, *Weaker Vessel*, p. 293.
53. Stiehm, "Man Question," p. 212.
54. See John D'Emilio and Estelle B. Freedman, *Intimate Matters: A History of Sexuality in America* (New York: Harper & Row, 1988), chap. 2, for a discussion of communal policing of sexuality in Anglo-American history.
55. Fige, *Female Advocate*, p. 18.
56. Tyrrell, *Patriarcha non Monarcha*, chap. 1, pp. 13–14; see also Montesquieu, *Spirit of Laws*, bk. 22, chap. 2, p. 301.
57. Montesquieu, *Spirit of Laws*, bk. 22, chap. 2, pp. 301–302.
58. Compare Stone, *Family, Sex and Marriage*, chap. 6 and Sidney, *Discourses*, chap. 1, sec. 17, p. 38.
59. See Tyrrell, *Patriarcha non Monarcha*, chap. 1, p. 36. Locke's ideas on father–son relations will be detailed in Chapter 4.
60. Chudleigh, *Ladies Defence*, p. 5.
61. Fraser, *Weaker Vessel*, p. 272.

62. Chudleigh, *Ladies Defence*, preface.
63. Toland, *Militia Reform'd*, p. 84.
64. Astell, *A Serious Proposal to the Ladies*, p. 144.
65. Pitkin, *Fortune Is a Woman*, p. 235.
66. See Kimmel, "Contemporary 'Crisis' of Masculinity," pp. 126–137.
67. Montesquieu, *Persian Letters*, Letters 154 and 161, pp. 274, 279–280.
68. Mary Lyndon Shanley and Peter G. Stillman, "Political and Marital Despotism: Montesquieu's *Persian Letters*," in *The Family in Political Thought*, ed. Jean Bethke Elshtain (Amherst: University of Massachusetts Press, 1982), p. 79.
69. *An Essay in Defence of the Female Sex*, pp. 10–23.
70. Astell, *Reflections upon Marriage*, p. 86.
71. Fraser, *Weaker Vessel*, p. 327.
72. Astell, *A Serious Proposal to the Ladies*, pp. 167–168; see also *An Essay in Defence of the Female Sex*, pp. 135–141.
73. Stone, *Family, Sex and Marriage*, pp. 655–656.
74. See Tyrrell, *Patriarcha non Monarcha*, chap. 1, p. 14; and Shanley, "Marriage Contract and Social Contract," p. 86.
75. See *The Fifteen Comforts of a Wanton Wife* [1706–1707] and *A Humble Remonstrance Of the Bachelors* [1693?], quoted in Kimmel, "Contemporary 'Crisis' of Masculinity," pp. 130–132.
76. Montesquieu, *Spirit of Laws*, bk. 8, chap. 2, p. 171.
77. *The Provoked Wife*, quoted in Stone, *Family, Sex and Marriage*, p. 240.
78. See Michael Grossberg, *Governing the Hearth: Law and the Family in Nineteenth-Century America* (Chapel Hill: University of North Carolina Press, 1985), for a study of the contract-status ambiguities of Anglo-American family law.
79. Hirschman, *Passions and the Interests*, p. 53.

CHAPTER 3

1. Sidney, *Discourses*, chap. 2, sec. 21, p. 140.
2. Lloyd, "Selfhood, War, and Masculinity," p. 75; see also Hartock, *Money, Sex and Power*, pp. 187–188.
3. Harrington, *Commonwealth of Oceana*, pp. 208–209.
4. Tyrrell, *Patriarcha non Monarcha*, chap. 1, p. 24.
5. Thomas L. Pangle, *The Spirit of Modern Republicanism: The Moral Vision of the American Founders and the Philosophy of Locke* (Chicago: University of Chicago Press, 1988), p. 215.
6. Locke, *Some Thoughts Concerning Education*, p. 213.
7. *Mundus Foppensis: or, the Fop Display'd*, reprinted in *Mundus Foppensis and*

The Levellers, pp. 8–17; and *A Farther Essay Relating to the Female-Sex*, pp. 105–115.

8. For example, see Fige, *Female Advocate*, p. 16.
9. Harrington, *Commonwealth of Oceana*, p. 228, and Trenchard, *An Argument*, p. 22.
10. Andrew Marvell, quoted in Schwoerer, *"No Standing Armies!"* p. 120.
11. William Prynne, quoted in ibid., p. 62; Toland, *Militia Reform'd*, pp. 17, 22; and Fletcher, *A Discourse of Government*, p. 29.
12. John Trenchard, *A Short History of Standing Armies in England*, 3d ed. (London: A. Baldwin, 1698), pp. 11–12, 29–30.
13. Pitkin, *Fortune Is a Woman*, p. 65.
14. Machiavelli, *The Discourses*, bk. 3, chap. 41, p. 528.
15. Ibid., chap. 36, pp. 516–517.
16. Machiavelli, *The Prince*, chap. 14, p. 55.
17. See Machiavelli, *The Discourses*, bk. 2, chap. 16, pp. 462–464.
18. Ibid., "Introduction," p. 274.
19. See Pocock, *Machiavellian Moment*, chaps. 12–13, for an analysis of the English debates over the militia and standing army.
20. Schwoerer, *"No Standing Armies!"* p. 170.
21. Toland, *Militia Reform'd*, pp. 5–58.
22. Fletcher, *A Discourse of Government*, pp. 33–34, 44–45, 53–56, 60–61.
23. Sidney, *Discourses*, chap. 2, sec. 21, p. 139.
24. Locke, *Some Thoughts Concerning Education*, pp. 128, 220–225.
25. Fletcher, *A Discourse of Government*, p. 55; see also Pitkin, *Fortune Is a Woman*, p. 72.
26. Locke, *Some Thoughts Concerning Education*, pp. 220–221, 223, 225–227.
27. Toland, *Militia Reform'd*, pp. 27, 65.
28. Western, *English Militia*, pp. 115–116, 254.
29. Kimmel, "Contemporary 'Crisis' of Masculinity," pp. 133–137.
30. Western, *English Militia*, p. 440.
31. *An Essay in Defence of the Female Sex*, p. 132.
32. See Hobbes, *Leviathan*, chap. 17, p. 132.
33. Ibid., p. 129; chap. 20, p. 154.
34. Ibid., chap. 21, p. 164.
35. Ibid., p. 165.
36. Ibid.
37. Michael Walzer, *Obligations: Essays on Disobedience, War, and Citizenship* (New York: Simon & Schuster, 1970), p. 87.
38. Ibid., p. 89.
39. Compare Locke, *A Letter from a Person of Quality*, pp. 55–149, and *Two Treatises*, II, par. 130, p. 186; par. 147, pp. 195–196.
40. Locke, *Two Treatises*, II, par. 139, p. 193.

41. M. Seliger, "Locke, Liberalism and Nationalism," in *John Locke: Problems and Perspectives*, ed. John W. Yolton (London: Cambridge University Press, 1969), p. 29.
42. Richard Cox, *Locke on War and Peace* (London: Oxford University Press, 1960), p. 172.
43. See Locke, *Some Thoughts Concerning Education*, pp. 226–227, and *Further Considerations Concerning Raising the Value of Money* (London: A. and J. Churchil, 1695), pp. 15–16; see also Pangle, *Spirit of Modern Republicanism*, pp. 225–227.
44. See Montesquieu, *Spirit of Laws*, bk. 1, chap. 3, p. 103; bk. 9, chap. 1, p. 183; and bk. 11, chap. 6, p. 212.
45. Trenchard, *An Argument*, p. 18.
46. Harrington, *Commonwealth of Oceana*, pp. 58, 266.
47. See Western, *English Militia*, pp. 25–27, 440.
48. Trenchard, *An Argument*, p. 11.
49. Robbins, *Eighteenth-Century Commonwealthman*, pp. 20, 112–113.
50. Sidney, *Discourses*, chap. 2, sec. 15, p. 109; secs. 22–23, pp. 143, 146.
51. Locke, *Two Treatises*, II, par. 45, p. 143.
52. See *Fundamental Constitutions of Caroline*, pp. 49–50; and Seliger, "Locke, Liberalism, and Nationalism," pp. 27–28.
53. See Robbins, *Eighteenth-Century Commonwealthman*, pp. 151–152.

CHAPTER 4

1. Locke, *Two Treatises*, II, par. 77, p. 159.
2. Ibid., par. 4, p. 122; par. 87, p. 163; par. 97, p. 169; par. 131, p. 186 (emphasis added).
3. Ashcraft, *Revolutionary Politics*, pp. 210, 228.
4. Locke, *Two Treatises*, II, par. 61, p. 150.
5. Ibid., par. 6, p. 123; see also Joseph Tussman, *Obligation and the Body Politic* (London: Oxford University Press, 1968), p. 25.
6. See Hanna Fenichel Pitkin, "Obligation and Consent—I," p. 996–997; Robert Booth Fowler, "Political Obligation and the Draft," in *Obligation and Consent*, ed. Donald Hanson and Robert Booth Fowler (Boston: Little, Brown, 1971), p. 57; and Carole Pateman, *Problem of Political Obligation*, pp. 72–74.
7. Compare J. W. Gough, *John Locke's Political Philosophy*, 2d ed. (London: Oxford University Press, 1973), pp. 69–70, 150; Dunn, *Political Thought of John Locke*, p. 112; and Macpherson, *Political Theory of Possessive Individualism*, pp. 232–234. Scholars also argue that Locke's assessment of women's rationality determined his expectations for women's citizenship. Compare

Elshtain, *Public Man, Private Woman*, p. 117, and Butler, "Early Liberal Roots of Feminism," p. 149.

8. See Locke, *Two Treatises*, esp. II, chap. 19, pp. 228–247.

9. John Locke, "Extract from Journals," in Lord King, *The Life of John Locke* (London: Henry Coburn, 1829), p. 119.

10. Locke, *On the Reasonableness of Christianity*, par. 241, pp. 170–171.

11. Locke, *On the Conduct of Understanding*, pp. 4–5.

12. Ibid., pp. 20, 37–38, 74, 77, 87–88; and Locke, *Some Considerations*, p. 42.

13. Locke, "Old England's Legal Constitution," pp. 320–321; and *A Letter Concerning Toleration*, p. 47.

14. Richard W. Krouse, "Patriarchal Liberalism and Beyond," in *Family in Political Thought*, p. 149.

15. Butler, "Early Liberal Roots of Feminism," p. 142; see also Hinton, "Husbands, Fathers and Conquerors," p. 294; and Schochet, *Authoritarian Family*, pp. 57–58.

16. For example, see Locke, *Two Treatises*, I, par. 40, p. 33.

17. Locke, *On the Conduct of Understanding*, pp. 25, 81.

18. Locke, *Two Treatises*, I, par. 54, p. 42.

19. Ibid., par. 59, p. 45; II, par. 66, p. 153; pars. 105–106, pp. 173–174. See also Lorenne M. G. Clark, "Women and Locke: Who Owns the Apples in the Garden of Eden," in *The Sexism of Social and Political Thought: Women and Reproduction from Plato to Nietzsche*, ed. Lorenne M. G. Clark and Lynda Lange (Toronto: University of Toronto Press, 1979), p. 33.

20. Locke, *Two Treatises*, I, par. 56, p. 44 (emphasis added).

21. John Locke, *An Essay Concerning Human Understanding*, I, p. 356.

22. Locke, *On the Reasonableness of Christianity*, par. 245, p. 185.

23. Locke, *Two Treatises*, II, pars. 77–81, pp. 159–161, and Dunn, *Political Thought of John Locke*, p. 98.

24. Locke himself was a lifelong bachelor. Still, he took great interest in children and was something of a surrogate father to Lady Masham's children. See Sheryl O'Donnell, " 'My Idea in Your Mind': John Locke and Damaris Cudworth Masham," in *Mothering the Mind: Twelve Studies of Writers and Their Silent Partners*, ed. Ruth Perry and Martine Watson Brownley (New York: Holmes & Meier, 1984), esp. p. 42.

25. Pangle, *Spirit of Modern Republicanism*, pp. 231–232.

26. Locke, *Two Treatises*, I, par. 45, p. 36; II, pars. 42–43, p. 142; see also Wolin, *Politics and Vision*, p. 315.

27. Locke, *Some Considerations*, p. 85.

28. Macpherson, *Political Theory of Possessive Individualism*, p. 207.

29. Compare Locke, *Some Thoughts Concerning Education*, pp. 213–214, and Harrington, *Commonwealth of Oceana*, p. 107.

30. Locke, *Two Treatises*, II, par. 111, p. 178; par. 8, p. 124; par. 123, p. 184.

31. Locke, *Some Considerations*, p. 115.

32. Compare John Rawls, *A Theory of Justice* (Cambridge: Harvard University Press, 1971), pp. 152–153, and Wood, *John Locke and Agrarian Capitalism*, p. 102.

33. Locke, *Two Treatises*, II, par. 82, p. 161.

34. See Locke, *Some Thoughts Concerning Education*, pp. 116, 213, 218, 252–253, 317.

35. Locke, *Two Treatises*, II, par. 107, p. 175.

36. Ibid., par. 182, pp. 214–215.

37. See Clark, "Women and Locke," p. 33.

38. Locke, *Two Treatises*, II, par. 50, p. 145; see also Ashcraft, *Revolutionary Politics*, pp. 266–274.

39. Locke, *Two Treatises*, II, par. 72, p. 156, and par. 190, p. 218.

40. Ashcraft, *Revolutionary Politics*, p. 270; see also Locke, *Some Considerations*, pp. 85, 115, 117–118.

41. Locke, *Two Treatises*, II, pars. 2–3, pp. 121–122; pars. 67–68, pp. 154–155.

42. Ibid., par. 92, p. 166, and I, par. 59, p. 45.

43. Locke, *Some Thoughts Concerning Education*, pp. 146, 150.

44. Locke, *Two Treatises*, II, par. 66, p. 153; pars. 72–73, p. 165.

45. Locke, *Some Thoughts Concerning Education*, p. 146.

46. Locke, *Two Treatises*, II, par. 69, p. 154.

47. Locke, *Some Thoughts Concerning Education*, p. 146.

48. Ibid., pp. 153, 204.

49. Ibid., pp. 155–156, 314.

50. Tarcov, *Locke's Education for Liberty*, p. 85.

51. Locke, *Some Thoughts Concerning Education*, pp. 218, 220.

52. Ibid., pp. 220–221.

53. Pangle, *Spirit of Modern Republicanism*, p. 227.

54. Locke, *Some Thoughts Concerning Education*, pp. 151, 246–249; see also Laura Greyson, "Fathers and Sons: Locke and the Problem of Democratic Authority," *Political Chronicle* 1, no. 1 (1989): 4–5.

55. Locke, *Some Thoughts Concerning Education*, pp. 247, 249.

56. Locke, *Two Treatises*, II, par. 120, p. 182; see also Greyson, "Fathers and Sons," p. 6.

57. Schochet, *Authoritarian Family*, p. xx.

58. Locke, *Some Thoughts Concerning Education*, p. 171.

59. Ibid., p. 145.

60. See Schochet, *Authoritarian Family*, p. 66; and Ashcraft, *Revolutionary Politics*, chap. 6.

61. Locke, *Some Thoughts Concerning Education*, pp. 228, 253.

62. See Pateman, *Sexual Contract*, p. 78.

63. Locke, *Some Thoughts Concerning Education*, pp. 177, 185.

64. Ibid., p. 149.

65. Ibid., p. 168.
66. Ibid., pp. 320–321.
67. Tarcov, *Locke's Education for Liberty*, p. 98.
68. See Locke, *Two Treatises*, II, par. 75, p. 158.
69. Locke, *Some Thoughts Concerning Education*, p. 187.
70. Hanna Fenichel Pitkin, "Obligation and Consent—II," *American Political Science Review* 60 (March 1966): 46.
71. See Gilligan, *In a Different Voice*, passim.
72. Appleby, *Capitalism and a New Social Order*, p. 15, and Diggins, *Lost Soul of American Politics*, p. 42.

CHAPTER 5

1. Locke, "Old England's Constitution," II, p. 321.
2. Locke, *Some Thoughts Concerning Education*, p. 111; and "Some Thoughts concerning Reading and Study for a Gentleman," in *A Collection of Several Pieces of Mr. John Locke*, p. 232.
3. For example, see Elshtain, *Public Man, Private Woman*, chap. 3.
4. Pangle, *Spirit of Modern Republicanism*, p. 227.
5. See Appleby, *Capitalism and a New Social Order*, p. 15, and Diggins, *Lost Soul of American Politics*, p. 42; see also Pocock, *Virtue, Commerce, and History*, p. 67.
6. Peter Laslett, *The World We Have Lost*, 2d ed. (New York: Scribner's, 1971), pp. 182, 188.
7. Schochet, *Authoritarian Family*, p. xx.
8. Locke, *Two Treatises*, II, pars. 74–75, pp. 157–158; par. 105, p. 173.
9. Ibid., par. 107, pp. 174–175; par. 110, p. 177.
10. Ibid., par. 107, p. 175.
11. Seliger, "Locke, Liberalism, and Nationalism," pp. 22–23.
12. Locke, *Two Treatises*, II, par. 110, pp. 177–178.
13. Ibid., par. 111, p. 178.
14. Ibid.
15. Ibid.
16. See Ibid., par. 138, p. 191; see also Macpherson, *Political Theory of Possessive Individualism*, chap. 5.
17. Ashcraft, *Revolutionary Politics*, pp. 259–261; see also Laslett, "Introduction," p. 43; Dunn, *Political Thought of John Locke*, p. 255; Wood, *John Locke and Agrarian Capitalism*, p. 113.
18. Locke, *Some Considerations*, pp. 2–4, 13, 102–104, 117–118 (emphasis added).
19. See Wood, *John Locke and Agrarian Capitalism*, p. 33.
20. Brennan and Pateman, " 'Mere Auxiliaries to the Commonwealth,' " p. 195.
21. Locke, *Two Treatises*, II, par. 173, p. 210.

22. Ibid., par. 112, p. 178.

23. Ibid., pars. 85–86, p. 162.

24. Ibid., par. 87, p. 163; and par. 95, pp. 168–169.

25. Ibid., par. 96, p. 169.

26. Ibid., par. 119, p. 182.

27. J. P. Plamenatz, *Consent, Freedom, and Political Obligation* (London: Oxford University Press, 1968), p. 8.

28. Patrick Riley, "On Finding an Equilibrium between Consent and Natural Law in Locke's Political Philosophy," *Political Studies* 22 (December 1974): 436.

29. Locke, *Two Treatises*, II, par. 122, p. 183.

30. Ibid., par. 110, p. 177.

31. Pangle, *Spirit of Modern Republicanism*, pp. 270–271.

32. Locke, *Two Treatises*, II, par. 131, p. 186; pars. 159–160, pp. 203–204; par. 186, p. 217.

33. Ibid., par. 124, p. 184.

34. Ibid., par. 136, p. 190; par. 219, p. 232.

35. Ibid., par. 158, p. 202; par. 160, p. 204.

36. Locke, "Old England's Legal Constitution," II, pp. 322–323.

37. Ibid.

38. Locke, *Two Treatises*, II, par. 209, p. 228.

39. Locke, "Old England's Legal Constitution," II, p. 319.

40. See Tarcov, *Locke's Education for Liberty*, p. 5; and Greyson, "Fathers and Sons," p. 7.

41. Locke, *Two Treatises*, II, par. 80, pp. 160–161.

42. Ibid., par. 59, p. 149; par. 65, p. 152; par. 80–83, p. 160–161.

43. Ibid., pars. 67–68, pp. 153–154.

44. Locke, *Some Thoughts Concerning Education*, pp. 168–169.

45. John Locke, "Report on the Poor," in Bourne, *Life of John Locke*, 2:378–385.

46. John Locke, "Report on Irish Linen Manufactures," in ibid., pp. 364–371.

47. Grossberg, *Governing the Hearth*, esp. chap. 8; see also Mimi Abramovitz, *Regulating the Lives of Women: Social Welfare Policy from Colonial Times to the Present* (Boston: South End Press, 1988); and Linda Gordon, *Heroes of Their Own Lives: The Politics and History of Family Violence* (New York: Penguin, 1988).

48. Refer to Chapter 4.

49. Locke, *Two Treatises*, II, par. 132, pp. 186–187.

50. Ibid., par. 161, p. 204; par. 209, p. 228.

51. Ibid., par. 168, p. 207.

52. Ibid., par. 222, p. 234.

53. Locke, "Old England's Legal Constitution," II, p. 321.

54. Wolin, "The Idea of the State in America," p. 46.

55. Locke, "Old England's Legal Constitution," II, p. 321.

CHAPTER 6

1. Locke, *Two Treatises*, II, par. 131, p. 186.
2. Butler, "Early Liberal Roots of Feminism," p. 149, and Samuel P. Huntington, *The Soldier and the State: The Theory and Politics of Civil–Military Relations* (Cambridge: Harvard University Press, 1957), pp. 149–155.
3. Pateman, *Sexual Contract*, p. 95; see also Brennan and Pateman, " 'Mere Auxiliaries to the Commonwealth,' " p. 187.
4. Locke, *Two Treatises*, II, par. 86, p. 162.
5. See Locke, *Some Thoughts Concerning Education*, pp. 168–169, 296–319.
6. See Jean Bethke Elshtain, "Aristotle, the Public-Private Split, and the Case of the Suffragists," in *Family in Political Thought*, p. 55, where she traces men's double existence back to Aristotle.
7. Zillah R. Eisenstein, *The Radical Future of Liberal Feminism* (New York: Longman, 1981), p. 37.
8. Locke, *Some Thoughts Concerning Education*, pp. 226–227.
9. Ibid., p. 155.
10. Locke, *An Essay Concerning Human Understanding*, I, p. 87.
11. Locke, *Two Treatises*, I, par. 47, pp. 36–37; par. 61, pp. 46–47; II, par. 52, p. 146; and *Some Thoughts Concerning Education*, p. 153.
12. Locke, *Two Treatises*, I, pars. 47–48, pp. 36–38.
13. Ibid.
14. Butler, "Early Liberal Roots of Feminism," p. 143; and Shanley, "Marriage Contract and Social Contract," pp. 87–88; see also Stone, *Family, Sex and Marriage*, p. 240.
15. Locke, *Two Treatises*, II, pars. 78–83, pp. 159–162.
16. Ibid.
17. Pateman, *Sexual Contract*, p. 52; compare Stone, *Family, Sex and Marriage*, p. 655.
18. Schochet, *Authoritarian Family*, pp. 249–250; and Stiehm, "The Protected, the Protector, the Defender," pp. 367–376.
19. See Stone, *Family, Sex and Marriage*, chap. 6, and Degler, *At Odds*, chap. 1.
20. Locke, *Two Treatises*, II, par. 65, p. 152.
21. Locke, *Some Thoughts Concerning Education*, pp. 252–253; see also p. 119.
22. See Pateman, *Sexual Contract*, p. 123 and Locke, *A Letter Concerning Toleration*, pp. 14–15.
23. Astell, *Some Reflections upon Marriage*, p. 103.
24. Locke, *Some Thoughts Concerning Education*, pp. 117–118.
25. Ibid., p. 117.
26. Compare Locke, "Letter to Mrs. Clarke," in *Educational Writings of John Locke*, pp. 344–346, and Fraser, *Weaker Vessel*, chap. 16.
27. Butler, "Early Liberal Roots of Feminism," pp. 148–149.

28. Katherine Philips, "Untitled," in *Kissing the Rod: An Anthology of Seventeenth-Century Verse*, ed. Germaine Greer, Susan Hastings, Jeslyn Medoff, and Melinda Sansone (New York: Farrar Straus & Giroux, 1988), pp. 188–189.

29. Lerner, *Creation of Patriarchy*, pp. 219–220.

30. Clark, "Women and Locke: Who Owns the Apples in the Garden of Eden," p. 37; see also Brennan and Pateman, " 'Mere Auxiliaries to the Commonwealth,' " p. 187.

31. See Pateman, "Shame of the Marriage Contract," pp. 79–80; and Elshtain, *Public Man, Private Woman*, p. 119.

32. See Mary Wollstonecraft, *Vindication of the Rights of Women*, ed. Miriam Brody Kramnick (New York: Viking Penguin, 1985), esp. p. 263.

33. See Stiehm, "The Protected, the Protector, the Defender," p. 373.

34. See O'Donnell, " 'My Idea in Your Mind,' " pp. 26–46; and Lady Masham, "Untitled," in *Kissing the Rod*, p. 321.

35. Locke, "Letter to Mrs. Clarke," p. 345.

36. George Savile, Marquis of Halifax, "The Lady's New Year's Gift, or, Advice to a Daughter," in *Roots of Bitterness*, pp. 78–79.

37. Ibid., pp. 81–82.

38. Ibid., p. 79.

39. Astell, *Some Reflections Upon Marriage* and *A Serious Proposal*, pp. 129, 167, 177–178.

40. Montesquieu, *Spirit of Laws*, bk. 7, chap. 8, p. 168.

41. Fraser, *Weaker Vessel*, pp. 183, 222.

42. See Susan Moller Okin, "Philosopher Queens and Private Wives: Plato on Women and the Family," in *Family in Political Thought*, pp. 31–50.

43. Locke, *Two Treatises*, II, par. 3, p. 122.

44. Ibid., par. 88, p. 164; see also Cox, *Locke on War and Peace*, p. 178; and Wood, *John Locke and Agrarian Capitalism*, pp. 32–33, 54.

45. Locke, *Two Treatises*, II, par. 45, p. 143; pars. 145–146, p. 195; see also par. 38, p. 140.

46. Ashcraft, *Revolutionary Politics*, p. 268; and Locke, *Two Treatises*, II, par. 37, p. 139; par. 47, p. 144; par. 50, p. 145.

47. Locke, *Some Considerations*, pp. 16, 30.

48. Locke, *Two Treatises*, II, par. 176, p. 211; see also Cox, *Locke on War and Peace*, p. 179.

49. Locke, *Two Treatises*, II, par. 139, p. 193.

50. Ibid., pars. 177–183, pp. 212–216.

51. Locke, *Some Thoughts Concerning Education*, p. 170.

52. Ibid., p. 225.

53. Ibid., pp. 223–225.

54. Ibid., p. 226.

55. Locke, *Two Treatises*, II, par. 18, p. 130.

56. Ibid., par. 107, p. 175.
57. See Cox, *Locke on War and Peace*, p. 171.
58. Locke, *Two Treatises*, II, par. 147, p. 196.
59. Ibid., I, par. 56, p. 44.
60. Locke, *Some Thoughts Concerning Education*, p. 111.
61. Stiehm, "The Protected, the Protector, the Defender," p. 370.
62. Locke, *A Letter from a Person of Quality*, esp. pp. 100–101, 106.
63. Ashcraft, *Revolutionary Politics*, chap. 7.
64. Locke, *Two Treatises*, II, par. 45, p. 143; par. 49, p. 145.
65. Locke, *A Letter Concerning Toleration*, pp. 13–14, 16, 23, 57.
66. Locke, *Two Treatises*, II, pars. 36–37, pp. 138–139.
67. Locke, *Further Considerations*, pp. 15–16; and Cox, *Locke on War and Peace*, p. 178.
68. Locke, "Report on the Poor," II, pp. 379–380.
69. Locke, "Report on Irish Linen Manufacture," II, p. 365; see also *Two Treatises*, II, par. 41, p. 141; and *Fundamental Constitutions of Caroline*, pp. 46–47.

CHAPTER 7

1. Rogin, *Fathers and Children*, p. 34.
2. See Nancy F. Cott, "Passionlessness," p. 164; Demos, *Past, Present, and Personal*, p. 45–46; and Daniel Lewis, quoted in Melvin Yazawa, *From Colonies to Commonwealth: Familial Ideology and the Beginnings of the American Republic* (Baltimore: Johns Hopkins University Press, 1985), p. 23.
3. The Reverend John Robinson, quoted in Demos, *Past, Present, and Personal*, pp. 46, 153; Elizabeth Pleck, *Domestic Tyranny: The Making of Social Policy against Family Violence from Colonial Times to the Present* (New York: Oxford University Press, 1987), pp. 18–28; Nancy F. Cott, "Eighteenth-Century Family and Social Life Revealed in Massachusetts Divorce Records," in *A Heritage of Her Own*, pp. 107–135; and Mary P. Ryan, *Womanhood in America: From Colonial Times to the Present*, 3d ed. (New York: Franklin Watts, 1983), p. 37.
4. Jay Fliegelman, *Prodigals and Pilgrims: The American Revolution against Patriarchal Authority* (Cambridge: Cambridge University Press, 1982), p. 204.
5. Carol Shammas, Marylynn Salmon, and Michel Dahlin, *Inheritance in America: From Colonial Times to the Present* (New Brunswick, N.J.: Rutgers University Press, 1987), p. 62.
6. Ibid., p. 120.
7. Ryan, *Cradle of the Middle Class*, pp. 152, 172.
8. Degler, *At Odds*, chap. 9.
9. Ryan, *Cradle of the Middle Class*, p. 184.

10. See Peiss, *Cheap Amusements*, esp. chap. 3; and Richard Sennett and Jonathan Cobb, *The Hidden Injuries of Class* (New York: Knopf, 1972), pp. 128–129.

11. Yazawa, *From Colonies to Commonwealth*, p. 2.

12. Ryan, *Womanhood in America*, p. 32; and Abramovitz, *Regulating the Lives of Women*, pp. 45–46, 53–54; see also Stephanie Coontz, *The Social Origins of Private Life: A History of American Families, 1600–1900* (London: Verso, 1988), p. 89.

13. *Aristotle's Masterpiece*, quoted in D'Emilio and Freedman, *Intimate Matters*, p. 20; and William Gouge, quoted in Demos, *Past, Present, and Personal*, p. 27.

14. Cott, "Eighteenth-Century Family and Social Life," p. 120; and Kerber, *Women of the Republic*, p. 120.

15. Demos, *Past, Present, and Personal*, pp. 58, 80–81; see also Abramovitz, *Regulating the Lives of Women*, p. 91; Shammas, Salmon, and Dahlin, *Inheritance in America*, p. 95; and Grossberg, *Governing the Hearth*, p. 235.

16. George Mason, quoted in Schochet, *Authoritarian Family*, pp. 18–19.

17. Coontz, *Social Origins of Private Life*, p. 155; see also D'Emilio and Freedman, *Intimate Matters*, p. 49.

18. Norton, *Liberty's Daughters*, p. 67; Herbert G. Gutman, "Marital and Sexual Norms among Slave Women," in *A Heritage of Her Own*, pp. 305–306; Eugene D. Genovese, *Roll, Jordan, Roll: The World the Slaves Made* (New York: Random House, 1974), p. 485; and Grossberg, *Governing the Hearth*, p. 133.

19. Abramovitz, *Regulating the Lives of Women*, p. 127; Norton, *Alternative Americas*, p. 31; Ryan, *Womanhood in America*, p. 146; Coontz, *Social Origins of Private Life*, p. 213; and Demos, *Past, Present, and Personal*, p. 86.

20. See Werner Sombart, *Why Is There No Socialism in the United States?* ed. C. T. Husbands (White Plains, N.Y.: M. E. Sharpe, 1976), pp. 93–104, 106; and Kraditor, *Radical Persuasion*, p. 186.

21. See Dubbert, *A Man's Place*, pp. 104–105; Daniel Horowitz, *The Morality of Spending: Attitudes toward the Consumer Society in America, 1875–1940* (Baltimore: Johns Hopkins University Press, 1985), p. 84; and Theodore Roosevelt, quoted in Peter Filene, "The Secrets of Men's History," in *Making of Masculinities*, p. 104.

22. Quoted in Norton, *Liberty's Daughters*, p. 43.

23. Ehrenreich, *Hearts of Men*, p. 24.

24. Coontz, *Social Origins of Private Life*, p. 83; and Abramovitz, *Regulating the Lives of Women*, pp. 53–54, 94–96.

25. Tim Carrigan, Bob Connell, and John Lee, "Toward a New Sociology of Masculinity," in *Making of Masculinities*, p. 87; "Davis v. Maryland, 1810," quoted in *Gay American History: Lesbians and Gay Men in the U.S.A.*, ed. Jonathan Katz (New York: Harper & Row, 1976), p. 26 and pt. 1; Degler, *At Odds*, p. 157; and D'Emilio and Freedman, *Intimate Matters*, p. 30.

26. Cited in Coontz, *Social Origins of Private Life*, pp. 213, 224.

27. D'Emilio and Freedman, *Intimate Matters*, p. 209; see also Grossberg, *Governing the Hearth*, pp. 120–126.

28. See Pugh, *Sons of Liberty*, pp. 102–104.

29. Dubbert, *A Man's Place*, chap. 2; Coontz, *Social Origins of Private Life*, p. 234; and Filene, *Him/Her/Self*, chap. 3.

30. Katz, *Gay American History*, pp. 129–134; D'Emilio and Freedman, *Intimate Matters*, p. 122; and Gary Kinsman, "Men Loving Men: The Challenge of Gay Liberation," in *Beyond Patriarchy*, pp. 109–111.

31. Kinsman, "Men Loving Men," p. 105; and Bruce Kidd, "Sports and Masculinity," in *Beyond Patriarchy*, p. 254.

32. Fliegelman, *Prodigals and Pilgrims*, p. 267; Degler, *At Odds*, p. 74; and Diggins, *Lost Soul of American Politics*, p. 135 (emphasis added).

33. E. Anthony Rotundo, "Patriarchs and Participants: A Historical Perspective on Fatherhood in the United States," in *Beyond Patriarchy*, pp. 65–67; and Yazawa, *From Colonies to Commonwealth*, p. 46.

34. See Fliegelman, *Prodigals and Pilgrims*, chap. 6; see also Vetterli and Bryner, *In Search of the Republic*, chap. 3.

35. Rotundo, "Patriarchs and Participants," p. 67; Kenneth A. Lockridge, *A New England Town: The First One Hundred Years* (New York: Norton, 1970), p. 102; and Demos, *Past, Present, and Personal*, p. 99.

36. Fliegelman, *Prodigals and Pilgrims*, pp. 5, 33–34; see also Yazawa, *From Colonies to Commonwealth*, p. 42; and Pleck, *Domestic Tyranny*, pp. 35–37, 41.

37. Fliegelman, *Prodigals and Pilgrims*, p. 33; and Rogin, *Fathers and Children*, p. 21; see also Yazawa, *From Colonies to Commonwealth*, pt. 2; and Coontz, *Social Origins of Private Life*, p. 79.

38. Abramovitz, *Regulating the Lives of Women*, p. 140; Pleck, *Domestic Tyranny*, pp. 40–44; and Coontz, *Social Origins of Private Life*, p. 178.

39. Demos, *Past, Present, and Personal*, p. 102; and Fliegelman, *Prodigals and Pilgrims*, p. 67.

40. Rogin, *Fathers and Children*, p. 34.

41. Fliegelman, *Prodigals and Pilgrims*, p. 66 and chap. 8.

42. Garry Wills, *Cincinnatus: George Washington and the Enlightenment* (Garden City: N.Y.: Doubleday, 1984), pp. 23, 129–130.

43. Noah Webster, "On the Education of Youth in America," in *Essays on Education in the Early Republic*, ed. Frederick Rudolph (Cambridge: Harvard University Press, 1965), p. 57; William Ellery Channing, quoted in Henry F. May, *The Enlightenment in America* (Oxford: Oxford University Press, 1976), p. 225; and Yazawa, *From Colonies to Commonwealth*, p. 20.

44. See Garry Wills, *Inventing America: Jefferson's Declaration of Independence* (New York: Random House, 1978), p. 35.

45. Appleby, *Capitalism and a New Social Order*, pp. 54, 67; and Rogin, *Fathers and Children*, pp. 15, 36.

46. John William Ward, *Andrew Jackson—Symbol for an Age* (New York: Oxford University Press, 1962), p. 40.

47. Ibid., pp. 44, 59, 63, 185.

48. Hartz, *Liberal Tradition in America*, pp. 111–112.

49. See Norton, *Alternative Americas*, pt. 1.

50. See Diggins, *Lost Soul of American Politics*, p. 298; and H. Mark Roelofs, *Ideology and Myth in American Politics* (Boston: Little, Brown, 1976), p. 146.

51. Norton, *Alternative Americas*, p. 270.

52. Ibid., p. 271.

53. See Shammas, Salmon, and Dahlin, *Inheritance in America*, pp. 56–57; and Genovese, *Roll, Jordan, Roll*, pp. 3–7.

54. Linderman, *Embattled Courage*, pt. 1.

55. Ibid., pt. 2.

56. Wolin, "The Idea of the State in America," p. 51.

57. Pugh, *Sons of Liberty*, p. 111.

58. See Yazawa, *From Colonies to Commonwealth*, pt. 2; Shi, *Simple Life*, pp. 94–97; and Richard Sennett, *Authority* (New York: Knopf, 1980), p. 59.

59. See Edward M. Coffman, *The Old Army: A Portrait of the American Army in Peacetime, 1784–1898* (New York: Oxford University Press, 1986), p. 251.

60. Lyman Beecher, quoted in Norton, *Alternative Americas*, pp. 78–79; and Horace Mann, quoted in Shi, *Simple Life*, p. 122.

61. Abramovitz, *Regulating the Lives of Women*, pp. 159, 166.

62. Pleck, *Domestic Tyranny*, pp. 98–99, 111, 119.

63. Grossberg, *Governing the Hearth*, pp. xi–xii, 87, 291, 298.

64. Linda Gordon, *Heroes in Their Own Lives*, p. 6.

65. Harry Brod, "Pornography and the Alienation of Male Sexuality," *Social Theory and Practice* 14 (Fall 1988): 274.

66. Theodore Roosevelt, quoted in Dubbert, *A Man's Place*, pp. 76–77.

67. Robbins, *Eighteenth-Century Commonwealthman*, pp. 20–21.

68. Rogin, *Fathers and Children*, p. 54.

CHAPTER 8

1. Sennett, *Authority*, p. 4.

2. Vetterli and Bryner, *In Search of the Republic*, pp. 5, 52, 235.

3. Compare Norton, *Liberty's Daughters*, pt. 2, and Rogin, *Fathers and Children*, pp. 63–64.

4. Ryan, *Cradle of the Middle Class*, pp. 45–46; see also Coontz, *Social Origins of Private Life*, p. 123.

5. See Ross, *Workers on the Edge*, esp. chap. 2; Norton, *Alternative Americas*, chap. 5; Hartz, *Liberal Tradition in America*, chap. 7; and Shi, *Simple Life*, chap. 7.

6. Demos, *Past, Present, and Personal*, p. 52; and Rotundo, "Patriarchs and Participants," pp. 68–70.

7. Demos, *Past, Present, and Personal*, p. 55.

8. Filene, *Him/Her/Self*, p. 81.

9. Compare Shklar, *Ordinary Vices*, chap. 2, and Diggins, *Lost Soul of American Politics*, pp. 12–13.

10. See Rogin, *Fathers and Children*, p. 49; Ryan, *Cradle of the Middle Class*, pp. 31, 62.

11. Demos, *Past, Present, and Personal*, p. 205.

12. See Judith Hicks Stiehm, "Government and the Family: Justice and Acceptance," in *Changing Images of the Family*, ed. Virginia Tufte and Barbara Myerhoff (New Haven: Yale University Press, 1979), p. 368; Richard Hofstadter, *Social Darwinism in American Thought*, rev. ed. (Boston: Beacon, 1955), p. 201; Pugh, *Sons of Liberty*, p. 100; and Sanford Lakoff, "From the Common Good to the Public Interest," a paper presented at the annual meeting of the Western Political Science Association, Anaheim, California, March 1987.

13. Shi, *Simple Life*, p. 277.

14. Vetterli and Bryner, *In Search of the Republic*, pp. 102, 124.

15. Douglas, *Feminization of American Culture*, pp. 7, 32, 43, 165; see also Degler, *At Odds*, chap. 12.

16. Compare Ryan, *Cradle of the Middle Class*, chap. 2, and Ward, *Andrew Jackson*, chap. 6, entitled "God's Right-Hand Man."

17. See Dubbert, *A Man's Place*, pp. 137–140.

18. Bellah et al., *Habits of the Heart*, p. 223.

19. Norton, *Alternative Americas*, p. 85.

20. Ibid., p. 131.

21. Benjamin Rush, "A Plan for the Establishment of Public Schools and the Diffusion of Knowledge in Pennsylvania," in *Essays on Education in the Early Republic*, pp. 11, 14–15.

22. Ibid., pp. 6, 12, 14–15.

23. Rogin, *Fathers and Children*, p. 261.

24. For example, see Degler, *At Odds*, chap. 12; and Pleck, *Domestic Tyranny*, chap. 7.

25. Abramovitz, *Regulating the Lives of Women*, pp. 158–159; see also Rogin, *Fathers and Children*, p. 275; and Pleck, *Domestic Tyranny*, p. 132.

26. Rogin, *Fathers and Children*, p. 279.

27. Ryan, *Womanhood in America*, p. 203; Sara M. Evans, *Born for Liberty: A History of Women in America* (New York: Free Press, 1989), chap. 6; and Kimmel, "Men's Responses to Feminism," p. 270.

28. Steven Mintz and Susan Kellogg, *Domestic Revolutions: A Social History of American Family Life* (New York: Free Press, 1988), p. 54.

29. Dubbert, *A Man's Place*, p. 29.

30. Anne Bradstreet, "The Four Ages of Man," quoted in Demos, *Past, Present, and Personal*, pp. 156–157.

31. Cotton Mather, quoted in ibid., p. 145.

32. See Rogin, *Fathers and Sons*, pp. 97–98; Ryan, *Cradle of the Middle Class*, p. 130; and McWilliams, *Idea of Fraternity in America*, pp. 245–247.

33. Demos, *Past, Present, and Personal*, p. 61; see also Rotundo, "Patriarchs and Participants," p. 68.

34. McWilliams, *Idea of Fraternity in America*, p. 83.

35. See Pugh, *Sons of Liberty*, chap. 1.

36. Hofstadter, *Social Darwinism in American Thought*, p. 44.

37. McWilliams, *Idea of Fraternity in America*, p. 377; see also Mary Ann Clawson, *Constructing Brotherhood: Class, Gender, and Fraternalism* (Princeton: Princeton University Press, 1989), p. 7; and Mark C. Carnes, *Secret Ritual and Manhood in Victorian America* (New Haven: Yale University Press, 1989), p. 1.

38. McWilliams, *Idea of Fraternity in America*, p. 92.

39. Carnes, *Secret Ritual*, p. 125; and Clawson, *Constructing Brotherhood*, p. 164.

40. Pugh, *Sons of Liberty*, p. 118.

41. Clawson, *Constructing Brotherhood*, p. 72.

42. See Barbara and John Ehrenreich, "The Professional-Managerial Class," *Radical America* 11 (March–April 1977): 7–31; see also Richard Hofstadter, *The Age of Reform* (New York: Random House, 1955), pp. 148–164; and Mark E. Kann, *Middle Class Radicalism in Santa Monica* (Philadelphia: Temple University Press, 1986), pp. 44–49.

43. This section is largely based on the Center for Research on Criminal Justice's *The Iron Fist and the Velvet Glove: An Analysis of the U.S. Police*, 2d ed. (Berkeley: Center for Research on Criminal Justice, 1977), pp. 34–42.

44. August Vollmer, quoted in ibid., p. 39.

45. See Mintz and Kellogg, *Domestic Revolutions*, chap. 6.

46. See Harlan Hahn, "Alternative Paths to 'Professionalization': The Development of Municipal Personnel," in *Managing Human Resources: A Challenge to Urban Governments*, ed. Charles H. Levine (Beverly Hills, Calif.: Sage, 1977), pp. 48–53.

47. See Harry Braverman, *Labor and Monopoly Capital: The Degradation of Work in the Twentieth Century* (New York: Monthly Review Press, 1974), esp. pt. 1; Ehrenreich and English, *For Her Own Good*, esp. chaps. 2–3; and Evans and Boyte, *Free Spaces*, chap. 4.

48. Clawson, *Constructing Brotherhood*, pp. 133, 236; and Carnes, *Secret Ritual*, p. 142.

49. See Dubbert, *A Man's Place*, chaps. 4–5.

50. See Ehrenreich and Ehrenreich, "The Professional-Managerial Class," pp. 22–23.

51. See McWilliams, *Fraternity in America*, chap. 10.

52. See Ross, *Workers on the Edge*, esp. chaps. 2, 4.

53. McWilliams, *Fraternity in America*, pp. 7–8.

54. Rogin, *Fathers and Children*, p. 93; John D. Rockefeller, quoted in Hofstadter, *Social Darwinism in American Thought*, p. 45; and McWilliams, *Fraternity in America*, p. 383.

55. See Allan David Heskin, *Tenants and the American Dream: Ideology and the Tenant Movement* (New York: Praeger, 1983), pp. 9–15.

56. See McWilliams, *Fraternity in America*, p. 379; Carnes, *Secret Ritual*, pp. 22, 31–33; and Cunliffe, *Soldiers and Civilians*, p. 231.

57. See McWilliams, *Fraternity in America*, pp. 92–93, 246; and Dorothy Hammond and Alta Jablow, "Gilgamesh and the Sundance Kid: The Myth of Male Friendship," in *Making of Masculinities*, p. 246.

58. See Linderman, *Embattled Courage*, pp. 266–270; and Huntington, *Soldier and the State*, pp. 222–229.

59. See Peter Filene, "History, Men's History, and What's the Difference," a paper delivered to the Conference on the New Gender Scholarship, Los Angeles, February 13–15, 1987, for a brief discussion of Debs and masculinity; see also Lawrence Goodwyn, *Democratic Promise: The Populist Movement in America* (New York: Oxford University Press, 1976), p. 360; and David Noble, "Present Tense Technology—Part One," *democracy* 3 (Spring 1983): 23.

60. See Edward Bellamy, *Looking Backward, 2007–1887* (New York: New American Library, 1960); Daniel De Leon, *Socialist Landmarks* (New York: New York Labor News, 1952), pp. 57–58; and Mark E. Kann, "Challenging Lockean Liberalism in America: The Case of Debs and Hillquit," *Political Theory* 8 (May 1980): 203–222.

61. See Dubbert, *A Man's Place*, chap. 5.

62. Hirschman, *Passions and the Interests*, p. 128.

63. See R. Jeffrey Lustig, *Corporate Liberalism: The Origins of Modern American Political Theory 1890–1920* (Berkeley: University of California Press, 1982), chap. 5.

64. Wolin, "Idea of the State in America," p. 52; and Thomas A. Spragens, *The Dilemma of Contemporary Political Theory: Toward A Post-Behavioral Science of Politics* (New York: Dunellen, 1973), pp. 83–84.

65. Wolin, "Idea of the State in America," p. 48.

66. Huntington, *Soldier and the State*, chap. 10; Lustig, *Corporate Liberalism*, p. 216; and Wolin, "Idea of the State in America," p. 48.

67. Sylvester Judd, quoted in Douglas, *Feminization of American Culture*, p. 102.

CHAPTER 9

1. Abigail Alcott, quoted in Shi, *Simple Life*, pp. 137–138.

2. Helen Cooper, Adrienne Munich, and Susan Squier, "Introduction," in *Arms*

and the Woman: War, Gender, and Literary Representation, ed. Helen Cooper, Adrienne Munich, and Susan Squier (Chapel Hill: University of North Carolina Press, 1989), p. xvii.

3. Abramovitz, *Regulating the Lives of Women*, p. 47; Demos, *Past, Present, and Personal*, p. 45; and Cott, "Passionlessness," p. 163.

4. See Fliegelman, *Prodigals and Pilgrims*, pp. 44, 124–125, 234; Norton, *Liberty's Daughters*, chap. 6; Yazawa, *From Colonies to Commonwealth*, p. 95; Bailyn, *Ideological Origins of the American Revolution*, p. 86; and Kerber, *Women of the Republic*, p. 105.

5. Marybeth Hamilton Arnold, "'The Life of a Citizen in the Hands of a Woman': Sexual Assault in New York City, 1790–1820," in *Passion and Power: Sexuality in History*, ed. Kathy Peiss and Christina Simmons (Philadelphia: Temple University Press, 1989), pp. 40, 51–52; D'Emilio and Freedman, *Intimate Matters*, p. 45; and Norton, *Alternative Americas*, p. 42.

6. See Pugh, *Sons of Liberty*, chap. 2; Matthews, *"Just a Housewife,"* chap. 5; Norton, *Alternative Americas*, p. 69; D'Emilio and Freedman, *Intimate Matters*, p. 86; Ehrenreich and English, *For Her Own Good*, pp. 76, 133–140.

7. Grossberg, *Governing the Hearth*, pp. 42, 54, 62–63; and Gordon, *Heroes of Their Own Lives*, pp. 89, 92, 103, 215, 220.

8. Abramovitz, *Regulating the Lives of Women*, pp. 112–113.

9. Ryan, *Womanhood in America*, pp. 20, 51; Laurel Thatcher Ulrich, "Vertuous Women Found: New England Ministerial Literature, 1668–1735," in *A Heritage of Her Own*, p. 68.

10. Ryan, *Womanhood in America*, chap. 1; Norton, *Liberty's Daughters*, chap. 5; Demos, *Past, Present, and Personal*, p. 11; Matthews, *"Just a Housewife,"* pp. 3–4; Maxine L. Margolis, *Mothers and Such: Views of American Women and Why They Changed* (Berkeley: University of California Press, 1984), chap. 7; Norton, *Alternative Americas*, pp. 53, 57; and D'Emilio and Freedman, *Intimate Matters*, p. 148.

11. Evans, *Born for Liberty*, p. 42.

12. Norton, *Liberty's Daughters*, p. 61 and chap. 6; Kerber, *Women of the Republic*, pp. xi–xii; and Evans, *Born for Liberty*, p. 50.

13. See Kerber, *Women of the Republic*, p. 136; and Norton, *Liberty's Daughters*, p. 179.

14. Kerber, *Women of the Republic*, pp. 30–31; Coontz, *Social Origins of Private Life*, p. 147.

15. See Gerda Lerner, "The Lady and the Mill Girl: Changes in the Status of Women in the Age of Jackson, 1800–1840," in *A Heritage of Her Own*, pp. 182–196; and Ryan, *Womanhood in America*, p. 70.

16. Linda K. Kerber, "'History Can Do It No Justice': Women and the Reinterpretation of the American Revolution," in *Women in the Age of the American Revolution*, ed. Ronald Hoffman and Peter J. Albert (Charlottesville: University of Virginia Press, 1989), pp. 30–33, 40; see also Margaret R. Higonnet and

Patrice L. R. Higonnet, "The Double Helix," in *Behind the Lines: Gender and the Two World Wars*, ed. Margaret R. Higonnet, Jane Jenson, Sonya Michel, and Margaret Collins Weitz (New Haven: Yale University Press, 1987), p. 38.

17. Laurel Thatcher Ulrich, " 'Daughters of Liberty': Religious Women in Revolutionary New England," in *Women in the Age of the American Revolution*, p. 227.

18. Quoted in Norton, *Liberty's Daughters*, pp. 100–101; see also Kerber, *Women of the Republic*, p. 110.

19. Yazawa, *From Colonies to Commonwealth*, pp. 141, 171.

20. Coontz, *Social Origins of Private Life*, p. 155; and Evans, *Born for Liberty*, p. 59.

21. Kerber, *Women of the Republic*, pp. 199–200, 229.

22. Quoted in ibid., p. 205.

23. Rush, "A Plan for the Establishment of Public Schools" and "Thoughts upon Female Education, Accommodated to the Present State of Society, Manners and Government in the United States of America," in *Essays on Education in the Early Republic*, pp. 22, 36–37; see also Noah Webster, "On the Education of Youth in America," and Simeon Doggett, "A Discourse on Education," in *Essays on Education*, pp. 69, 159.

24. Kerber, *Women of the Republic*, p. 11; and Matthews, *"Just a Housewife,"* p. 7.

25. Ryan, *Womanhood in America*, p. 113; and Matthews, *"Just a Housewife,"* chap. 1.

26. Stiehm, "The Man Question," pp. 207–223; see also Stiehm, "Government and the Family," p. 369, for a discussion of how biology and family anchor individuals in history. To the extent men absented themselves from the family, they lost an anchor.

27. Compare Bonnie G. Smith, *Ladies of the Leisure Class: The Bourgeoises of Northern France in the Nineteenth Century* (Princeton: Princeton University Press, 1981), p. 56, and Mintz and Kellogg, *Domestic Revolutions*, p. 55.

28. Frances B. Cogan, *All-American Girl: The Ideal of Real Womanhood in Mid-Nineteenth-Century America* (Athens: University of Georgia Press, 1989), p. 4.

29. See ibid., pp. 75–76; D'Emilio and Freedman, *Intimate Matters*, pp. 143, 152; Pleck, *Domestic Tyranny*, pp. 91–94; and Margolis, *Mothers and Such*, chap. 2.

30. Rogin, *Fathers and Children*, p. 49; Demos, *Past, Present, and Personal*, p. 31; and Degler, *At Odds*, p. 153; see also Pitkin, *Fortune Is a Woman*, chap. 5.

31. See Degler, *At Odds*, chap. 1; Smith, "Family Limitation," p. 239; and Mintz and Kellogg, *Domestic Revolutions*, pp. 43–47.

32. See Cott, "Passionlessness," esp. pp. 168–169.

33. Degler, *At Odds*, pp. 74, 171; Cogan, *All-American Girl*, pp. 108, 154; Grossberg, *Governing the Hearth*, p. 251.

34. Margolis, *Mothers and Such*, p. 30; Demos, *Past, Present, and Personal*, p. 58; see also Joseph H. Pleck, "American Fathering in Historical Perspective," in *Changing Men: New Directions in Research on Men and Masculinity*, ed. Michael S. Kimmel (Newbury Park, Calif.: Sage Publications, 1987), p. 87; and Grossberg, *Governing the Hearth*, pp. 238–247.

35. Pleck, *Domestic Tyranny*, pp. 35–37, 40–41.

36. Thomas R. Dew, "Dissertation on the Characteristic Differences between the Sexes, and on the Position of Woman in Society [1835]," in *Up from the Pedestal*, p. 46; Smith, *Ladies of the Leisure Class*, p. 63; Ryan, *Cradle of the Middle Class*, pp. 172, 184–185; and Cogan, *All-American Girl*, chap. 6.

37. Quoted in Demos, *Past, Present, and Personal*, p. 32; see also Margolis, *Mothers and Such*, pp. 129–130.

38. Mintz and Kellogg, *Domestic Revolutions*, p. 54; Degler, *At Odds*, p. 28; and Smith, "Family Limitation," p. 231.

39. Matthews, *"Just a Housewife,"* p. 85; and Ehrenreich and English, *For Her Own Good*, p. 121.

40. Quoted in Evans, *Born for Liberty*, p. 63; Grossberg, *Governing the Hearth*, p. 301; Pateman, "The Shame of the Marriage Contract," p. 90; see also Shammas, Salmon, and Dahlin, *Inheritance in America*, pp. 76, 97–101.

41. Quoted in Filene, *Him/Her/Self*, p. 40.

42. Rogin, *Fathers and Children*, p. 15; Demos, *Past, Present, and Personal*, p. 31; Degler, *At Odds*, p. 472; see also Norton, *Alternative Americas*, p. 42.

43. Matthews, *"Just a Housewife,"* p. 35; Cogan, *All-American Girl*, pp. 81, 89; Coontz, *Social Origins of Private Life*, p. 193; D'Emilio and Freedman, *Intimate Matters*, p. 179; and Grossberg, *Governing the Hearth*, pp. 47–49.

44. Catharine Beecher, excerpted in Jeanne Boydston, Mary Kelley, and Anne Margolis, *The Limits of Sisterhood: The Beecher Sisters on Women's Rights and Woman's Sphere* (Chapel Hill: University of North Carolina Press, 1988), pp. 127–139; see also Douglas, *Feminization of American Culture*, p. 128.

45. Ryan, *Womanhood in America*, pp. 137–138; Dubbert, *A Man's Place*, pp. 39–46; and Samuel Jennings, "Proper Conduct of the Wife towards Her Husband," in *Roots of Bitterness*, p. 116.

46. Sara Josepha Hale, quoted in Shi, *Simple Life*, p. 116; Caroll Smith-Rosenberg, "Beauty, the Beast, and the Militant Woman: A Case Study of Sex Roles and Social Stress in Jacksonian America," in *A Heritage of Her Own*, p. 208; and Degler, *At Odds*, p. 98.

47. Karen J. Blair, *The Clubwoman as Feminist: True Womanhood Redefined, 1868–1914* (New York: Holmes & Meier, 1980), pp. 18, 28.

48. See Dubbert, *A Man's Place*, pp. 17–19; Filene, *Him/Her/Self*, chap. 3; and Kimmel, "The Contemporary 'Crisis' of Masculinity in Historical Perspective," pp. 121–153.

49. See Stone, *Family, Sex and Marriage*, pp. 666–673, 677; and Smith, *Ladies of the Leisure Class*, chap. 6.

50. Matthews, *"Just a Housewife,"* p. 35; see also Evans, *Born for Liberty,* p. 76.

51. Catharine Beecher, excerpted in *Limits of Sisterhood,* p. 132; and Smith-Rosenberg, "Beauty, the Beast, and the Militant Woman," p. 204; see also Ryan, *Womanhood in America,* p. 130.

52. Pleck, *Domestic Tyranny,* p. 100; and Blair, *Clubwoman as Feminist,* pp. 1, 40–42, 49, 80; see also Degler, *At Odds,* chap. 13.

53. Evans, *Born for Liberty,* pp. 130, 137, 142–143.

54. Ellen Carol DuBois, *Feminism and Suffrage: The Emergence of an Independent Women's Movement in America 1848–69* (Ithaca, N.Y.: Cornell University Press, 1978), pp. 45–46; and Orestes A. Brownson, "The Woman Question," in *Up from the Pedestal,* p. 192.

55. Isabella Hooker, excerpted in *Limits of Sisterhood,* pp. 202–203, 212; see also Filene, *Him/Her/Self,* p. 37.

56. See Matthews, *"Just a Housewife,"* p. 85; Coontz, *Social Origins of Private Life,* pp. 190, 267, 330; and Ross, *Workers on the Edge,* pp. 103, 169–170, 228.

57. Carroll D. Wright, quoted in Horowitz, *Morality of Spending,* p. 18; and Ryan, *Womanhood in America,* p. 209; see also Coontz, *Social Origins of Private Life,* p. 181.

58. See Peiss, *Cheap Amusements,* chap. 7; Blair, *Clubwoman as Feminist,* pp. 108–111; Horowitz, *Morality of Spending,* chaps. 4–5; and Matthews, *"Just a Housewife,"* p. 163.

59. Henrietta Goodrich, quoted in Ehrenreich and English, *For Her Own Good,* p. 168.

60. Mrs. A. J. Graves, "Women in America," in *Roots of Bitterness,* pp. 144–145.

61. Theodore Roosevelt, quoted in Ehrenreich and English, *For Her Own Good,* p. 190; Reverend Abbott, quoted in Margolis, *Mothers and Such,* p. 36; and Grover Cleveland, "Would Woman Suffrage Be Unwise?" in *Up from the Pedestal,* p. 200.

62. Lloyd, "Selfhood, War, and Masculinity," p. 76; Hartsock, *Money, Sex, and Power,* p. 236; and Elshtain, *Women and War,* p. 192.

63. Linderman, *Embattled Courage,* pp. 87, 91, 94; Evans, *Born for Liberty,* p. 114; and Blair, *Clubwoman as Feminist,* p. 13.

64. Jane E. Schultz, "Mute Fury: Southern Women's Diaries of Sherman's March to the Sea, 1864–1865," in *Arms and the Woman,* pp. 61, 74–75.

65. See Cynthia Enloe, *Does Khaki Become You? The Militarization of Women's Lives* (Boston: South End Press, 1983), chap. 2; and Coffman, *Old Army,* pp. 298, 322.

66. Ward, *Andrew Jackson,* p. 33; and Cunliffe, *Soldiers and Civilians,* p. 7; see also Samuel Keen, *Faces of the Enemy: Reflections of the Hostile Imagination* (San Francisco: Harper & Row, 1986), 58–59; and Judith Stiehm, *Bring Me Men and Women: Mandated Change at the U.S. Air Force Academy* (Berkeley: University of California Press, 1981), p. 2.

67. Stuart Chase, quoted in Horowitz, *The Morality of Spending,* p. 112; Joanne L.

Hayes, "Fare for Hard Times," *Country Living Magazine*, March 1989, pp. 110–111, 117; and Linderman, *Embattled Courage*, p. 64.

68. Elshtain, *Women and War*, p. 144.

69. Linderman, *Embattled Courage*, pp. 261–264. Contrast Margaret R. Higonnet, "Civil Wars and Sexual Territories," in *Arms and the Woman*, p. 93 where the author points out that women are less likely than men to see families as insulated from war.

70. Elshtain, *Women and War*, pp. 101–102, 165; Higonnet and Higonnet, "Double Helix," pp. 33–35; and Judith Hicks Stiehm, *Arms and the Enlisted Woman* (Philadelphia: Temple University Press, 1989), chap. 10.

71. See Christina Simmons, "Modern Sexuality and the Myth of Victorian Repression," in *Passion and Power*, p. 171; Blair, *Clubwoman as Feminist*, pp. 28, 58, 70; Abramovitz, *Regulating the Lives of Women*, pp. 191–192; Pleck, *Domestic Tyranny*, pp. 4, 143; Gordon, *Heroes of Their Own Lives*, pp. 73, 104; Coontz, *Social Origins of Private Life*, p. 197; and Mintz and Kellogg, *Domestic Revolutions*, pp. 108–109, 112–113.

72. See Pugh, *Sons of Liberty*, p. 37; Rogin, *Fathers and Children*, p. 50; Coffman, *Old Army*, pp. 312–313; Linderman, *Embattled Courage*, pp. 226–227; Kimmel, "Contemporary 'Crisis' of Masculinity," p. 147; Theodore Roosevelt, quoted in Ehrenreich and English, *For Her Own Good*, p. 168; D'Emilio and Freedman, *Intimate Matters*, pp. 211–212; and Enloe, *Does Khaki Become You?* p. 29.

CHAPTER 10

1. General Leonard Wood, quoted in Chambers, "Conscripting for the Colossus," p. 304.

2. George Washington, "Letter to Congress (May 1783)," in *American Military Thought*, ed. Walter Millis (Indianapolis: Bobbs-Merrill, 1966), p. 23; and Hugh Scott, "War Department Annual Report (1916)," in *American Military Thought*, p. 349; see also Stiehm, *Bring Me Men and Women*, p. 297.

3. "Massachusetts Body of Liberties" in *American Military Thought*, p. xviii; and Weigley, *History of the United States Army*, pp. 15–16.

4. George Washington, "Letter to the Continental Congress (September 24, 1776)," in *American Military Thought*, pp. 10–12.

5. See Coffman, *Old Army*, chap. 3; Enloe, *Does Khaki Become You?* chap. 1; Stiehm, "The Protected, the Protector, the Defender," pp. 367–370; and *Bring Me Men and Women*, p. 267.

6. See Coffman, *Old Army*, pp. 83, 193; Rogin, *Fathers and Children*, pp. 128–129 and chaps. 6–7; and Zinn, *A People's History*, pp. 127, 158–159.

7. See Stiehm, "The Protected, the Protector, the Defender," p. 372; *Bring Me Men and Women*, p. 284; Elshtain, *Women and War*, p. 22; Lifton, *Future of*

Immortality, p. 15; J. Glenn Gray, *The Warriors: Reflections on Men in Battle* (New York: Harper & Row, 1959, 1970), p. 46; and Hammond and Jablow, "Gilgamesh and the Sundance Kid," pp. 241–258.

8. Enloe, *Does Khaki Become You?* p. 5; and Coffman, *Old Army*, pp. 312–313.

9. George Washington, "Letter to the Continental Congress (September 24, 1776)," p. 12; Don Higginbotham, "The Early American Way of War: Reconnaissance and Appraisal," *William and Mary Quarterly* 44 (April 1987): 261–262, 267–268; and Peter Karsten, *Soldiers and Society: The Effects of Military Service and War on American Life* (Westport, Conn.: Greenwood Press, 1978), p. 19.

10. See Charles A. Lofgren, *"Government from Reflection and Choice": Constitutional Essays on War, Foreign Relations, and Federalism* (New York: Oxford University Press, 1986), p. 57.

11. See Don Higginbotham, *War and Society in Revolutionary America: The Wider Dimensions of Conflict* (Columbia: University of South Carolina Press, 1988), pp. 23–24; Weigley, *History of the United States Army*, p. 125; and Cunliffe, *Soldiers and Civilians*, p. 192 and chap. 7.

12. See Weigley, *History of the United States Army*, chap. 5.

13. Quoted in Ward, *Andrew Jackson*, pp. 8, 25.

14. Cunliffe, *Soldiers and Civilians*, p. 81.

15. Karstens, *Soldiers and Society*, pp. 15, 151, 283; and Cunliffe, *Soldiers and Civilians*, p. 88.

16. Dubbert, *A Man's Place*, p. 60; Karstens, *Soldiers and Society*, p. 17; Stephen Crane, *The Red Badge of Courage* (Mahwah, N.J.: Watermill Press, 1981), esp. pp. 8, 126; and Linderman, *Embattled Courage*, p. 57.

17. See Linderman, *Embattled Courage*, chap. 12; Kimmel, "Contemporary 'Crisis' of Masculinity in Historical Perspective," pp. 121–153; and Cunliffe, *Soldiers and Civilians*, p. 379 and chap. 10. Compare Huntington, *Soldier and the State*, pp. 217–221, and Weigley, *History of the United States Army*, chap. 8, on whether the Southern military tradition was myth or reality.

18. Dubbert, *A Man's Place*, chaps. 5–7; Filene, *Him/Her/Self*, pp. 97, 102, and chap. 4; and Shi, *Simple Life*, p. 53.

19. Higginbotham, *War and Society*, p. 22.

20. Coffman, *Old Army*, p. 16; see also Cunliffe, *Soldiers and Civilians*, p. 49.

21. Samuel Adams, quoted in Weigley, *History of the United States Army*, p. 75.

22. Cunliffe, *Soldiers and Civilians*, pp. 20–21; and Samuel Gompers, quoted in Weigley, *History of the United States Army*, p. 282.

23. Cunliffe, *Soldiers and Civilians*, p. 116.

24. Coffman, *Old Army*, pp. 62, 84–87; and Scott, "War Department Annual Report (1916)," p. 348.

25. Quoted in Cunliffe, *Soldiers and Civilians*, p. 177; and Emory Upton, *The Military Policy of the United States* [1880], in *American Military Thought*, p. 190.

26. Huntington, *Soldier and the State*, p. 70.

27. Norton, *Alternative Americas*, p. 31; see also Coffman, *Old Army*, pp. 71–73.

28. Millis, "Introduction," in *American Military Thought*, p. xxxiii.

29. See Higginbotham, *War and Society*, pp. 30–31; and Pocock, *Machiavellian Moment*, pp. 526–541.

30. See Higginbotham, "Early American Way of War," p. 245; and Norton, *Alternative Americas*, p. 119.

31. Quoted in Lofgren, *"Government from Reflection and Choice,"* pp. 40–41.

32. Robert Jackson and Friedrich von Steuben, quoted in *The Sword and the Pen*, ed. Adrian Liddell Hart (New York: Thomas Y. Crowell, 1976), pp. 60, 117; see also Cunliffe, *Soldiers and Civilians*, p. 50.

33. See Weigley, *History of the United States Army*, pp. 93, 104, 153–154; Cunliffe, *Soldiers and Civilians*, p. 36; Ward, *Andrew Jackson*, p. 26; and Jackson, quoted in Rogin, *Fathers and Children*, p. 142; see also pp. 150, 153.

34. Rogin, *Fathers and Children*, pp. 8, 188, 207; and Norton, *Alternative Americas*, p. 69.

35. Lewis Cass and Andrew Jackson, quoted in Zinn, *A People's History*, pp. 131, 139.

36. Rogin, *Fathers and Children*, p. 120.

37. See Ward, *Andrew Jackson*, p. 188; and Coffman, *Old Army*, p. 38.

38. Quoted in Zinn, *A People's History*, p. 161.

39. Cunliffe, *Soldiers and Civilians*, p. 74.

40. Upton, *Military Policy of the United States*, p. 184.

41. Compare Pugh, *Sons of Liberty*, p. 42, and Rogin, *Fathers and Children*, pp. 107, 312.

42. Ward, *Andrew Jackson*, p. 136.

43. See Cunliffe, *Soldiers and Civilians*, chap. 11 and pp. 416–417; Huntington, *Soldier and the State*, chap. 3 and pp. 222–229; Weigley, *History of the United States Army*, p. 271; and Coffman, *Old Army*, pp. 72–78.

44. Cunliffe, *Soldiers and Civilians*, pp. 106–107, 419.

45. See Coffman, *Old Army*, chap. 3; Enloe, *Does Khaki Become You?* chap. 3; and Elshtain, *Women and War*, p. 139.

46. Scott, "War Department Annual Report, 1916," pp. 346–347; see also Weigley, *History of the United States Army*, pp. 125, 360.

47. See Weigley, *History of the United States Army*, p. 208; and Zinn, *A People's History*, pp. 230–232.

48. Linderman, *Embattled Courage*, pp. 121, 154–156, 198–201; Weigley, *History of the United States Army*, p. 251; Shultz, "Mute Fury," pp. 59–79; and Keen, *Faces of the Enemy*, passim.

49. Michael Paul Rogin, *Ronald Reagan, the Movie and Other Episodes in Political Demonology* (Berkeley: University of California Press, 1987), pp. xiii–xvii.

50. James A. Garfield, quoted in Cunliffe, *Soldiers and Civilians*, p. 431.

51. Linderman, *Embattled Courage*, pp. 275–283, 287.

52. See Upton, *Military Policy of the United States*, pp. 191–192; see also Weigley, *History of the United States Army*, pp. 278–281.

53. Upton, *Military Policy of the United States*, pp. 185–186.

54. Theodore Roosevelt, "First Annual Message, December 3, 1901," in *American Military Thought*, p. 263.

55. Theodore Roosevelt, "Seventh Annual Message, December 3, 1907," in ibid., p. 271.

56. Elihu Root, "Army Reorganization," in ibid., pp. 242, 248, 254.

57. Roosevelt, "Seventh Annual Message," p. 269.

58. Root, "Army Reorganization," p. 241.

59. Chambers, "Conscripting for Colossus," p. 301.

60. Ibid., p. 301; Huntington, *Soldier and the State*, p. 286; and Leonard Wood, *Our Military History*, excerpted in *American Military Thought*, p. 278.

61. Wood, *Our Military History*, p. 274.

62. See Huntington, *Soldier and the State*, chap. 10.

63. Chambers, "Conscripting for Colossus," p. 301.

64. "War Department Annual Reports, 1912," in *American Military Thought*, p. 286.

65. Scott, "War Department Annual Reports, 1916," pp. 347–348.

66. "War Department Annual Reports, 1915," in *American Military Thought*, pp. 312–313.

67. Elshtain, *Women and War*, pp. 107, 117; and Bruce White, "The American Military and the Melting Pot in World War I," in *Military in America*, pp. 318–322.

68. William James, "The Moral Equivalent of War," in *International War: An Anthology*, 2d ed., ed. Melvin Small and J. David Singer (Chicago: Dorsey Press, 1989), pp. 328, 331, 334–335.

69. Stiehm, *Arms and the Enlisted Woman*, pp. 226–227.

70. Karsten, *Soldiers and Society*, pp. 150–151.

71. Stiehm, *Bring Me Men and Women*, p. 298.

CONCLUSION

1. Mary P. Ryan, *Women in Public: Between Banners and Ballots, 1825–1880* (Baltimore: Johns Hopkins University Press, 1990), p. 55.

2. See Kann, "Costs of Being on Top," pp. 29–37.

3. Okin, *Women in Western Political Thought*, p. 282.

4. Jane J. Mansbridge, *Why We Lost the ERA* (Chicago: University of Chicago Press, 1986), pp. 22, 35.

5. See Richard Lemon, *The Troubled American* (New York: Simon & Schuster, 1970); and Donald Warren, *The Radical Center: Middle Americans and the Politics of Alienation* (South Bend, Ind.: Notre Dame University Press, 1976).

6. Alexis de Tocqueville, *Democracy in America*, ed. J. P. Mayer (Garden City, N.Y.: Doubleday, 1969), pp. 13, 600–603.

7. George F. Gilder, *Sexual Suicide* (New York: New York Times Books, 1973), pp. 6, 14, 22–23, 57.

8. Fitzgerald, *Cities on a Hill*, pp. 137, 140–141.

9. George F. Gilder, *Wealth and Poverty* (New York: Bantam Books, 1981), chap. 3, "The Returns of Giving."

10. Phyllis Schlafly, *The Power of the Positive Woman* (New York: Harcourt Brace Jovanovich, 1977), pp. 17, 55, 88–89, 177, 214–215.

11. Ibid., pp. 34–35, 60, 63.

12. Ibid., pp. 13, 20, 218.

13. Ibid., p. 67.

14. Ibid., pp. 39, 218–219.

15. Huntington, "United States," pp. 104–106, 113–114.

16. Huntington, *Soldier and the State*, p. 144 and chap. 3.

17. U.S. Army White Paper, "Values," endorsed by Chief of Staff John A. Wickham, Jr., May 5, 1986, available in the U.S. Army War College Library, Carlisle, Pennsylvania.

18. Lt. Colonel Hugh A. Kelly, "The United States Army Ethic," submitted to the 1984 Officer Personnel Management System Study Group, available in the U.S. Army War College Library, Carlisle, Pennsylvania; and General John W. Vessey, Jr., "A Concept of Service," reprinted in the *Naval War College Review* (November–December 1984)—emphasis added.

19. *The Selective Service: Its Concepts, History, and Operation* (Washington, D.C.: U.S. Government Printing Office, 1967), in Karsten, *Soldiers and Society*, pp. 104–105.

20. Miriam Brody Kramnick, "Introduction," in *Vindication*, p. 7.

21. Wollstonecraft, *Vindication*, pp. 104, 122, 218, 251, 255–256, 283, 287, 306.

22. Ehrenreich, *Hearts of Men*, pp. 11, 118–119, 122, 134, 167, 171.

23. Ibid., pp. 175–177, 179, 181–182.

24. Compare Wolin, "Idea of the State in America," pp. 54–55; and Kathy E. Ferguson, *The Feminist Case against Bureaucracy* (Philadelphia: Temple University Press, 1984), pp. 133, 145, 153, 180.

25. Benjamin Barber, *Strong Democracy: Participatory Politics for a New Age* (Berkeley: University of California Press, 1984), pp. 4, 25, 299–302.

26. Ehrenreich, *Hearts of Men*, p. 179; and Ferguson, *Feminist Case*, p. 174.

27. Compare Bellah et al., *Habits of the Heart*, p. 296; and Bloom, *Closing of the American Mind*, p. 35.

28. See Warren Farrell, *The Liberated Man* (New York: Random House, 1974), chap. 10; and "Berkeley Men's Center Manifesto," in *Men and Masculinity*, ed. Joseph Pleck and Jack Sawyer (Englewood Cliffs, N.J.: Prentice-Hall, 1974), pp. 173–174.

29. Harry Brod, "Eros Thanatized: Pornography and Male Sexuality," *Humanities in Society* 7 nos. 1–2 (1984): 47.
30. Carrigan, Connell, and Lee, "Toward a New Sociology of Masculinity," p. 80.
31. Stiehm, *Bring Me Men and Women*, pp. 297–301.
32. Stiehm, *Arms and the Enlisted Woman*, pp. 224–232; and *Bring Me Men and Women*, pp. 292–293.
33. Mansbridge, *Why We Lost the ERA*, pp. 55–56; Kathleen Jones, "Dividing the Ranks: Women and the Draft," in *Women, Militarism, and War: Essays in History, Politics, and Social Theory*, ed. Jean Bethke Elshtain and Sheila Tobias (Savage, Md.: Rowman & Littlefield, 1990), p. 127; and Gilligan, *In a Different Voice*, pp. 163–165.
34. Carole Pateman, "Women and Democratic Citizenship," The Jefferson Memorial Lectures delivered at the University of California, Berkeley, February 1985, pt. 3.
35. Ibid.; and Joyce Berkman, "Feminism, War, and Peace Politics: The Case of World War I," in *Women, Militarism, and War*, pp. 141–160.
36. Los Angeles Consumer Task Force on Marital Status Discrimination report cited in *Los Angeles Times*, March 29, 1990, pp. 1, 26; Rhode Island Rape Crisis Center report cited in the *San Pedro News Pilot*, May 3, 1988, p. A2; and Riane Eisler, "Violence and Male Dominance: The Ticking Time Bomb," *Humanities in Society* 7 (Winter–Spring 1984): 3–18.
37. Pitkin, *Fortune Is a Woman*, esp. chap. 6.

Index